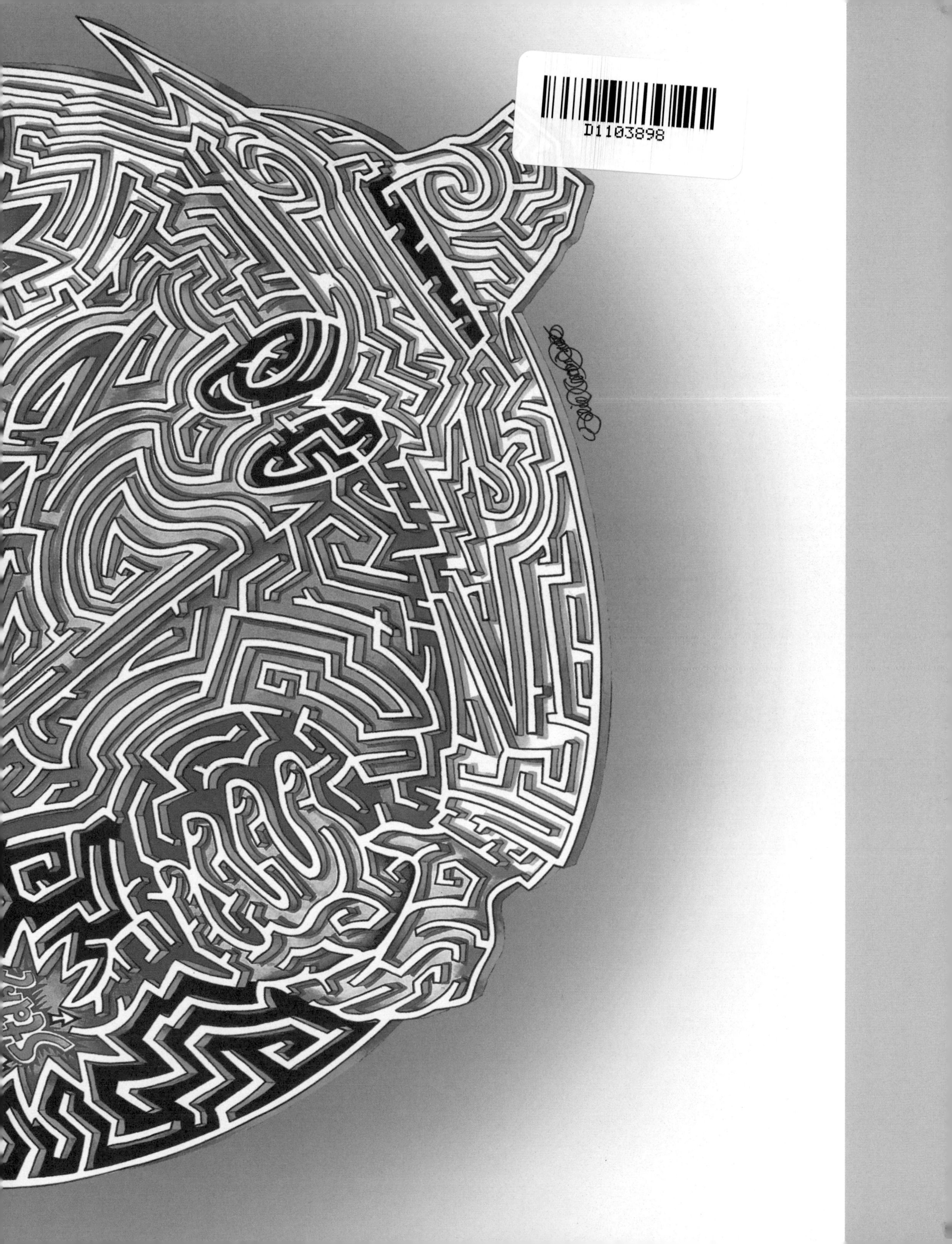
Start

MAD™

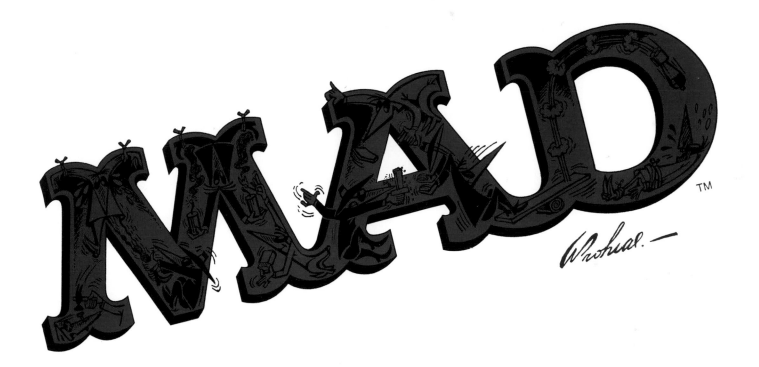

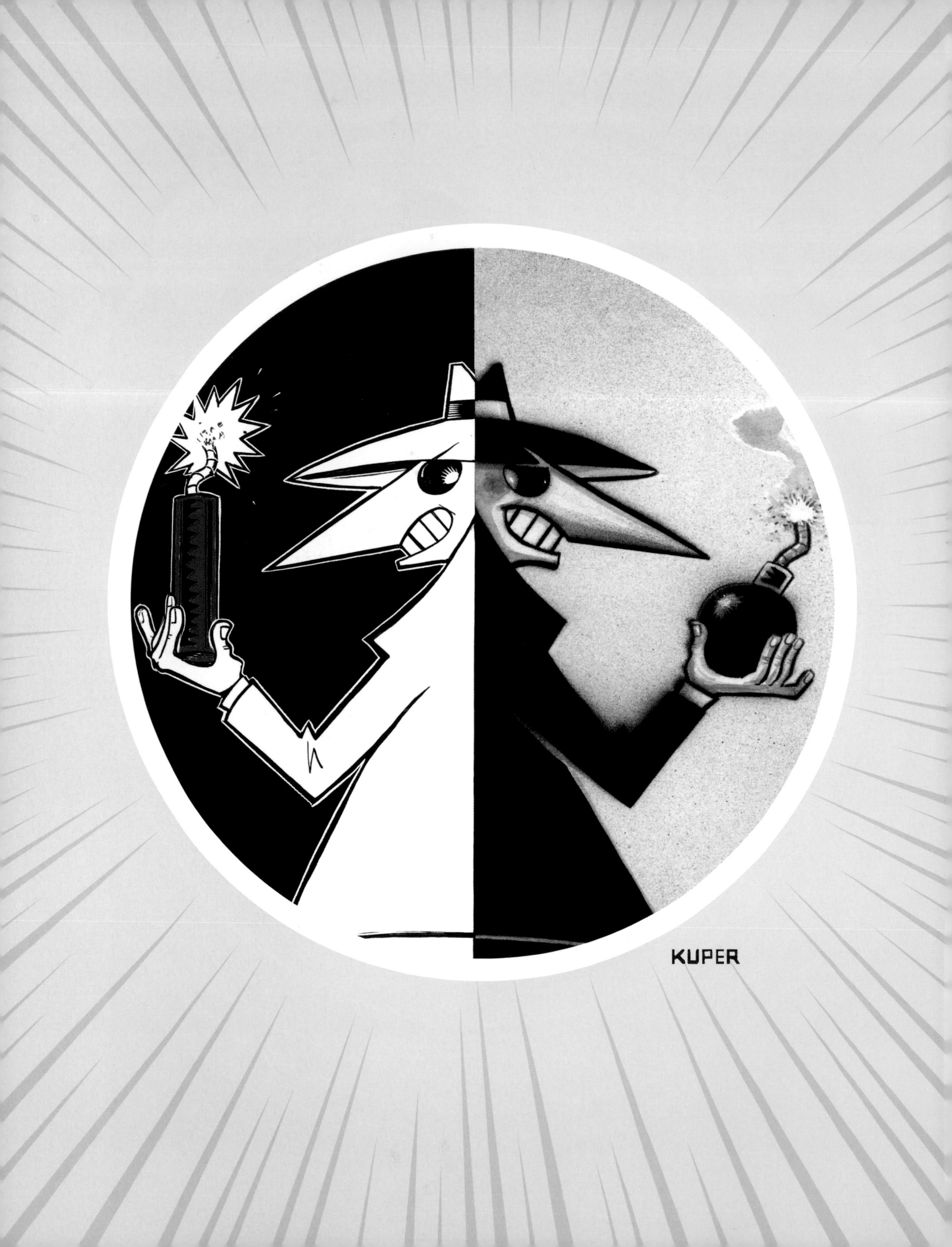
KUPER

MAD PRESENTS

SPY vs SPY

AN EXPLOSIVE CELEBRATION

Edited by John Ficarra

LIBERTY
STREET

MAD Magazine

John Ficarra	Senior VP & Executive Editor
Charlie Kadau, Joe Raiola	Senior Editors
Dave Croatto	Editor
Jacob Lambert	Associate Editor
Sam Viviano	VP – Art & Design
Ryan Flanders	Associate Art Director

Front matter and introductory sections designed by Patricia Dwyer

MAD THANKS

To Al Feldstein and Nick Meglin, who originally edited many of the pages in this book, and to John Putnam and Lenny Brenner, who art directed them. Thanks to Jim Campbell, Mike Carlin, Jacq Cohen, Susan Karlin, Kevin Kiniry, Greg Lockard, Bobbie Page and Brian Walters. Special thanks to the Prohias family. Extra special thanks to Bill Gaines, who started it all and whose spirit lives on in the MAD offices.

End pages maze art by David Anson Russo.

Spy vs. Spy created by Antonio Prohias.

Compilation and new material Copyright © 2015 E.C. Publications Inc.

LIBERTY STREET   Published by Liberty Street, an imprint of Time Inc. Books
1271 Avenue of the Americas, 6th floor, New York, NY 10020

LIBERTY STREET is a trademark of Time Inc.

ISBN 10: 1-61893-159-8
ISBN 13: 978-1-61893-159-7

Library of Congress Control Number: 2015946735

We welcome your comments and suggestions about Time Inc. Books. Please write to us at: Time Inc. Books, Attention: Book Editors, P.O. Box 361095, Des Moines, IA 50336-1095. If you would like to order any of our hardcover Collector's Edition books, please call us at 800-327-6388, Monday through Friday, 7 a.m.-9 p.m. Central Time.

Please send any glowing comments and flattering letters to:
MAD 1325 Avenue of the Americas New York, NY 10019

Please send any cheap shots, nasty complaints or thinly-veiled threats to Time Inc. Books at the address above.

To subscribe to MAD, visit madmagazine.com
Download the MAD app for the iPad at the iTunes store

TABLE OF CONTENTS

FOREWORD

by Lewis Black

MAD is a funny magazine. *Spy vs. Spy* is a funny work of comic art. If you want funny, skip this, turn a few pages, and have a good time. Truly the genius of Antonio Prohias speaks for itself.

(I can't help it but when I am asked to write about something that I know is funny, I immediately want to talk about why I find it funny. I can't make it funnier.)

Anyway…

About a thousand years ago, when I was twelve and twelve was still young, I stumbled onto MAD Magazine. The year was 1960 and what first grabbed my eye was the perverse little grin of Alfred E. Neuman with one tooth missing. Who the hell puts an idiot on the cover of their magazine? He spoke to me immediately as I, too, was an idiot. Little did I know, as I reached for the magazine and opened it, that Alfred was going to lead me into my first few baby steps toward becoming an adult.

What has MAD got to do with being an adult? It exposed my young and oh-so-innocent mind to satire. Even though I didn't know it at the time, I was moving into a land beyond fart jokes.

Sure, there was lot of silliness going on inside the covers of MAD, but in the self-reverential world of the suburbs I was raised in, silly was good. But beyond the silly, MAD was making fun of the world I lived in: the leaders, the movies, the television shows, the commercials, the fads, the mores, the clothing I was wearing, everything that encompassed my world. I knew the world I lived in was funny, seriously funny, but I just didn't have the words to explain why. MAD gave me that language in the simplest and funniest way. I felt like a kid my age was writing this stuff. For

Illustration by Sam Viviano

all I knew it might have been Alfred E. Neuman himself. Whoever was writing it, it made me feel less crazy, and at the age of twelve feeling less crazy was a good thing.

And then there was *Spy vs. Spy* and it was perfect. (It was as if the Road Runner cartoons had taken higher physics!) One Spy dressed in white and the other in black, like everything else at the time, it was either black or white. We hadn't gotten into any grey areas as of yet. (Maybe it took the invention of Color TV to help us get to the grey.)

We lived in the midst of a Cold War and as it raged on around us, this short strip nailed, in the simplest fashion, the paranoia of the times. It made it funny. It showed that the road we were traveling on was paved with our collective stupidity and ended in death. And it made me laugh, and I needed to laugh.

For God's sake, people were building bomb shelters in their backyards as if they would survive in a tiny hellhole long enough to eventually return to their homes after the radiation had cleared. We were told by our teachers that if there was a nuclear attack to hide under our wooden desks. Those morons thought we were going to survive a nuclear holocaust by hiding under kindling. It was at that moment I decided you really couldn't trust adults. Some of them were obviously insane.

And nothing has changed. I am an adult now and I am surrounded by a multitude of adults, who for all intents and purposes are insane. The landscape and the enemies have changed but the road is still paved with stupidity. *Spy vs. Spy* still applies. Be it the Chinese, the Russians, ISIS, or whomever has stepped up to the plate to wear the black outfit (because the United States always has to be wearing white) Antonio Prohias's work remains timeless. And so we still laugh.

When I was young, MAD Magazine was my safe haven because it was insane in a good way. It was the kind of insanity that keeps you sane.

INTRODUCTION

Welcome to *Spy vs. Spy: An Explosive Celebration*. This book is an appreciation of the enduring black and white characters created by Antonio Prohias in the pages of MAD Magazine from 1961 to 1987 and also the current Spy strips by artist/writer Peter Kuper.

This is by no means the first collection of Spy adventures, but it's certainly the most colorful and diverse. A little MAD history: from 1955 through 2000, MAD was a proudly black-and-white production. MAD's founding publisher Bill Gaines insisted on it. He believed young readers would be more likely to think of a black-and-white magazine printed on cheap paper as something "underground" and tacitly forbidden, and therefore more desirable. By the end of the twentieth century, however, the world had changed: full color was now the standard in movies, television, video games and, most importantly, magazines. Quipped MAD Senior Editor Joe Raiola at the time, "MAD looks like it was printed in Mexico in 1959!" As much as I hated to admit it, he had a point. It was time for MAD to (belatedly) join the color revolution.

Thus, in December 2000, with issue number 400, MAD magazine published its first all-color edition. That same year, MAD also began experimenting with adding color to reprints of older MAD articles, in a semi-annual magazine called MAD *Color Classics*.

To be sure, not every older MAD article improved with colorization, but one of the clear winners was *Spy vs. Spy*, this despite the fact that the entire strip was predicated on the literal dichotomy between "Black" and "White." It turned out, however, that this ongoing battle of diametric opposites was enhanced by taking place in a Technicolor world.

It has long been my hope to add color to all of Prohias' Spy adventures, and this volume goes a long way to fulfilling that dream. In *Spy vs. Spy: An Explosive Celebration*, we present, for the first time, 150 strips by Antonio Prohias — over 60% of his total output — colorized by master colorist Carrie Strachan. While Prohias was an extraordinary draftsman, designer, and cartoonist who crafted a fully-realized black-and-white world, his strips are amazingly transformed by Strachan's expansive color sense and attention to detail. (Be sure to read her in-depth essay on the challenges of adding color, introduced by MAD Art Director Sam Viviano, on page 13.)

In addition, long-time MAD artist/writer and close friend of Prohias, Sergio Aragonés, has written and illustrated a warm remembrance of Prohias' early life and how the two became close friends.

The last part of the book is devoted to *Spy vs. Spy*'s current writer/artist, Peter Kuper. It tracks Peter's own artistic journey from black-and-white to his distinctive airbrush and stencil technique to the bold line and color technique he now employs.

But wait! I'm not finished! Scattered throughout the book are Spy illustrations and posters by 15 artists from the worlds of illustration, animation, comics and even Lego sculpting. Their assignment was simple: Take the Spy characters and make them your own. I don't think you'll be disappointed with the results!

I hope you enjoy *Spy vs. Spy: An Explosive Celebration*!

— John Ficarra, Editor

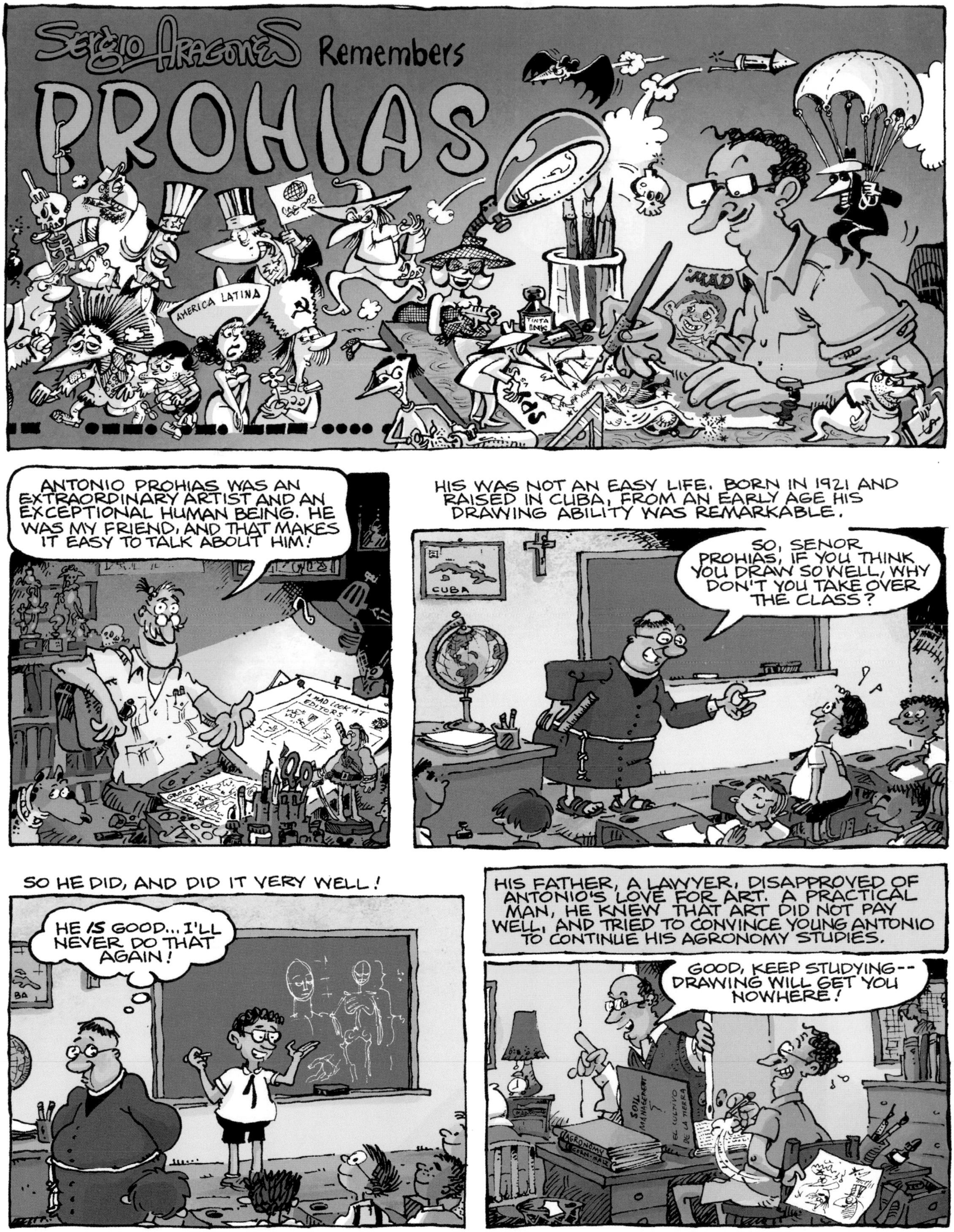

Sergio Aragonés Remembers
PROHIAS
AMERICA LATINA
TINTA INK
MAD
ANTONIO PROHIAS WAS AN EXTRAORDINARY ARTIST AND AN EXCEPTIONAL HUMAN BEING. HE WAS MY FRIEND, AND THAT MAKES IT EASY TO TALK ABOUT HIM!
A MAD LOOK AT EDITORS
HIS WAS NOT AN EASY LIFE. BORN IN 1921 AND RAISED IN CUBA, FROM AN EARLY AGE HIS DRAWING ABILITY WAS REMARKABLE.
CUBA
SO, SENOR PROHIAS, IF YOU THINK YOU DRAW SO WELL, WHY DON'T YOU TAKE OVER THE CLASS?
SO HE DID, AND DID IT VERY WELL!
HE *IS* GOOD... I'LL NEVER DO THAT AGAIN!
HIS FATHER, A LAWYER, DISAPPROVED OF ANTONIO'S LOVE FOR ART. A PRACTICAL MAN, HE KNEW THAT ART DID NOT PAY WELL, AND TRIED TO CONVINCE YOUNG ANTONIO TO CONTINUE HIS AGRONOMY STUDIES.
GOOD, KEEP STUDYING-- DRAWING WILL GET YOU NOWHERE!
SOIL MANAGEMENT
EL CULTIVO DE LA TIERRA
AGRONOMY

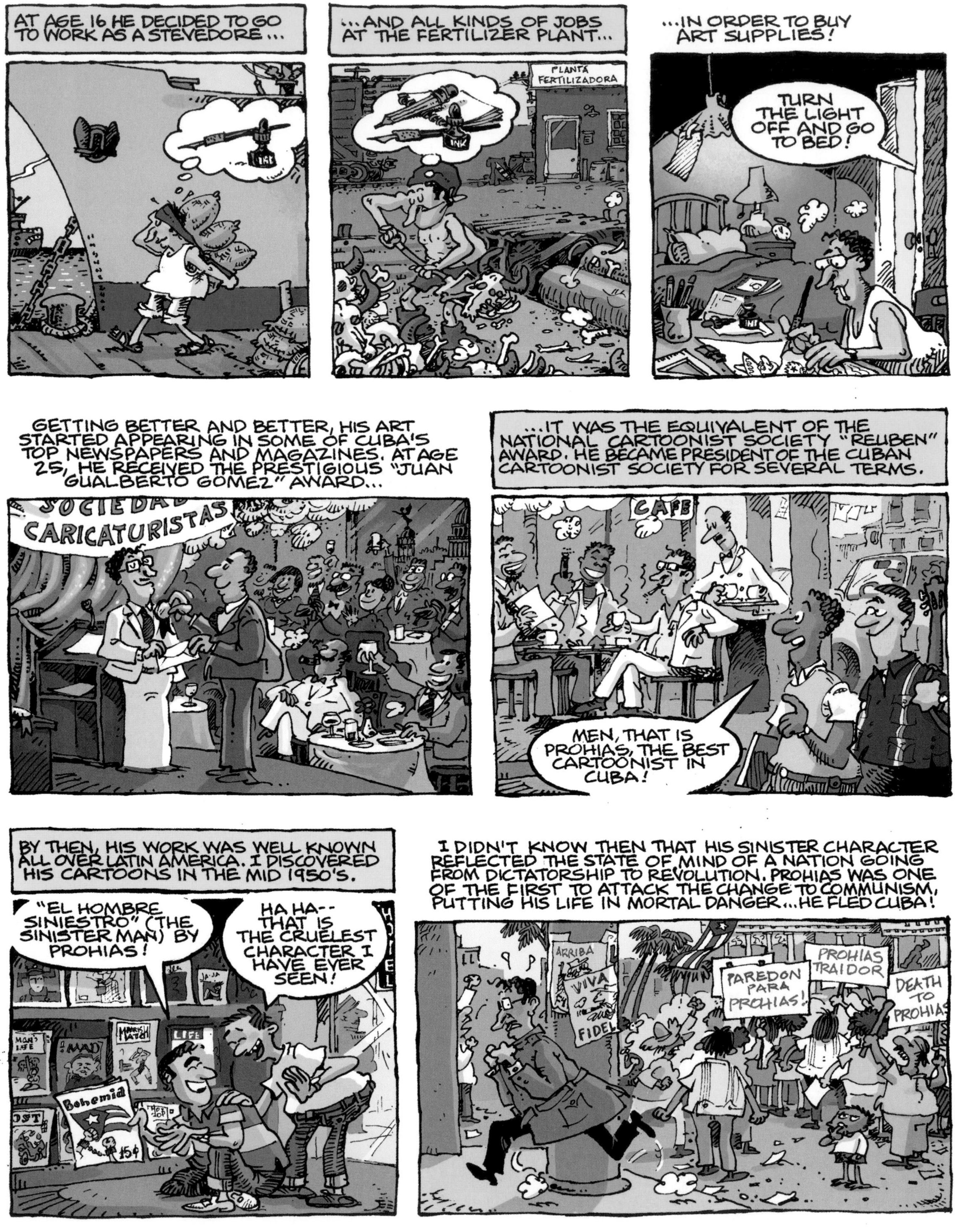
AT AGE 16 HE DECIDED TO GO TO WORK AS A STEVEDORE...
INK
...AND ALL KINDS OF JOBS AT THE FERTILIZER PLANT...
PLANTA FERTILIZADORA
INK
...IN ORDER TO BUY ART SUPPLIES!
TURN THE LIGHT OFF AND GO TO BED!
INK
GETTING BETTER AND BETTER, HIS ART STARTED APPEARING IN SOME OF CUBA'S TOP NEWSPAPERS AND MAGAZINES. AT AGE 25, HE RECEIVED THE PRESTIGIOUS "JUAN GUALBERTO GOMEZ" AWARD...
CARICATURISTAS
...IT WAS THE EQUIVALENT OF THE NATIONAL CARTOONIST SOCIETY "REUBEN" AWARD. HE BECAME PRESIDENT OF THE CUBAN CARTOONIST SOCIETY FOR SEVERAL TERMS.
CAFE
MEN, THAT IS PROHIAS, THE BEST CARTOONIST IN CUBA!
BY THEN, HIS WORK WAS WELL KNOWN ALL OVER LATIN AMERICA. I DISCOVERED HIS CARTOONS IN THE MID 1950'S.
"EL HOMBRE SINIESTRO" (THE SINISTER MAN) BY PROHIAS!
HA HA-- THAT IS THE CRUELEST CHARACTER I HAVE EVER SEEN!
HOTEL
LIFE
MAD
Bohemia
15¢
I DIDN'T KNOW THEN THAT HIS SINISTER CHARACTER REFLECTED THE STATE OF MIND OF A NATION GOING FROM DICTATORSHIP TO REVOLUTION. PROHIAS WAS ONE OF THE FIRST TO ATTACK THE CHANGE TO COMMUNISM, PUTTING HIS LIFE IN MORTAL DANGER...HE FLED CUBA!
ARRIBA
VIVA
FIDEL
PAREDON PARA PROHIAS!
PROHIAS TRAIDOR
DEATH TO PROHIAS

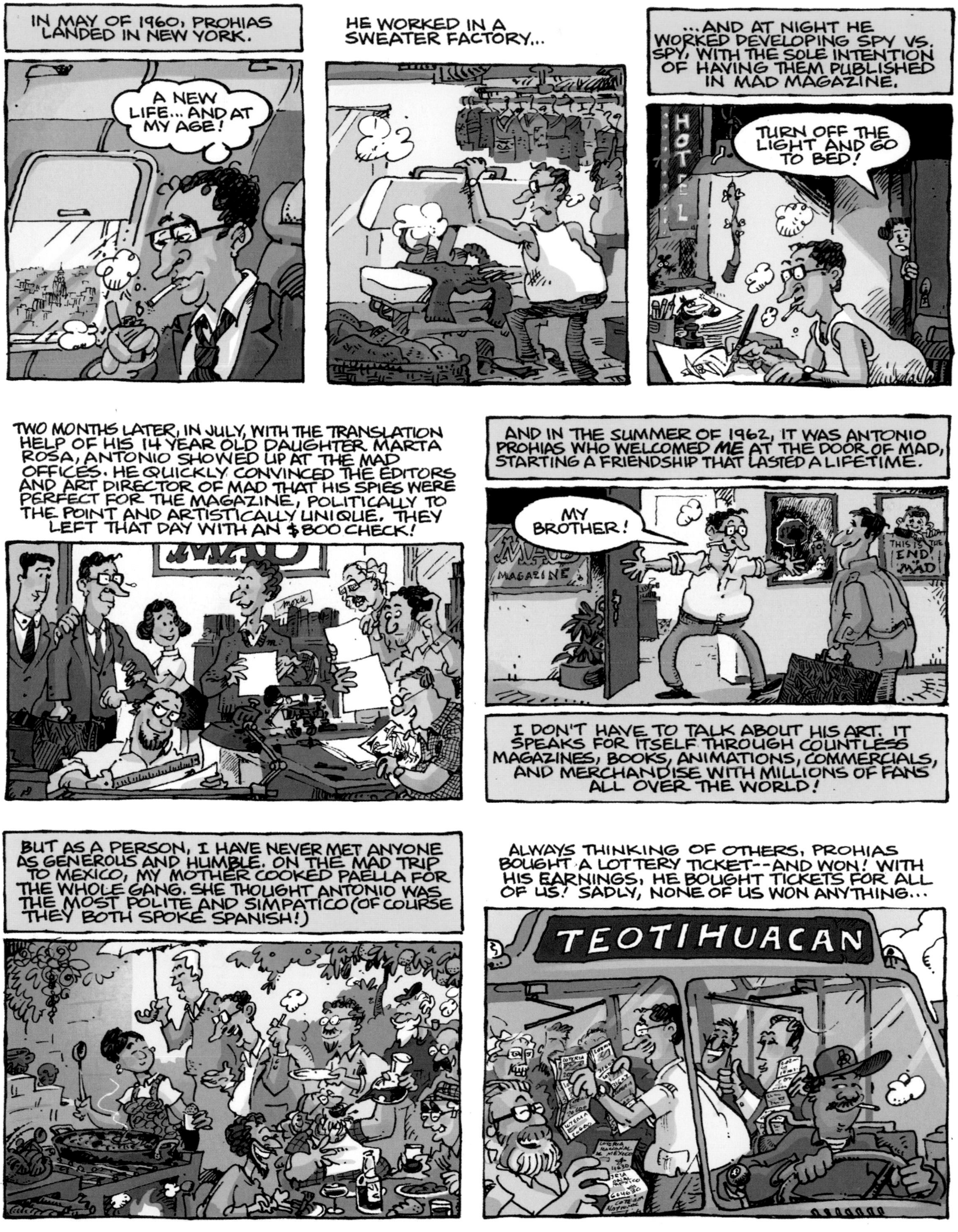
IN MAY OF 1960, PROHIAS LANDED IN NEW YORK.
A NEW LIFE... AND AT MY AGE!
HE WORKED IN A SWEATER FACTORY...
...AND AT NIGHT HE WORKED DEVELOPING SPY VS. SPY, WITH THE SOLE INTENTION OF HAVING THEM PUBLISHED IN MAD MAGAZINE.
HOTEL
TURN OFF THE LIGHT AND GO TO BED!
TWO MONTHS LATER, IN JULY, WITH THE TRANSLATION HELP OF HIS 14 YEAR OLD DAUGHTER MARTA ROSA, ANTONIO SHOWED UP AT THE MAD OFFICES. HE QUICKLY CONVINCED THE EDITORS AND ART DIRECTOR OF MAD THAT HIS SPIES WERE PERFECT FOR THE MAGAZINE, POLITICALLY TO THE POINT AND ARTISTICALLY UNIQUE. THEY LEFT THAT DAY WITH AN $800 CHECK!
AND IN THE SUMMER OF 1962, IT WAS ANTONIO PROHIAS WHO WELCOMED *ME* AT THE DOOR OF MAD, STARTING A FRIENDSHIP THAT LASTED A LIFETIME.
MY BROTHER!
MAD MAGAZINE
THIS IS THE END of MAD
I DON'T HAVE TO TALK ABOUT HIS ART. IT SPEAKS FOR ITSELF THROUGH COUNTLESS MAGAZINES, BOOKS, ANIMATIONS, COMMERCIALS, AND MERCHANDISE WITH MILLIONS OF FANS ALL OVER THE WORLD!
BUT AS A PERSON, I HAVE NEVER MET ANYONE AS GENEROUS AND HUMBLE. ON THE MAD TRIP TO MEXICO, MY MOTHER COOKED PAELLA FOR THE WHOLE GANG. SHE THOUGHT ANTONIO WAS THE MOST POLITE AND SIMPATICO (OF COURSE THEY BOTH SPOKE SPANISH!)
ALWAYS THINKING OF OTHERS, PROHIAS BOUGHT A LOTTERY TICKET--AND WON! WITH HIS EARNINGS, HE BOUGHT TICKETS FOR ALL OF US! SADLY, NONE OF US WON ANYTHING...
TEOTIHUACAN

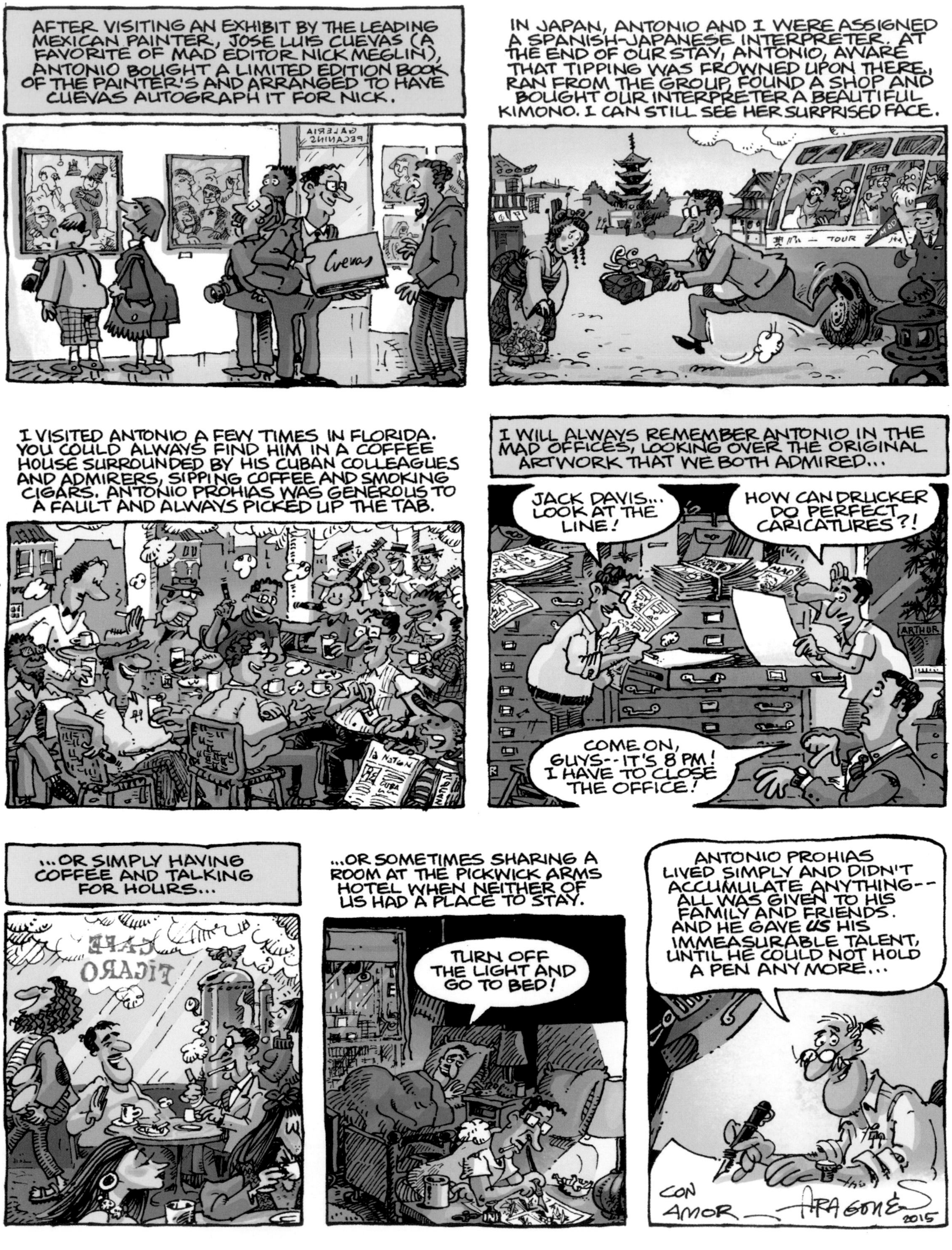
AFTER VISITING AN EXHIBIT BY THE LEADING MEXICAN PAINTER, JOSE LUIS CUEVAS (A FAVORITE OF MAD EDITOR NICK MEGLIN), ANTONIO BOUGHT A LIMITED EDITION BOOK OF THE PAINTER'S AND ARRANGED TO HAVE CUEVAS AUTOGRAPH IT FOR NICK.
GALERIA PECANINS
Cuevas
IN JAPAN, ANTONIO AND I WERE ASSIGNED A SPANISH-JAPANESE INTERPRETER. AT THE END OF OUR STAY, ANTONIO, AWARE THAT TIPPING WAS FROWNED UPON THERE, RAN FROM THE GROUP, FOUND A SHOP AND BOUGHT OUR INTERPRETER A BEAUTIFUL KIMONO. I CAN STILL SEE HER SURPRISED FACE.
TOUR
I VISITED ANTONIO A FEW TIMES IN FLORIDA. YOU COULD ALWAYS FIND HIM IN A COFFEE HOUSE SURROUNDED BY HIS CUBAN COLLEAGUES AND ADMIRERS, SIPPING COFFEE AND SMOKING CIGARS. ANTONIO PROHIAS WAS GENEROUS TO A FAULT AND ALWAYS PICKED UP THE TAB.
CUBA
I WILL ALWAYS REMEMBER ANTONIO IN THE MAD OFFICES, LOOKING OVER THE ORIGINAL ARTWORK THAT WE BOTH ADMIRED...
JACK DAVIS... LOOK AT THE LINE!
HOW CAN DRUCKER DO PERFECT CARICATURES?!
COME ON, GUYS--IT'S 8 PM! I HAVE TO CLOSE THE OFFICE!
ARTHUR
MAD
...OR SIMPLY HAVING COFFEE AND TALKING FOR HOURS...
CAFE FIGARO
...OR SOMETIMES SHARING A ROOM AT THE PICKWICK ARMS HOTEL WHEN NEITHER OF US HAD A PLACE TO STAY.
TURN OFF THE LIGHT AND GO TO BED!
ANTONIO PROHIAS LIVED SIMPLY AND DIDN'T ACCUMULATE ANYTHING-- ALL WAS GIVEN TO HIS FAMILY AND FRIENDS. AND HE GAVE US HIS IMMEASURABLE TALENT, UNTIL HE COULD NOT HOLD A PEN ANY MORE...
CON AMOR — ARAGONÉS 2015

Coloring Spy vs. Spy
SECRETS REVEALED!

Here at MAD,

we've been talking about colorizing the entire library of Antonio Prohias' over two hundred black-and-white *Spy vs. Spy* strips for a long time. It started, as John Ficarra noted in his introduction, when we first began experimenting with color in the magazine nearly two decades ago. While the Spies were, by the very nature of their conception, black and white beings, their adventures seemed to take on new vividness when taking place in a full-color world.

When the decision was made to publish this book, featuring a huge number of *Spy vs. Spy* adventures never before seen in color, we knew that one person was qualified to tackle the job: Carrie Strachan. Many skilled artisans have added color to Prohias' work over the years, but the consistently impressive results coming from Carrie had made her our go-to colorist for the Spies.

None of her previous assignments, however, were as daunting as this one: colorize 150 *Spy vs. Spy* strips in a period of six months. She came through, may I say, with — *ahem* — flying colors. Not only did she complete the job in the alloted time, but the work she did was astounding. Even we jaded old pros asked ourselves, "How'd she do it?"

You may be wondering the same thing, so here, in Carrie's own words, is the answer.

— Sam Viviano, Art Director

When I tell people that I'm coloring Spy vs. Spy*, the response I often get is, "But, aren't those guys black and white?" "Well, yeah," I say, "but, I'm coloring them." This is generally met with looks of confusion — especially when I tell people that this is my actual job. To help clear things up a bit, here's an explanation of the process.*

The scans I receive from MAD come from different sources. If available, negatives used to make the original printing plates provide the best scans. In the worst-case scenario, pages of the printed magazine are used. In both instances, what looked like solid gray areas on the page are actually lots of little black dots clustered together to create what is called a halftone.

JOKE AND DAGGER DEPT.
SPY VS SPY
BOOM
Prohias

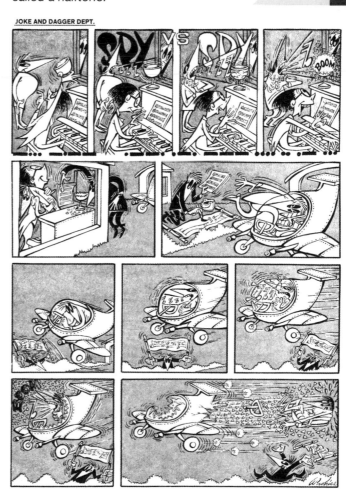

The first thing I have to do is remove the halftone dots. While fine for black and white printing, having the dots on top of color can often make the colors look "muddy." Think of looking at a painting through a dirty window. Removing the dots and cleaning up the line art is often the most time-consuming part of the process.

Once the line art is cleaned up and ready to go, it's time to start putting in the color. First I'll put down flat versions of the colors I plan on using; the shading or "rendering" come later. I'll generally put in the darkest version of the color I plan on using and add midtones and highlights when I render the page later. This is to keep the colors on the page from getting too dark.

One of the challenges of coloring 150 Spy vs. Spy comics is to keep the pages from all looking the same. You don't want page after page of the same blue sky. Since Spy vs. Spy isn't exactly known for its gritty realism, you can have orange skies, green water and yellow grass.

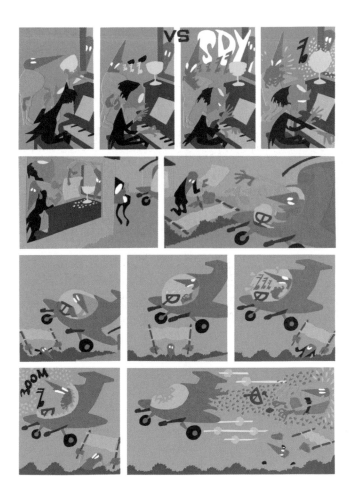

The next step is rendering. This is when I add midtones and highlights to the drawings to give them a more three-dimensional look. I'll use a special brush to add texture to some things like grass, trees or walls. I don't want to get too detailed in the rendering, though — I want the color to complement the artwork, not overwhelm it.

Finally, I add "special effects." For Spy vs. Spy this is generally limited to "knocking out" some of the line art. This just means turning the line into a color other than black. I also add some glare to windows or bottles to make it look like an object or a character is actually behind some glass. Although it does seem like a lot of the windows in these strips don't have glass in them. I mean, the Spies are always just reaching in and taking things. Time to step up security, guys! But that probably wouldn't be as fun, would it?

—Carrie Strachan, Colorist

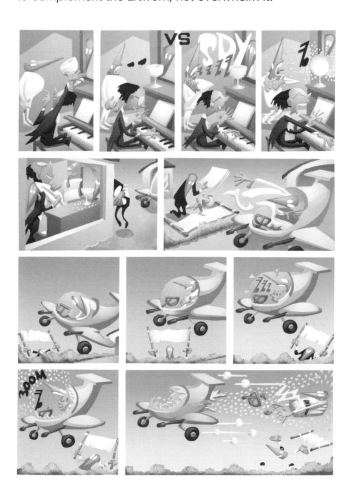

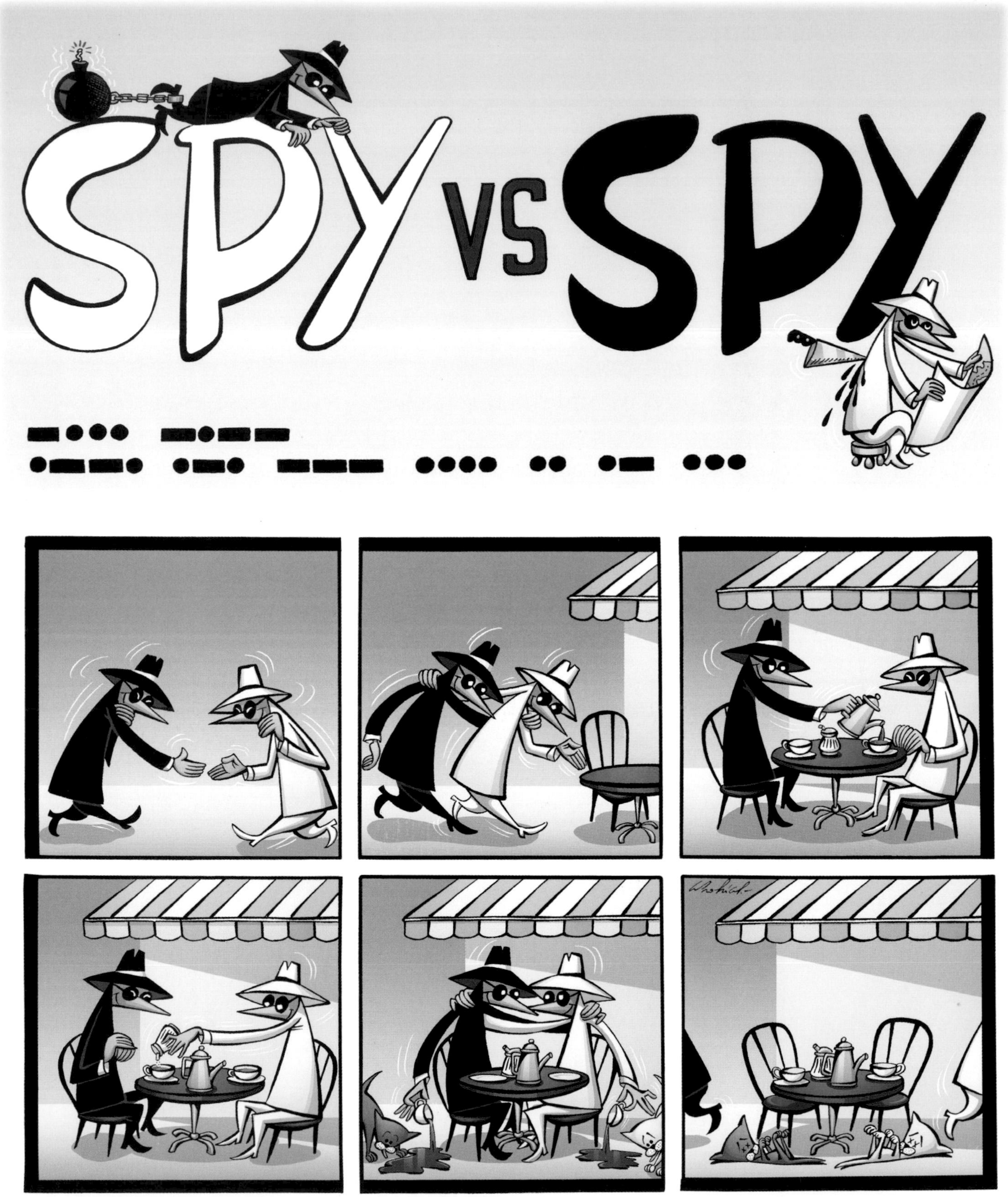
SPY VS SPY

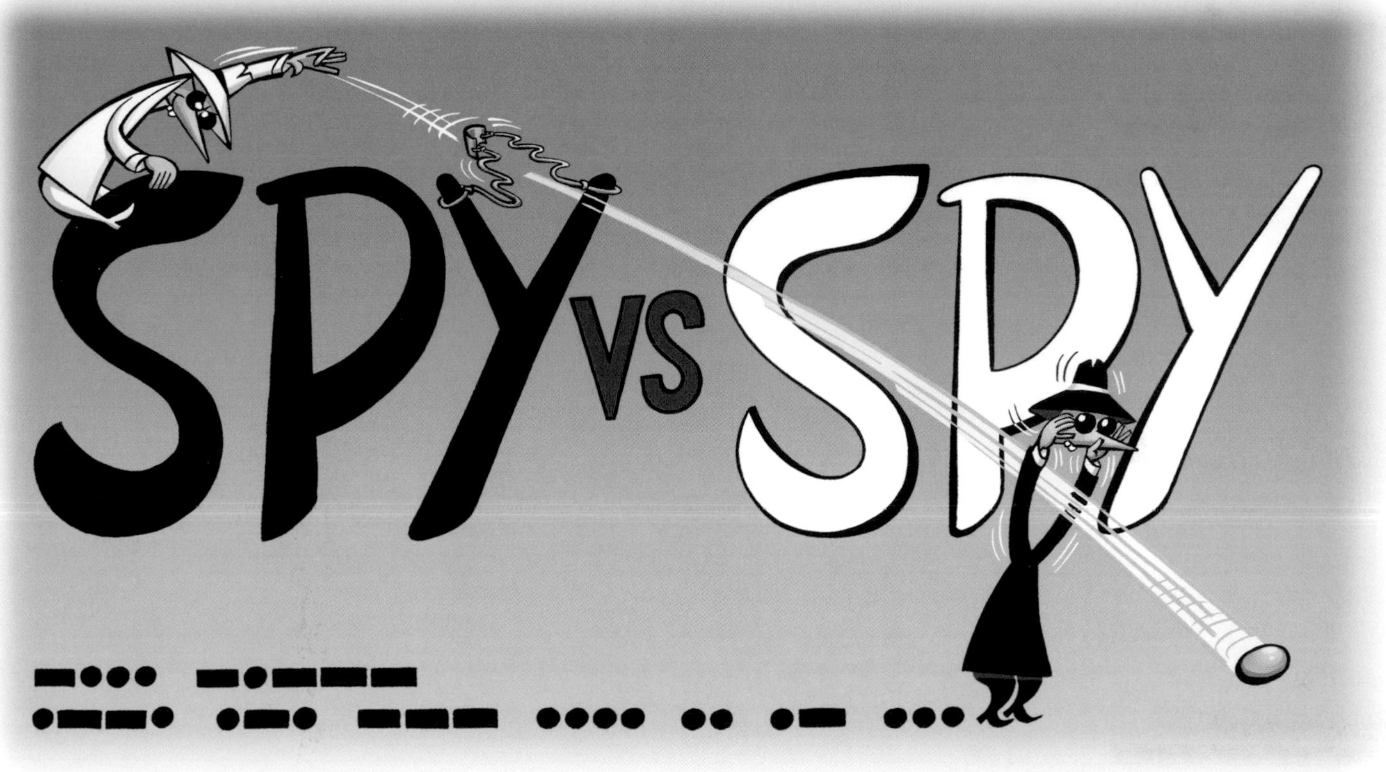
SPY vs SPY

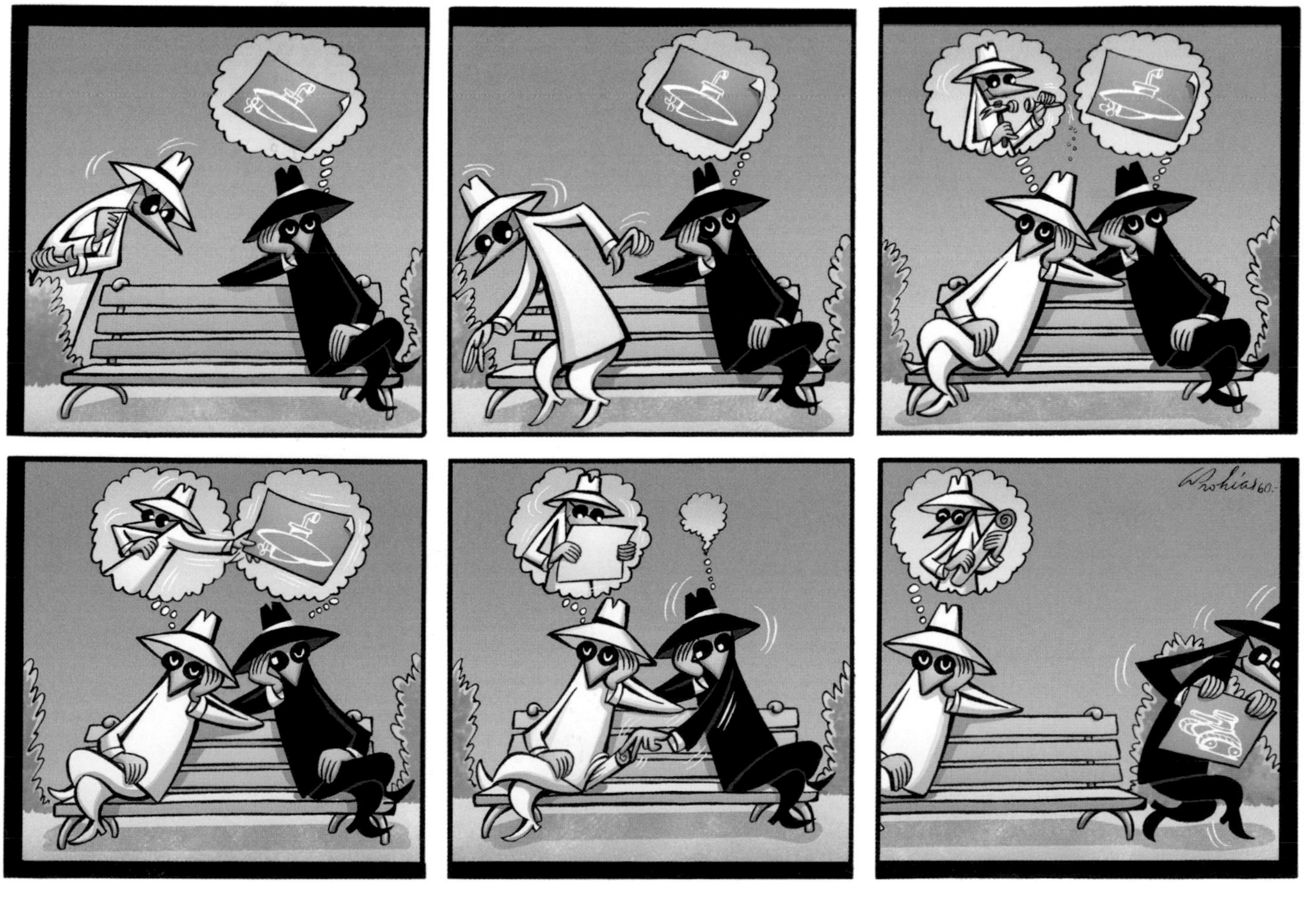

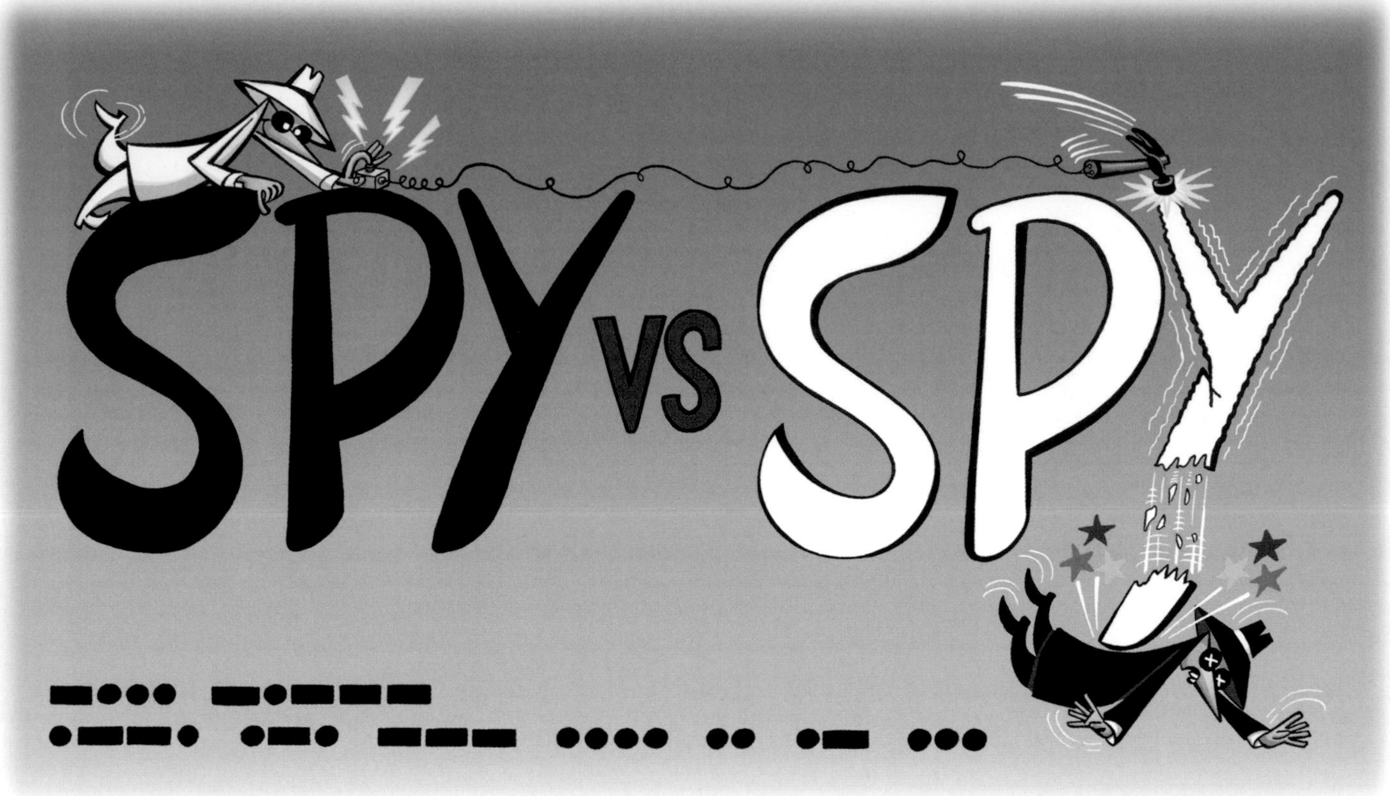
SPY VS SPY

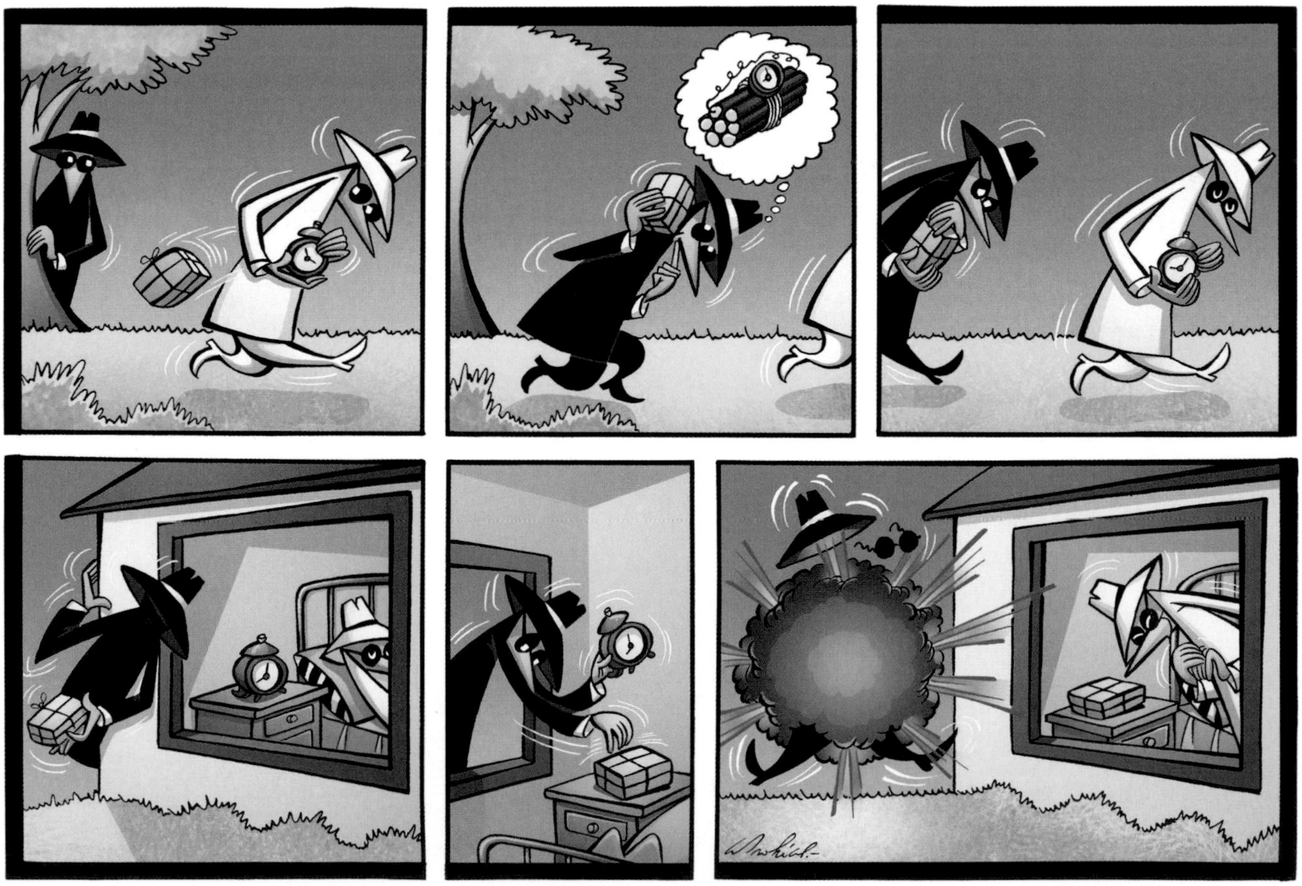

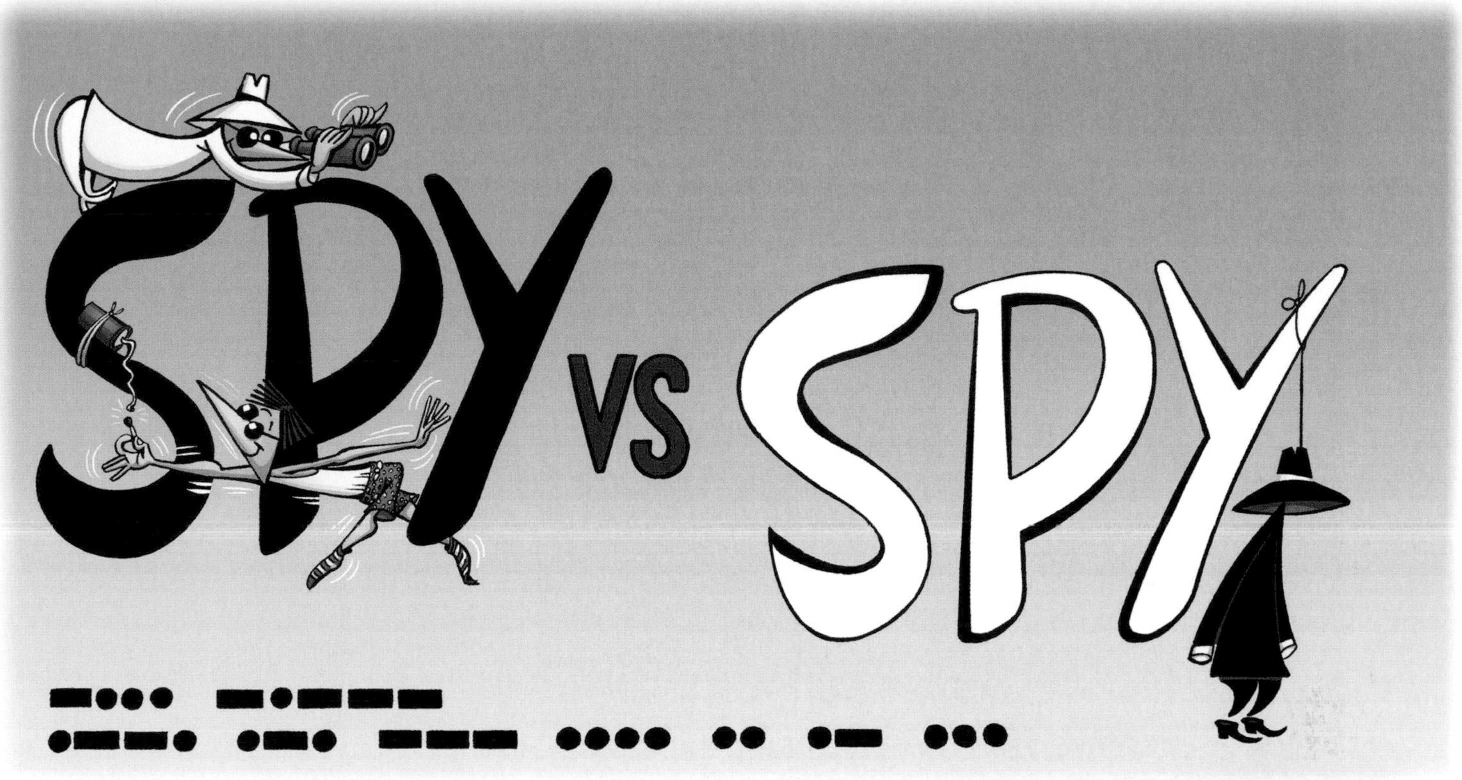
SPY vs SPY

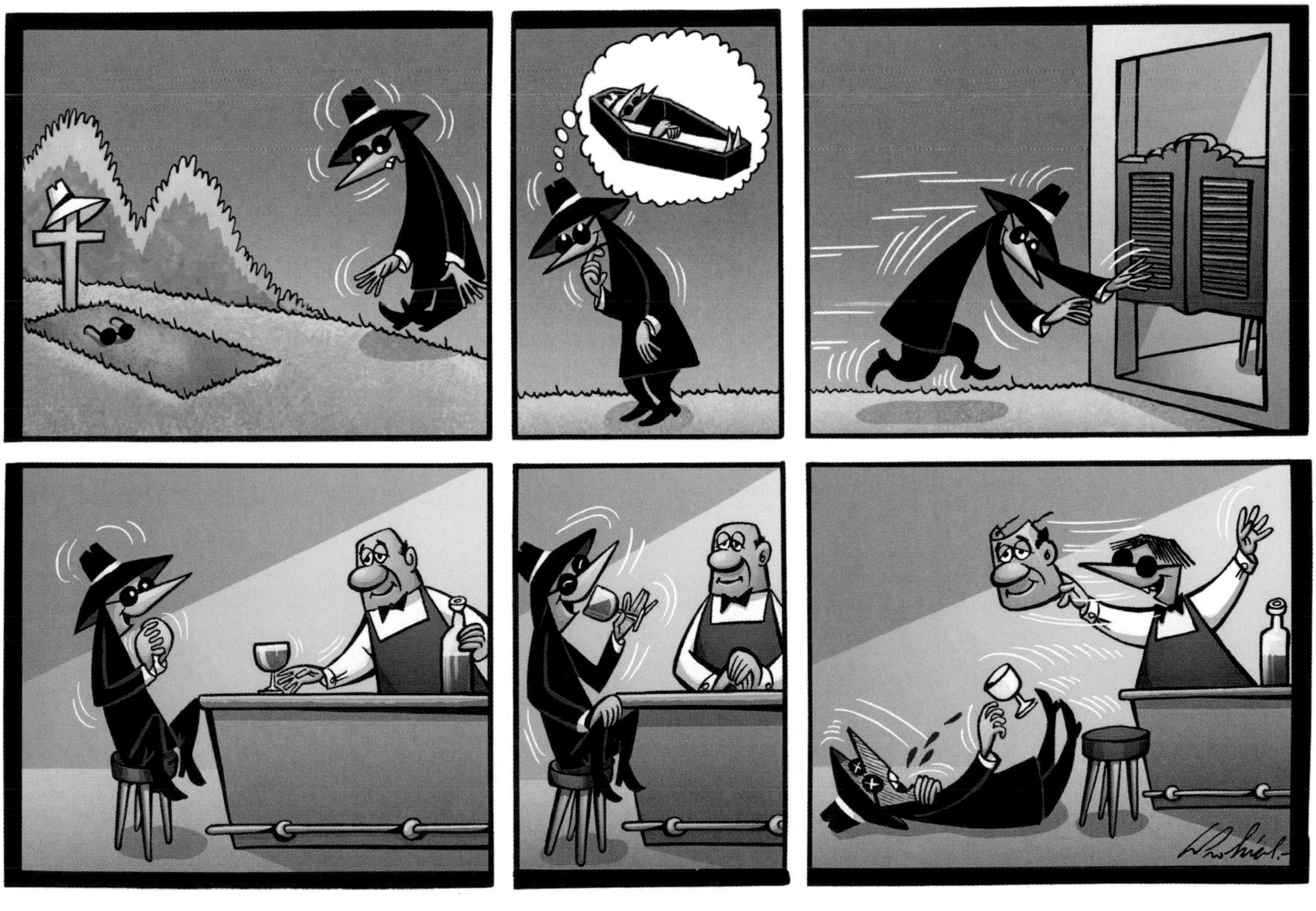

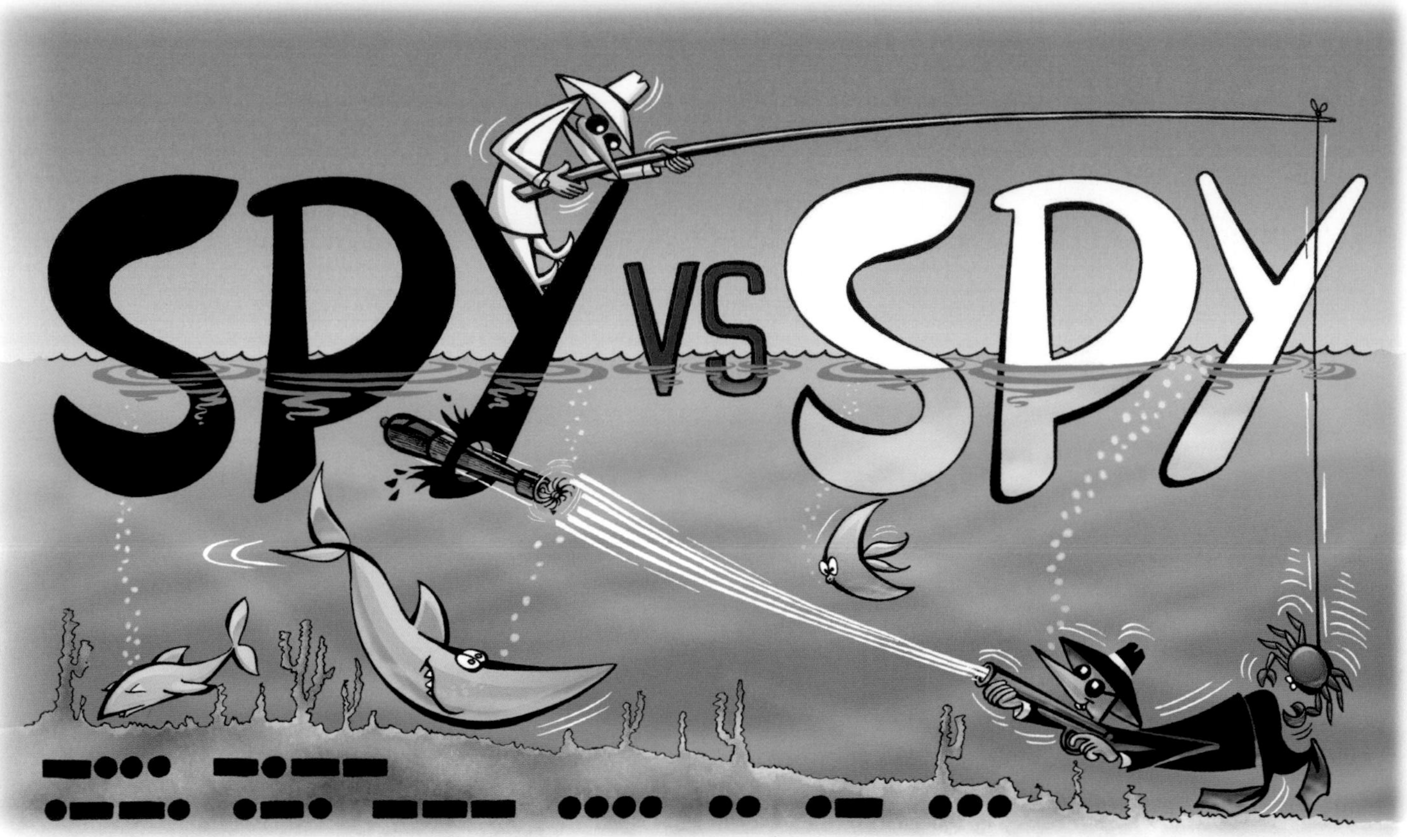
SPY vs SPY

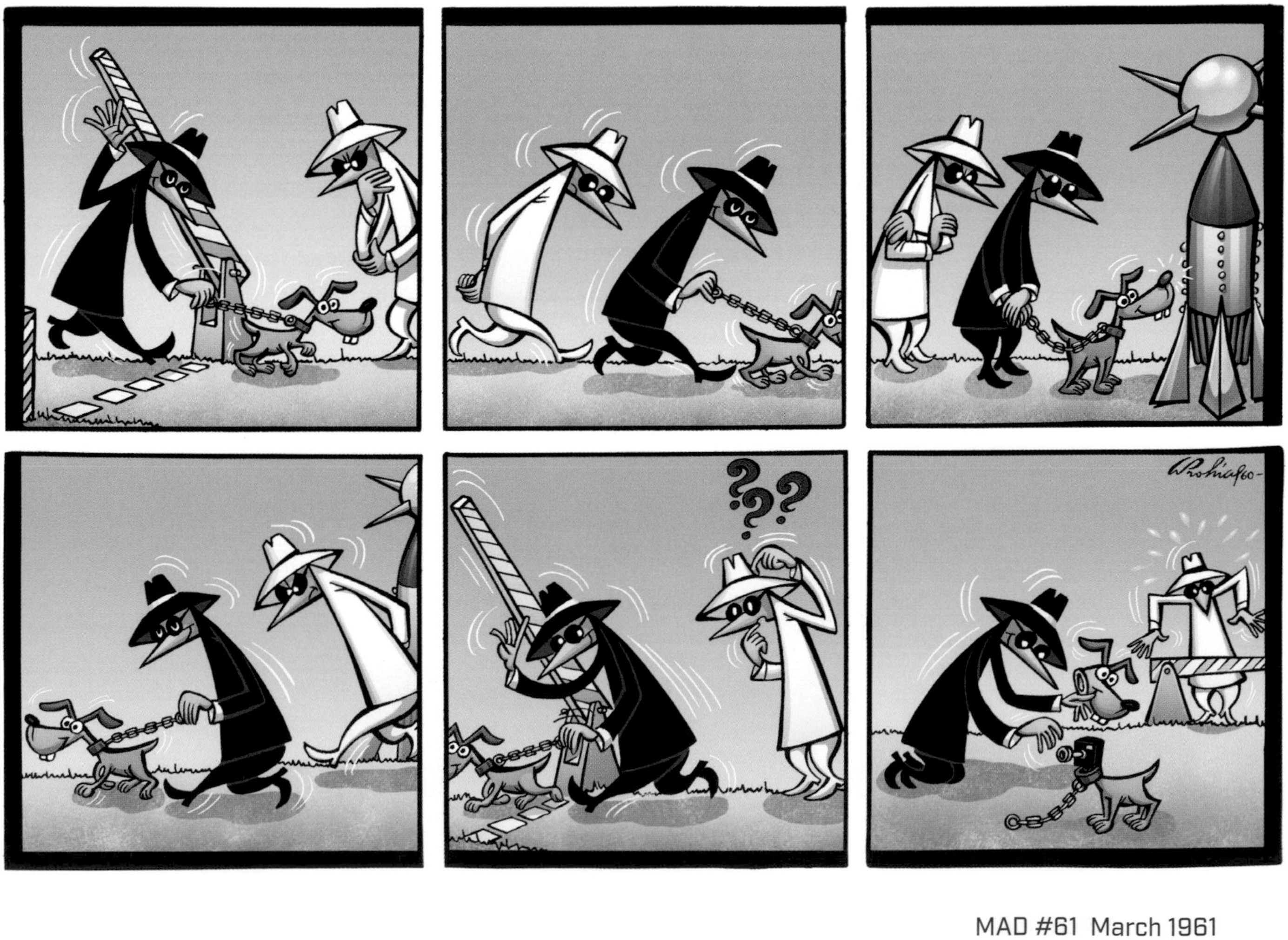

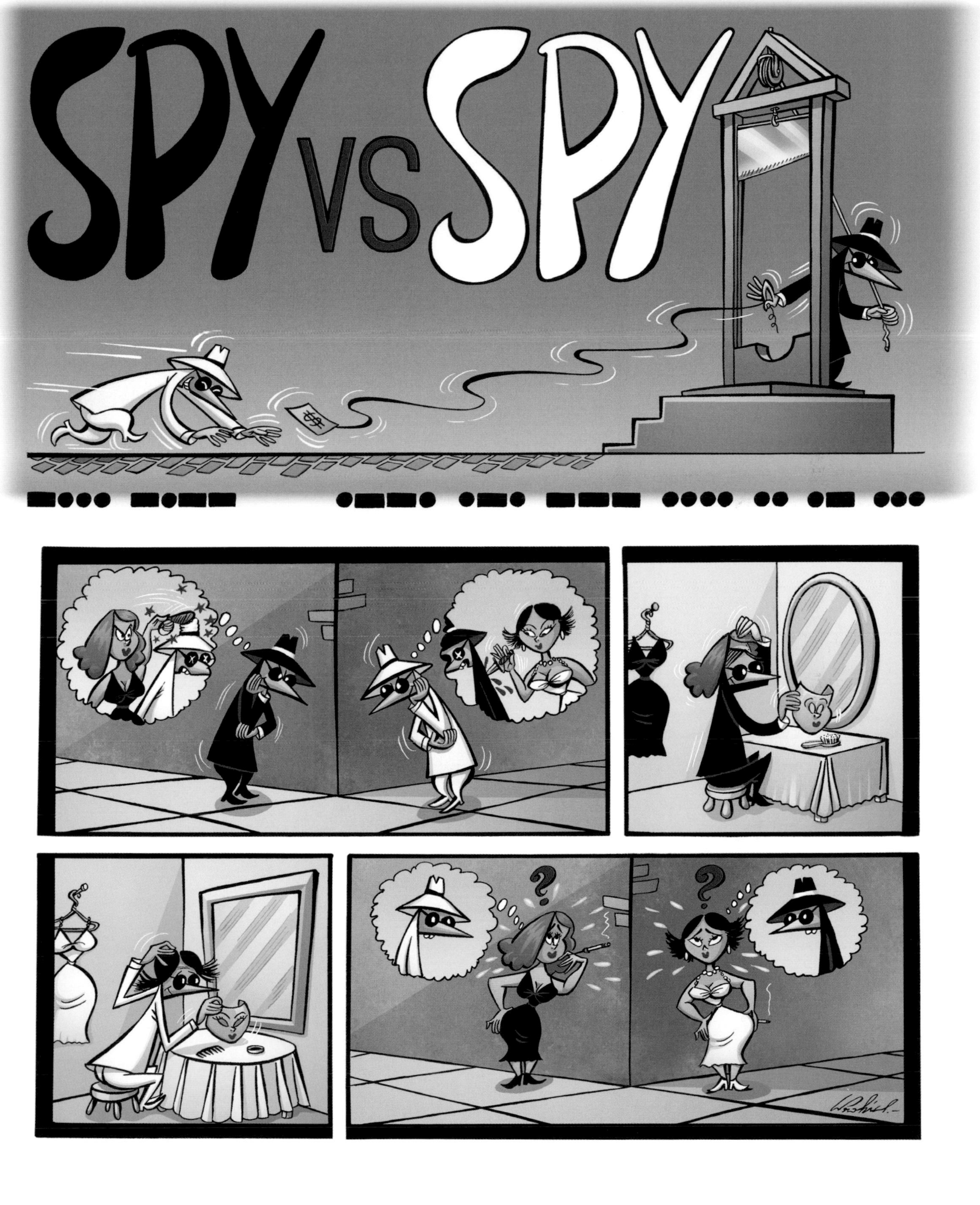
SPY VS SPY

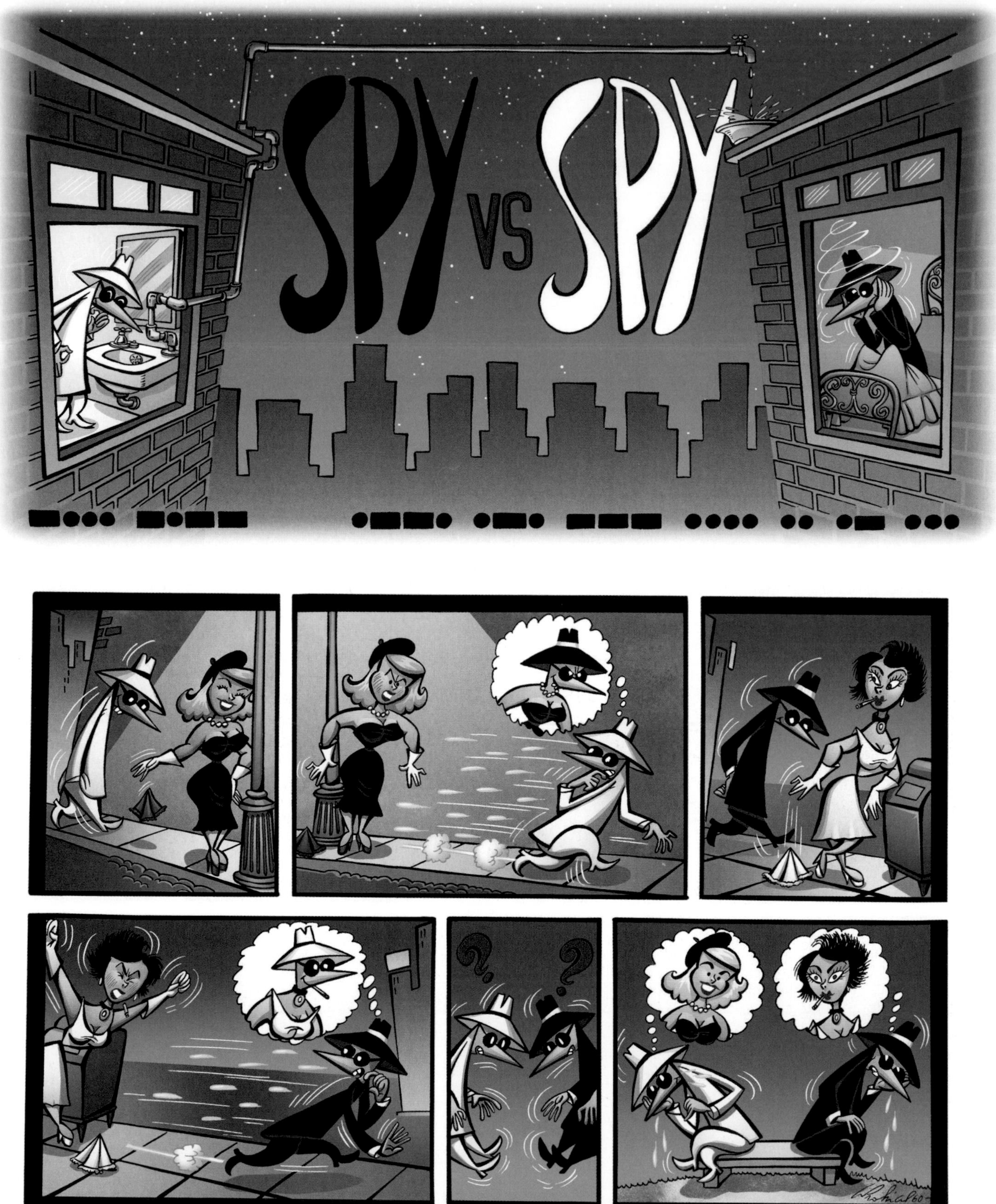
SPY vs SPY

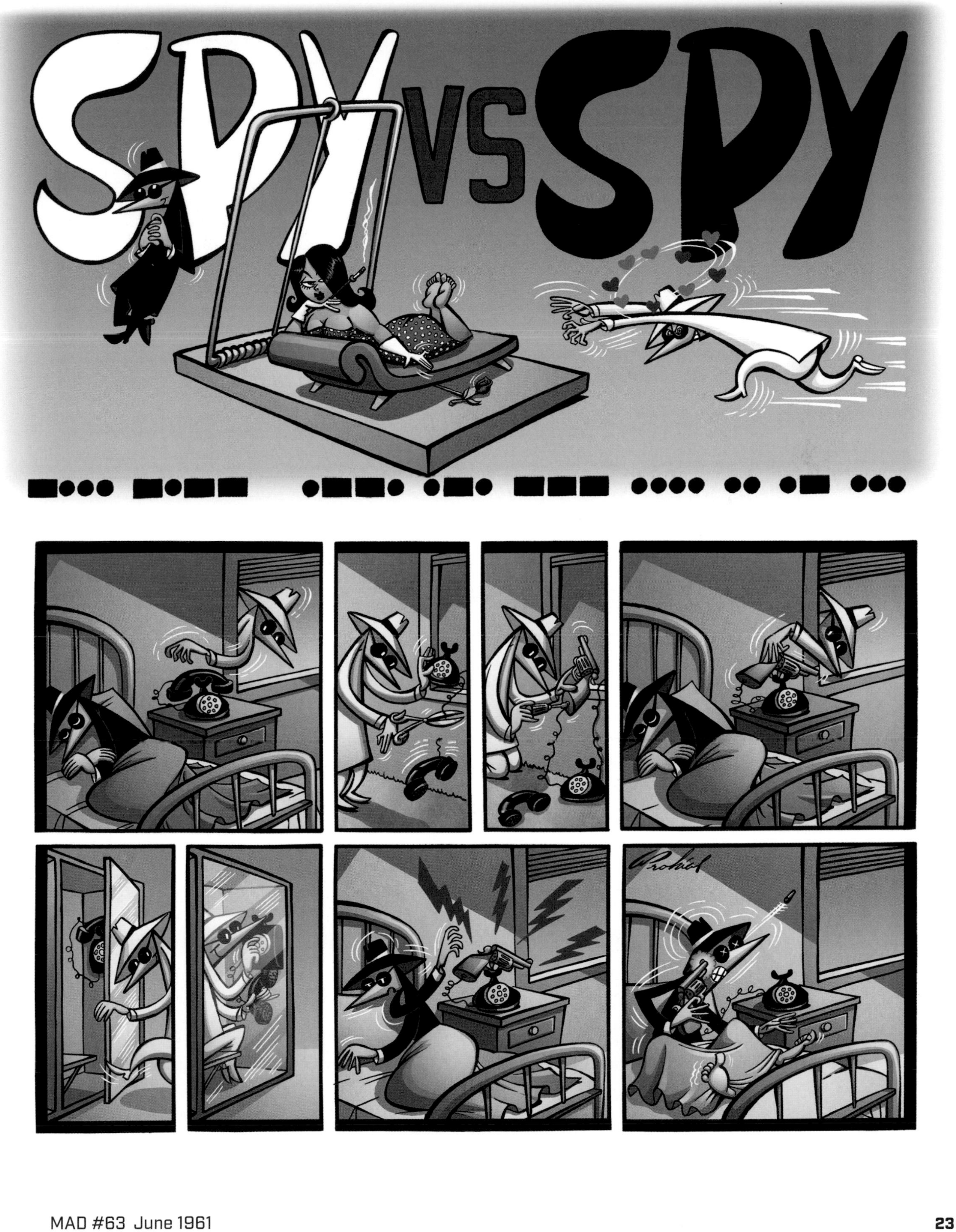
SPY VS SPY

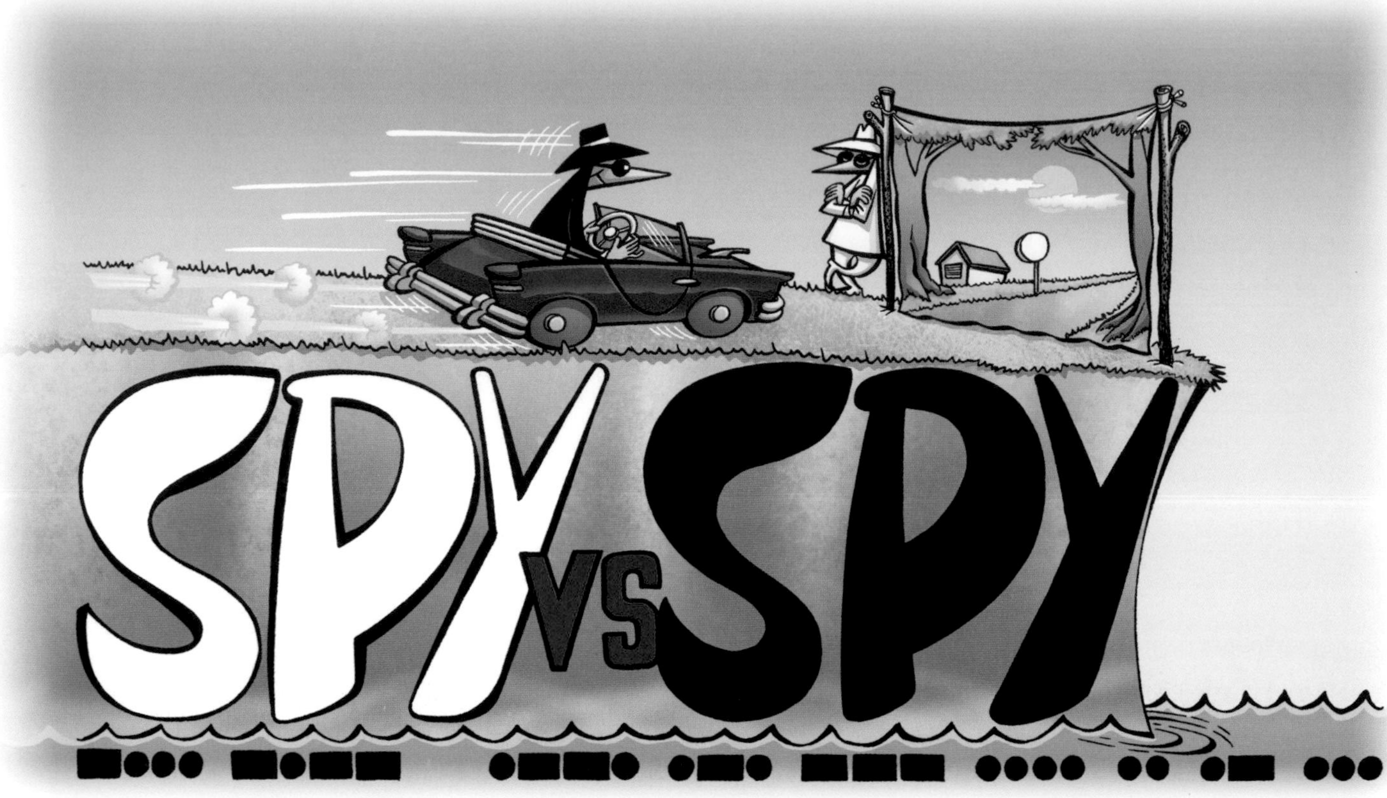
SPY vs SPY

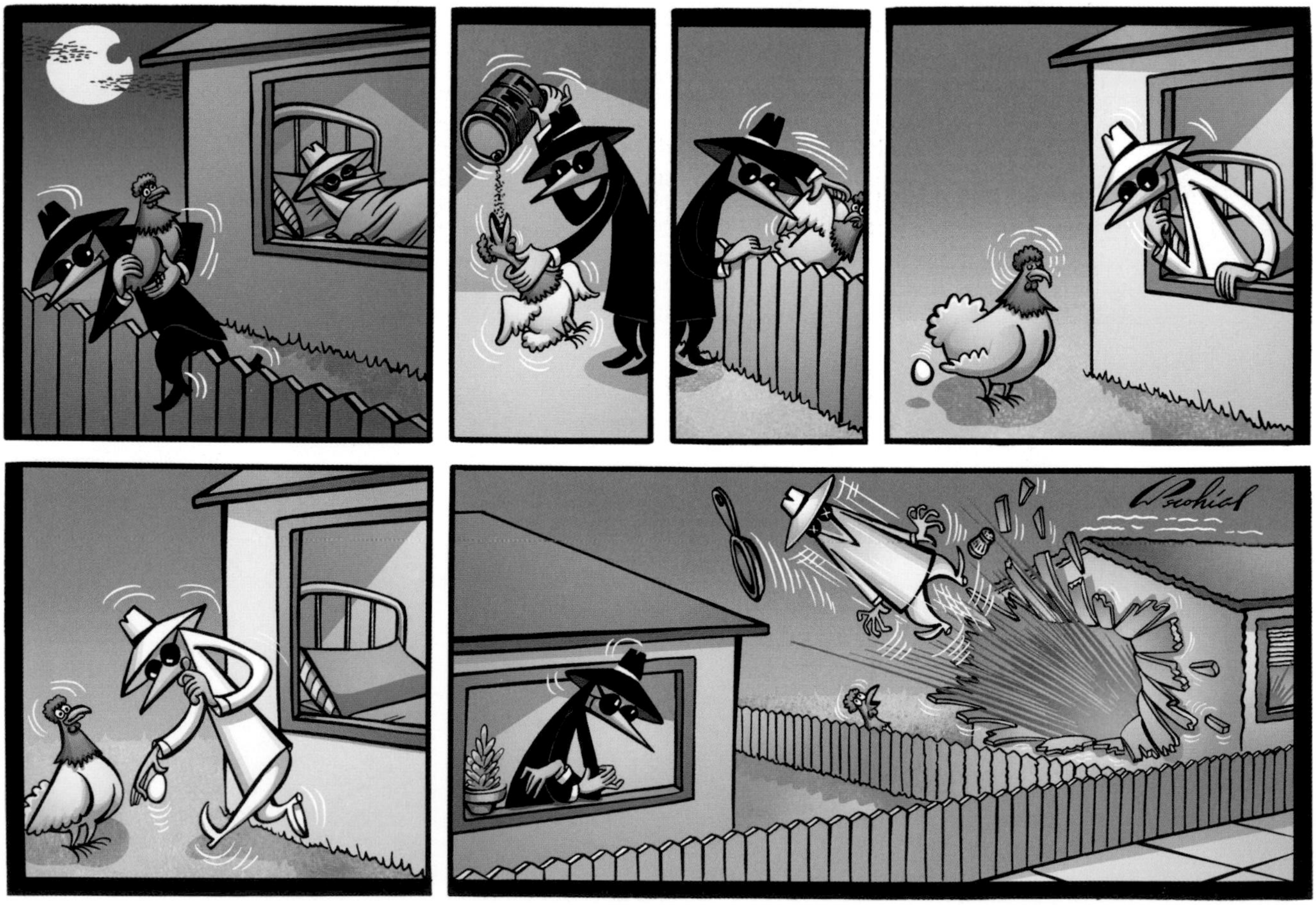

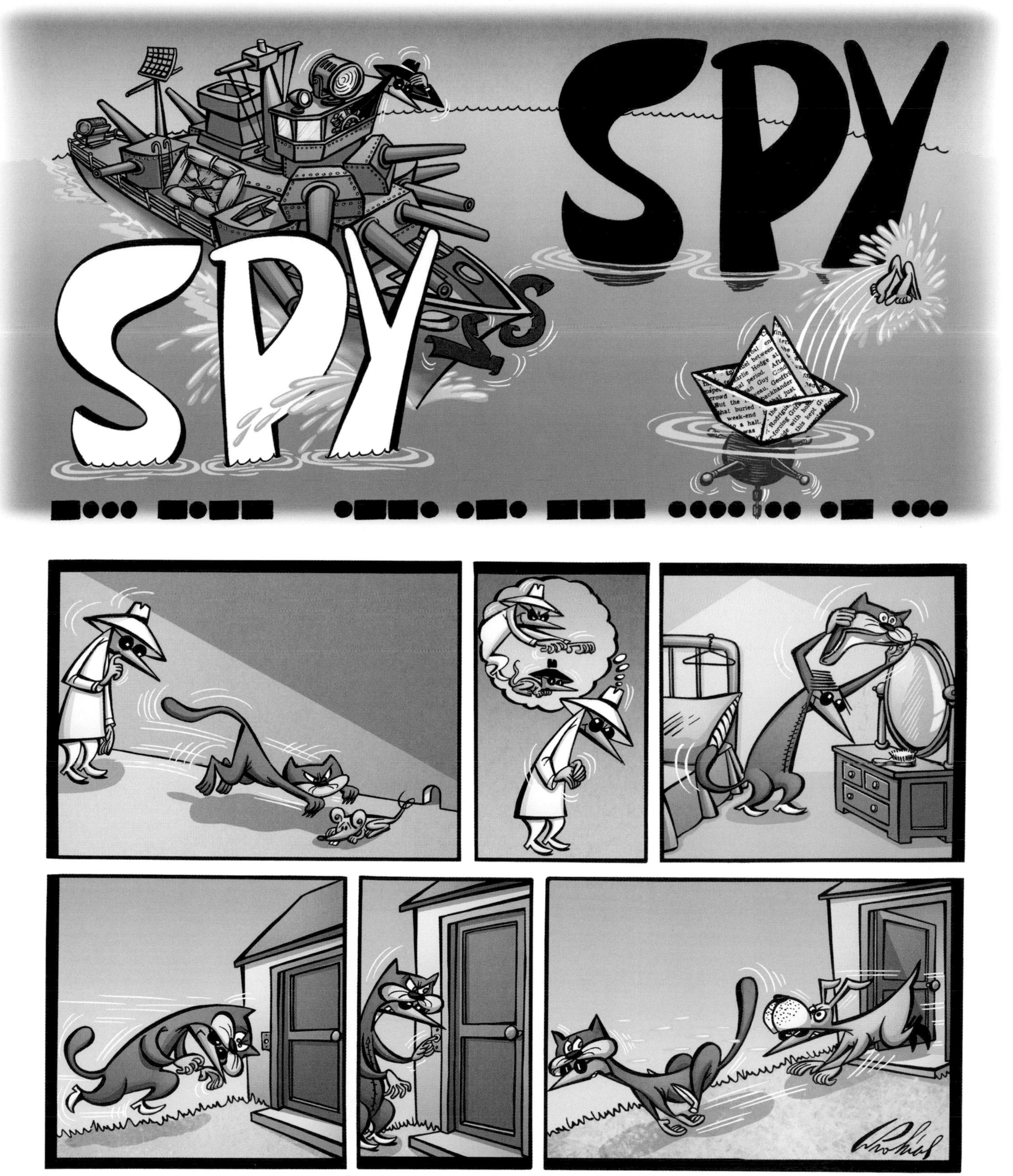
SPY
vs
SPY

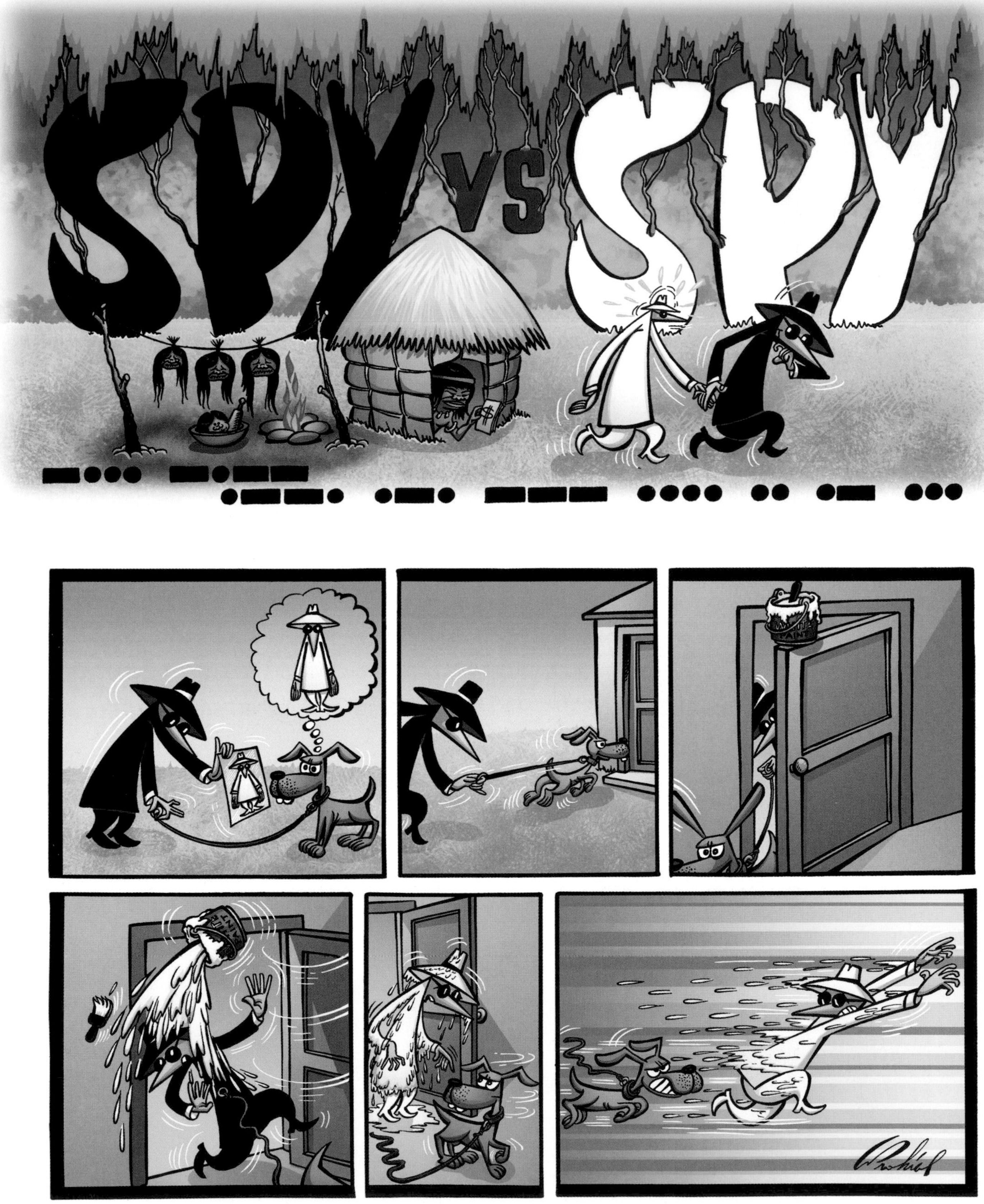
SPY vs SPY

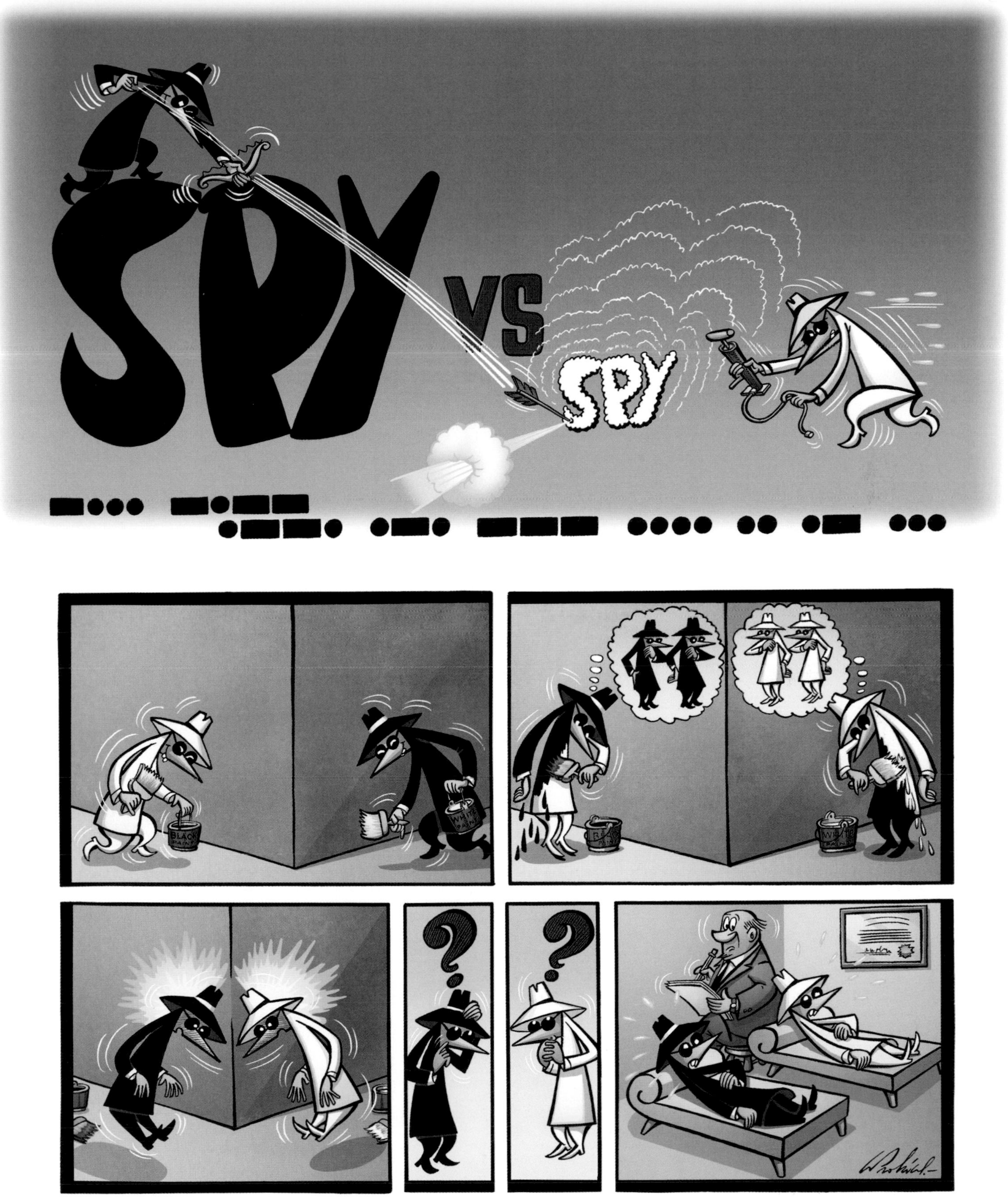
SPY VS SPY
BLACK PAINT
WHITE PAINT

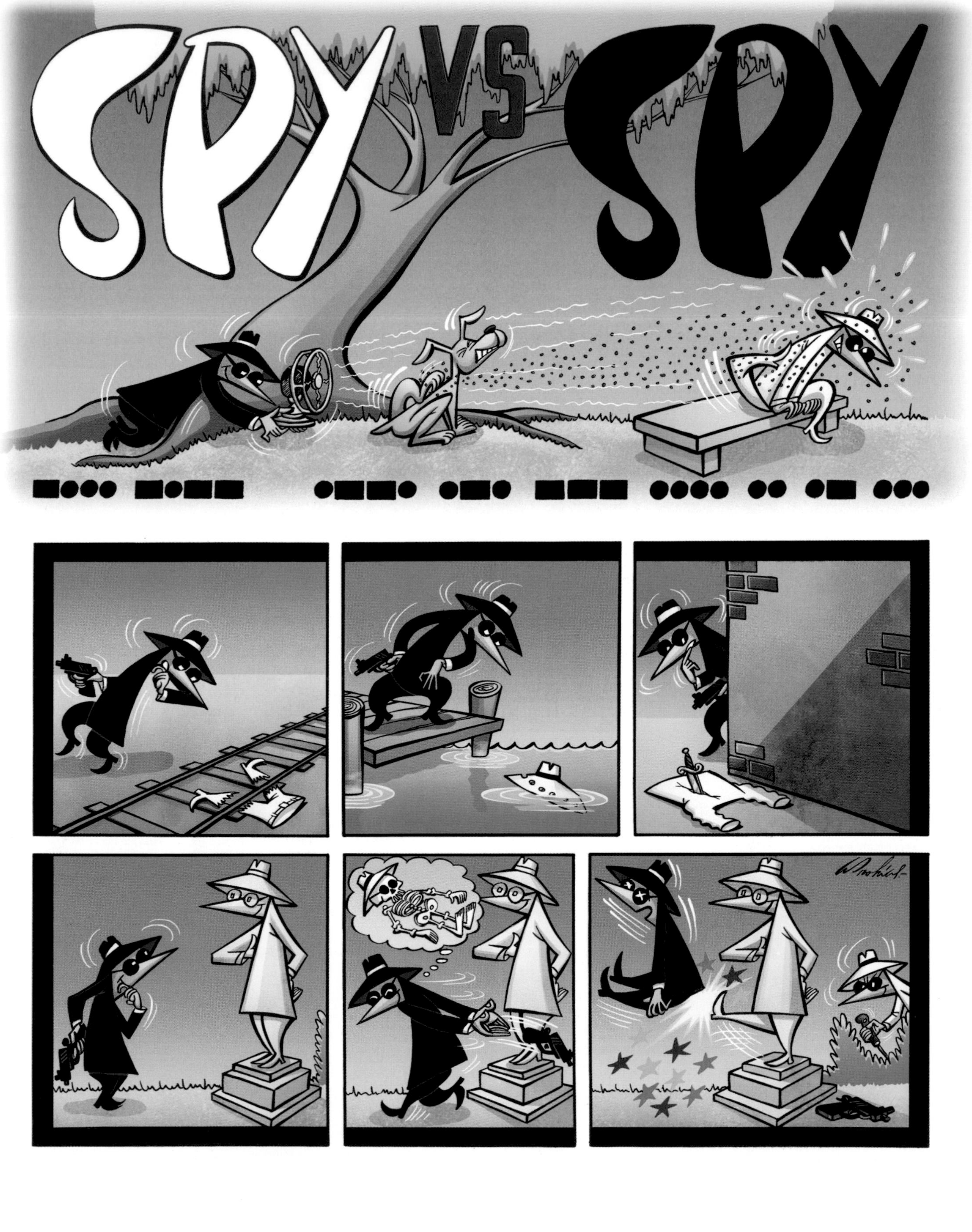
SPY VS SPY

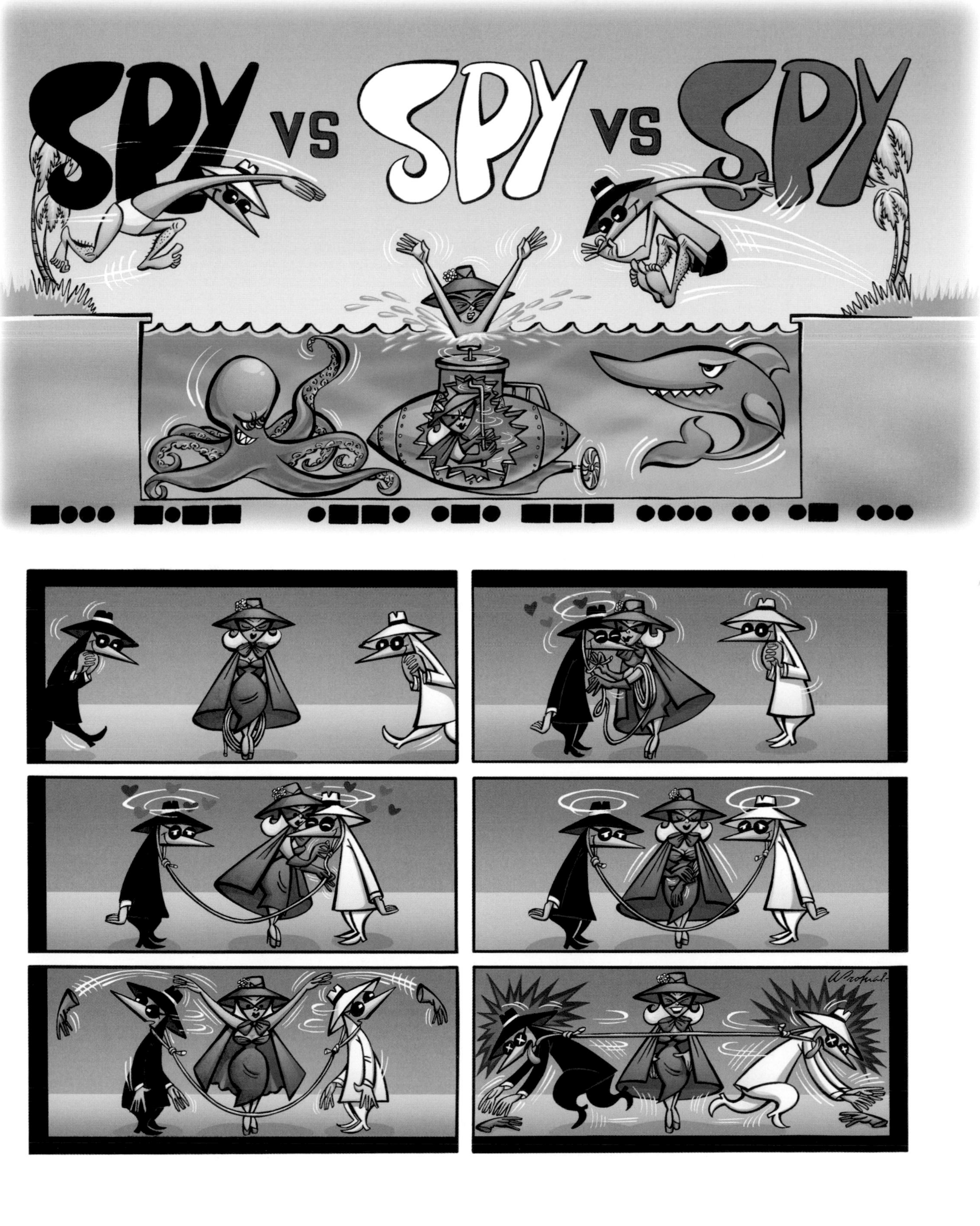
SPY VS SPY VS SPY

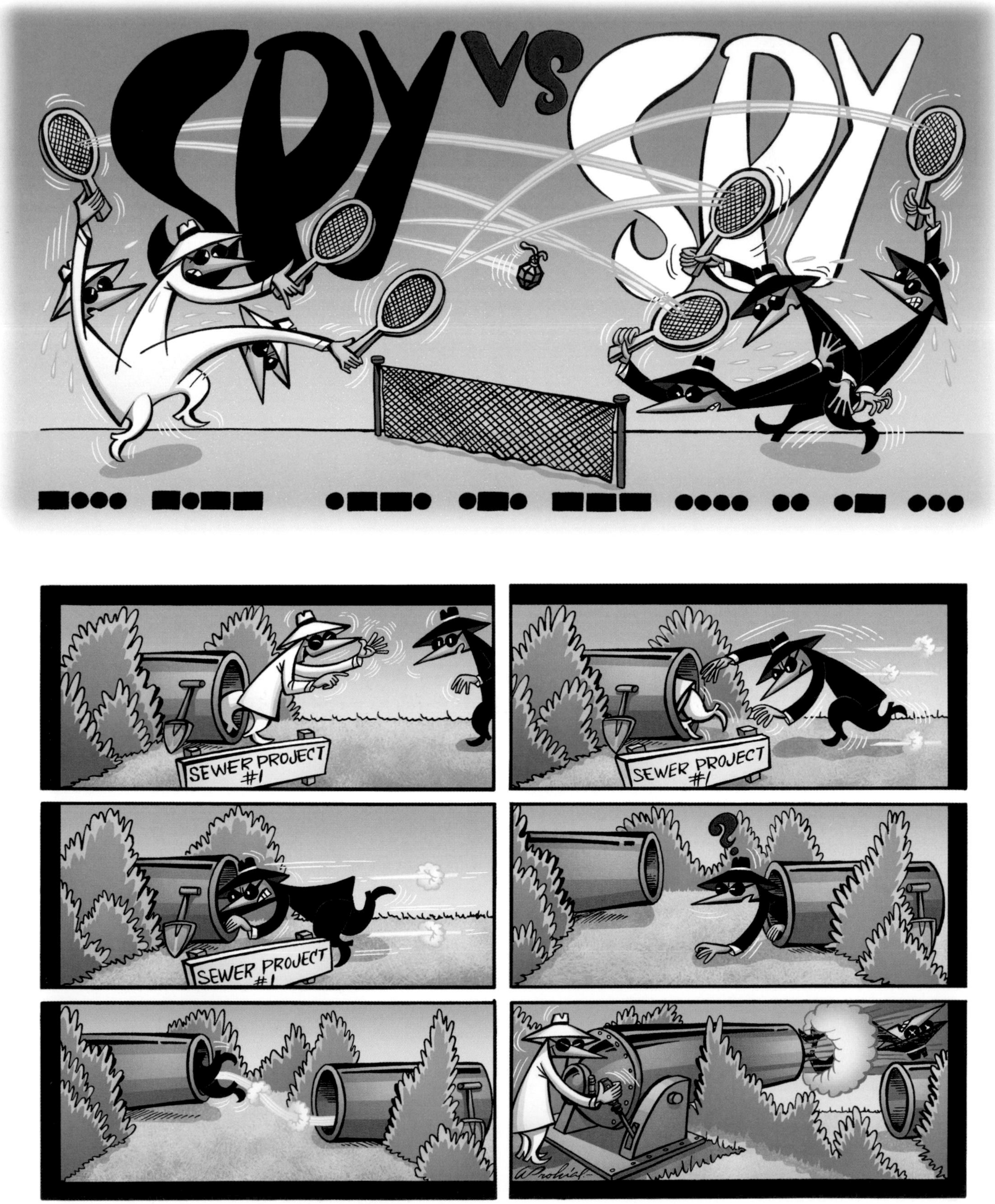
SPY vs SPY
SEWER PROJECT #1
SEWER PROJECT #1
SEWER PROJECT #1

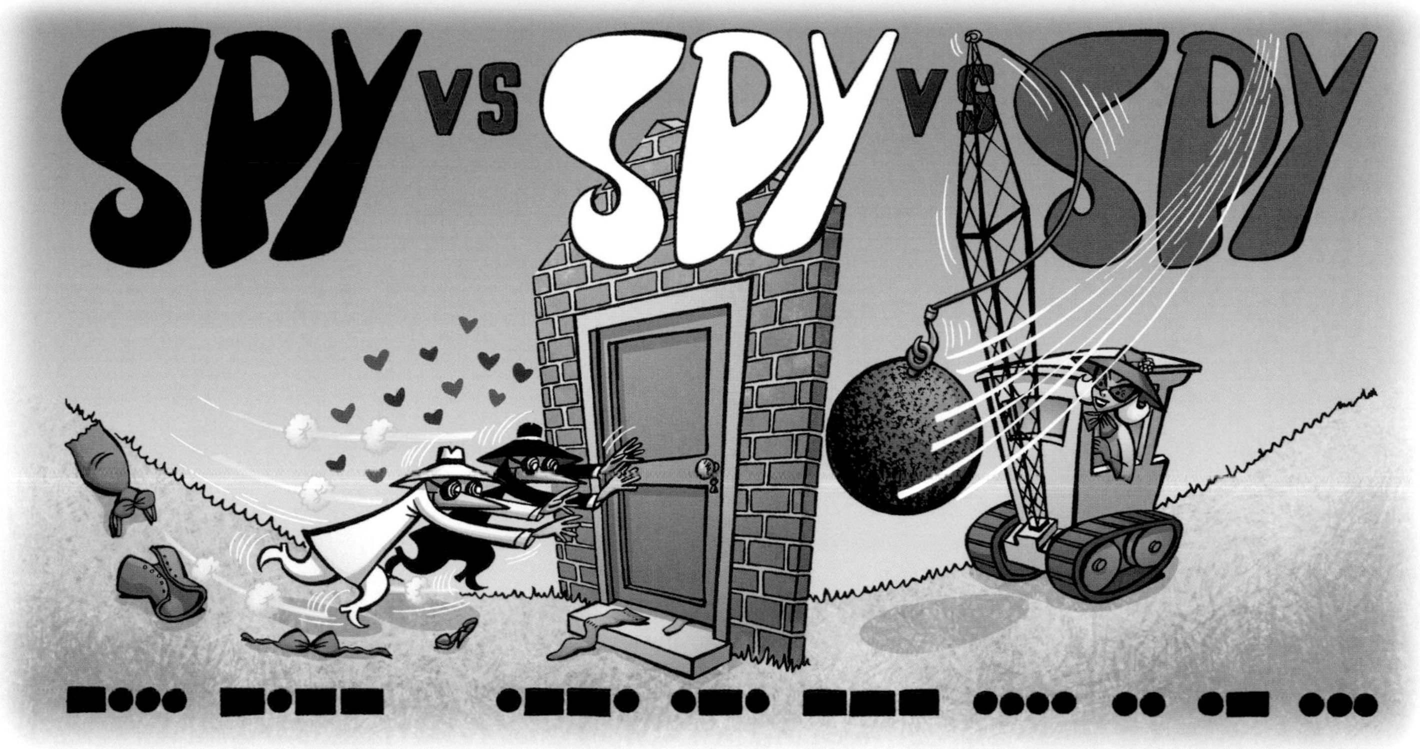
SPY vs SPY vs SPY

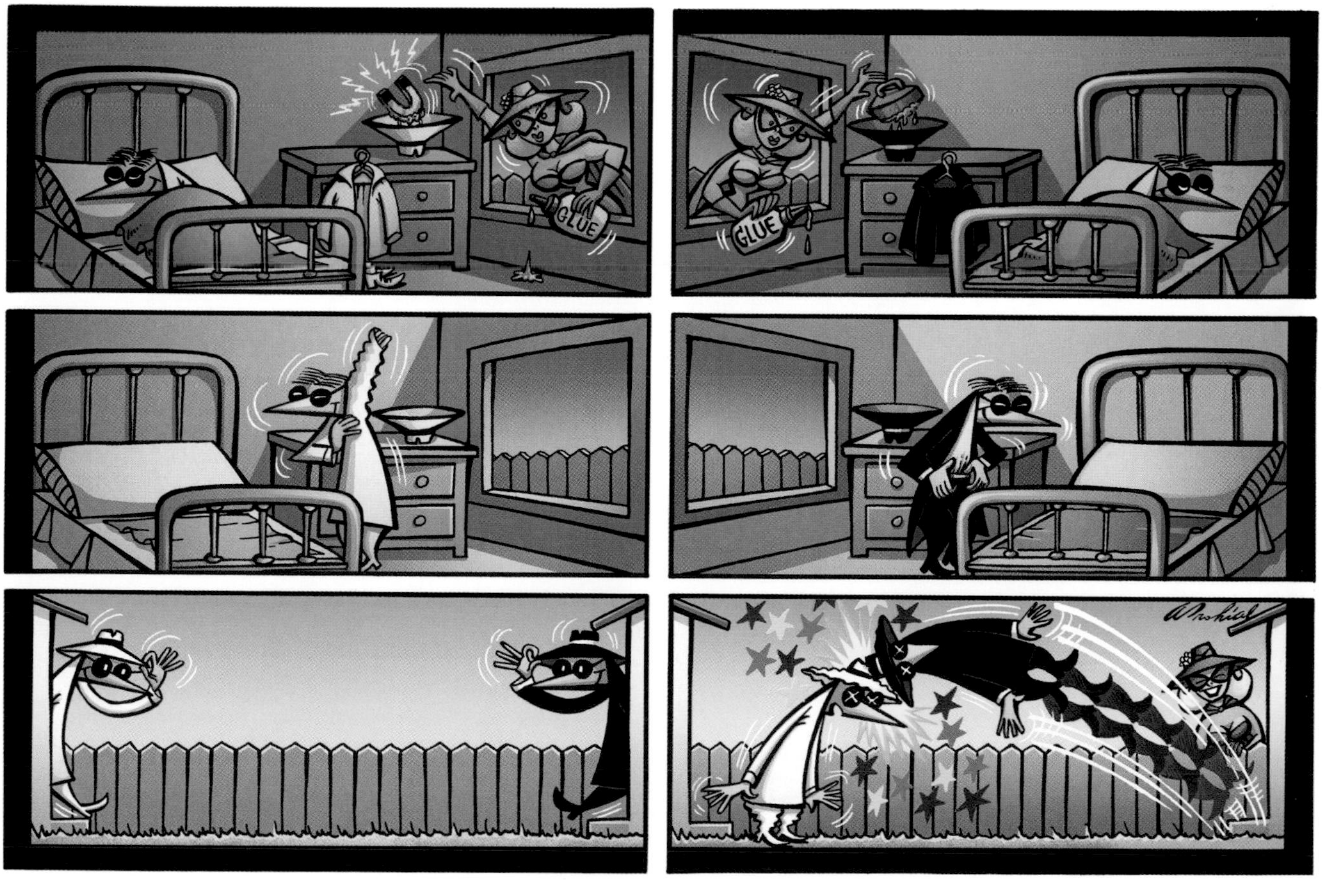
GLUE
GLUE
Prohias

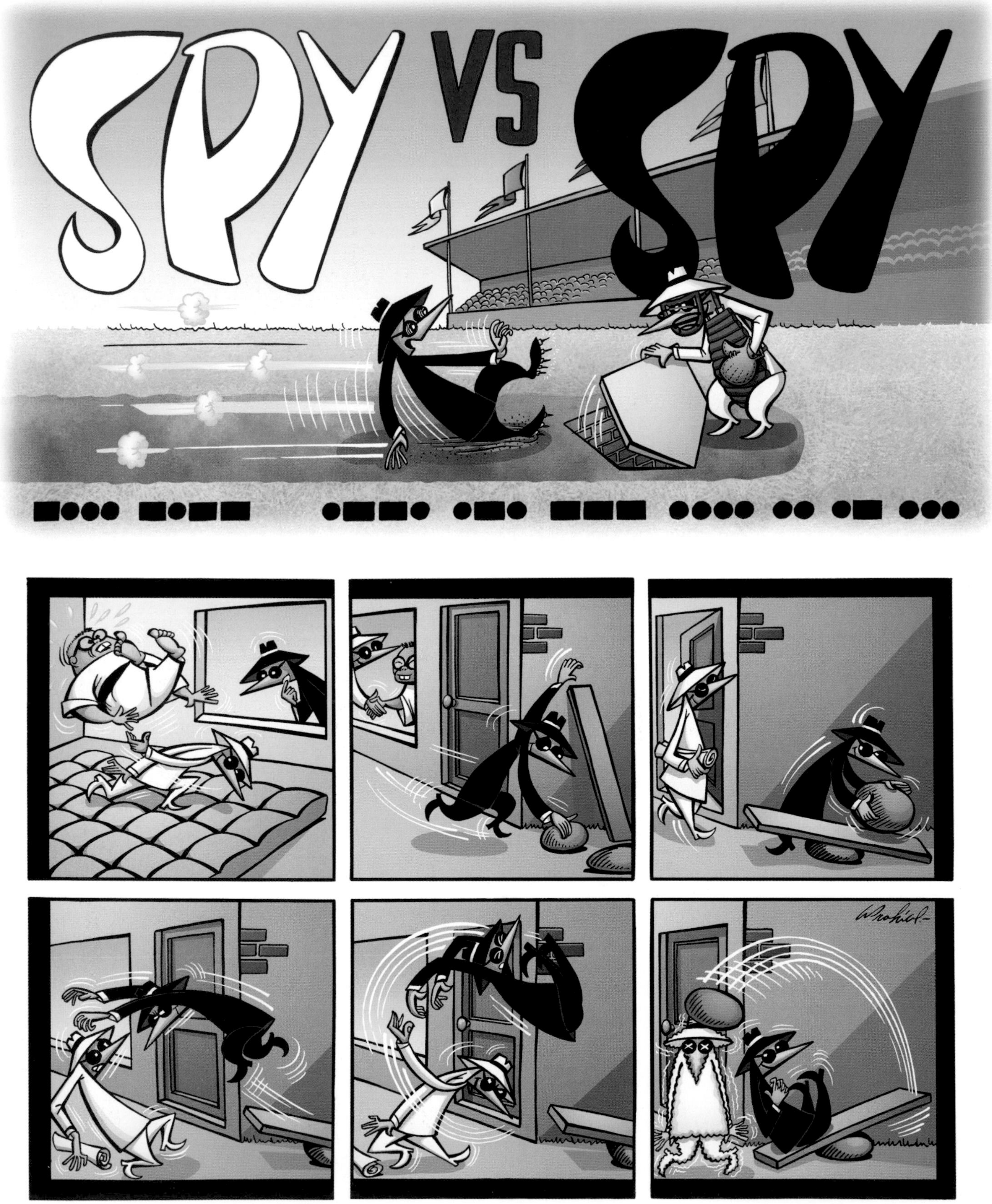
SPY VS SPY

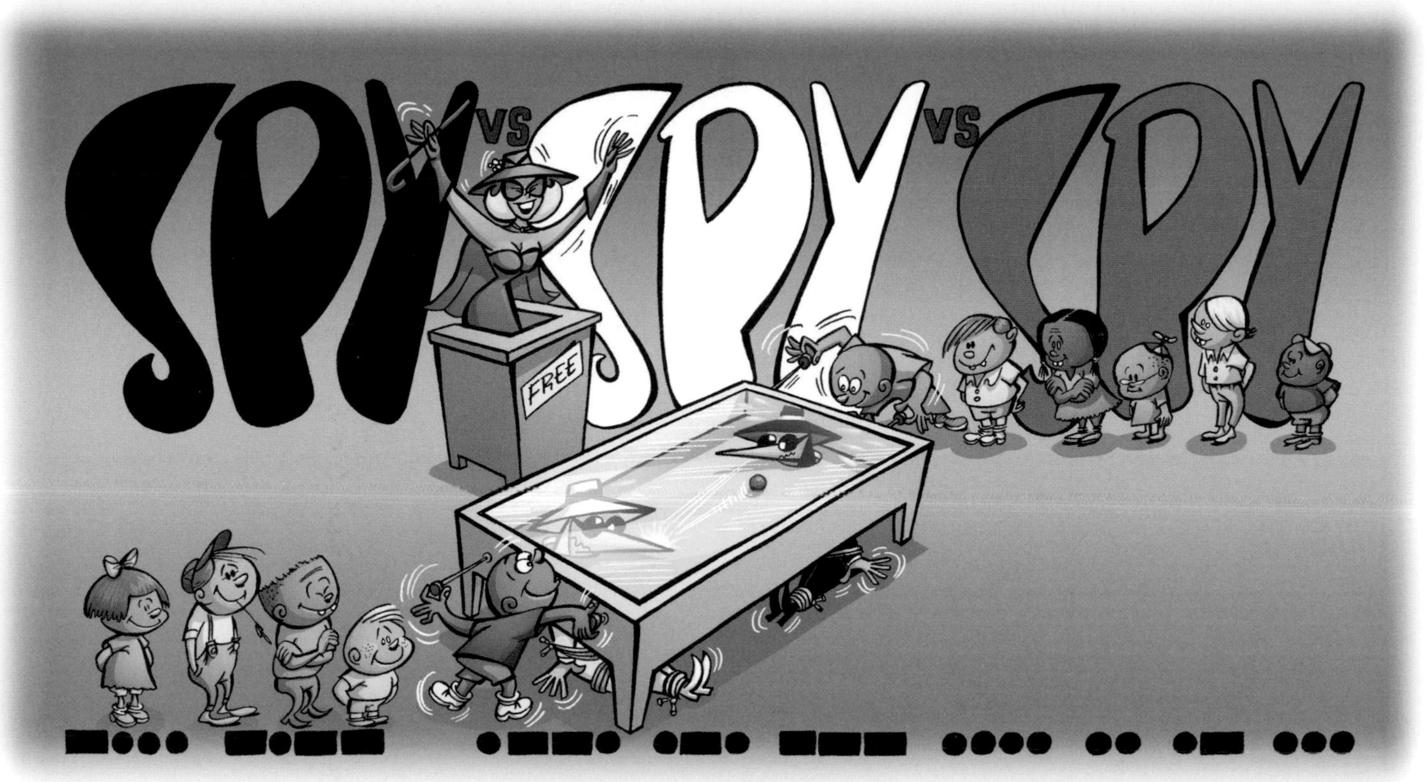
SPY vs SPY vs SPY
FREE

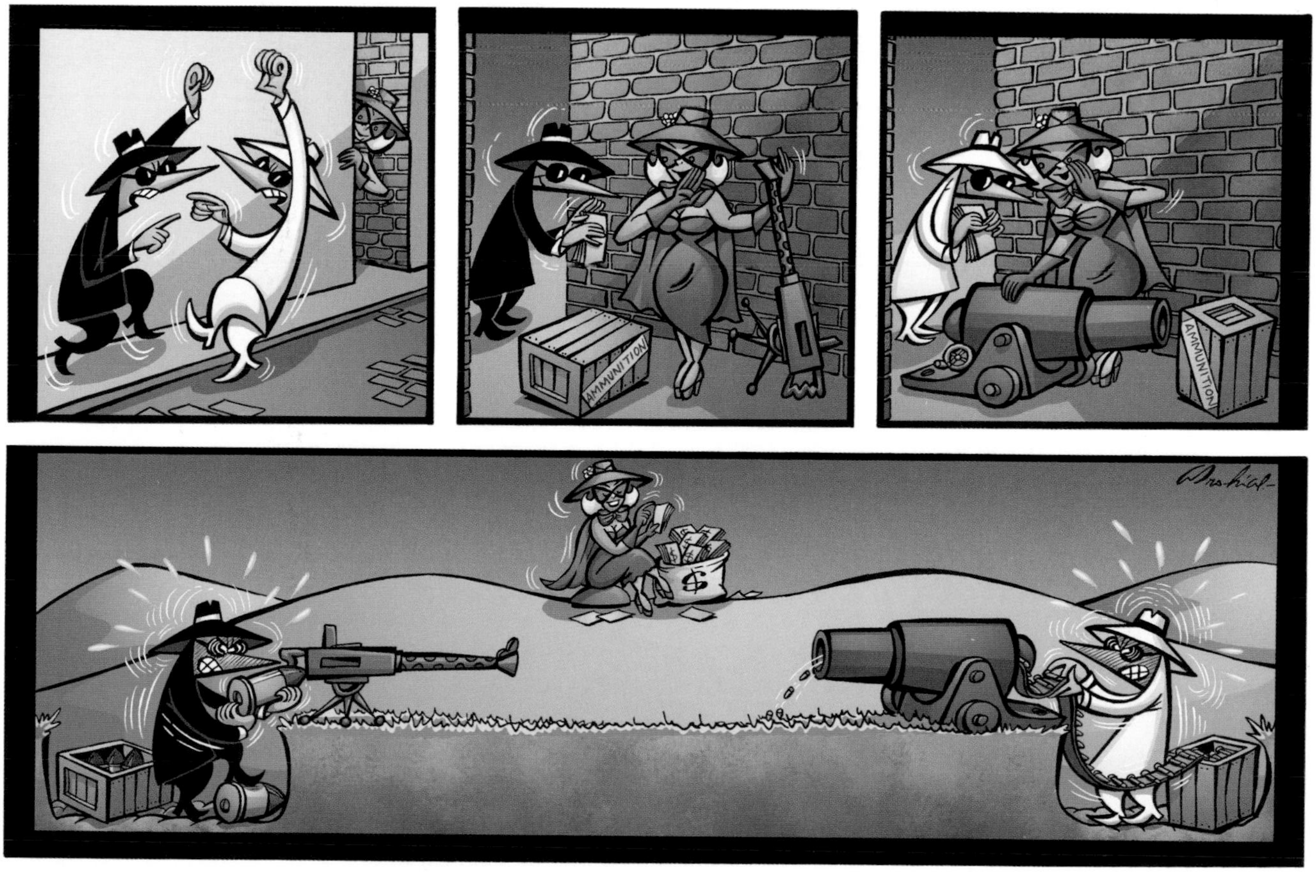
AMMUNITION
AMMUNITION

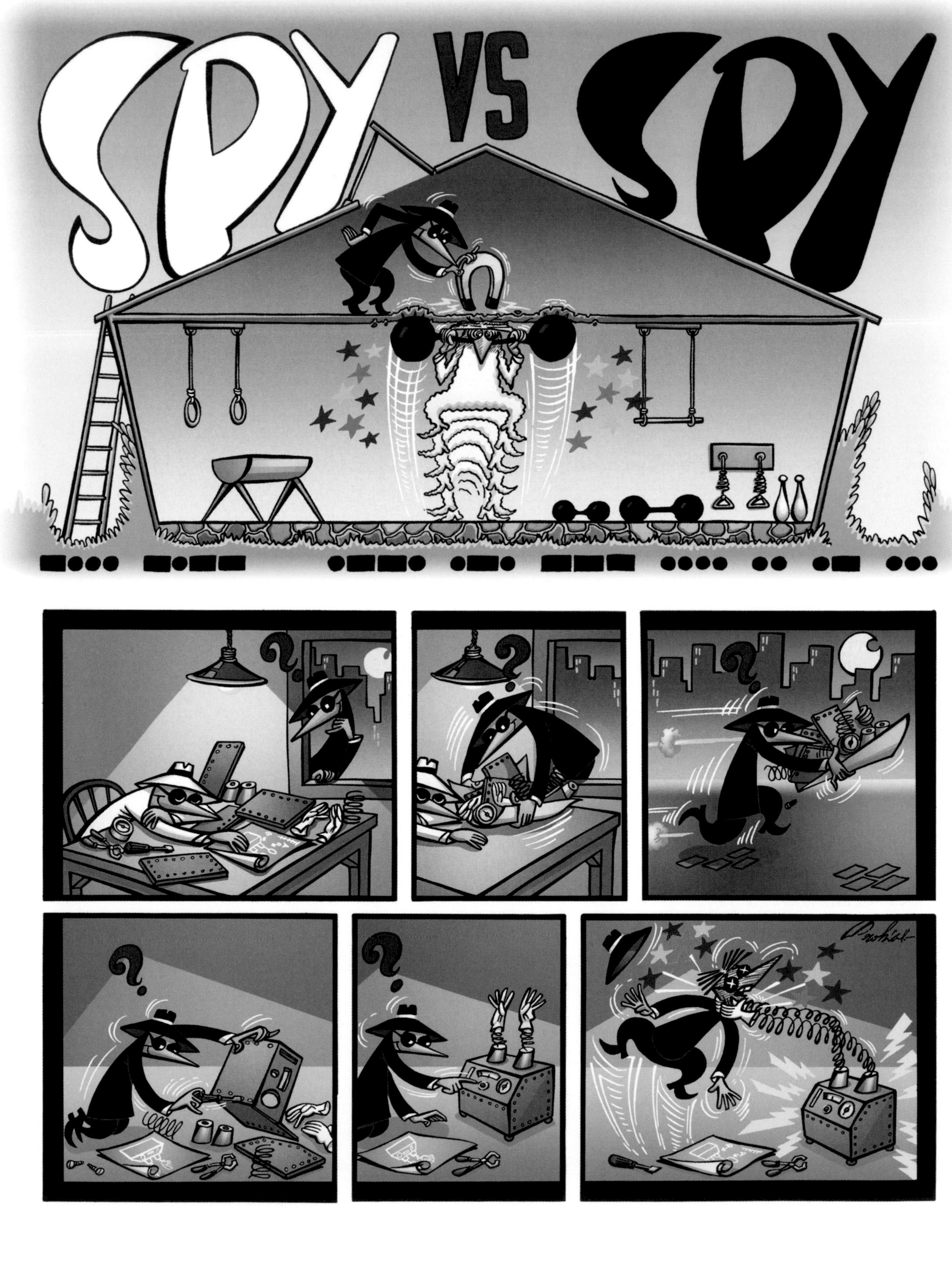
SPY VS SPY

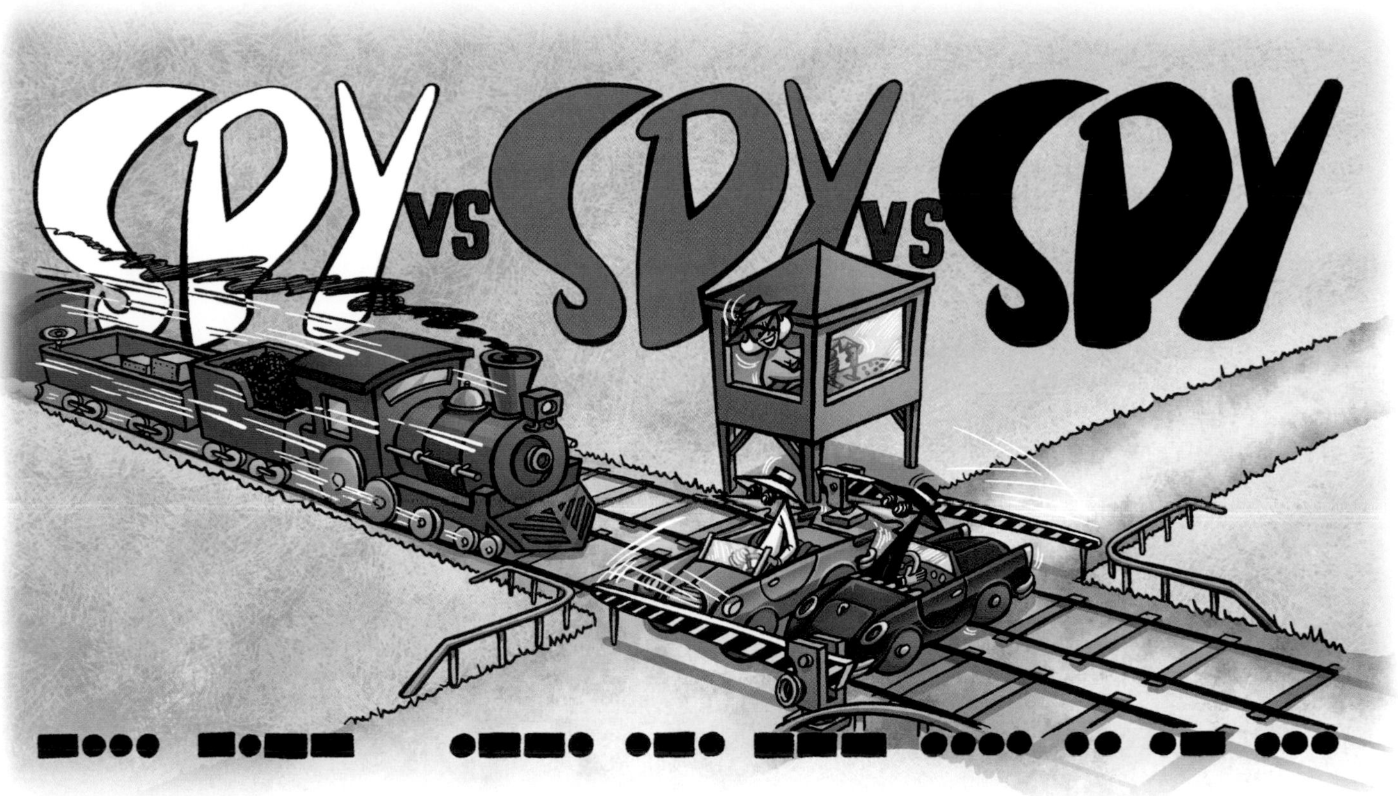
SPY VS SPY VS SPY

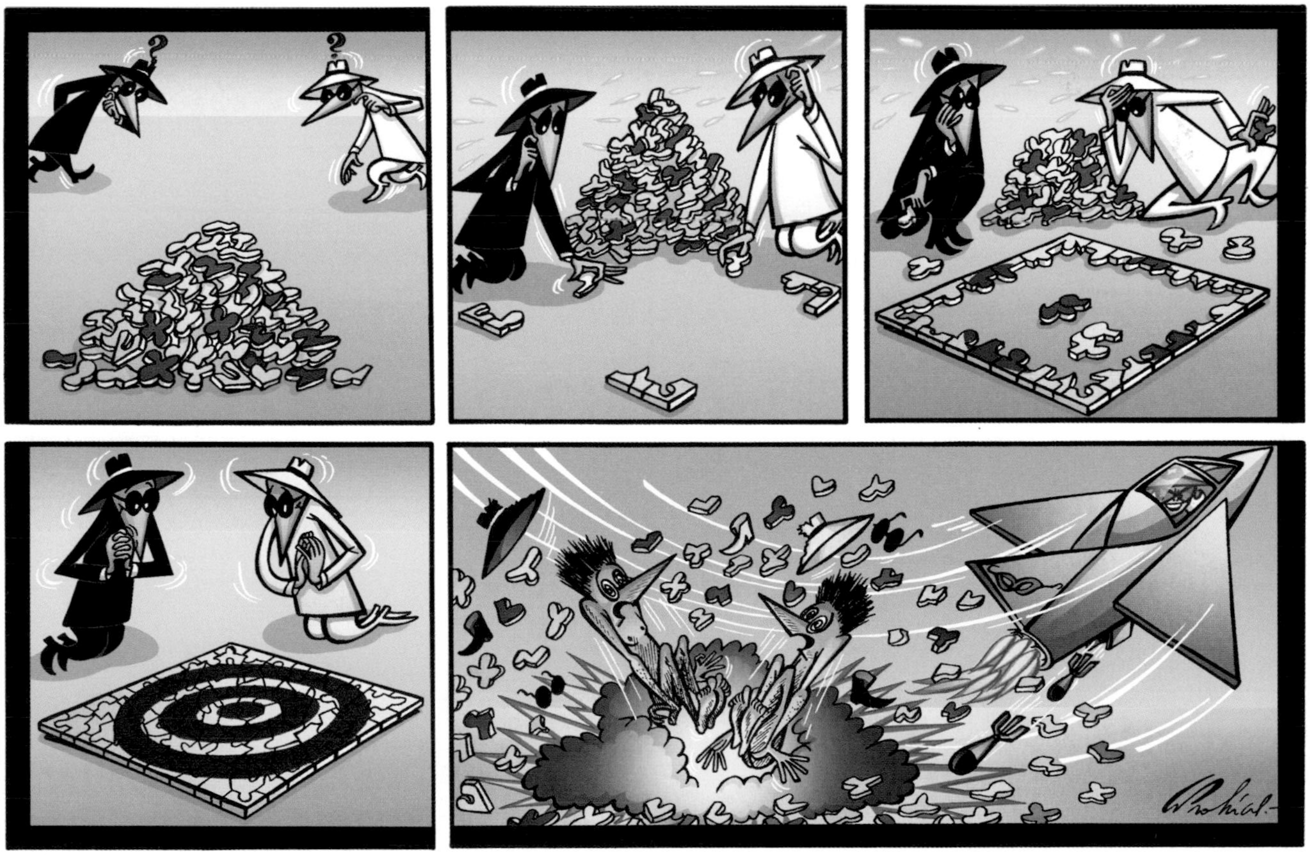

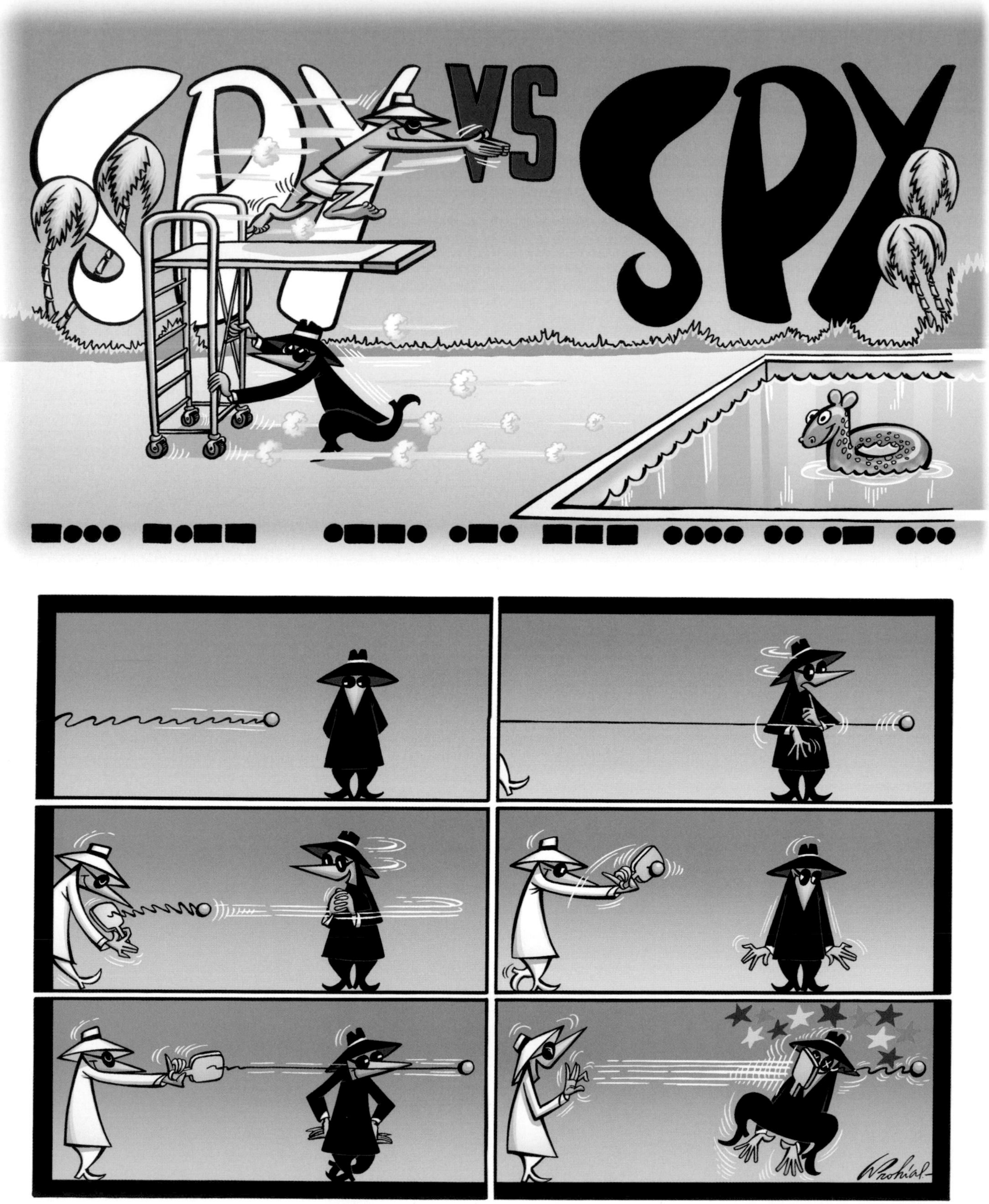
SPY VS SPY

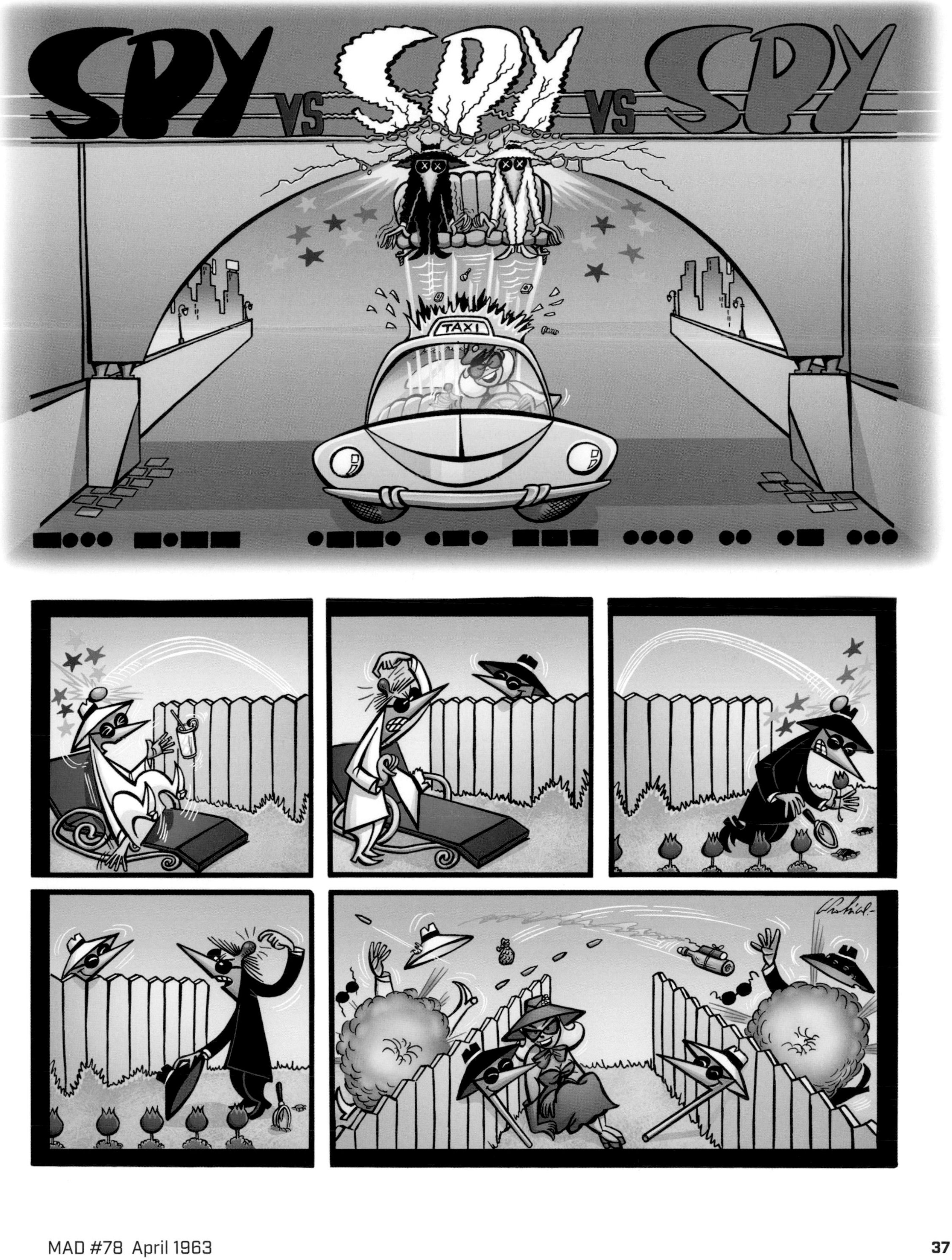
SPY VS SPY VS SPY
TAXI

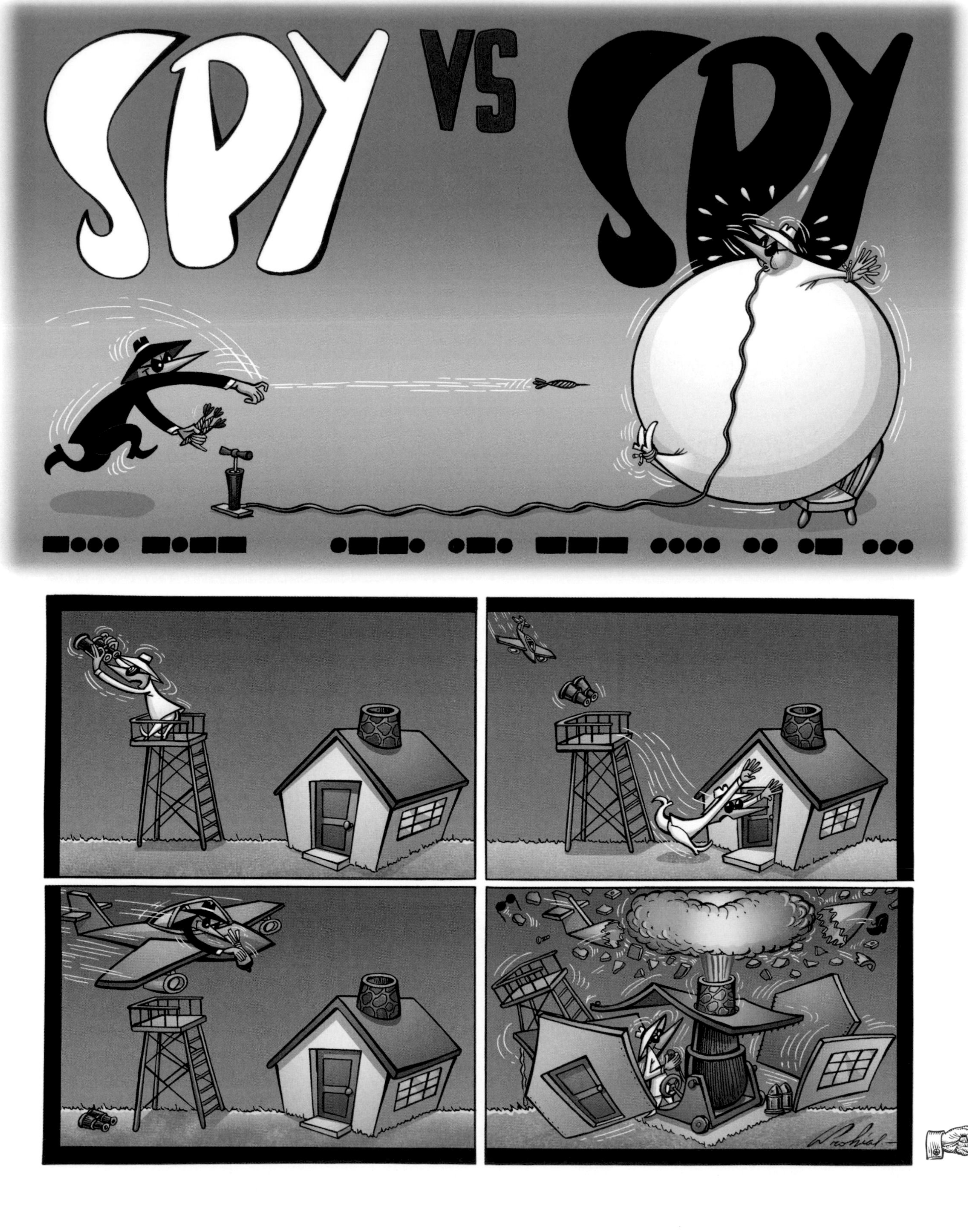
SPY VS SPY

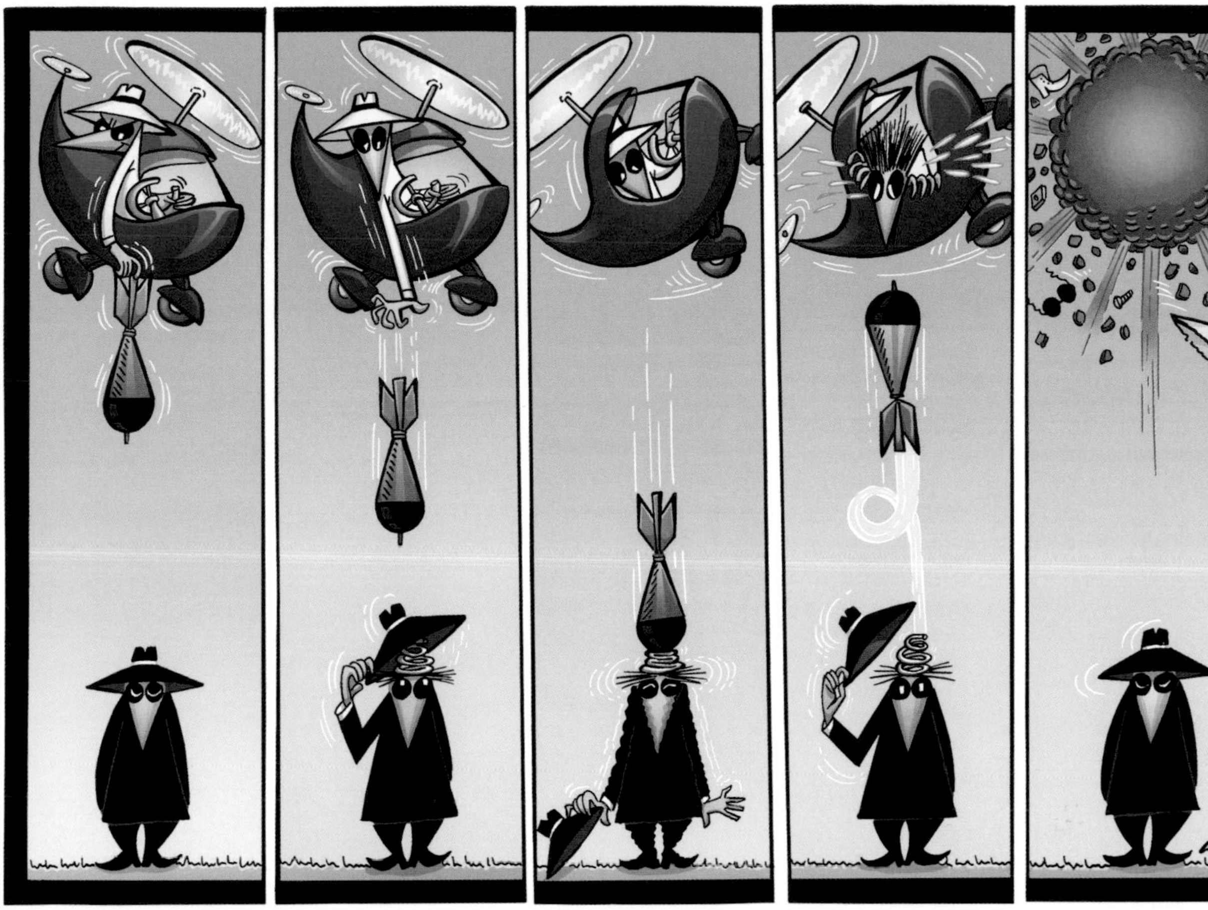

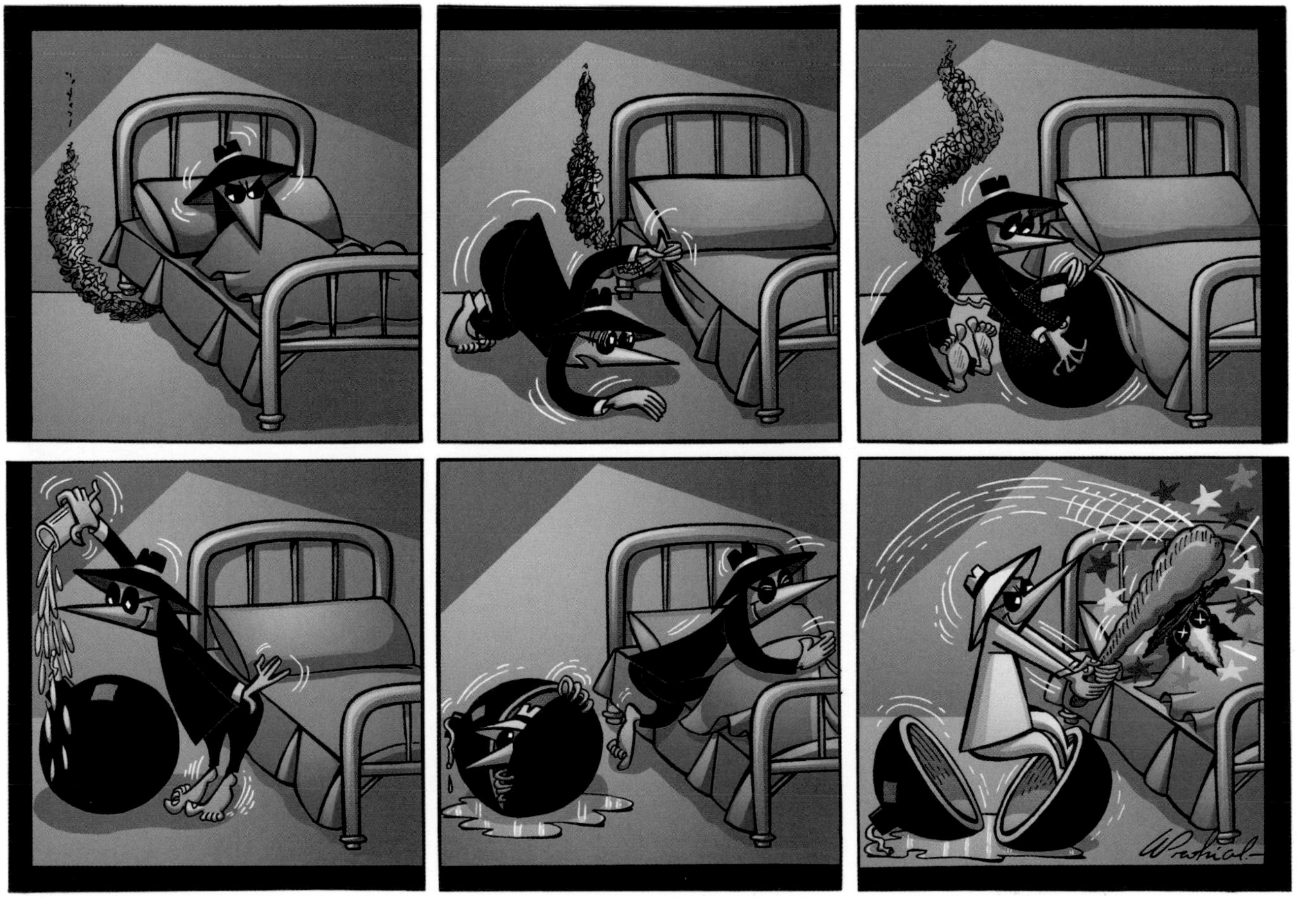

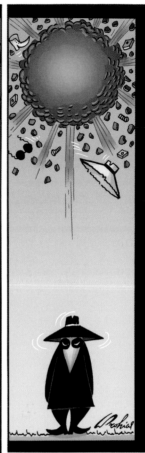

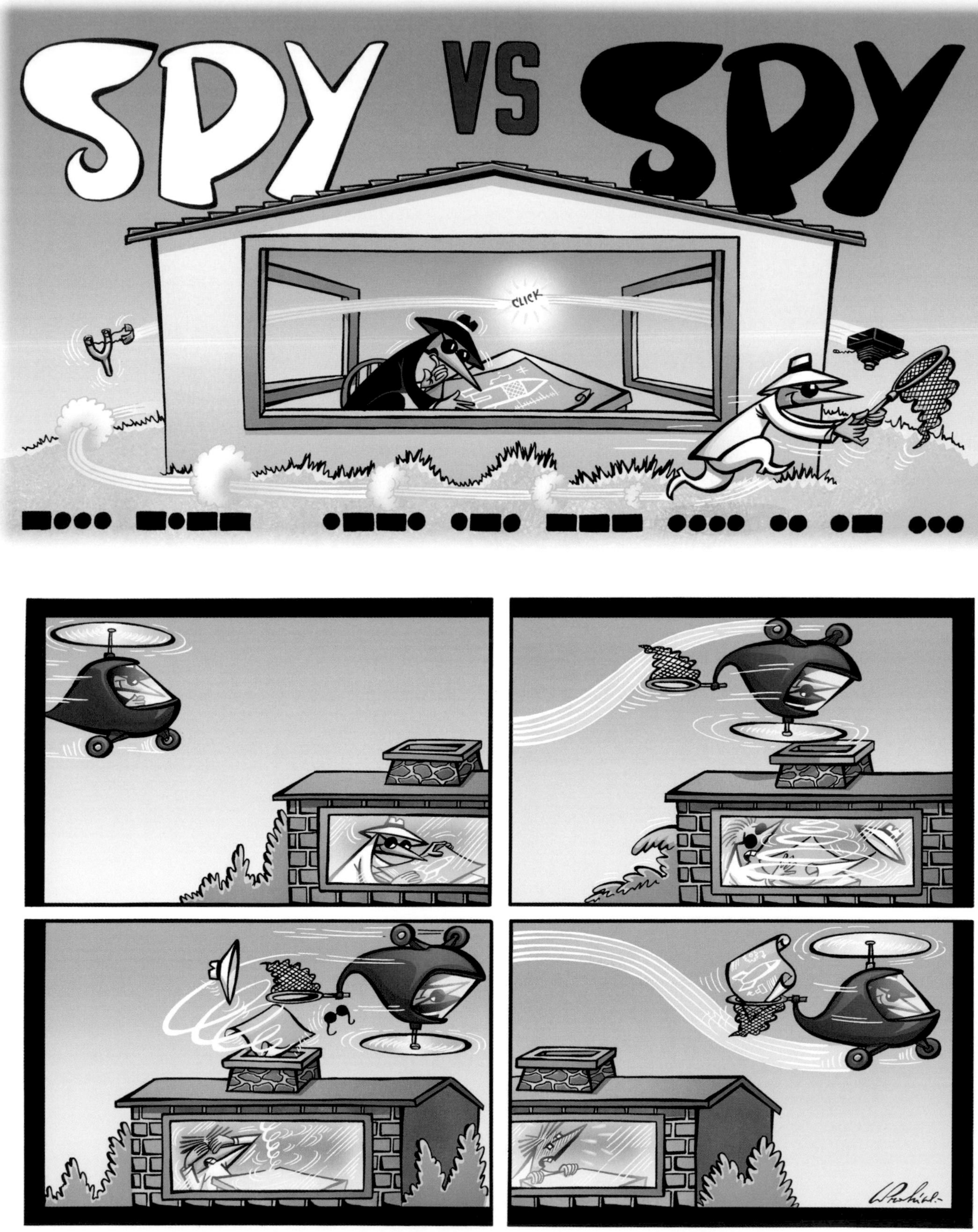
SPY VS SPY
CLICK

SPY vs SPY vs SPY

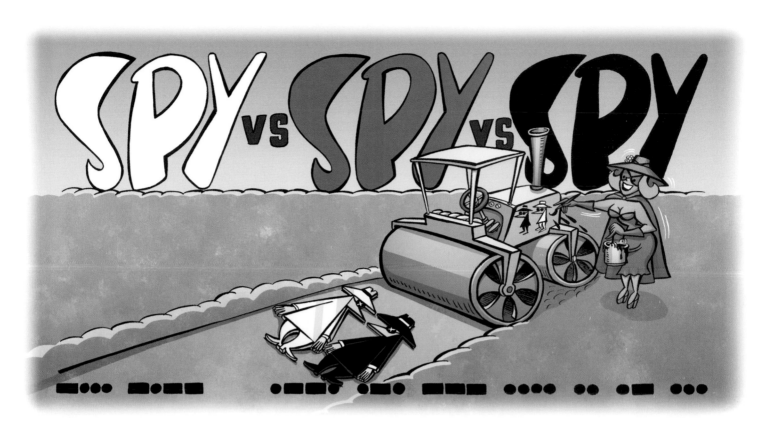

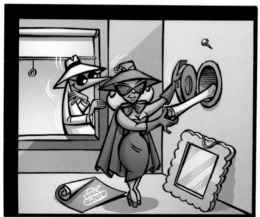

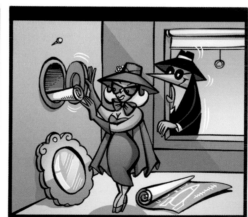

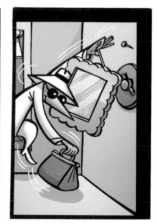

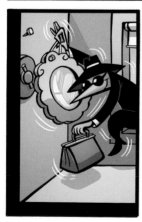

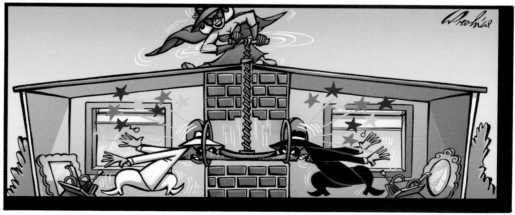

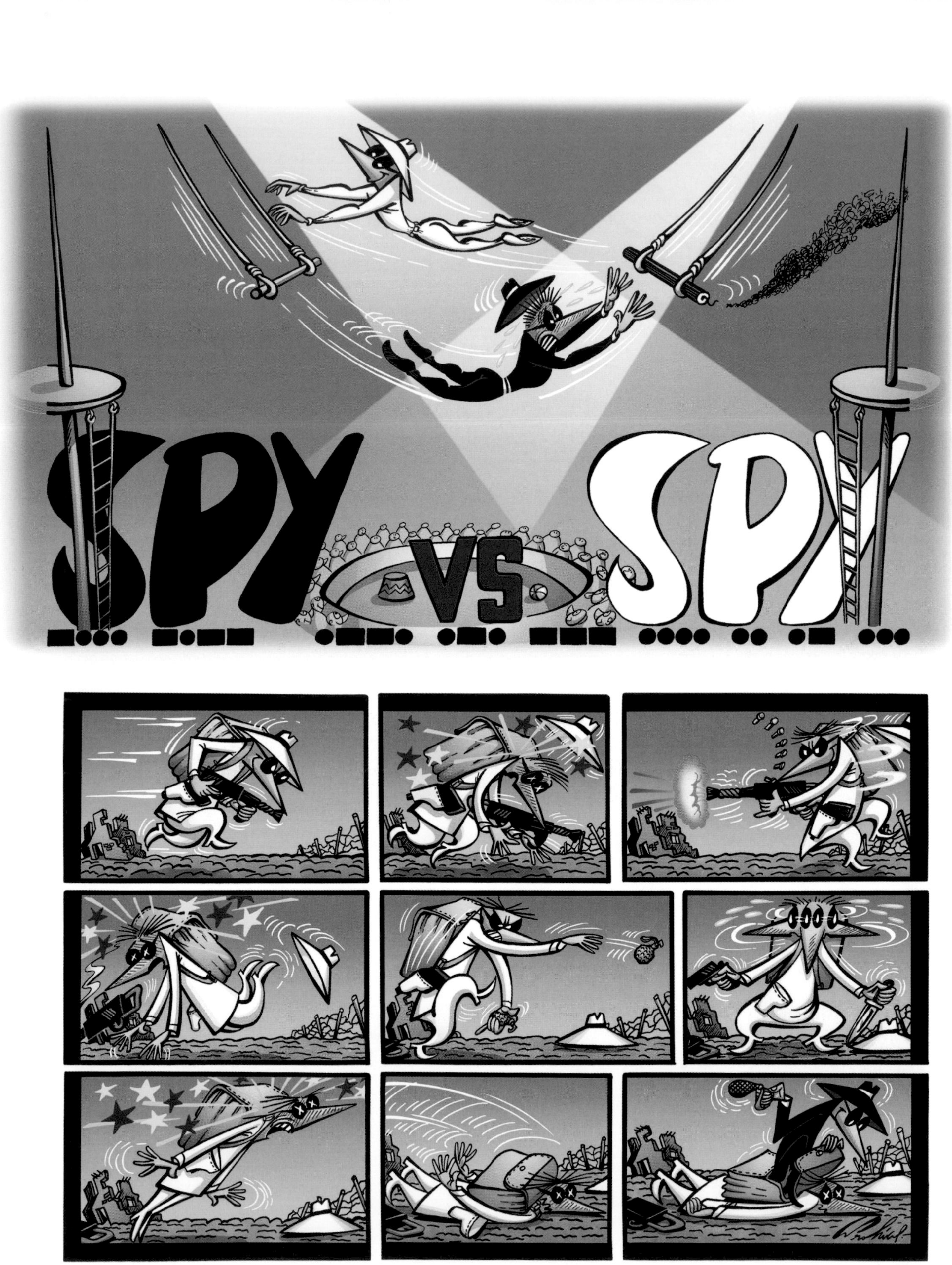
SPY VS SPY

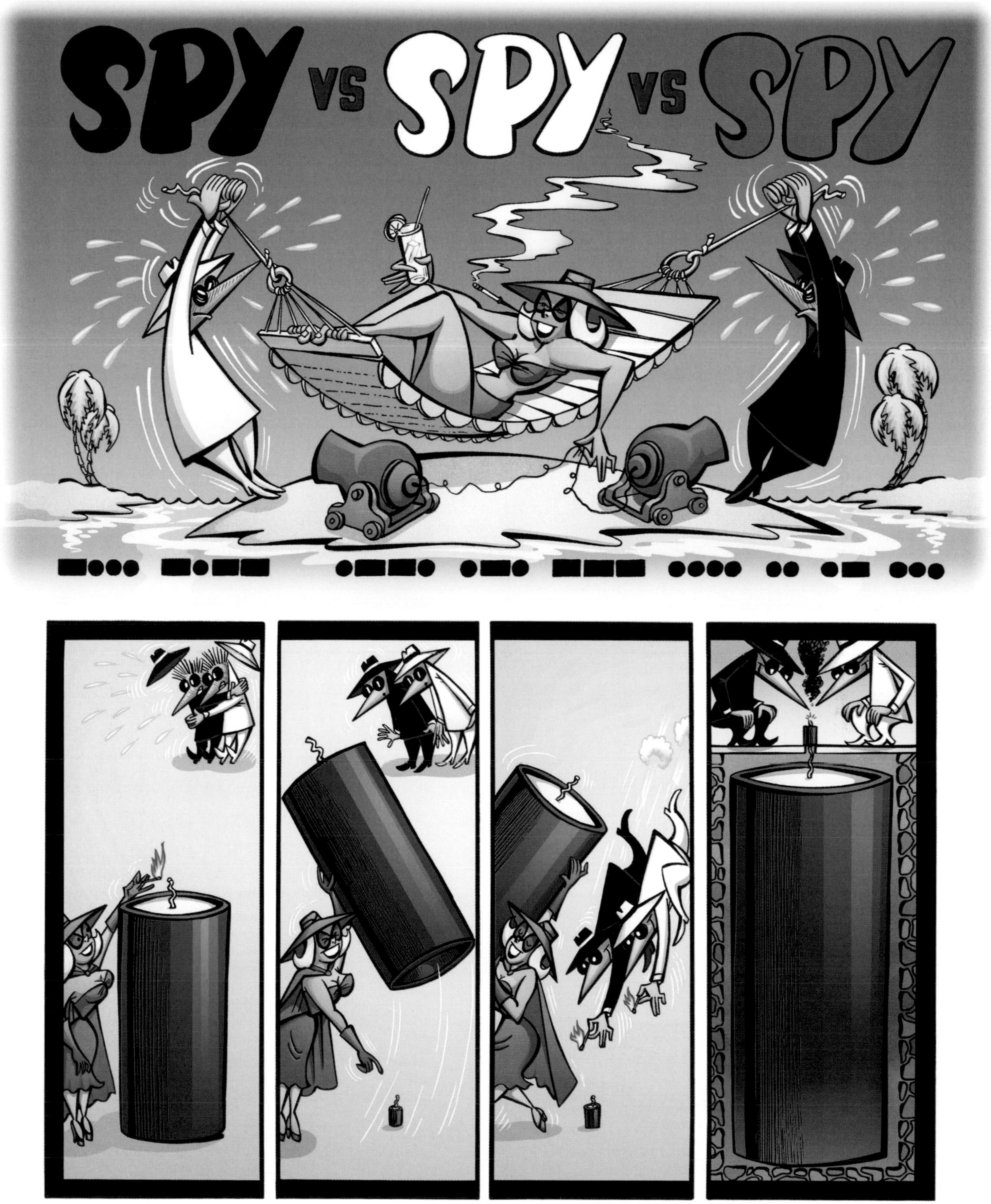
SPY vs SPY vs SPY

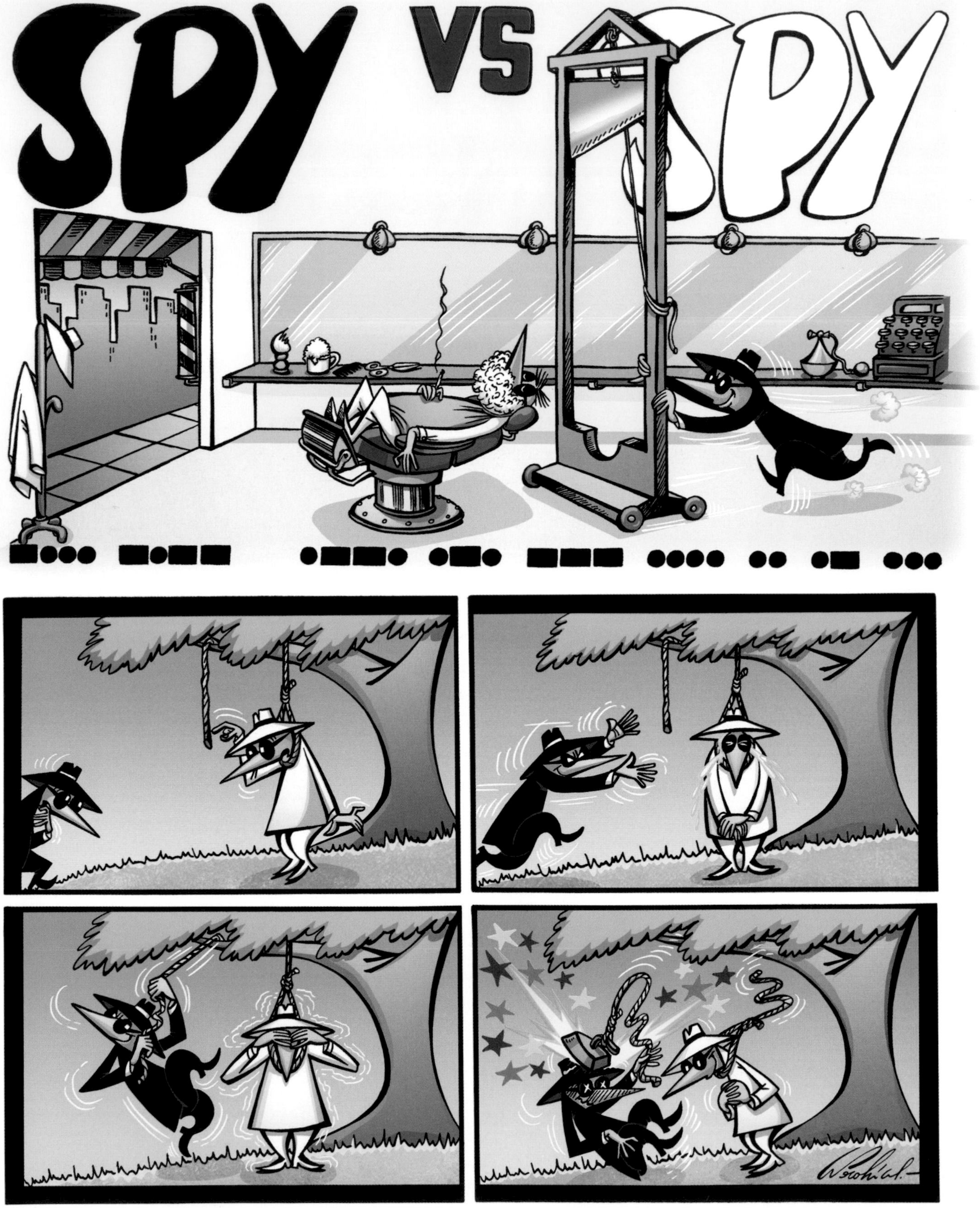
SPY VS SPY

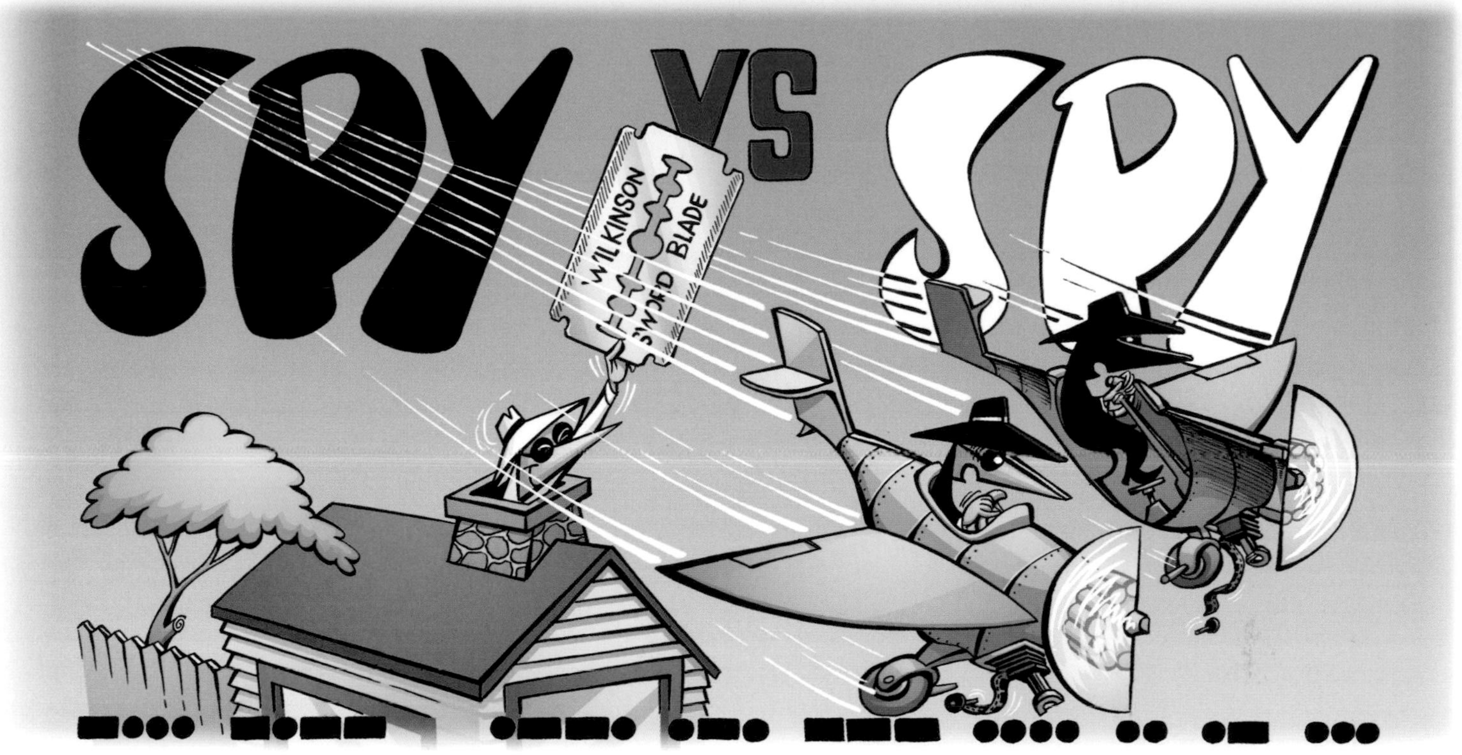
SPY vs SPY
WILKINSON SWORD BLADE

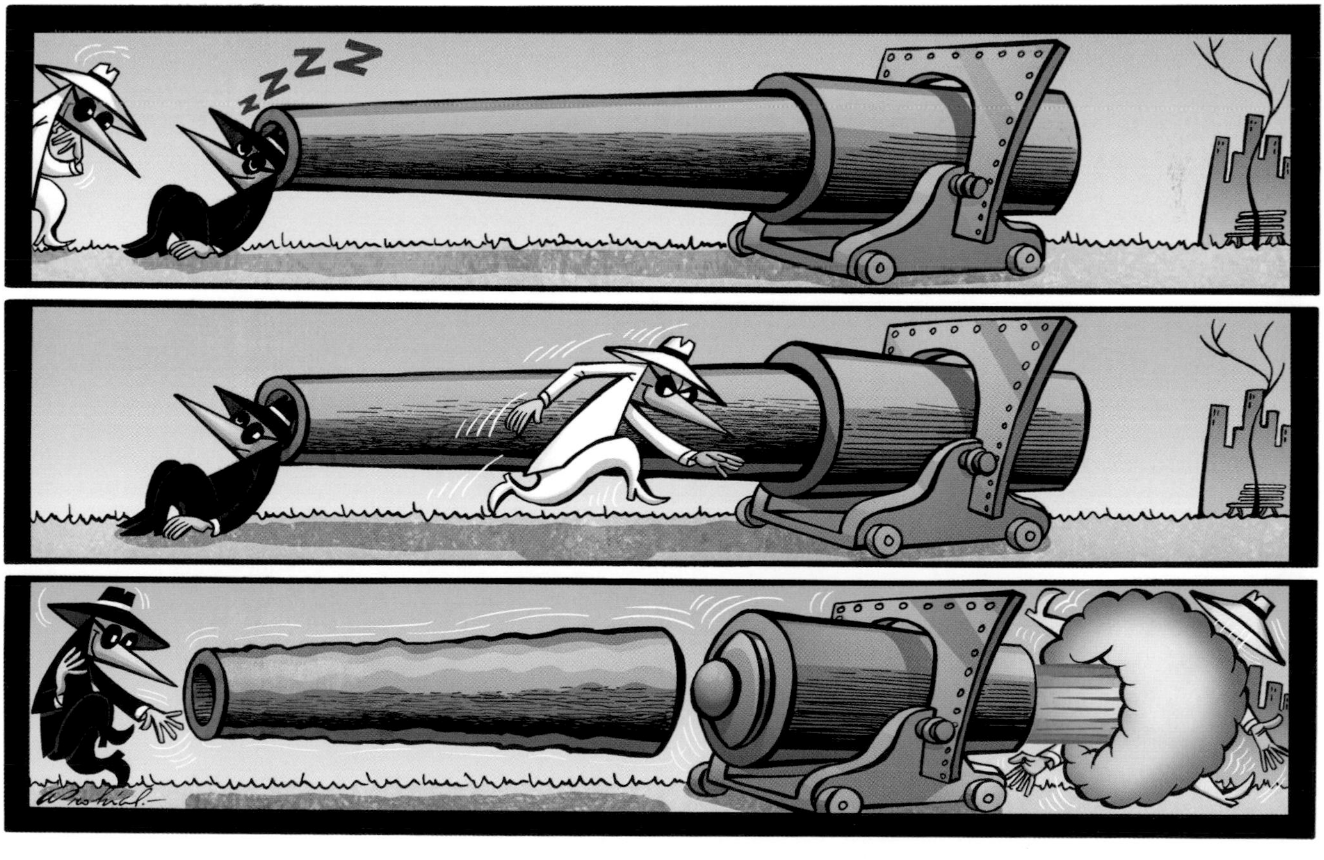
ZZZZ

SPY vs SPY vs SPY

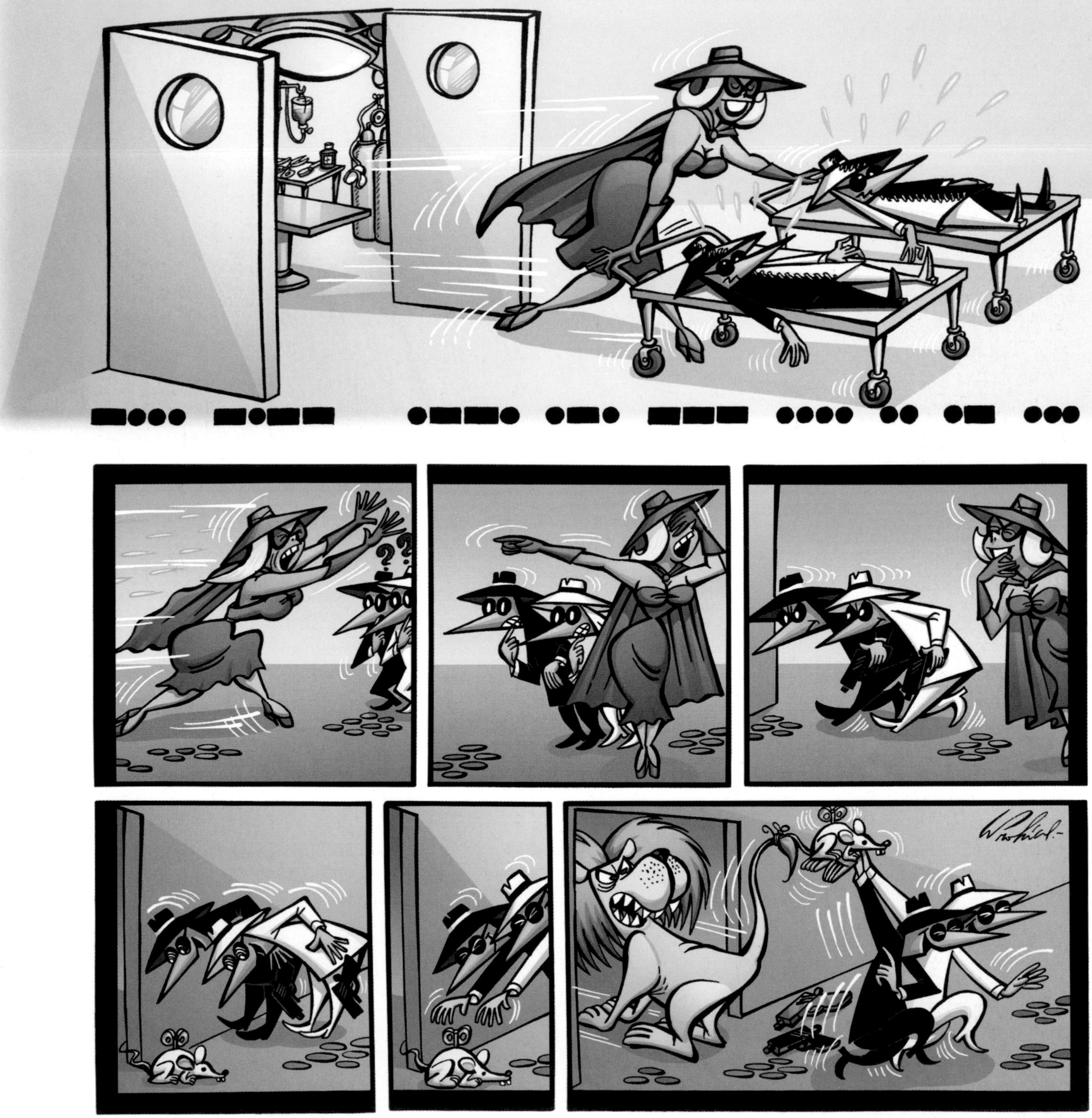

The **Diabolical Duo** of **Double-Cross** and **Deceit**
as **Depicted** by **Some** of the **World's Most Renowned Artists**.

THE SPY VS. SPY POSTER COLLECTION

GALLERY I

Bob Staake

Tony Millionaire

Gilbert and Jaime Hernandez

Jim Lee (Colorist: Alex Sinclair)

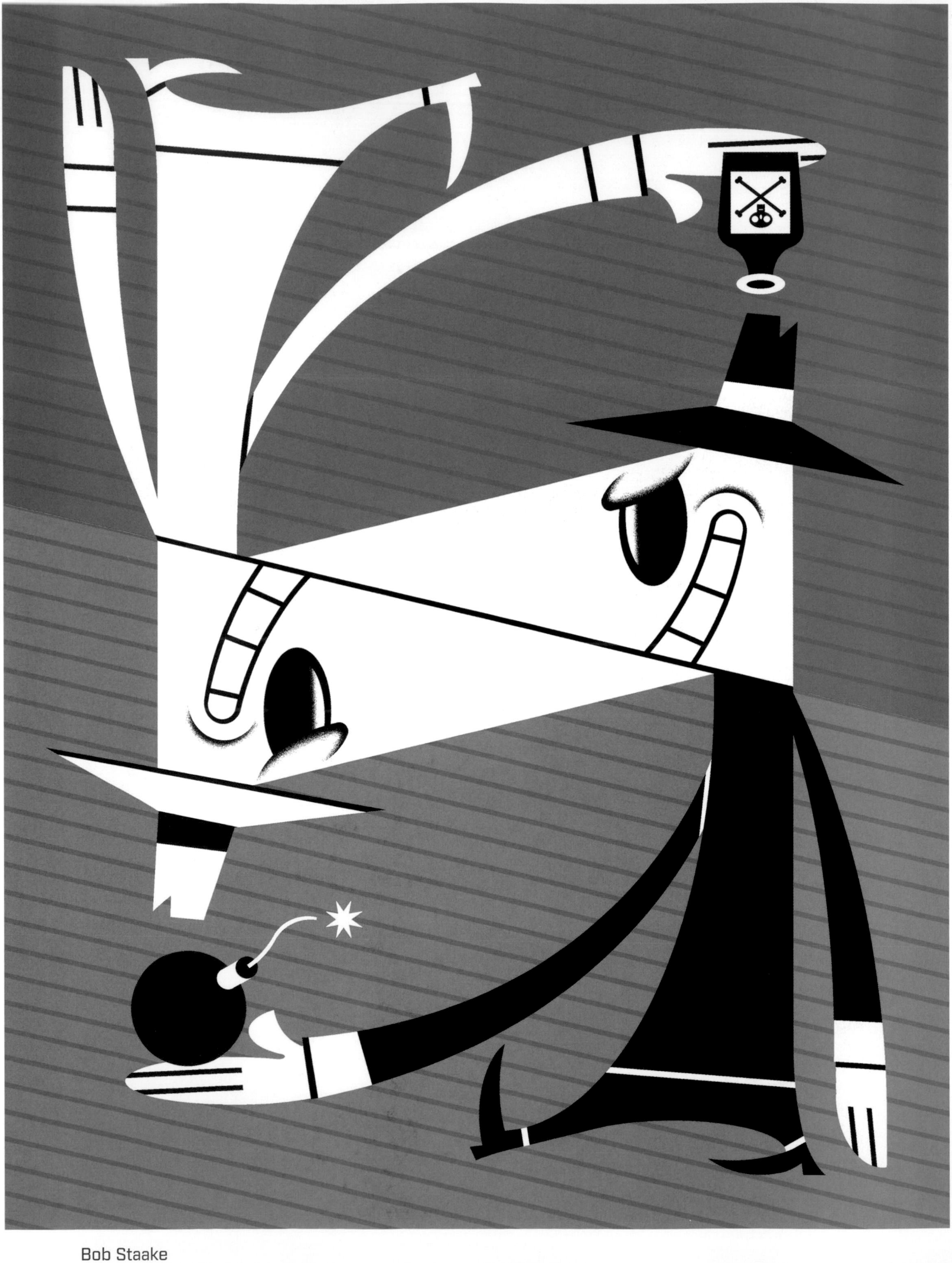

Bob Staake

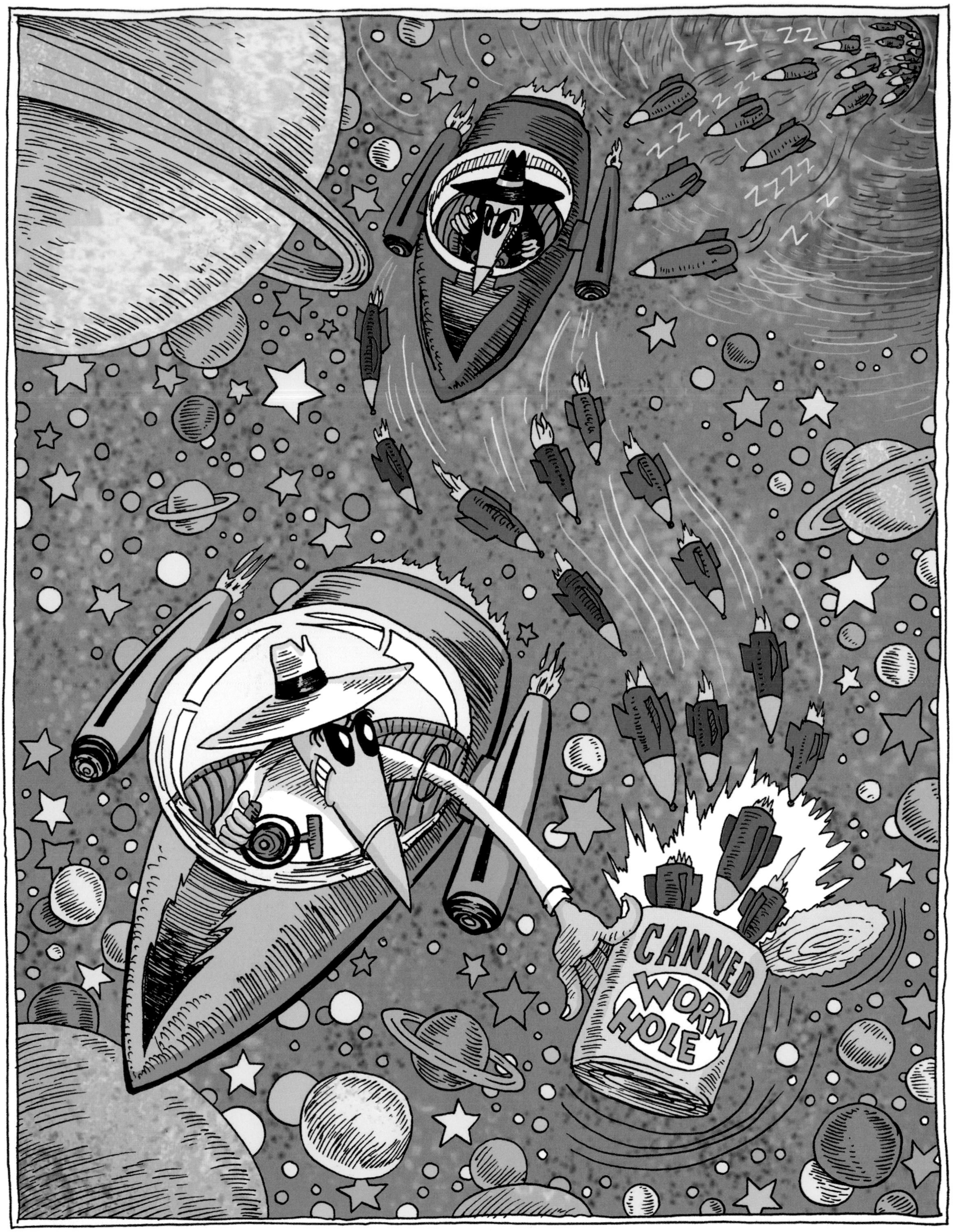
CANNED WORM HOLE

Tony Millionaire

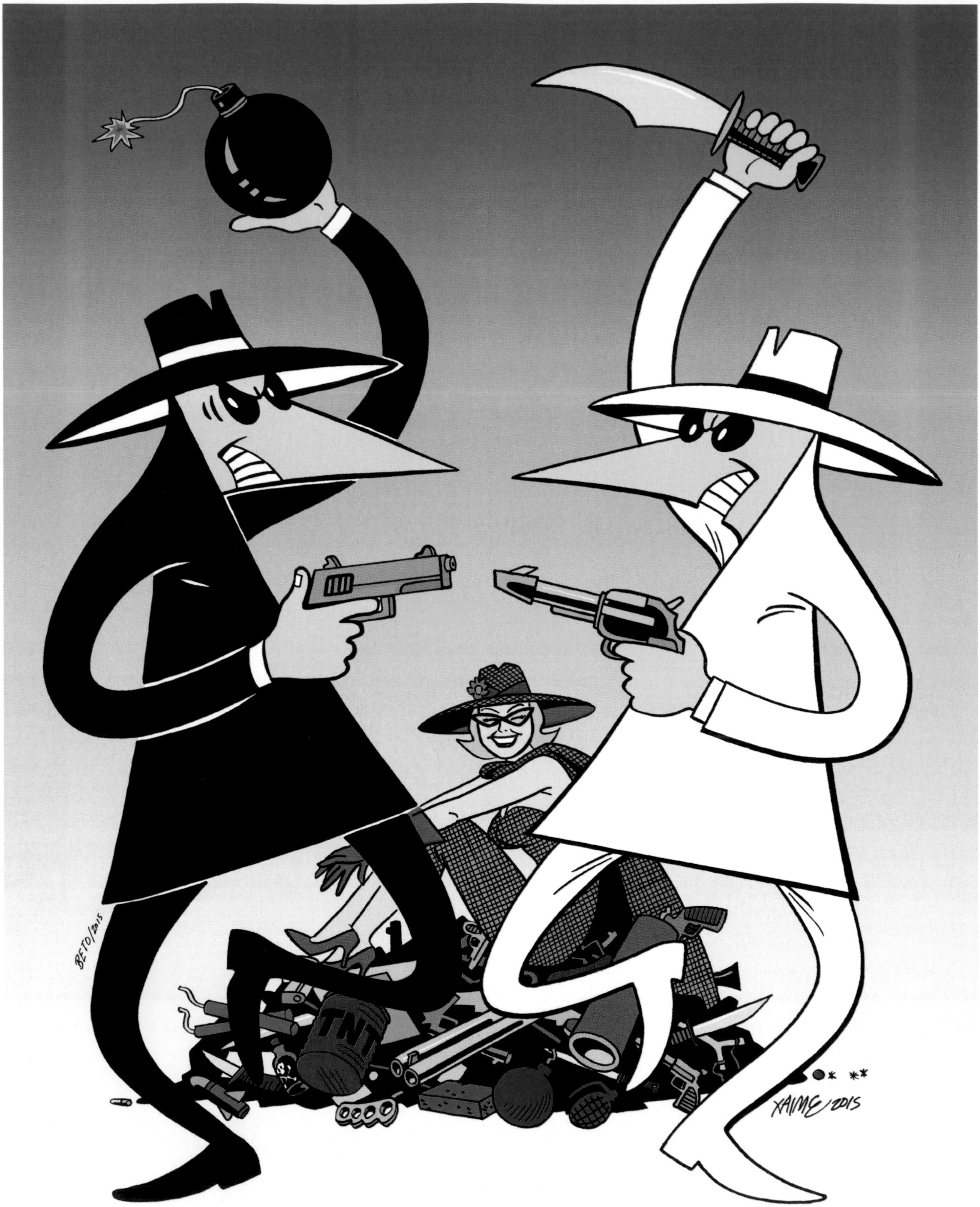

BETO/2015
TNT
XAIME/2015

Gilbert and Jaime Hernandez

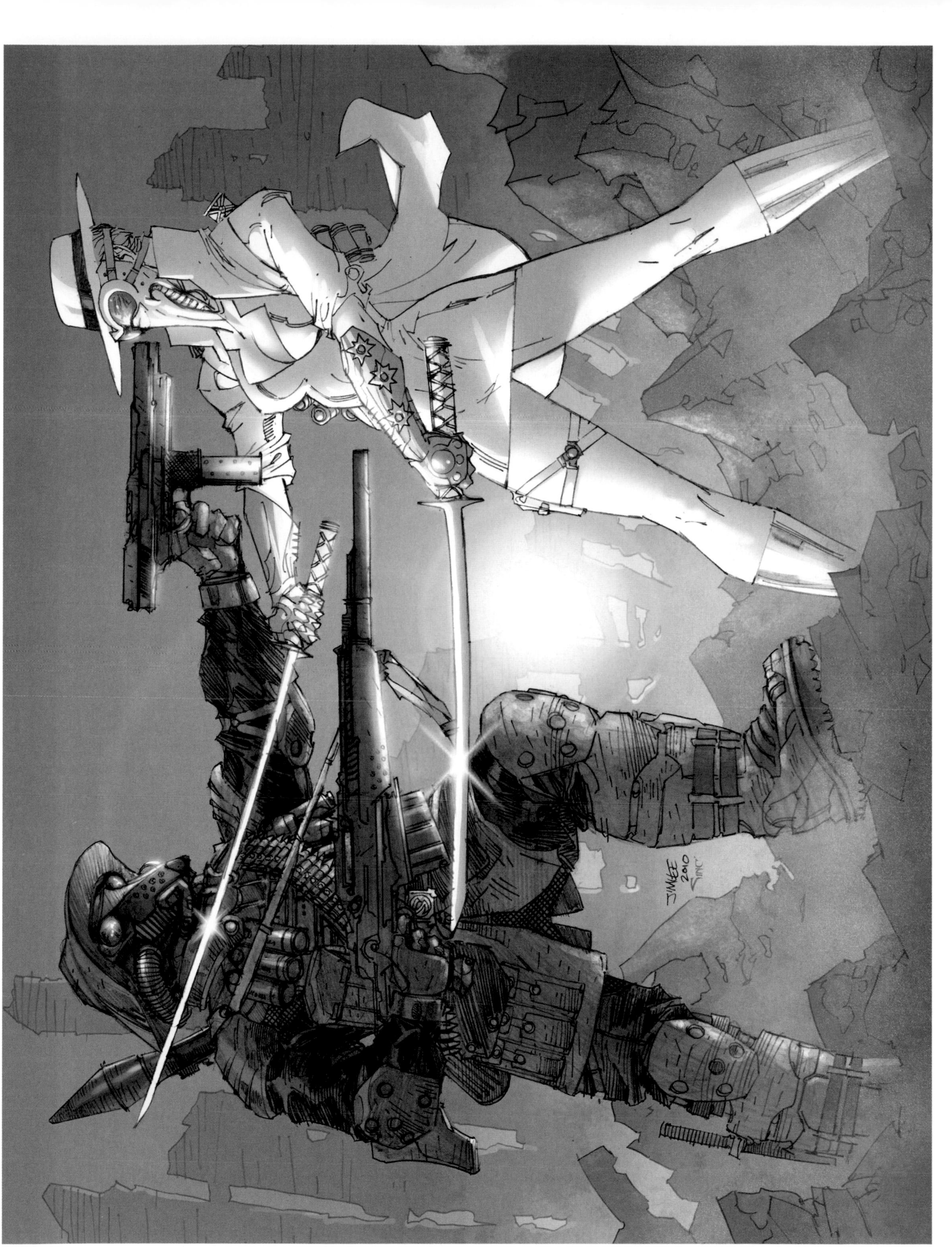

Jim Lee (Colorist: Alex Sinclair)

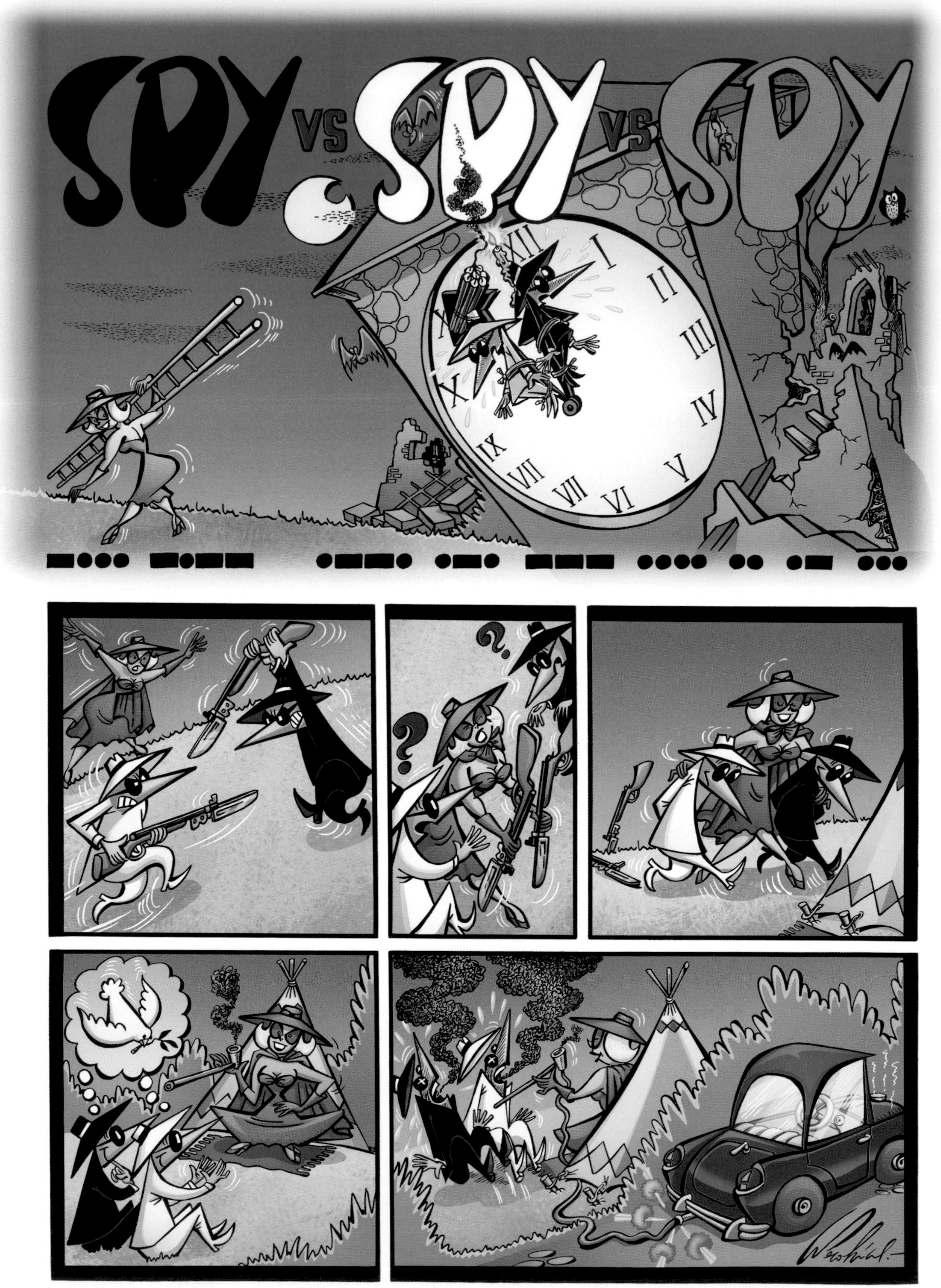
SPY VS SPY VS SPY

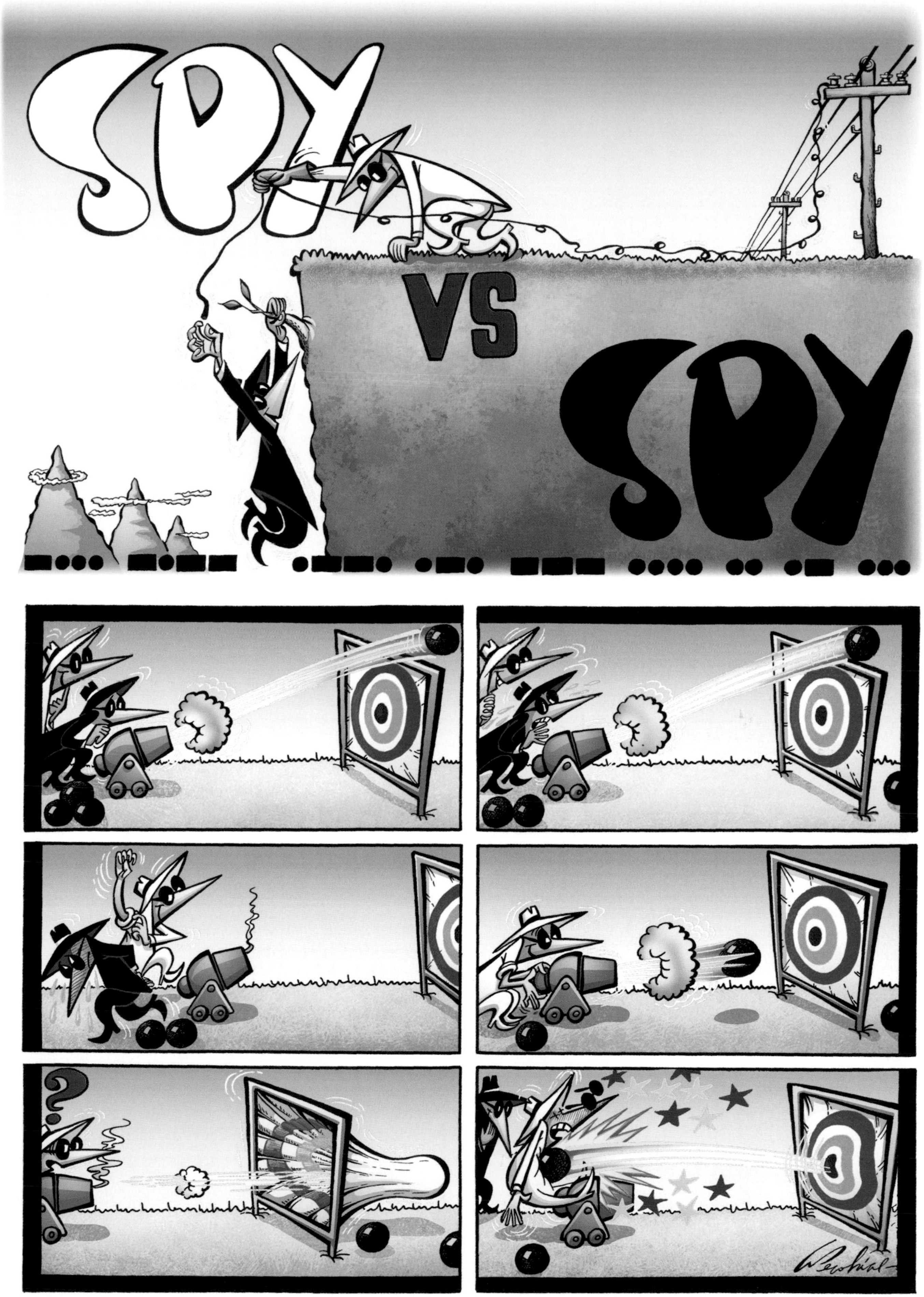
SPY
VS
SPY

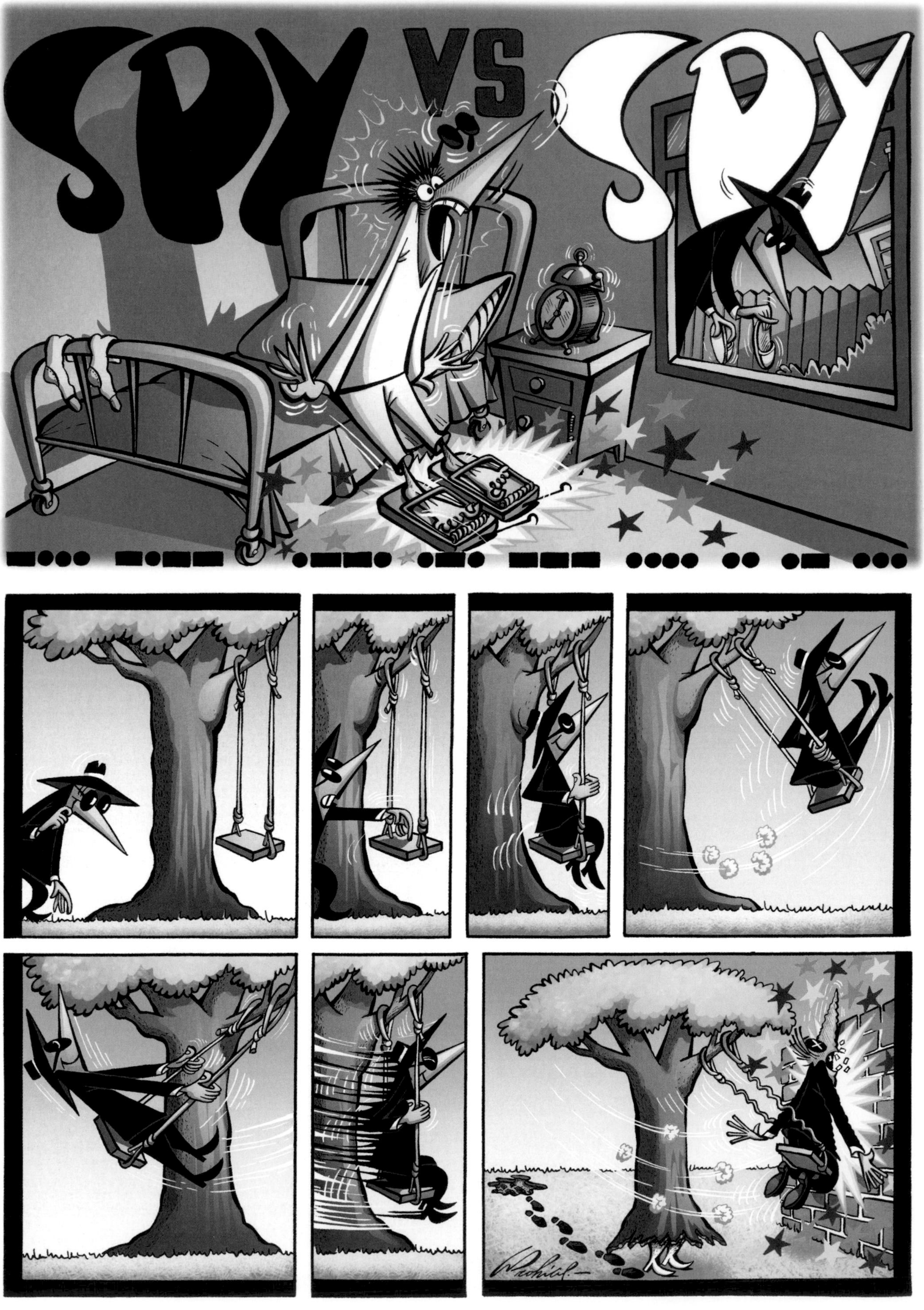
SPY VS SPY

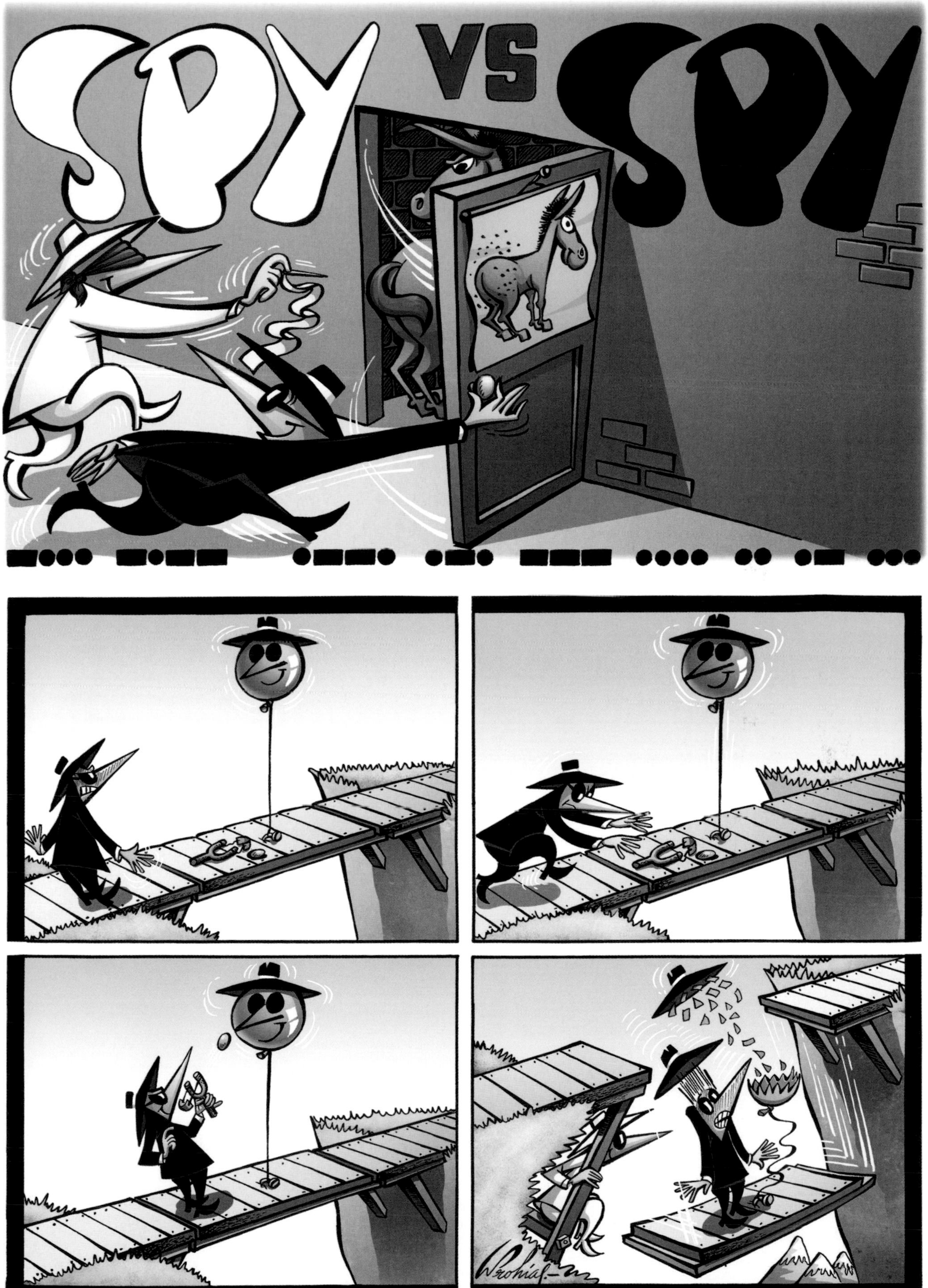
SPY VS SPY

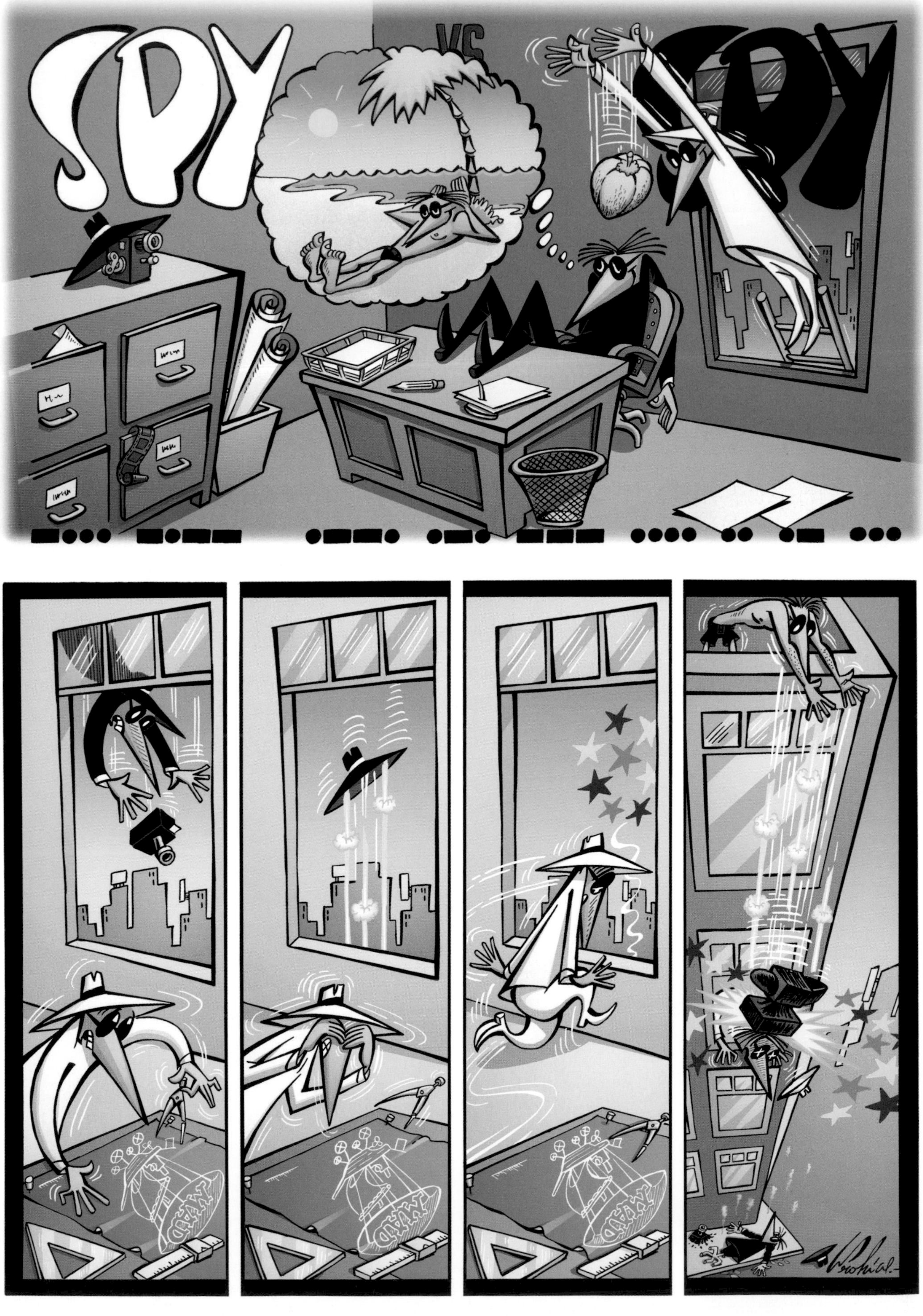
SPY
VS
SPY

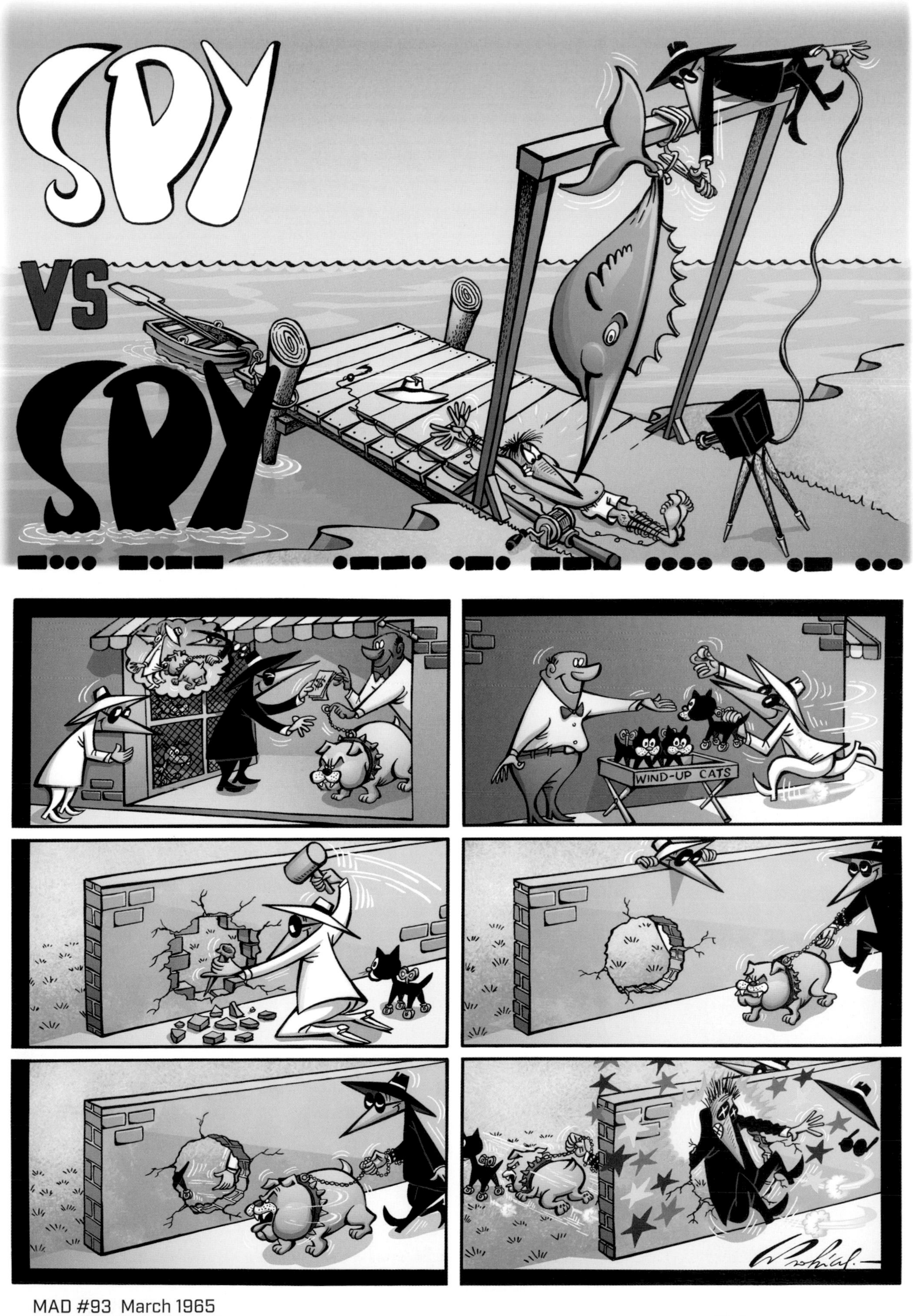
SPY
VS
SPY
WIND-UP CATS

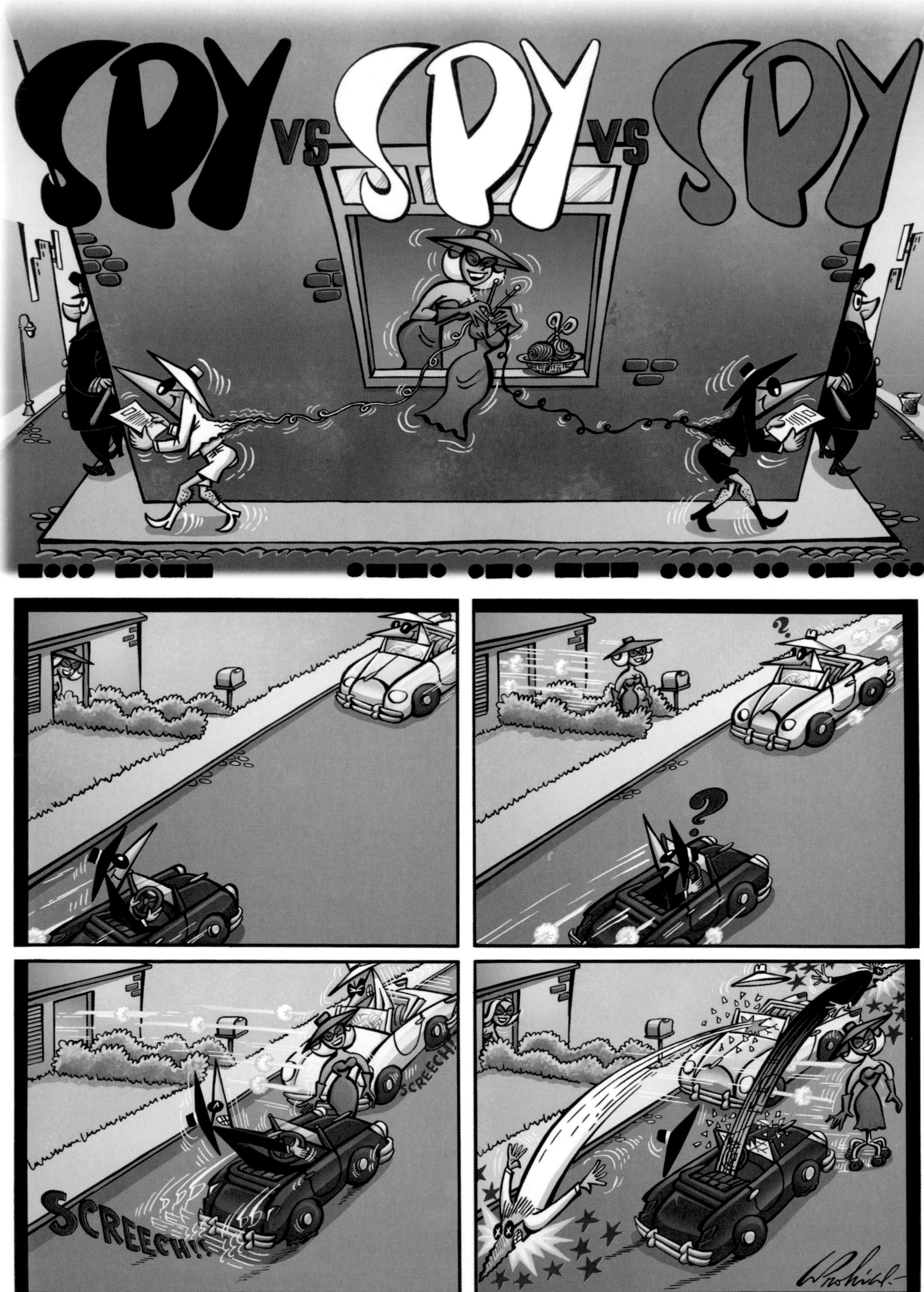
SPY VS SPY VS SPY
?
?
SCREECH!!
SCREECH!!

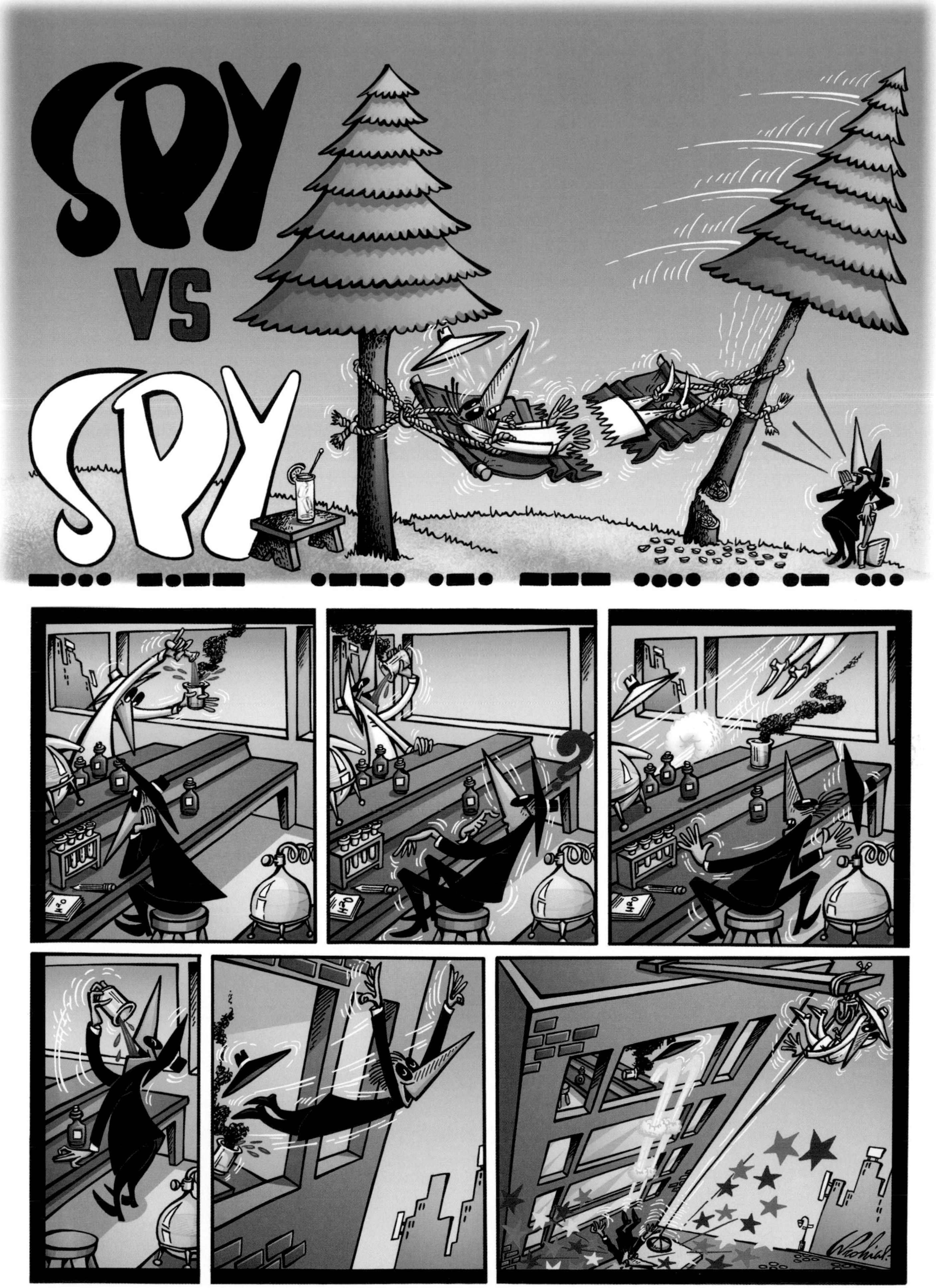
SPY
VS
SPY

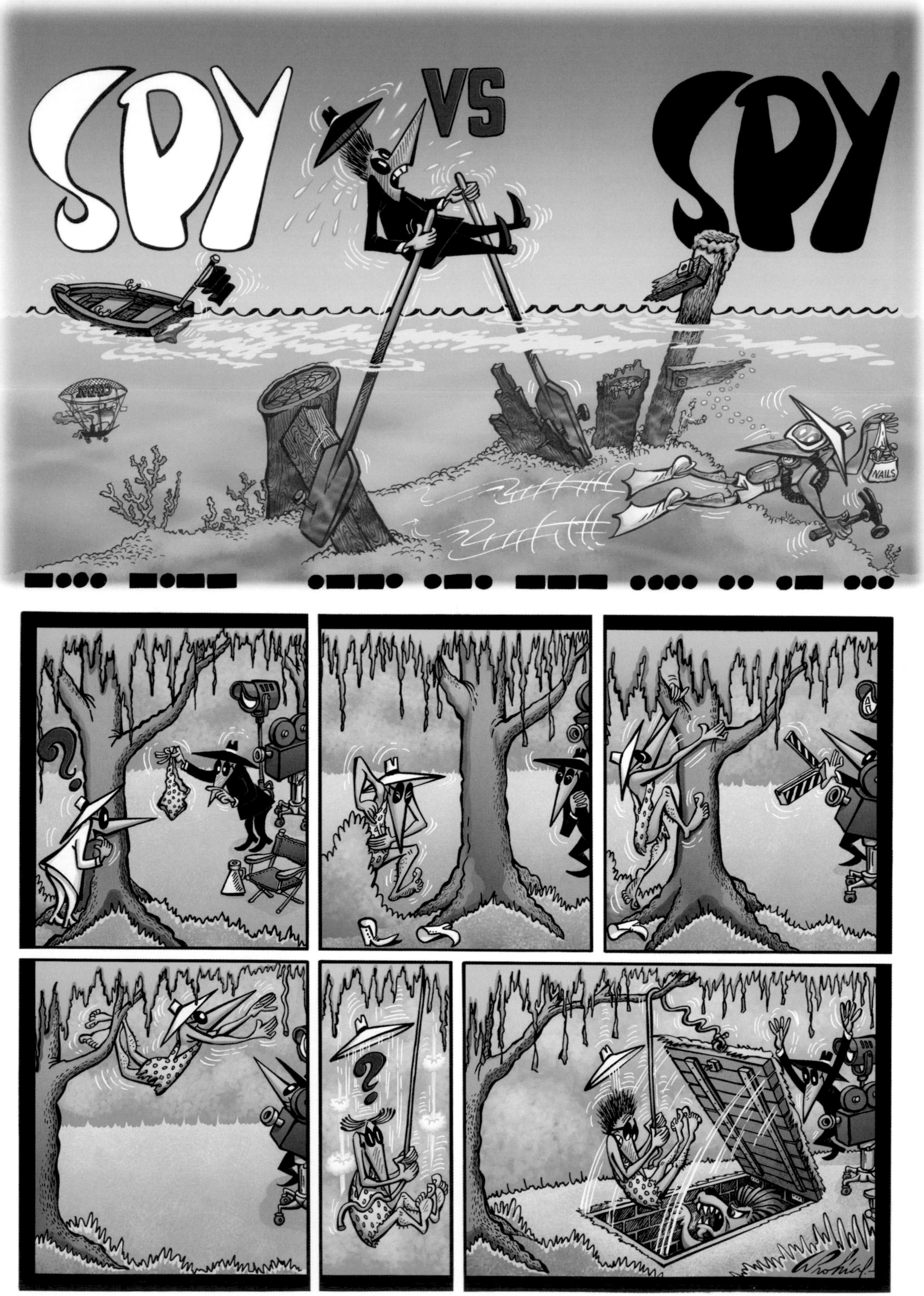
SPY
VS
SPY
MAD
NAILS
Prohias

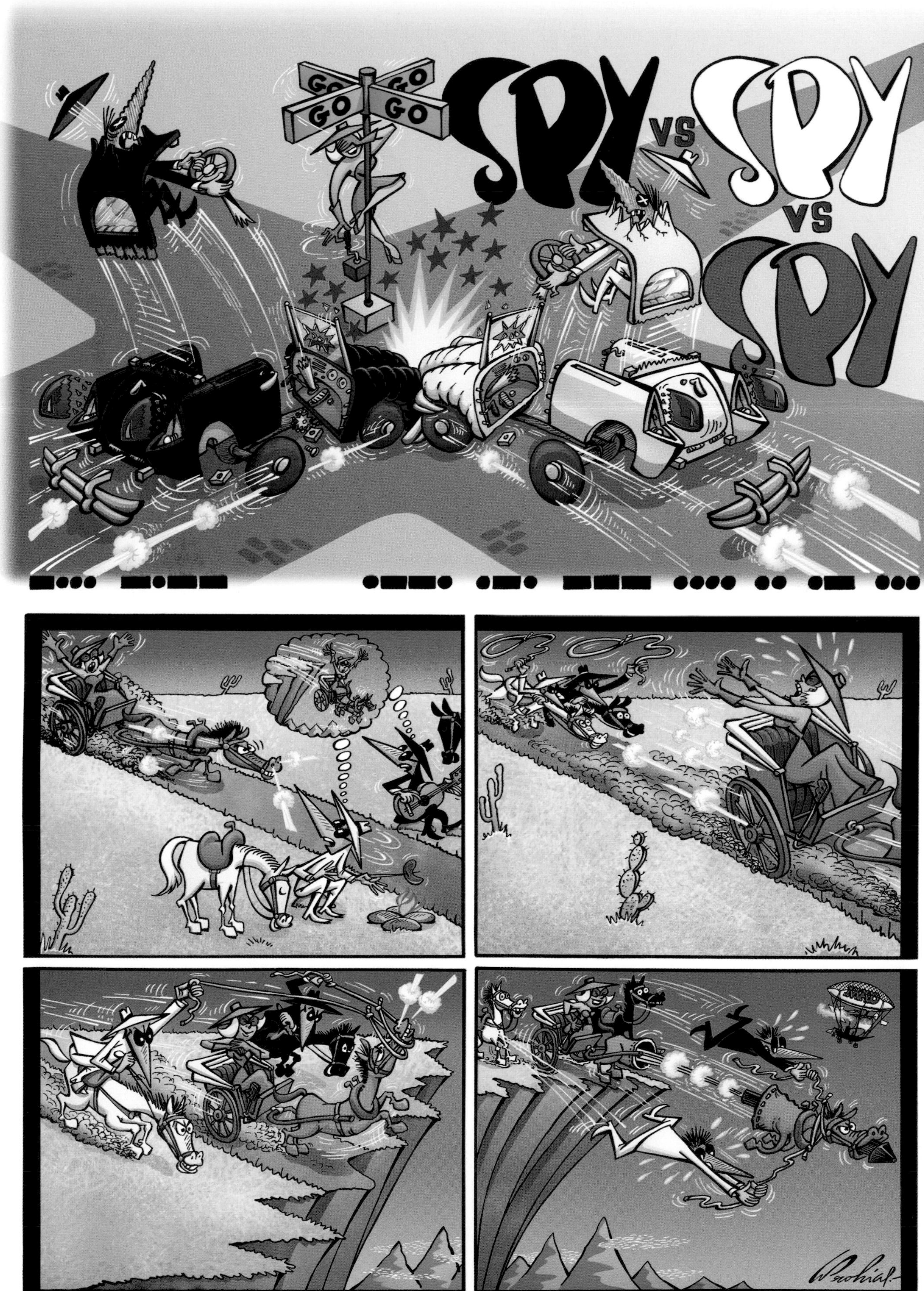
SPY vs SPY vs SPY
GO
GO
GO
GO

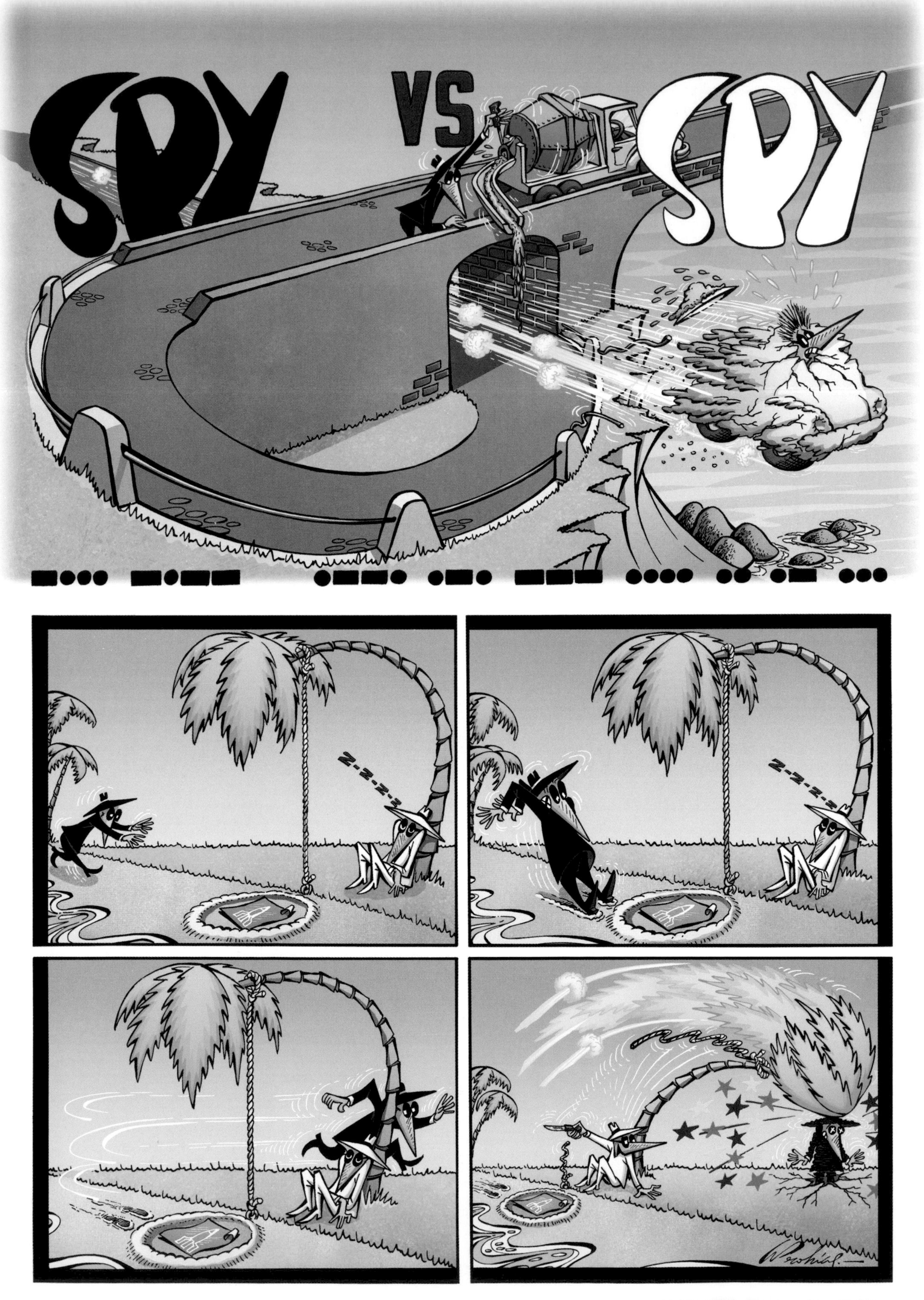
SPY VS SPY
Z-Z-Z-Z
Z-Z-Z-Z

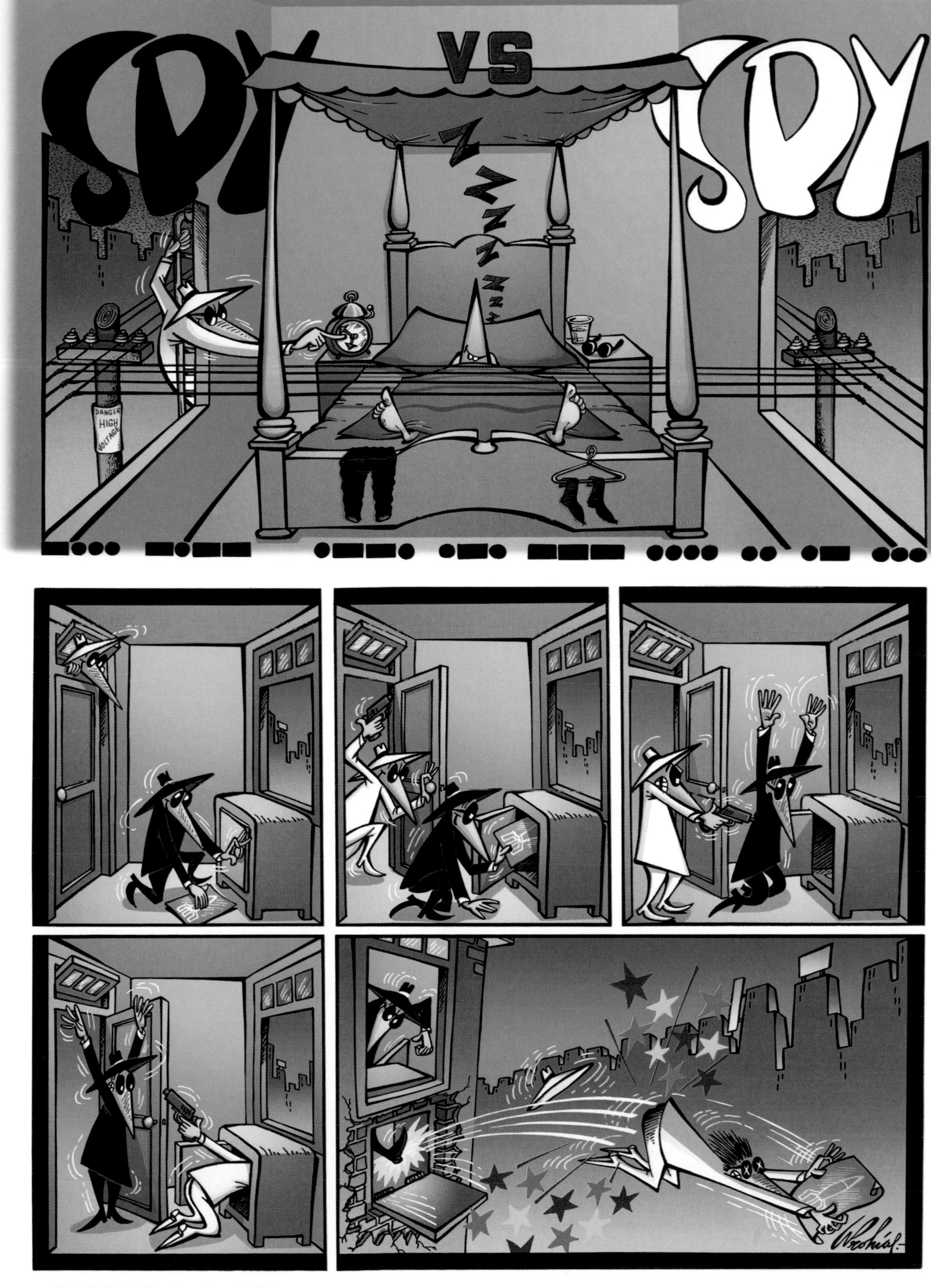
SPY VS SPY
DANGER HIGH VOLTAGE

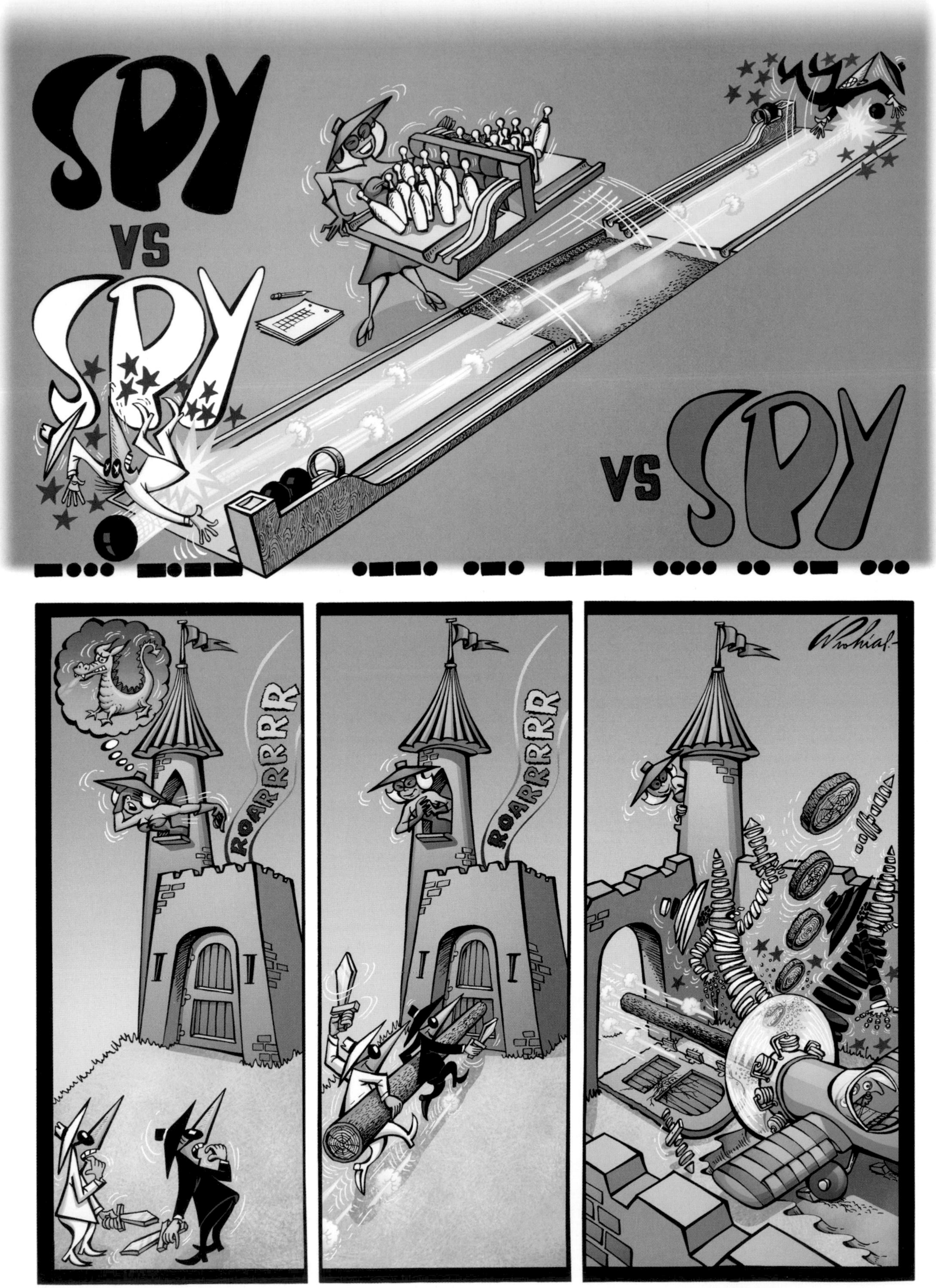
SPY
VS
SPY
VS
SPY
ROARRRRR
ROARRRRR
Prohias

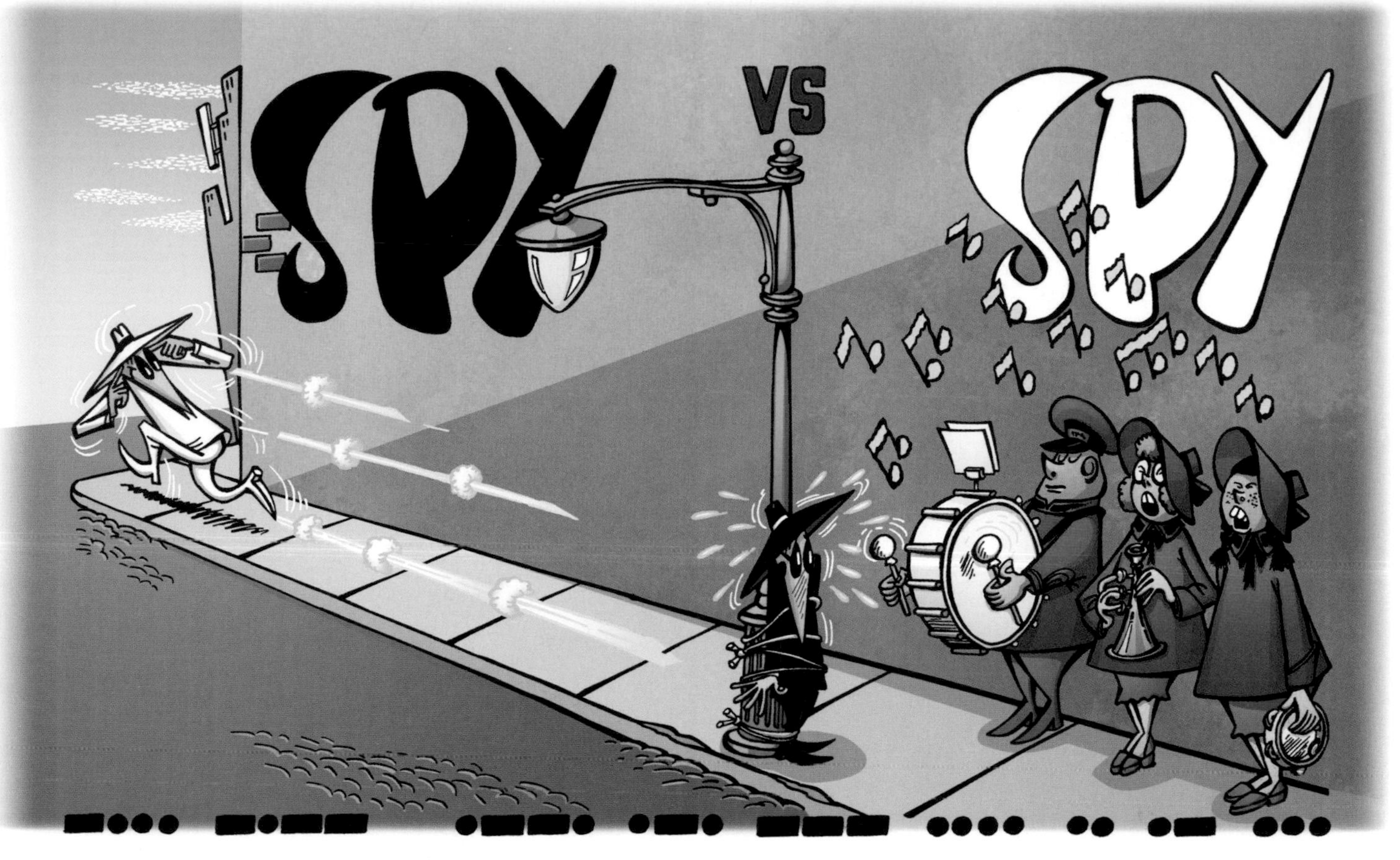
SPY vs SPY

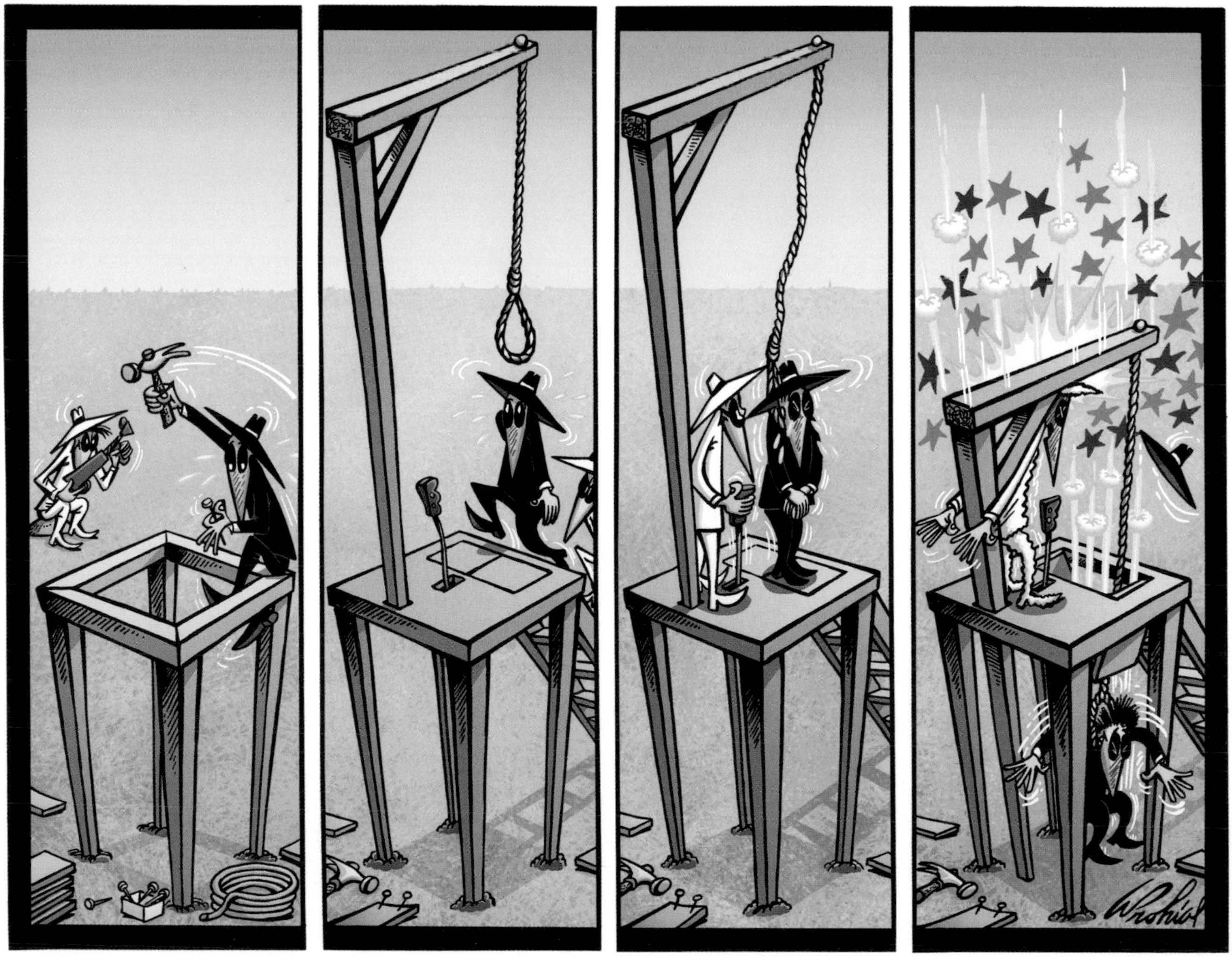

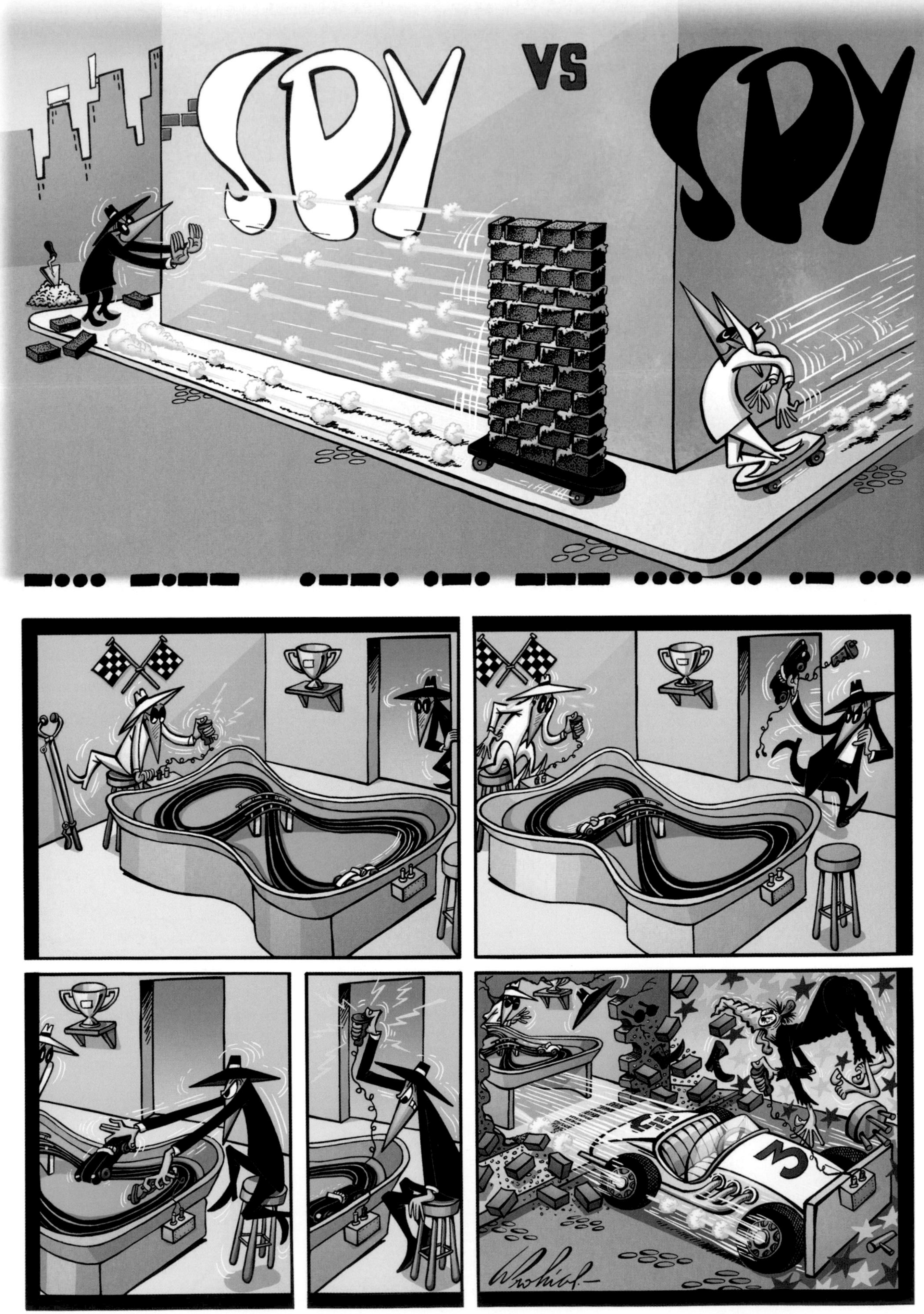
SPY VS SPY

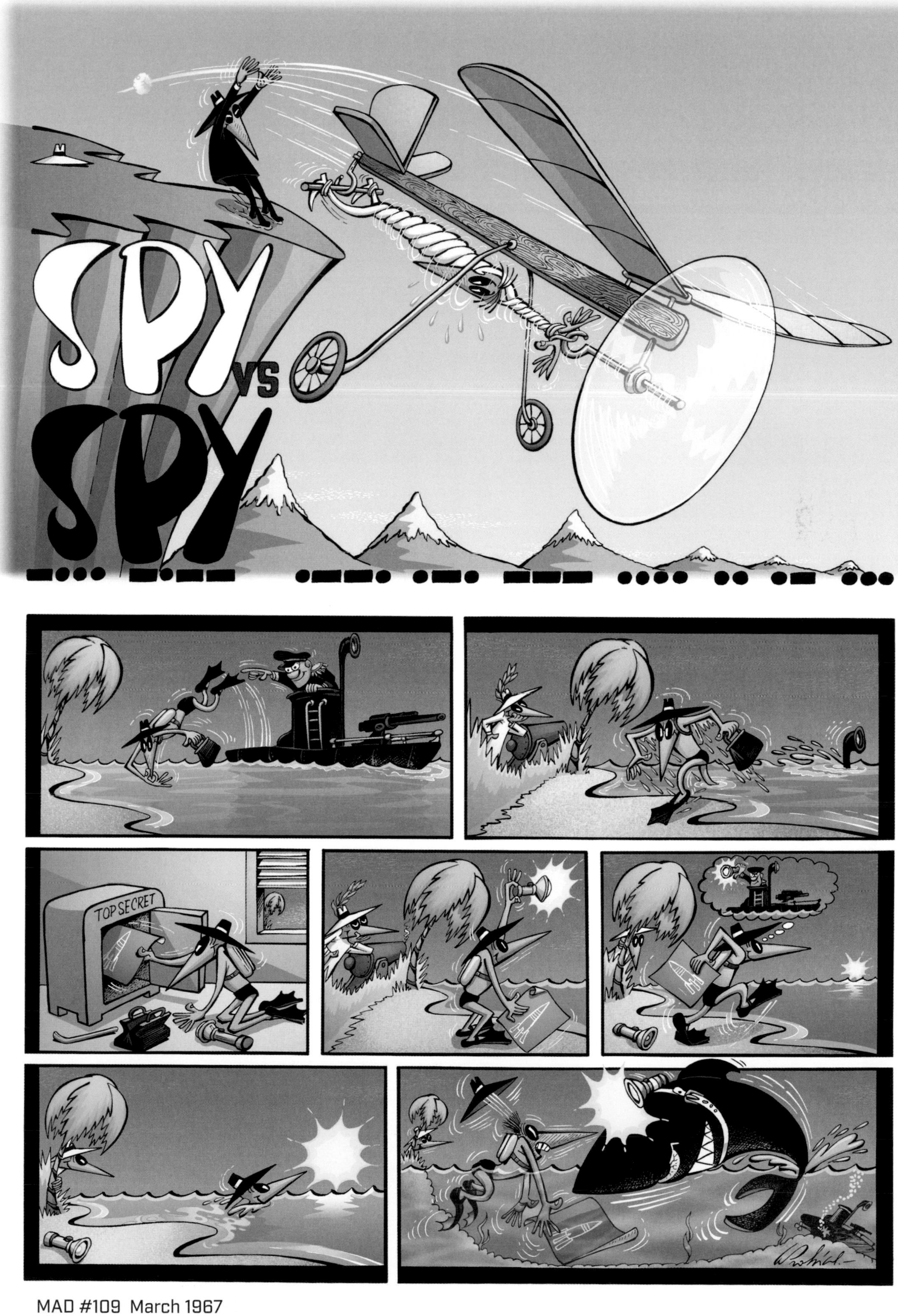
SPY VS SPY
TOP SECRET

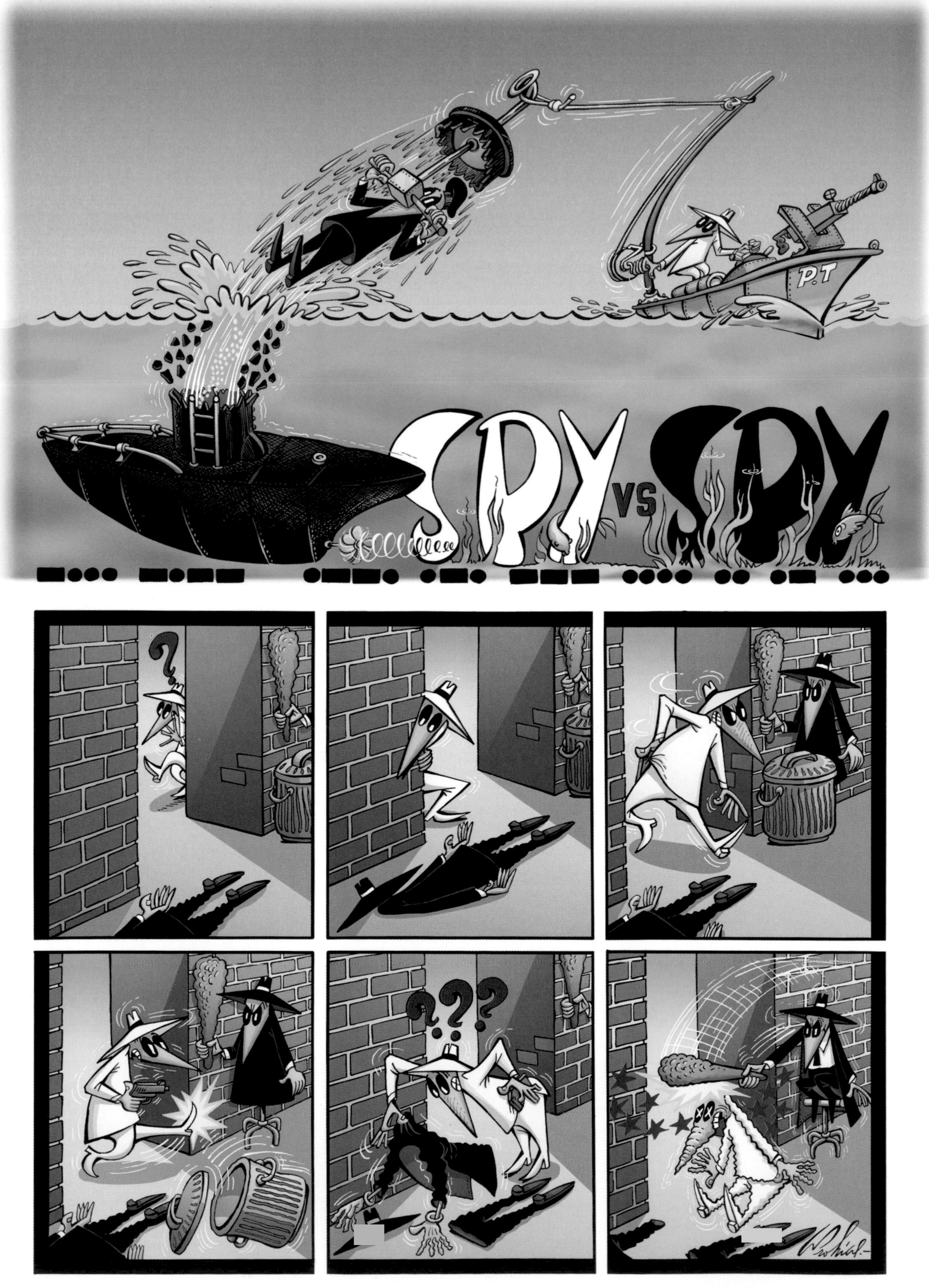
P.T
SPY vs SPY

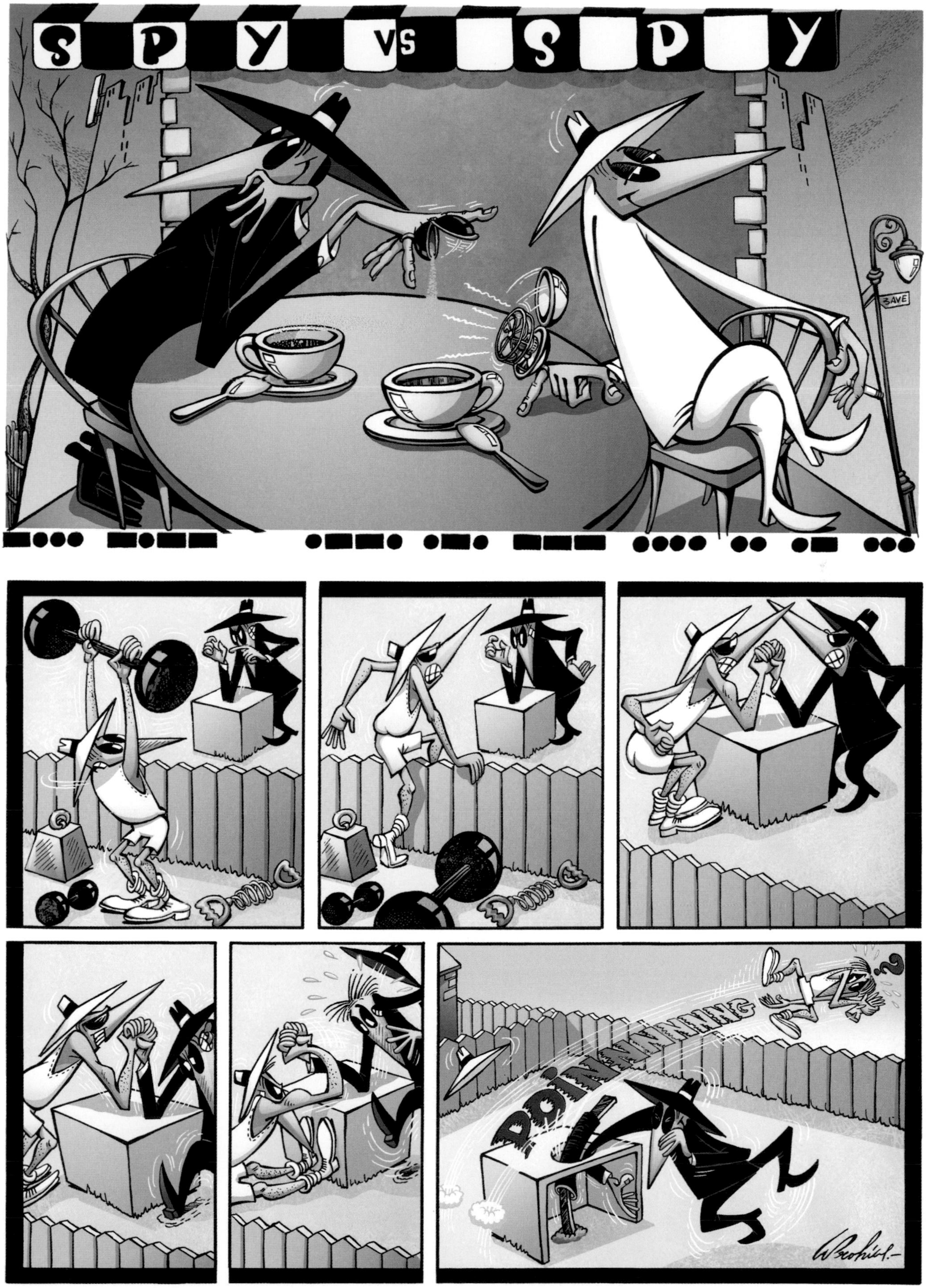
SPY vs SPY
3AVE
DOINNNNNNG
Prohias

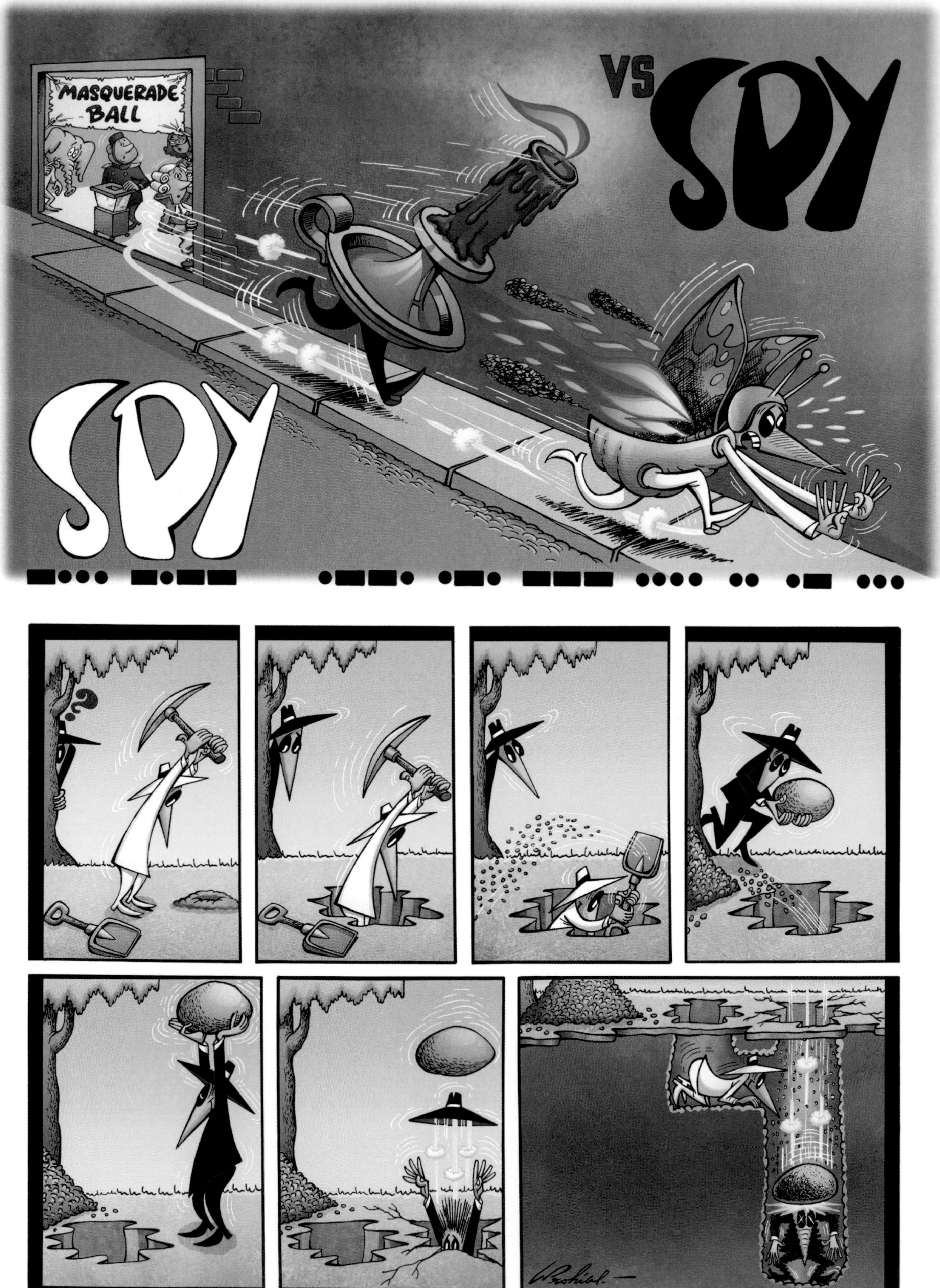
MASQUERADE BALL
SPY VS SPY

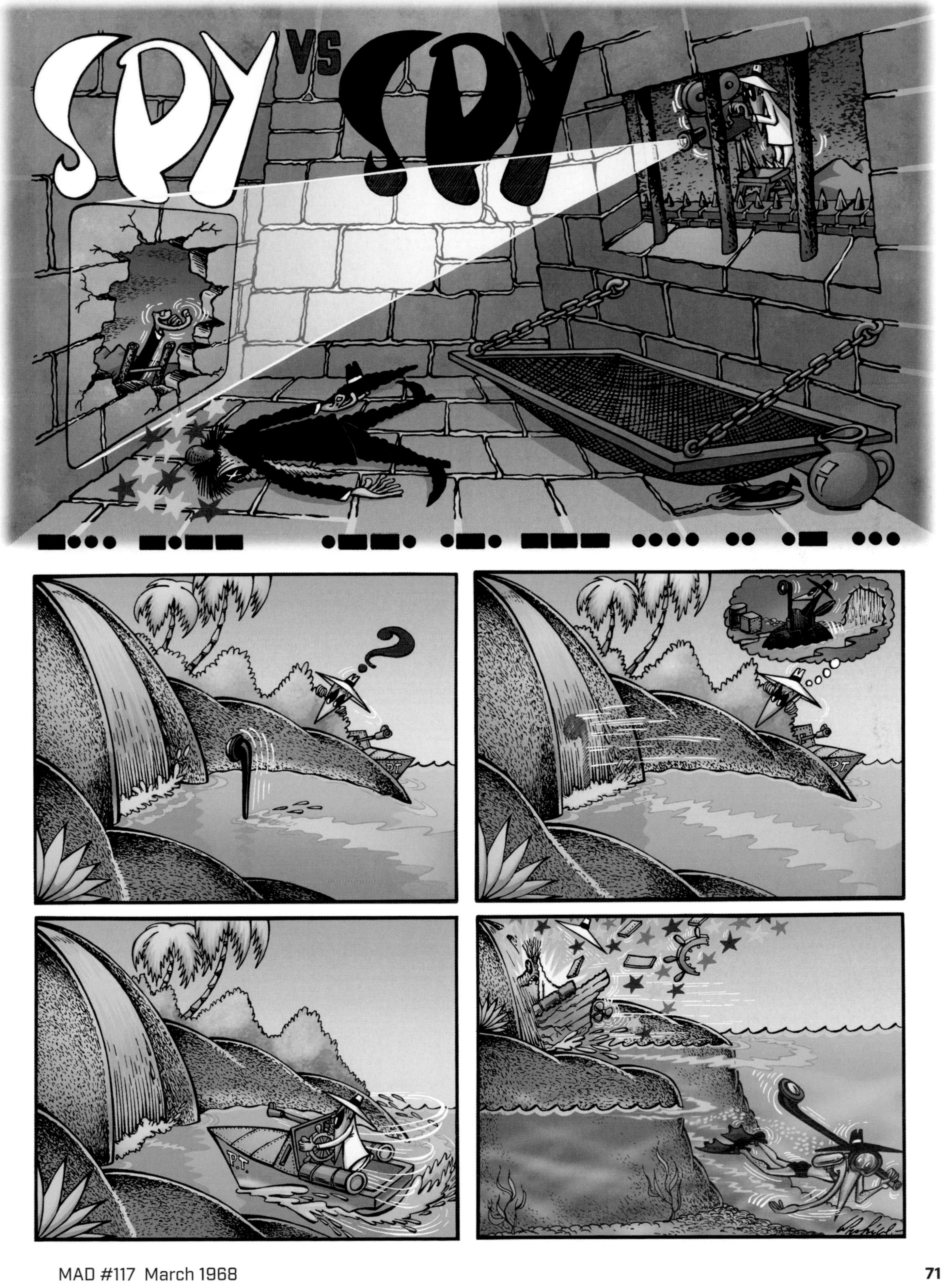
SPY VS SPY
PT
P.T.

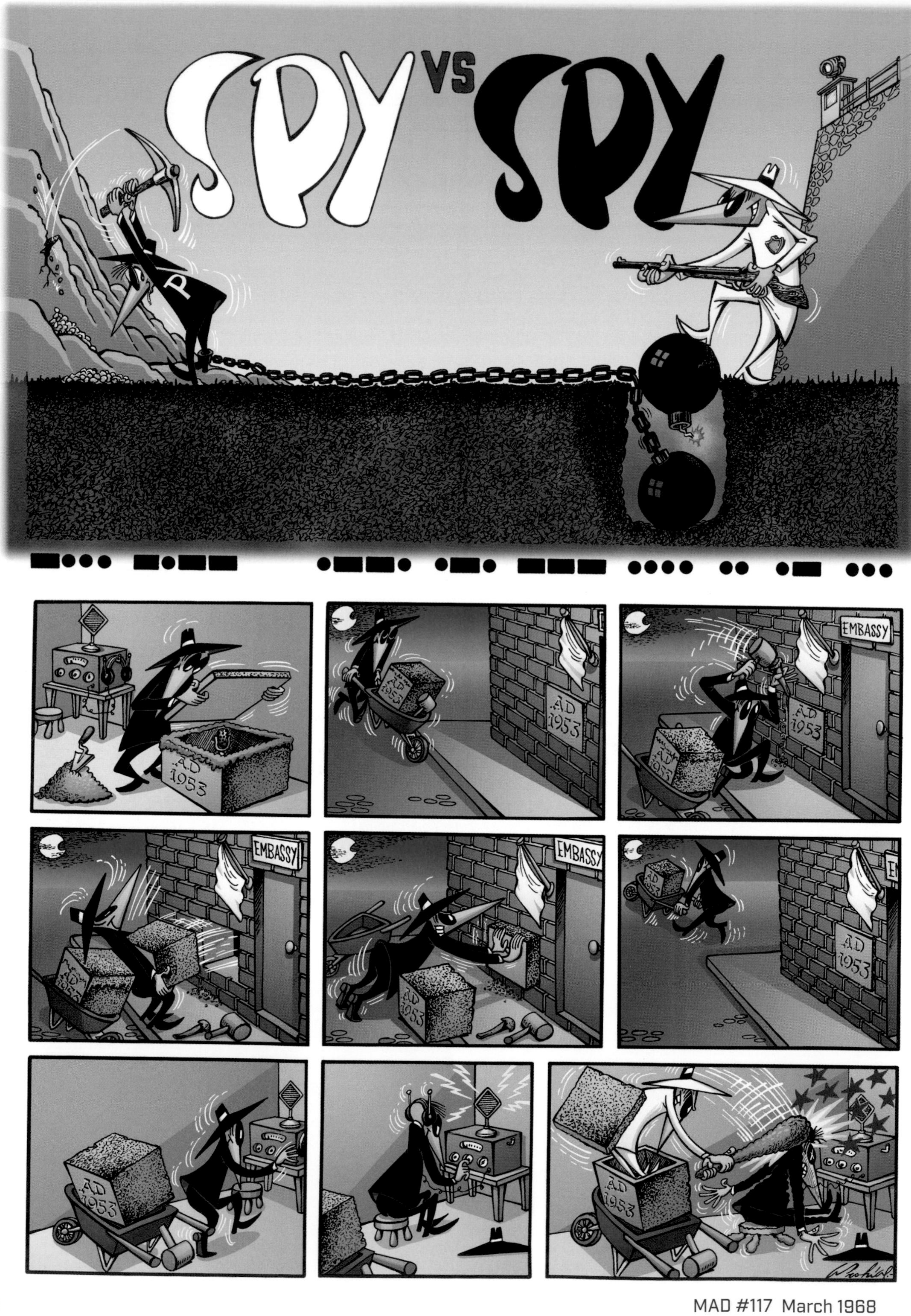
SPY VS SPY
A.D. 1953
EMBASSY

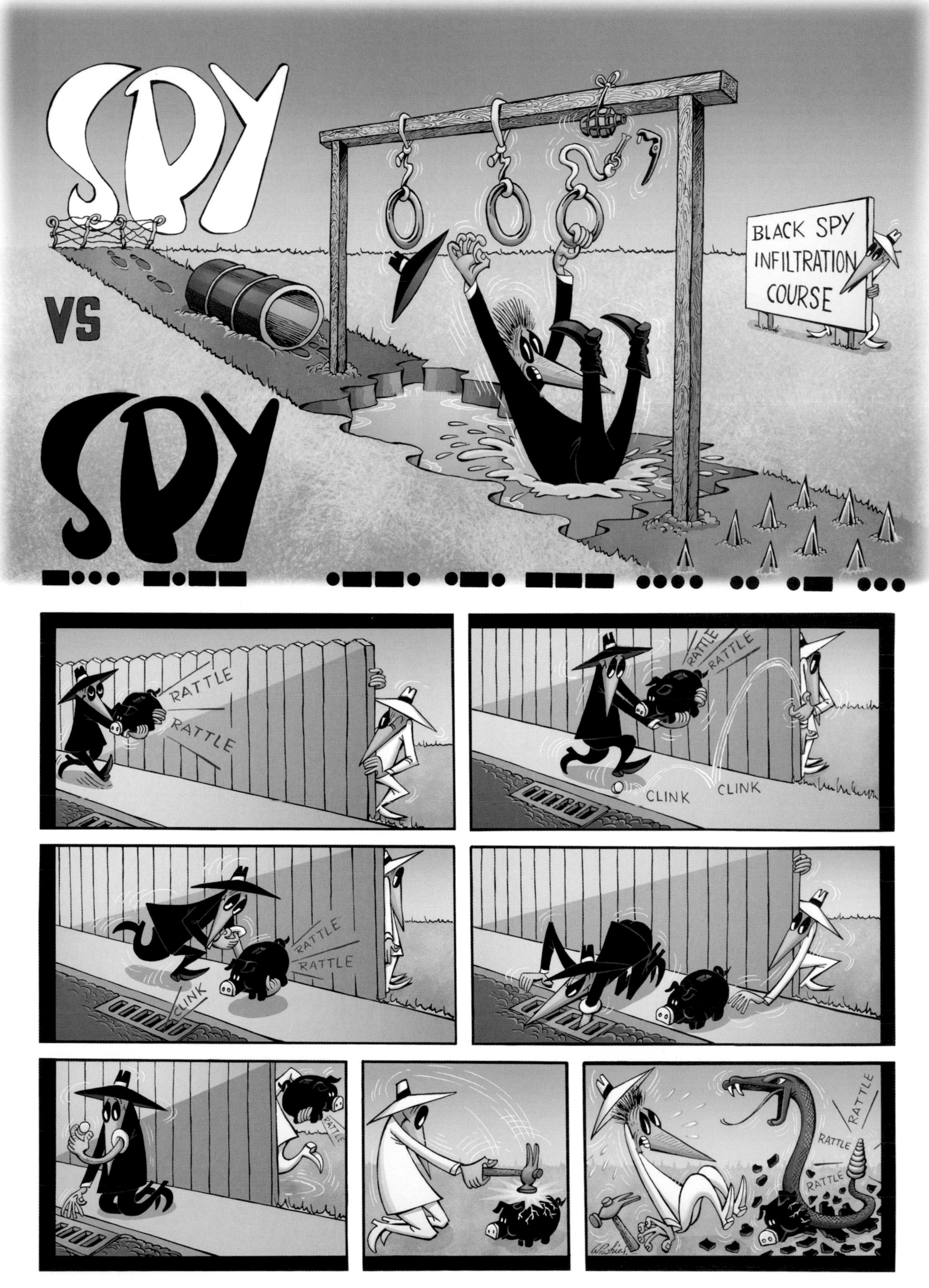
SPY
VS
SPY
BLACK SPY INFILTRATION COURSE
RATTLE
RATTLE
RATTLE
RATTLE
CLINK
CLINK
RATTLE
RATTLE
CLINK
RATTLE
RATTLE
RATTLE
RATTLE
RATTLE

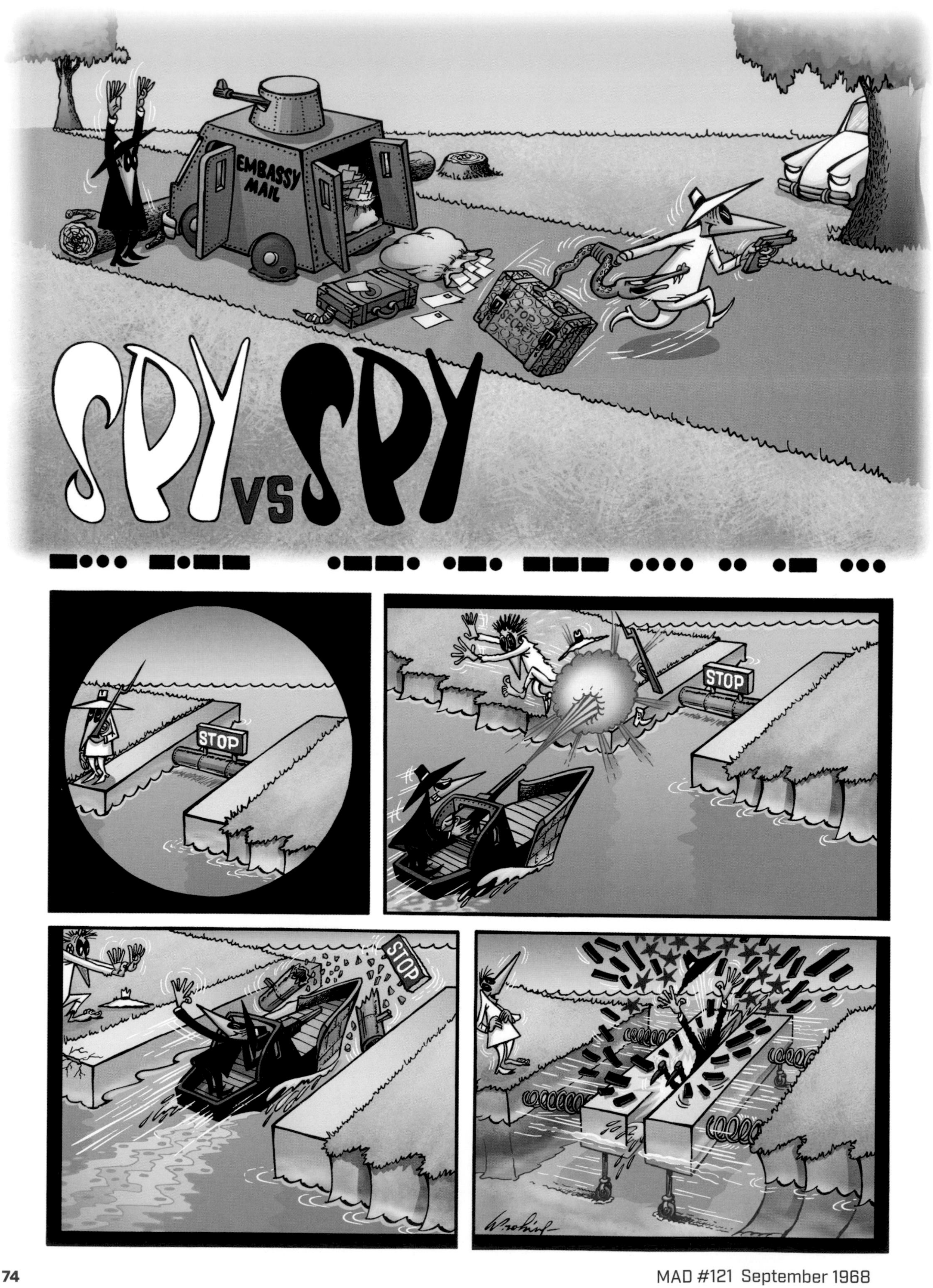
EMBASSY MAIL
TOP SECRET
SPY vs SPY
STOP
STOP
STOP

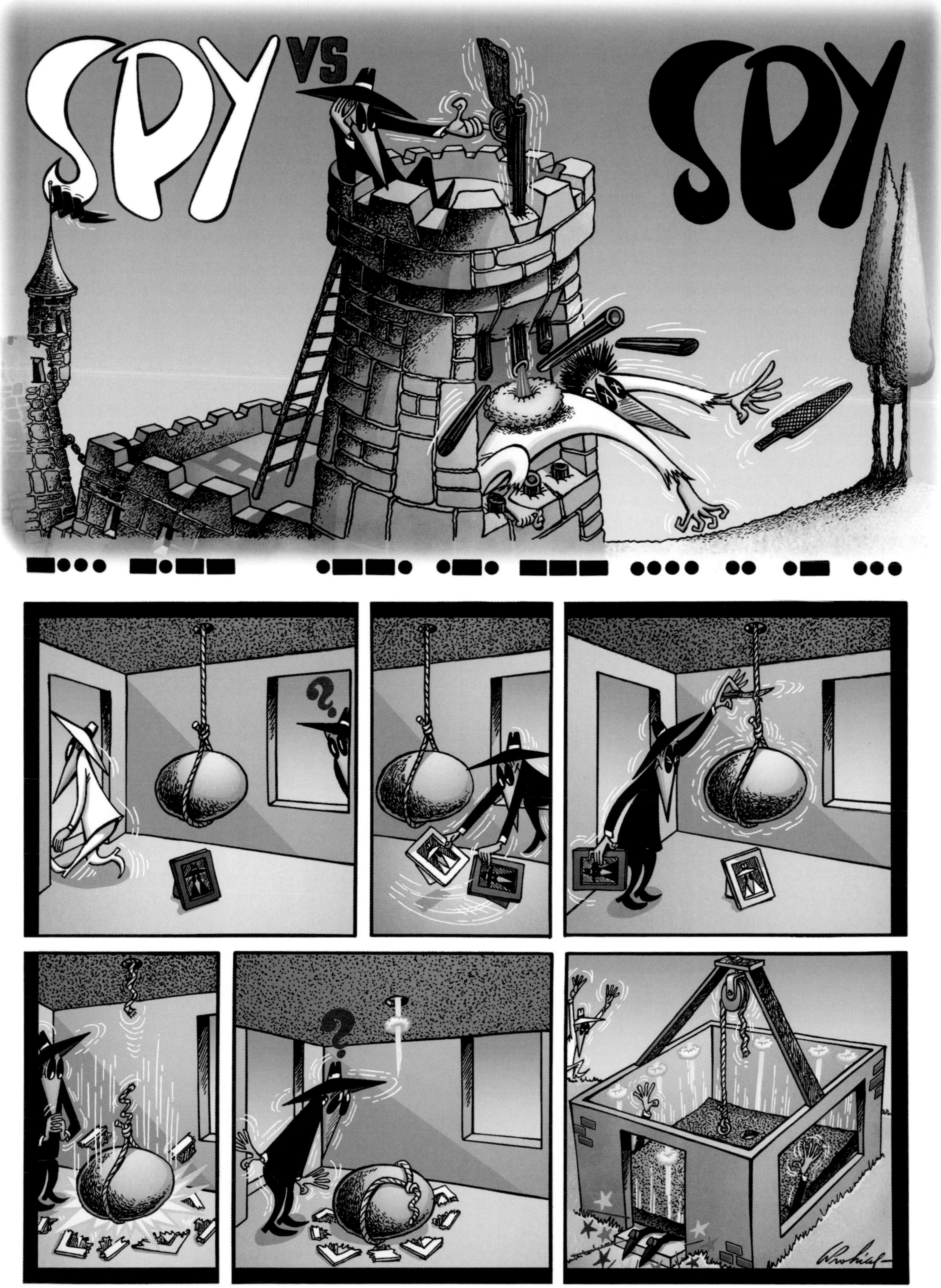
SPY
VS
SPY
Prohias

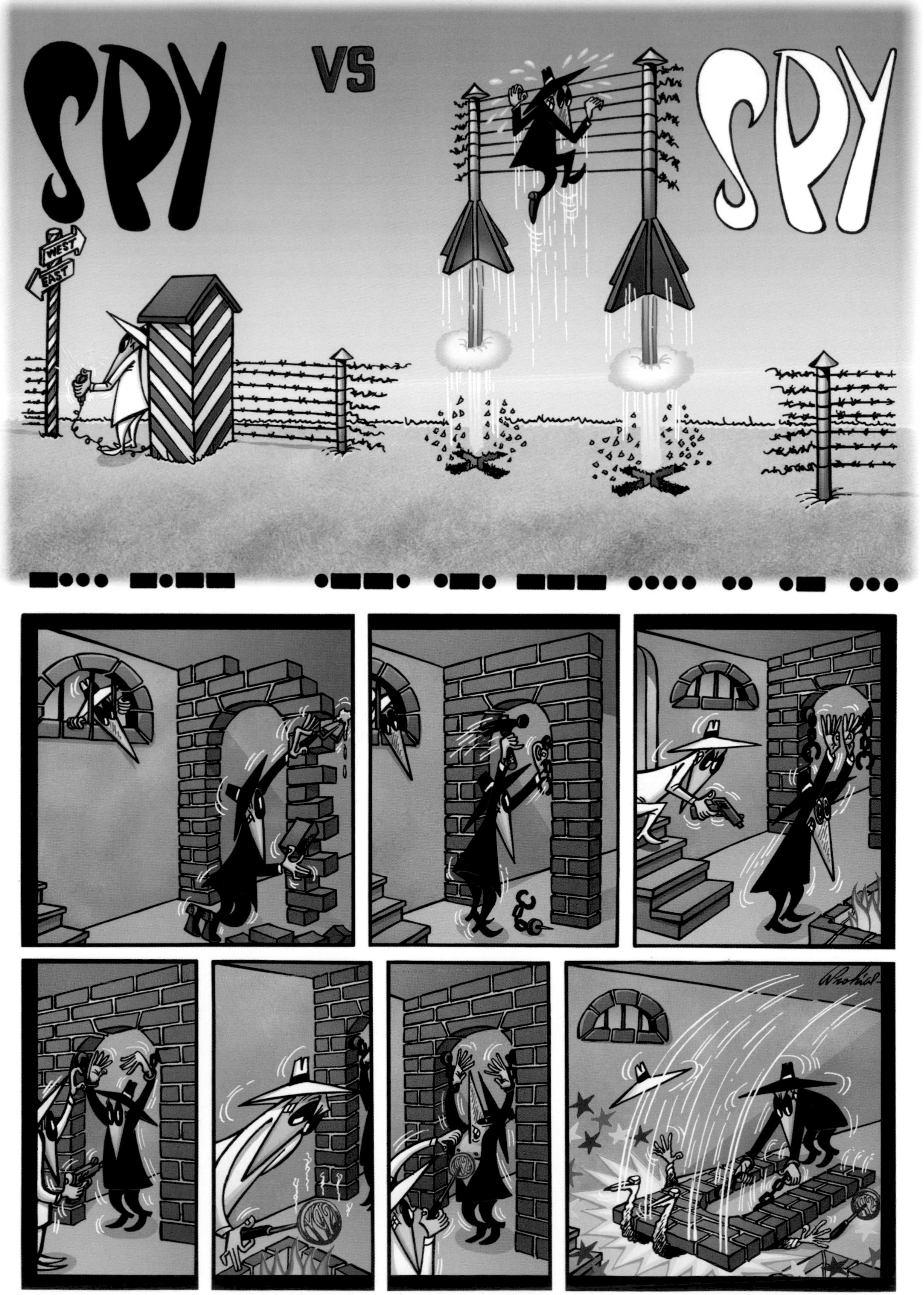
SPY
VS
SPY
WEST
EAST
Prohias

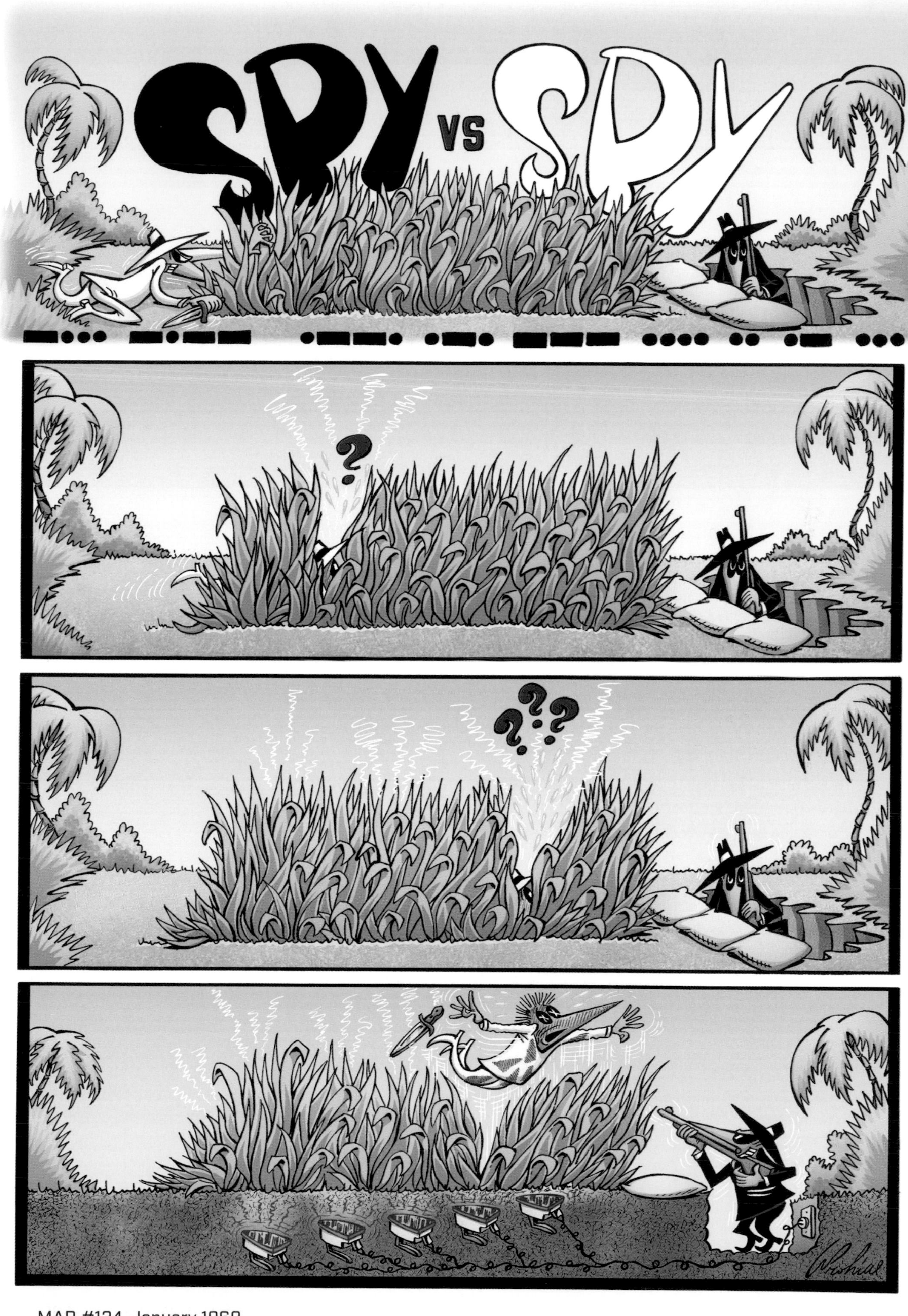
SPY vs SPY

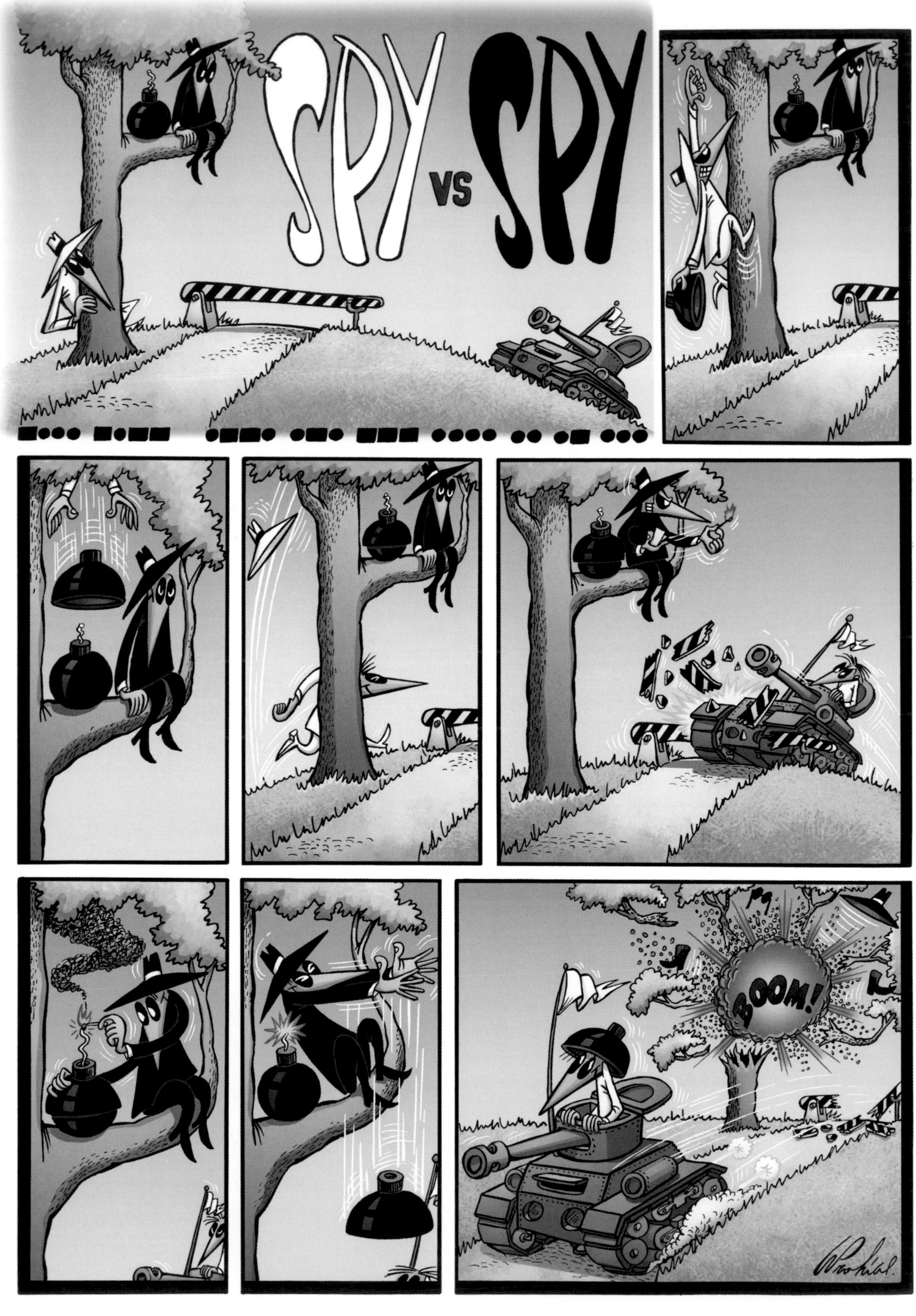
SPY vs SPY
BOOM!
Prohías

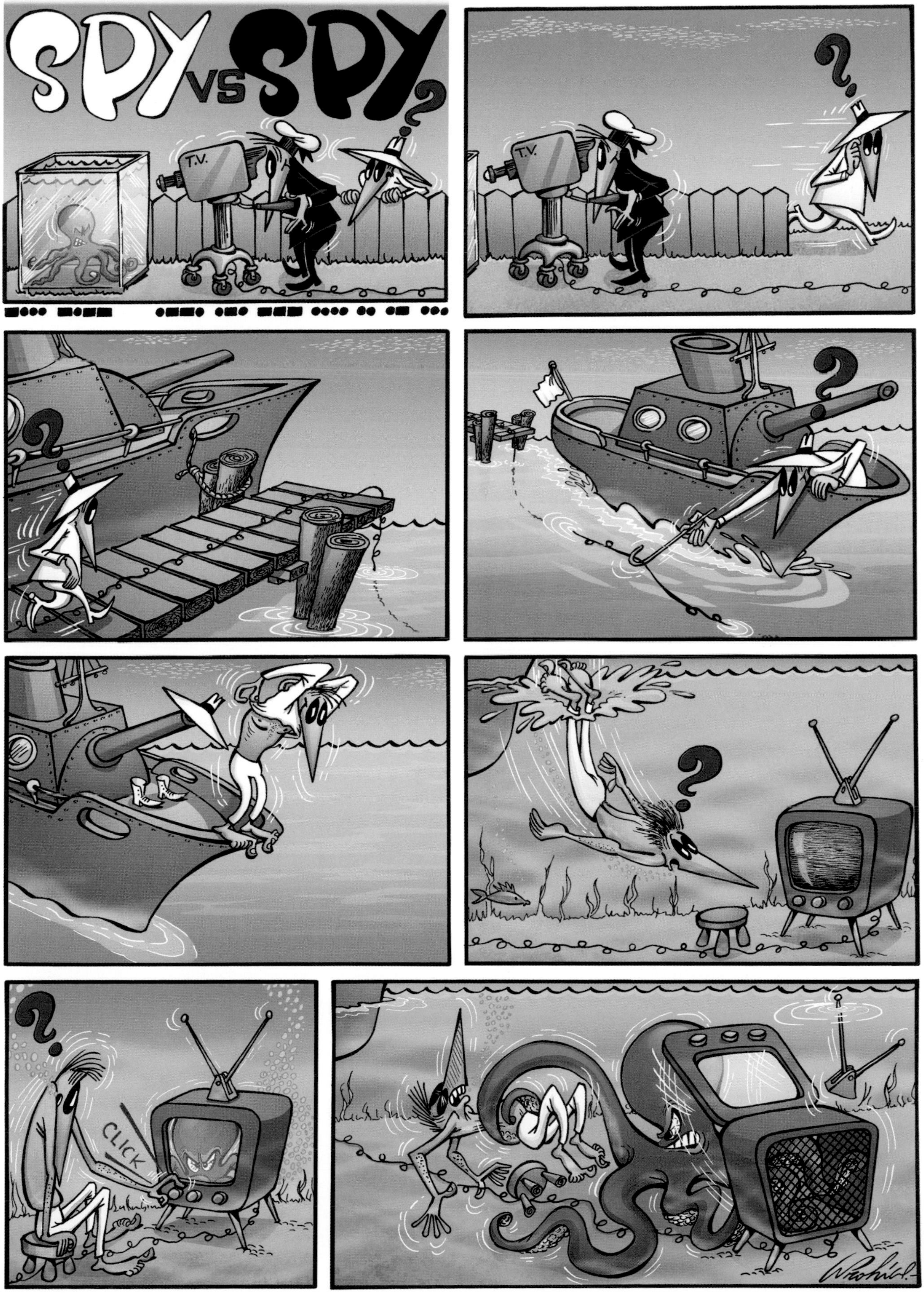

SPY vs SPY
T.V.
T.V.
CLICK

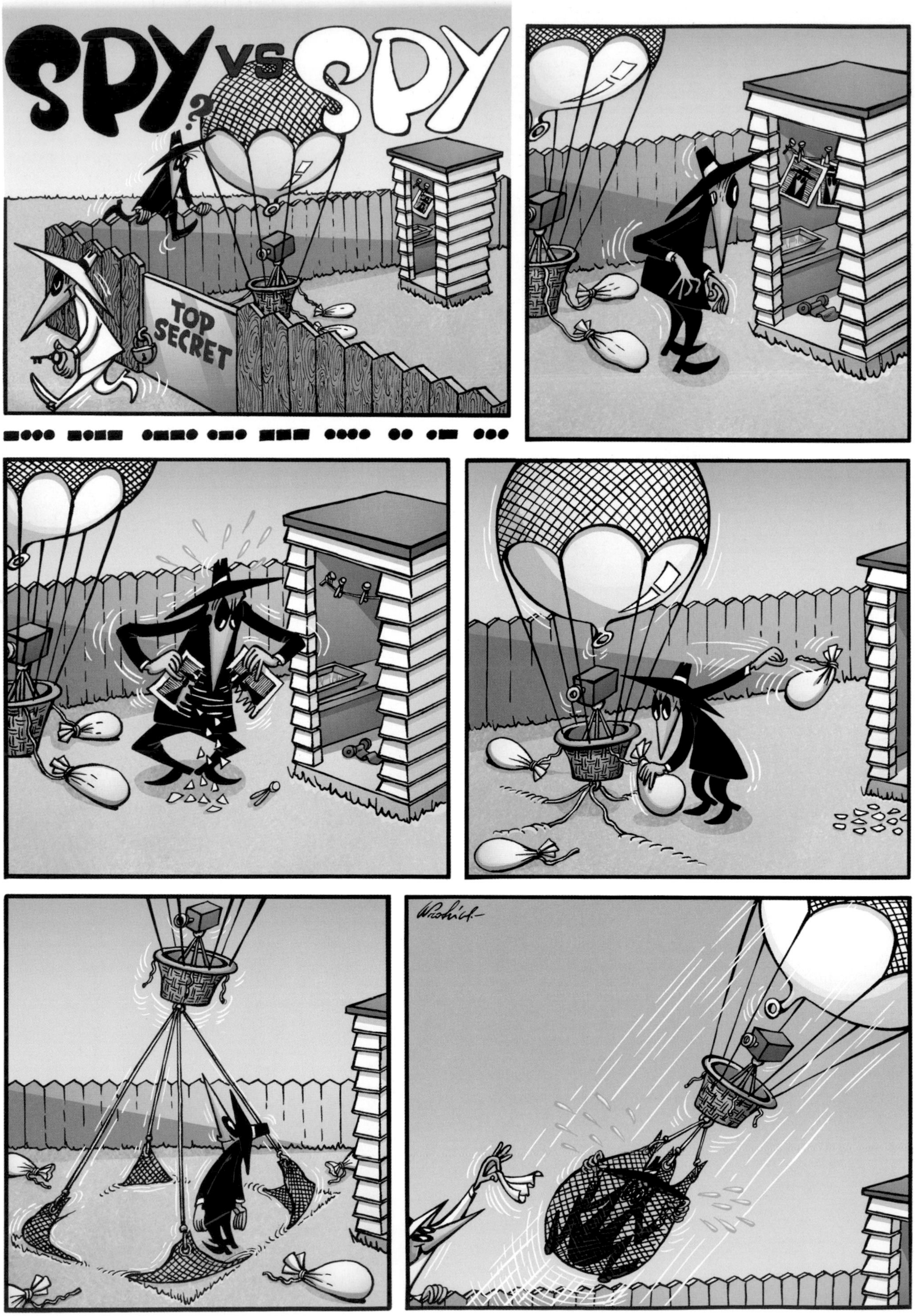
SPY vs SPY
TOP SECRET

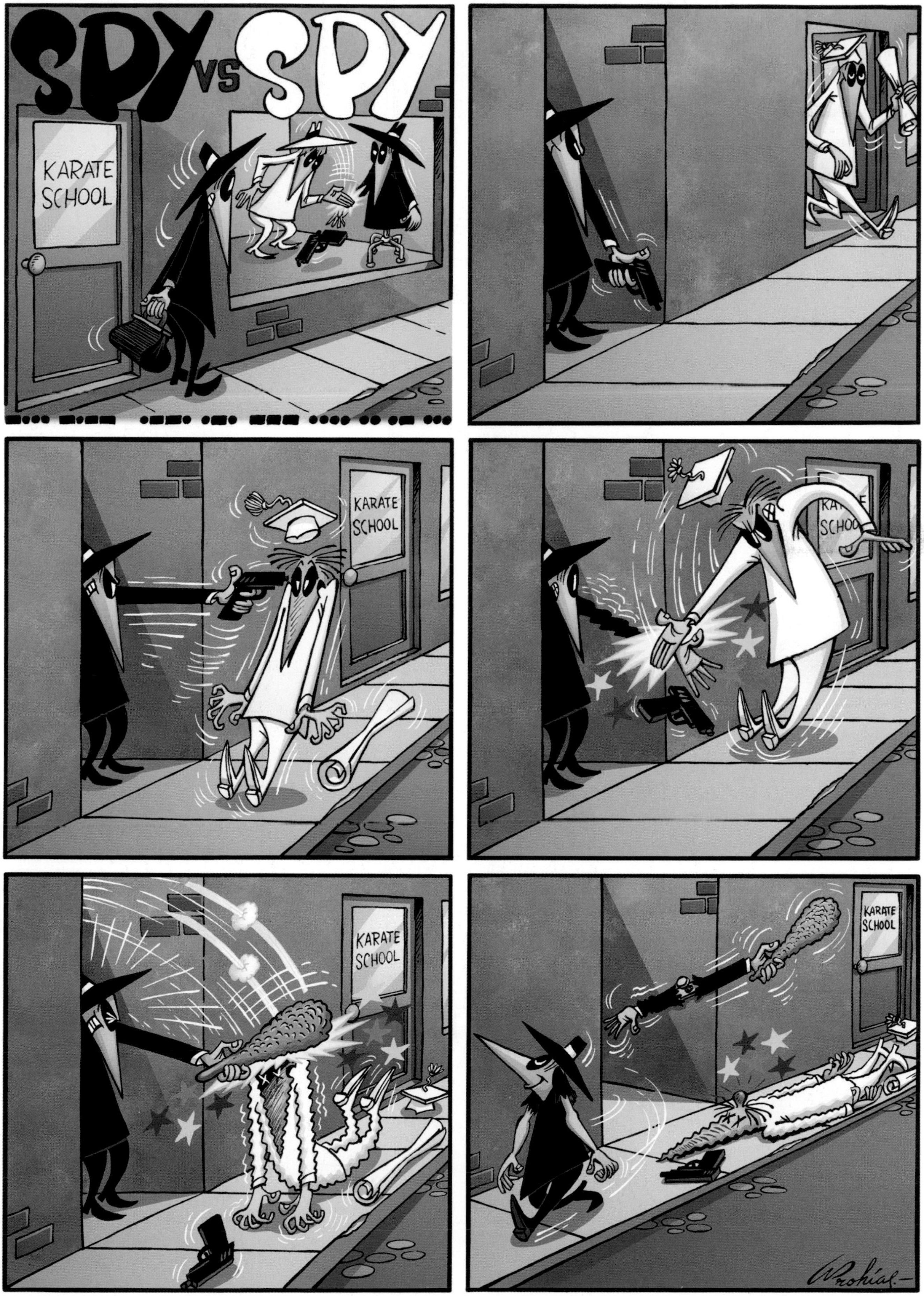
SPY VS SPY
KARATE SCHOOL
KARATE SCHOOL
KARATE SCHOOL
KARATE SCHOOL
KARATE SCHOOL
Prohias

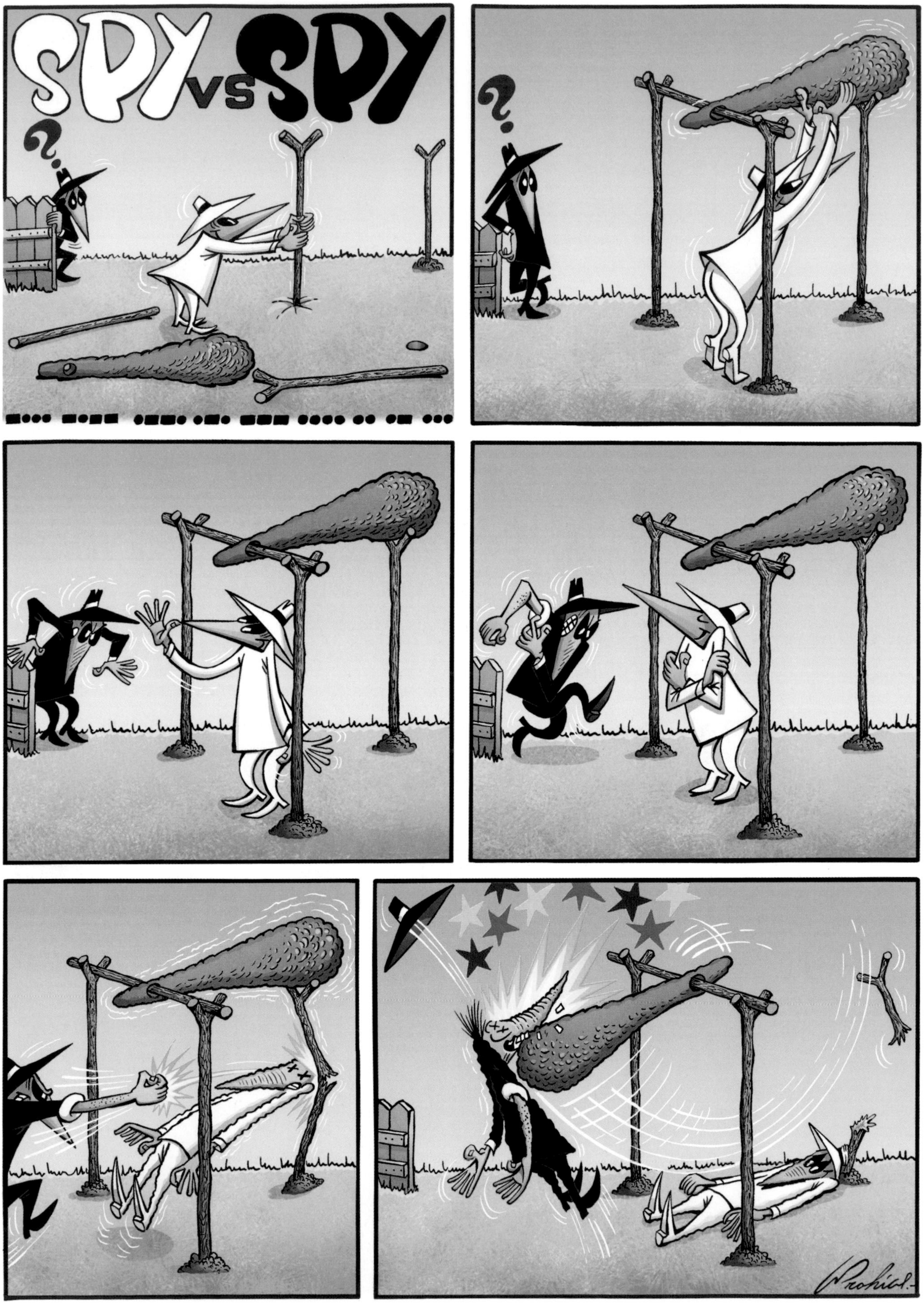
SPY vs SPY
Prohias

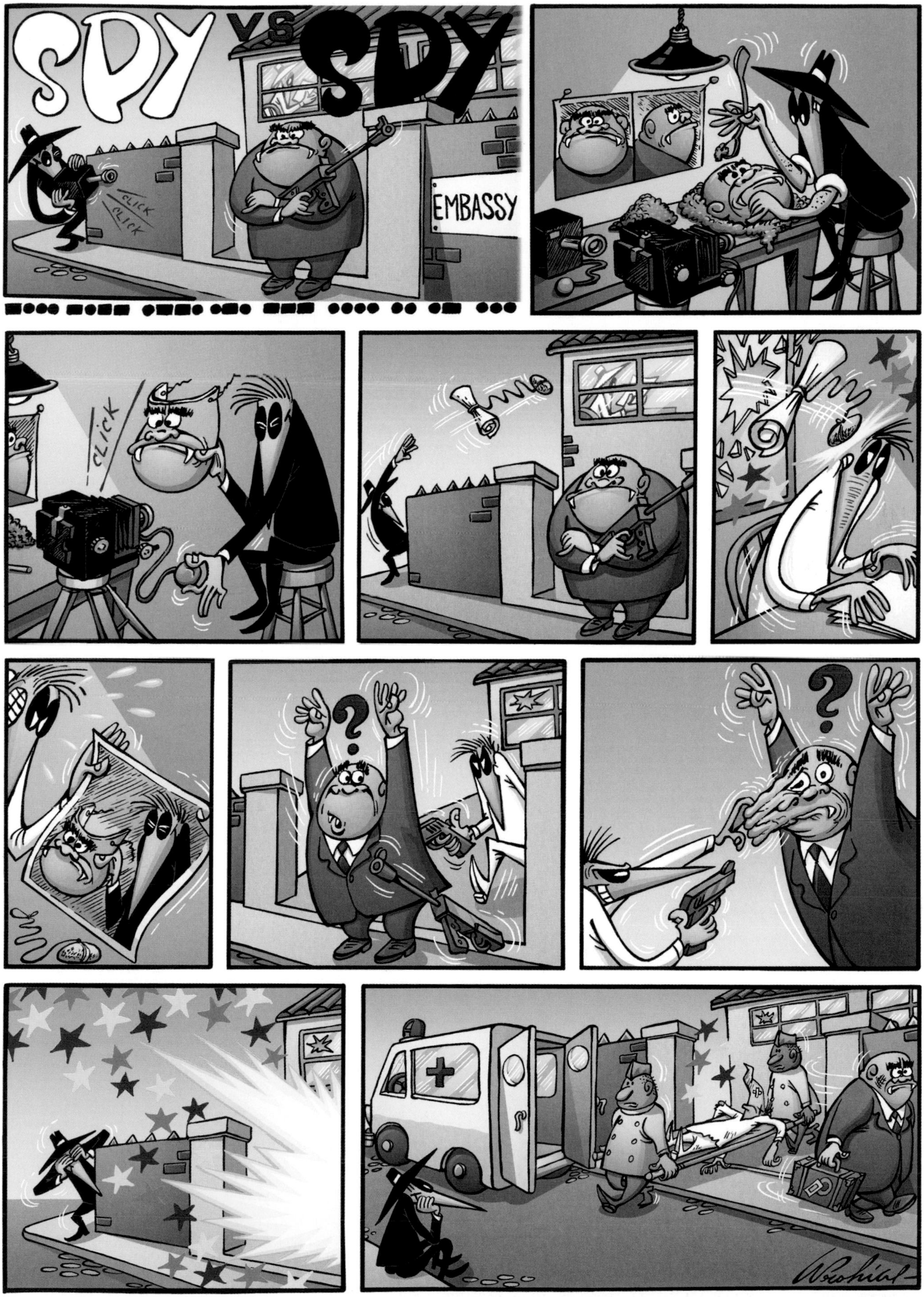
SPY VS SPY
CLICK
CLICK
EMBASSY
CLICK
?
?

SPY vs SPY

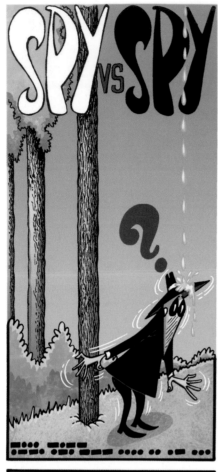

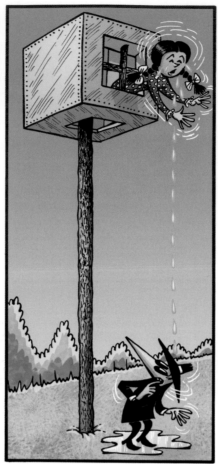

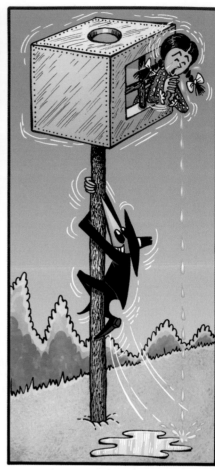

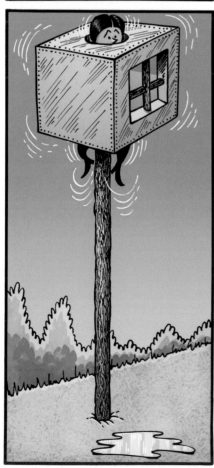

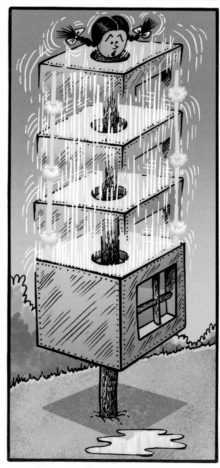

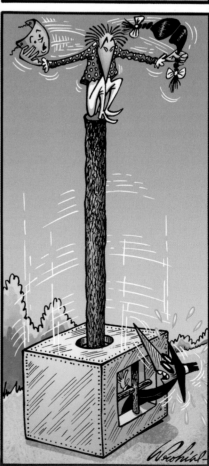

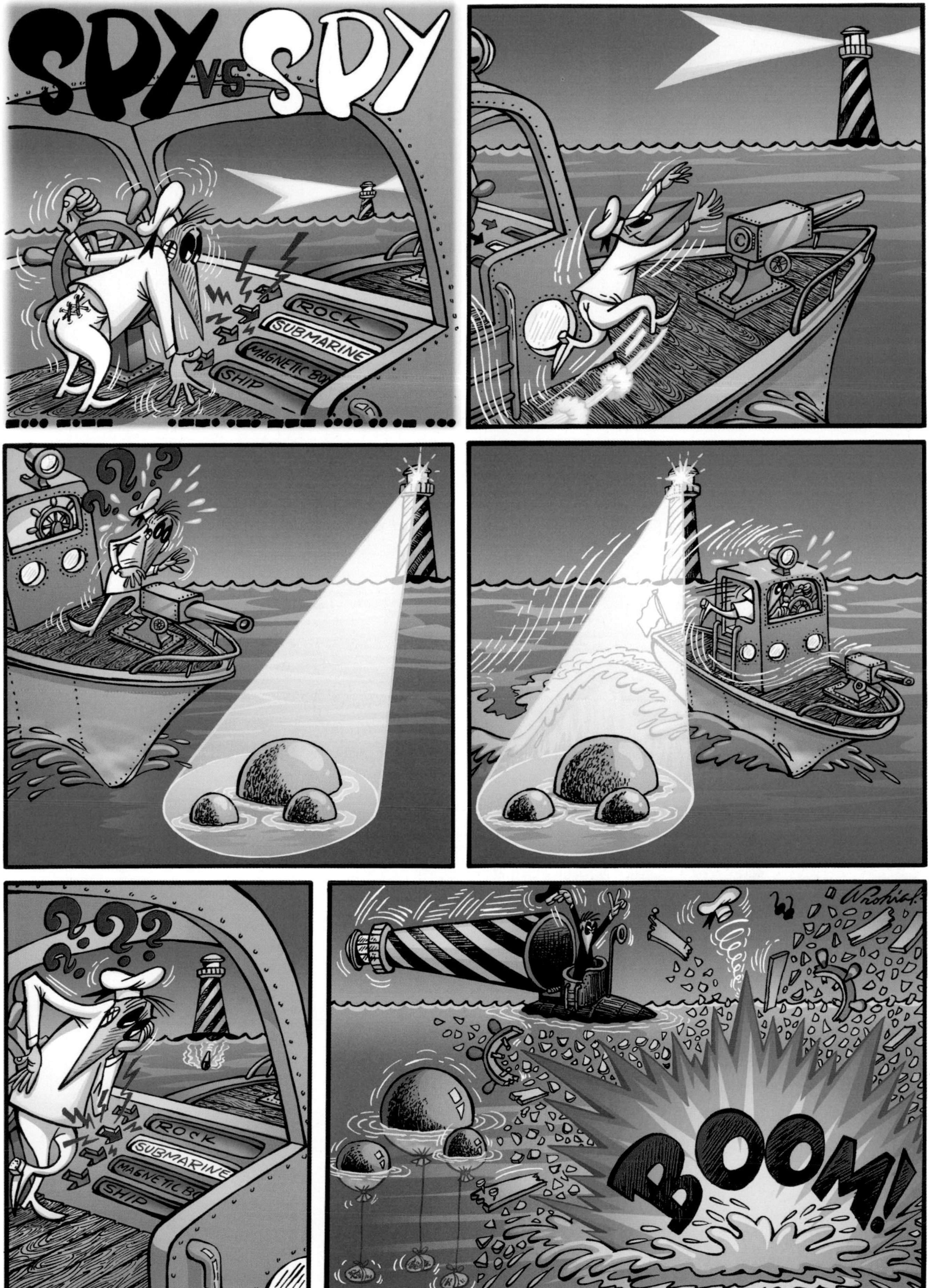
SPY vs SPY
ROCK
SUBMARINE
MAGNETIC BO
SHIP
ROCK
SUBMARINE
MAGNETIC BO
SHIP
BOOM!

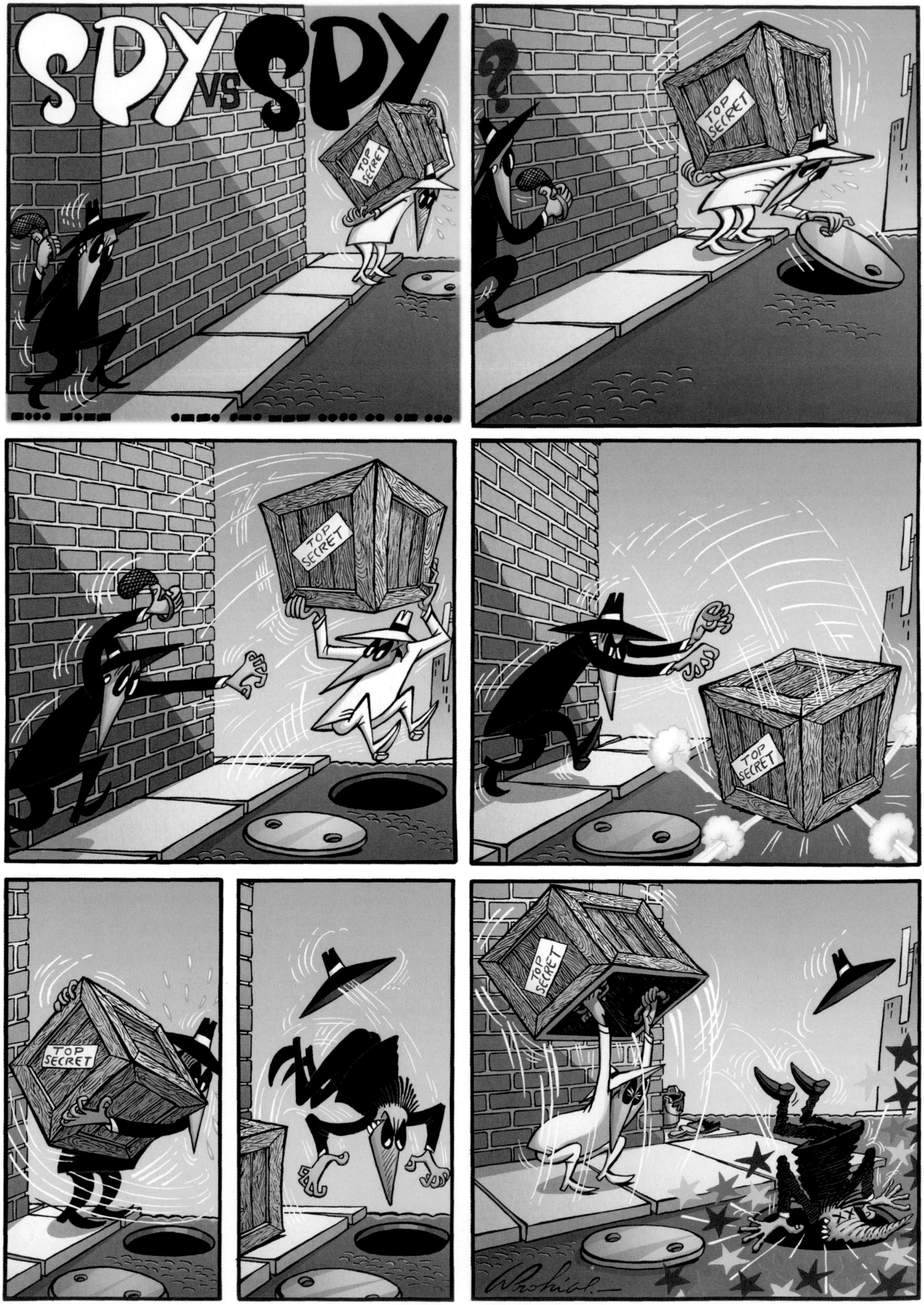
SPY vs SPY
TOP SECRET
TOP SECRET
TOP SECRET
TOP SECRET
TOP SECRET
TOP SECRET

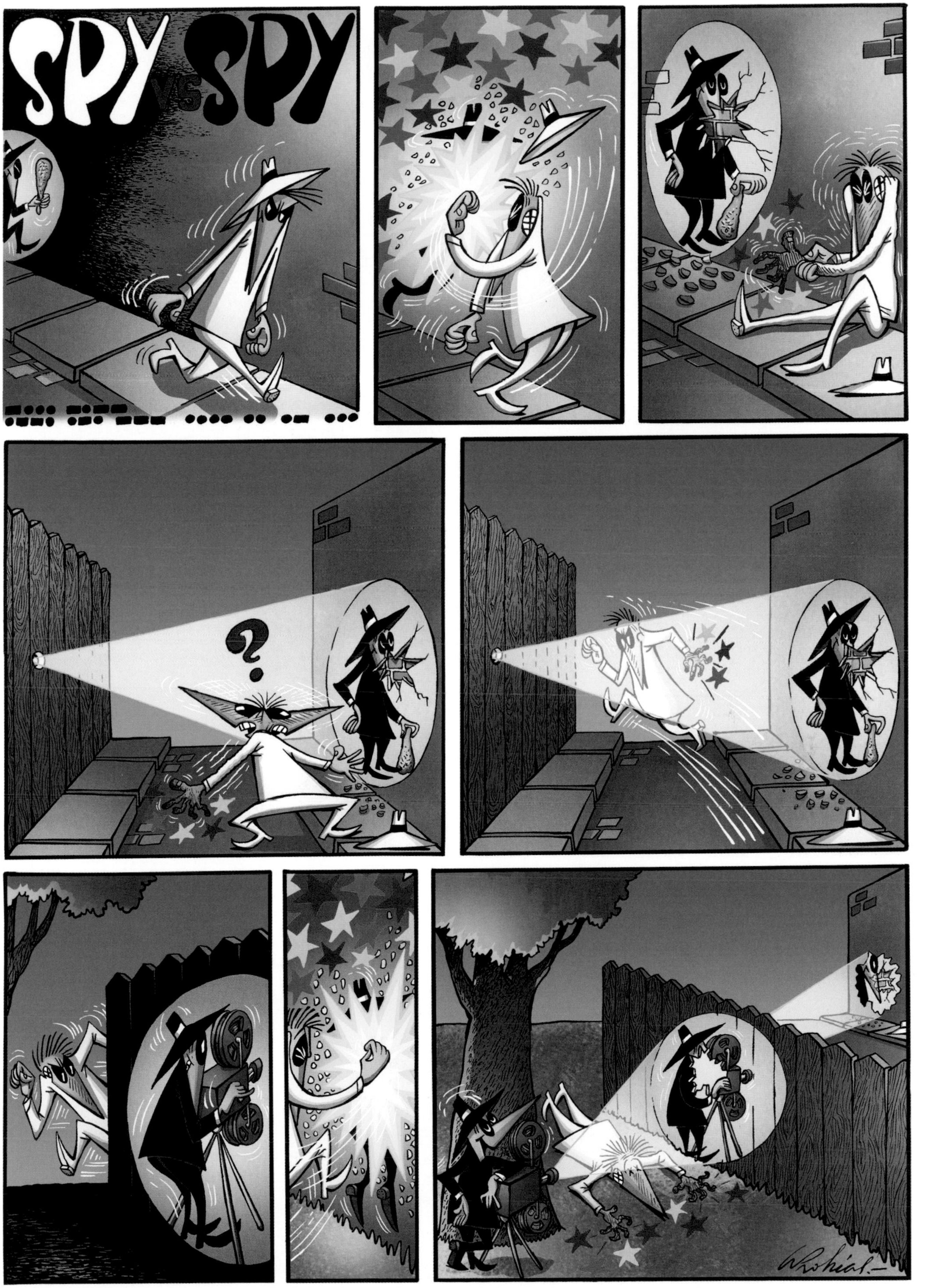
SPY vs SPY

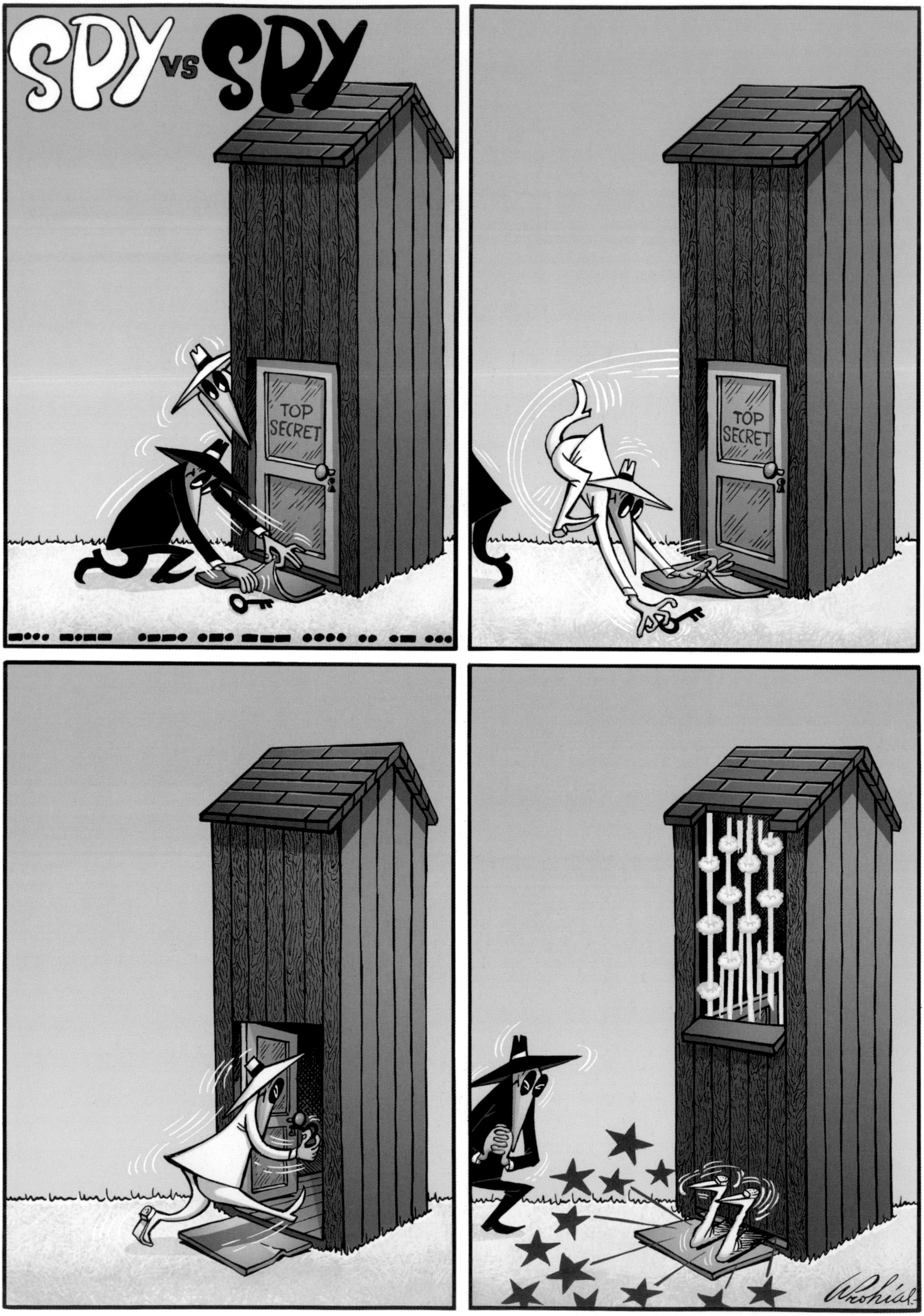
SPY vs SPY
TOP SECRET
TOP SECRET
Prohias

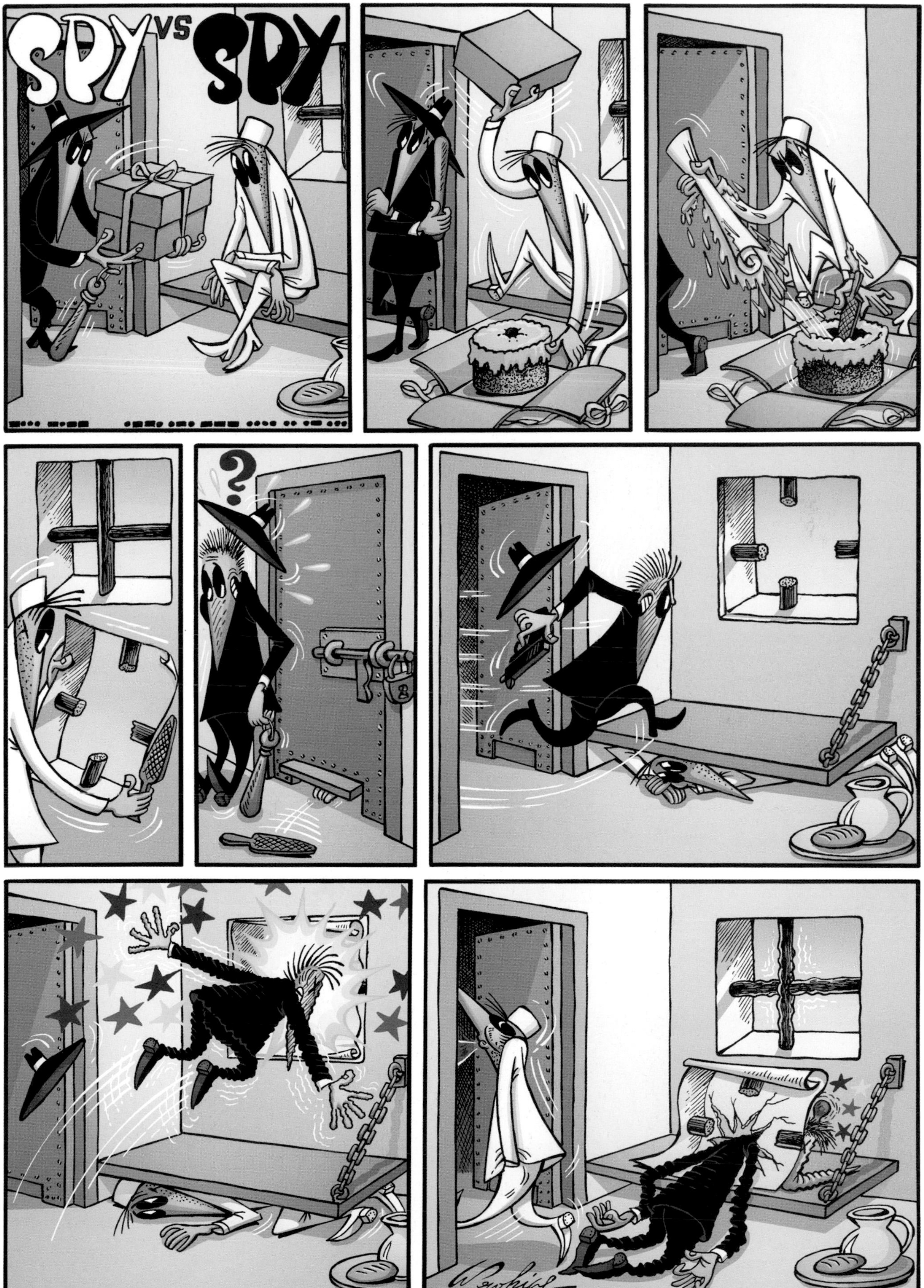
SPY VS SPY

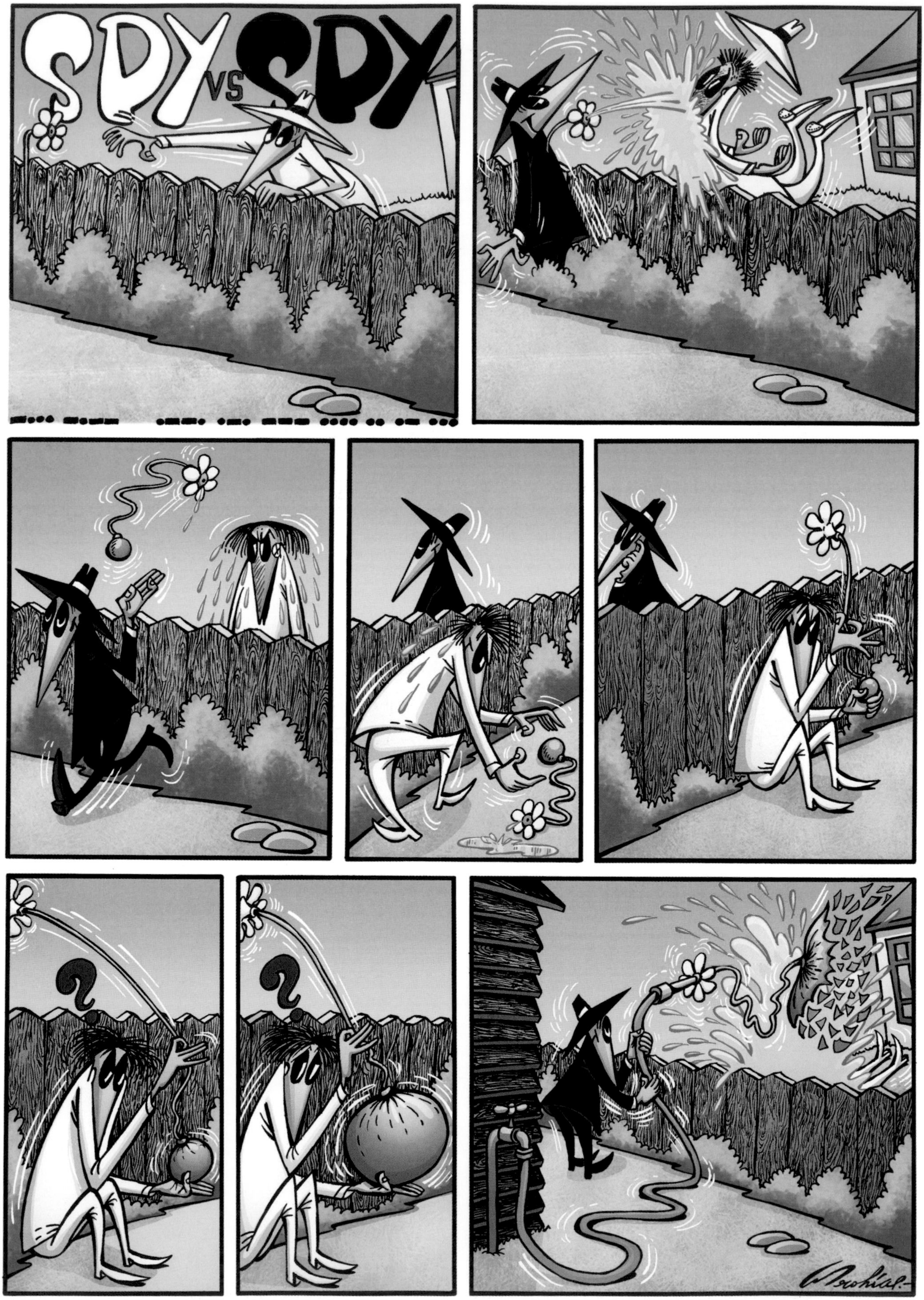
SPY vs SPY

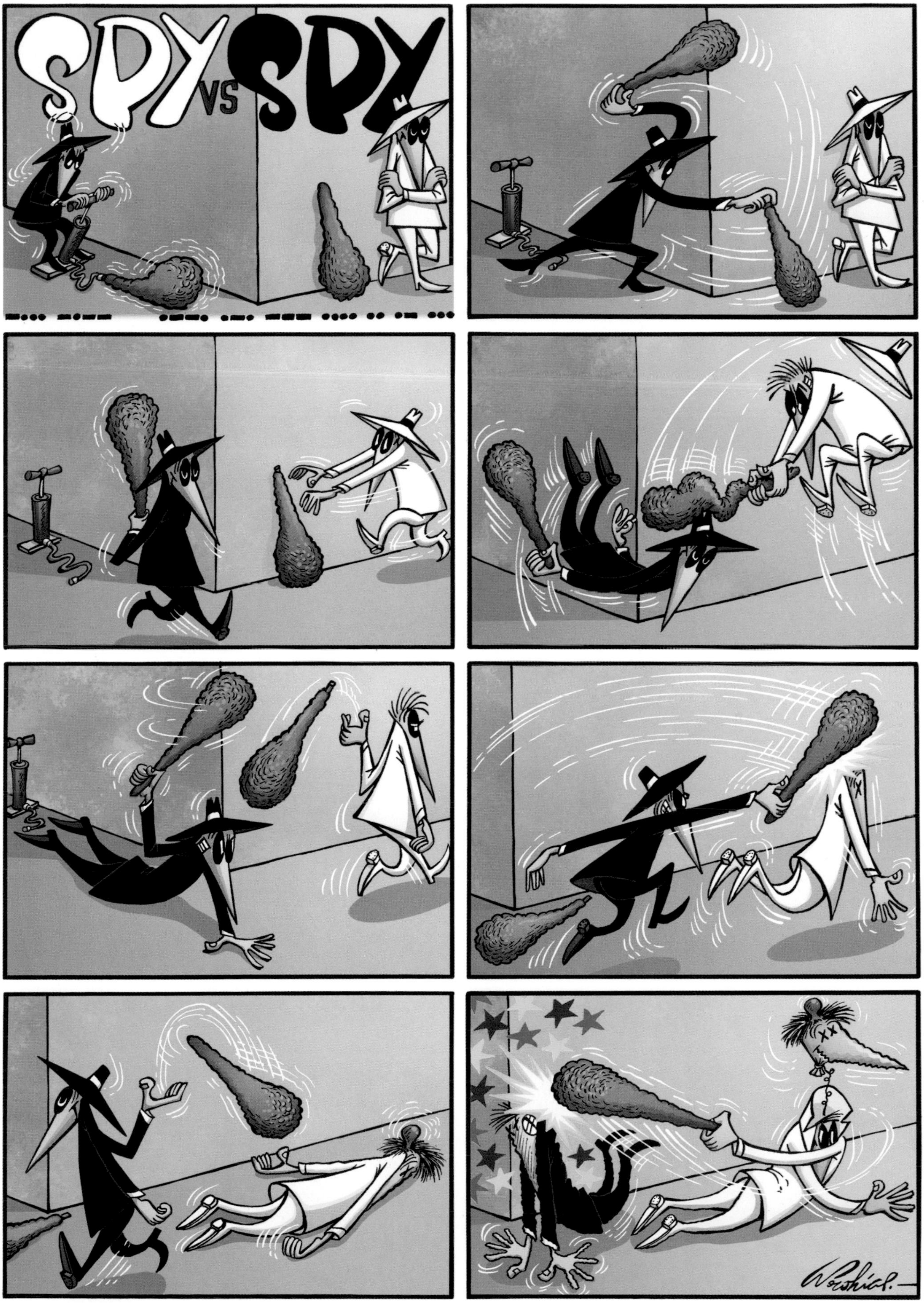
SPY VS SPY

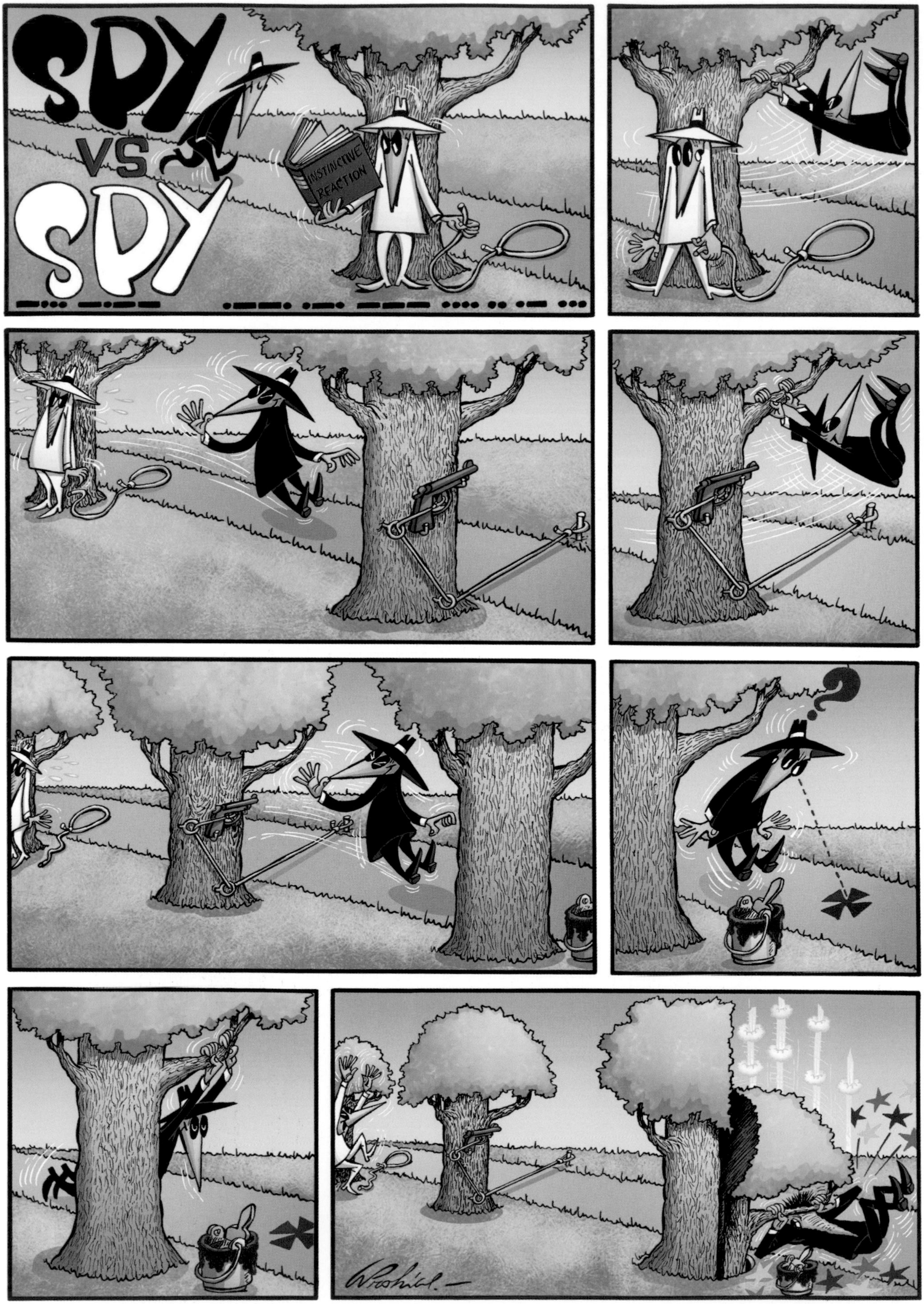
SPY vs SPY
INSTINCTIVE REACTION

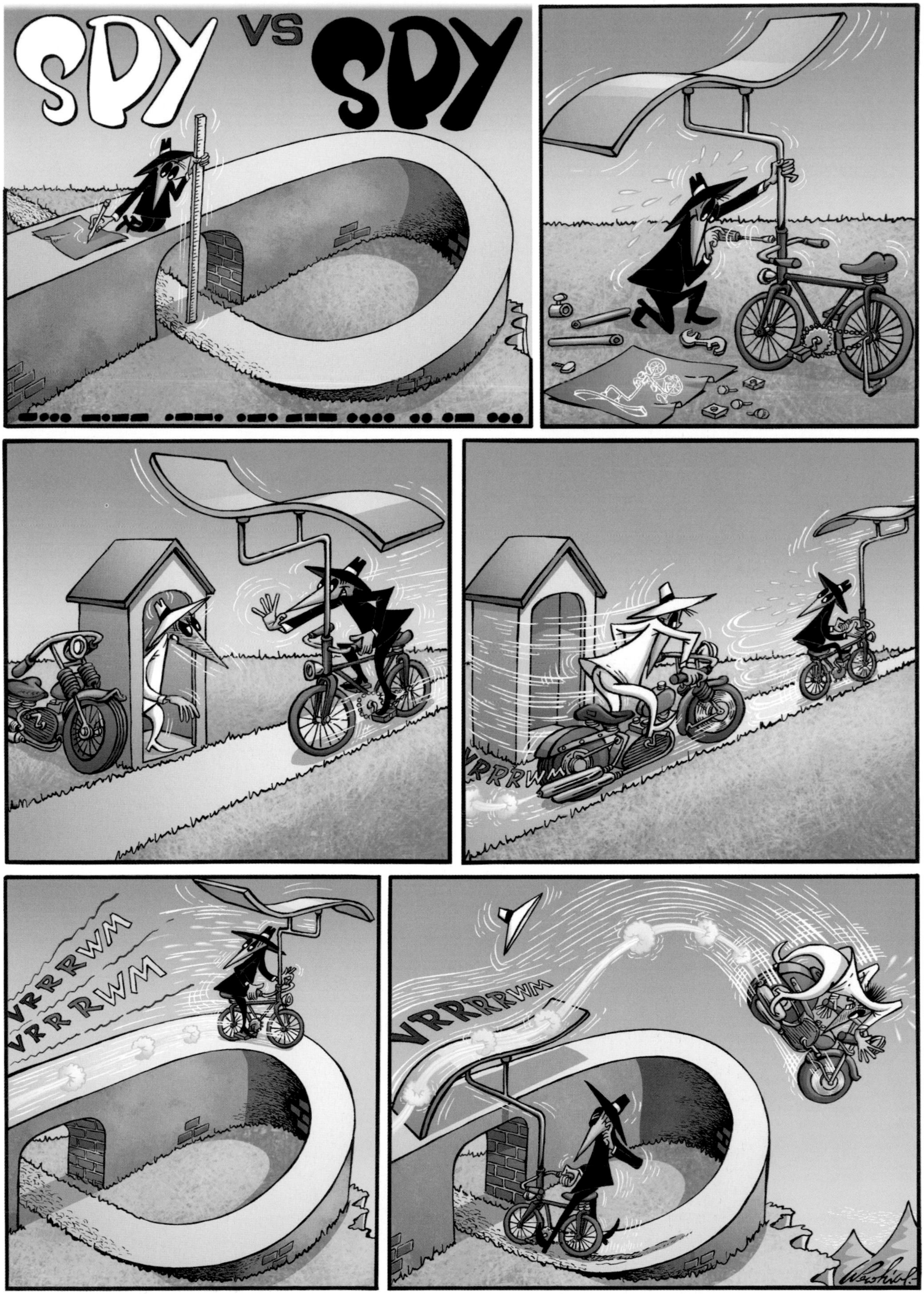
SPY vs SPY
VRRRWM
VRRRWM
VRRRWM
VRRRRWM

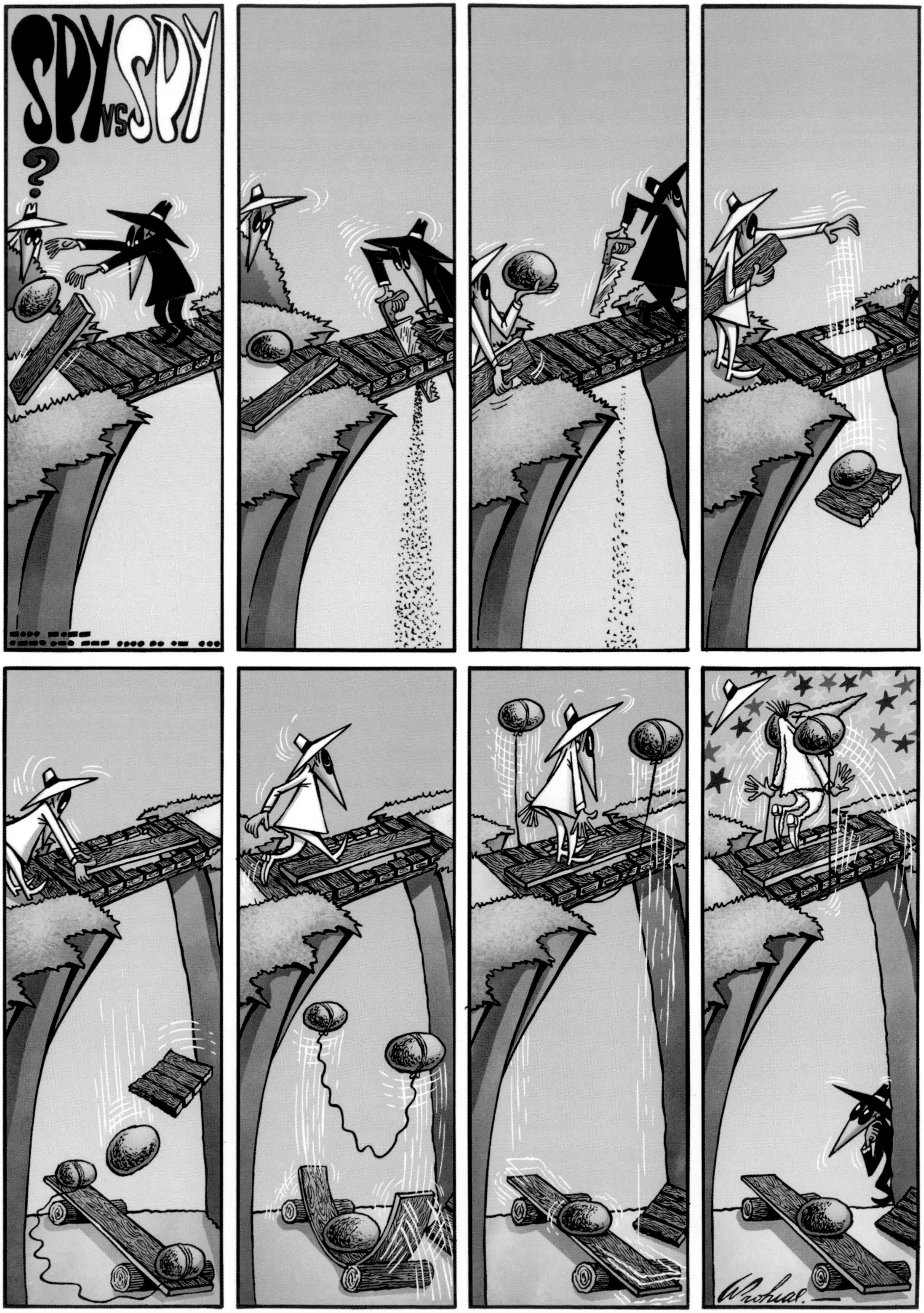
SPY vs SPY

The **Diabolical Duo** of **Double-Cross** and **Deceit**
as **Depicted** by **Some** of the **World's Most Renowned Artists**.

THE SPY VS. SPY POSTER COLLECTION

GALLERY II

Evan Dorkin (Colorist: Sarah Dyer)

Hermann Mejia

Orlando Arocena

Darwyn Cooke

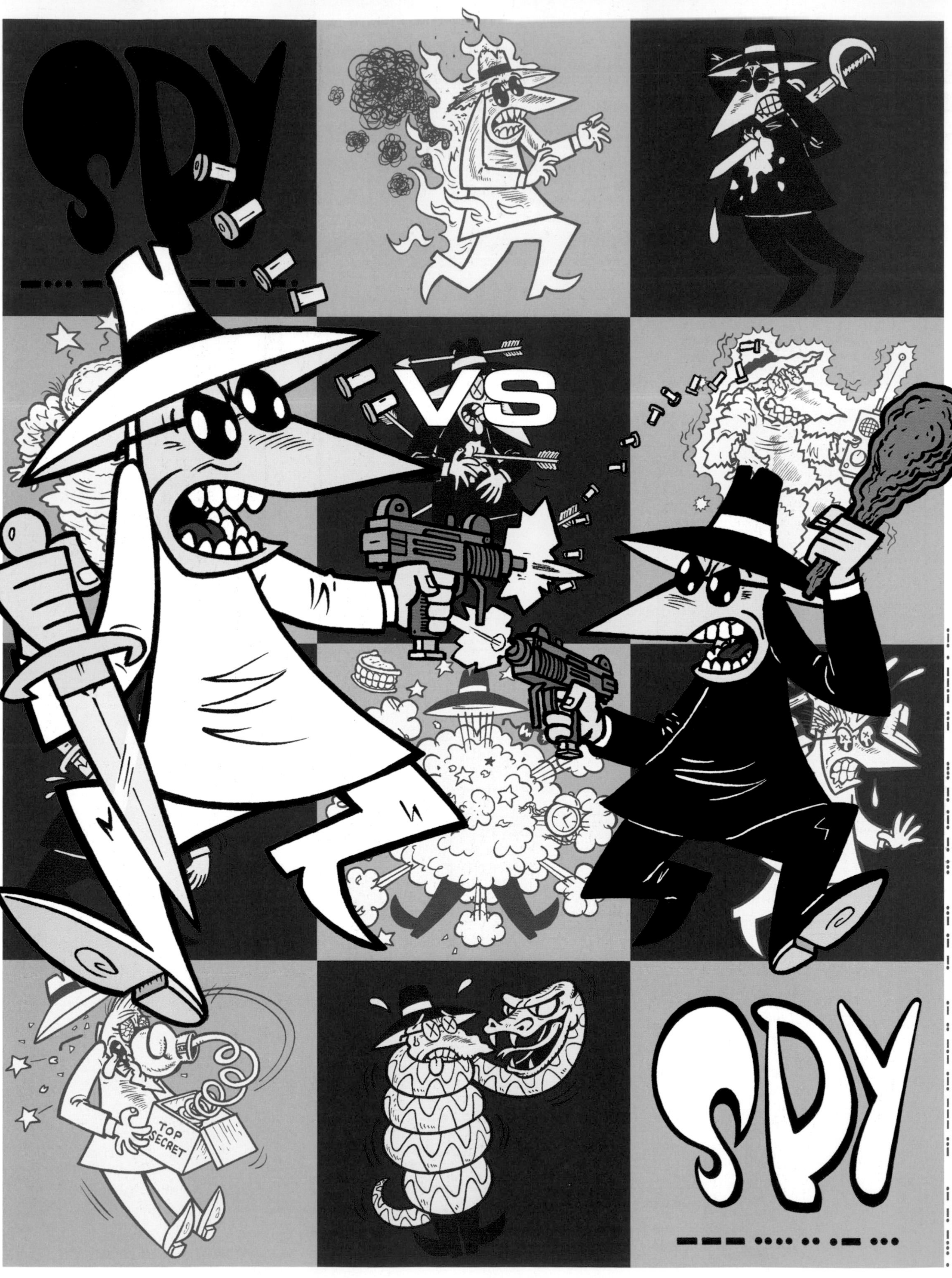
SPY
VS
SPY
TOP SECRET

Evan Dorkin (Colorist: Sarah Dyer)

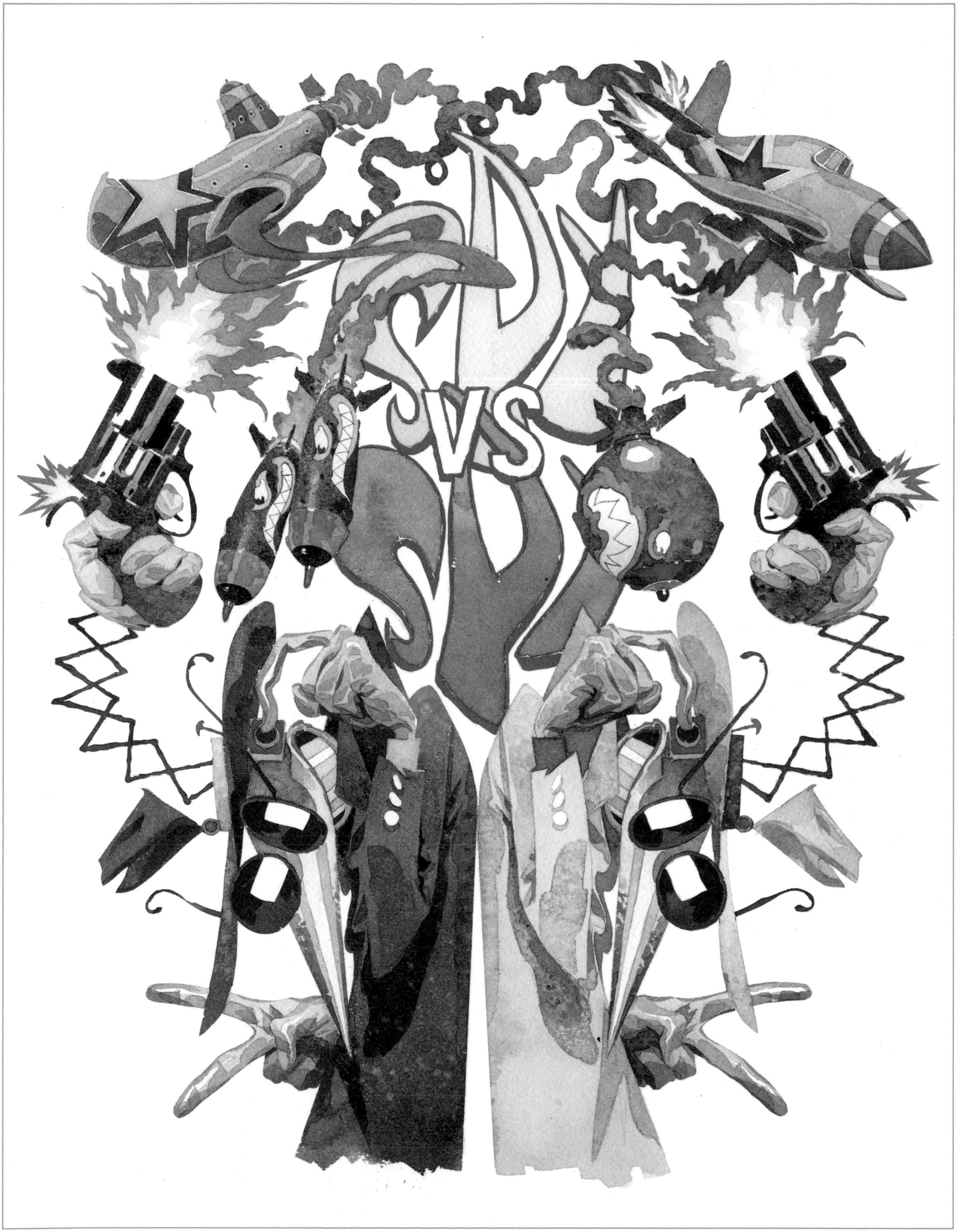
VS

Hermann Mejia

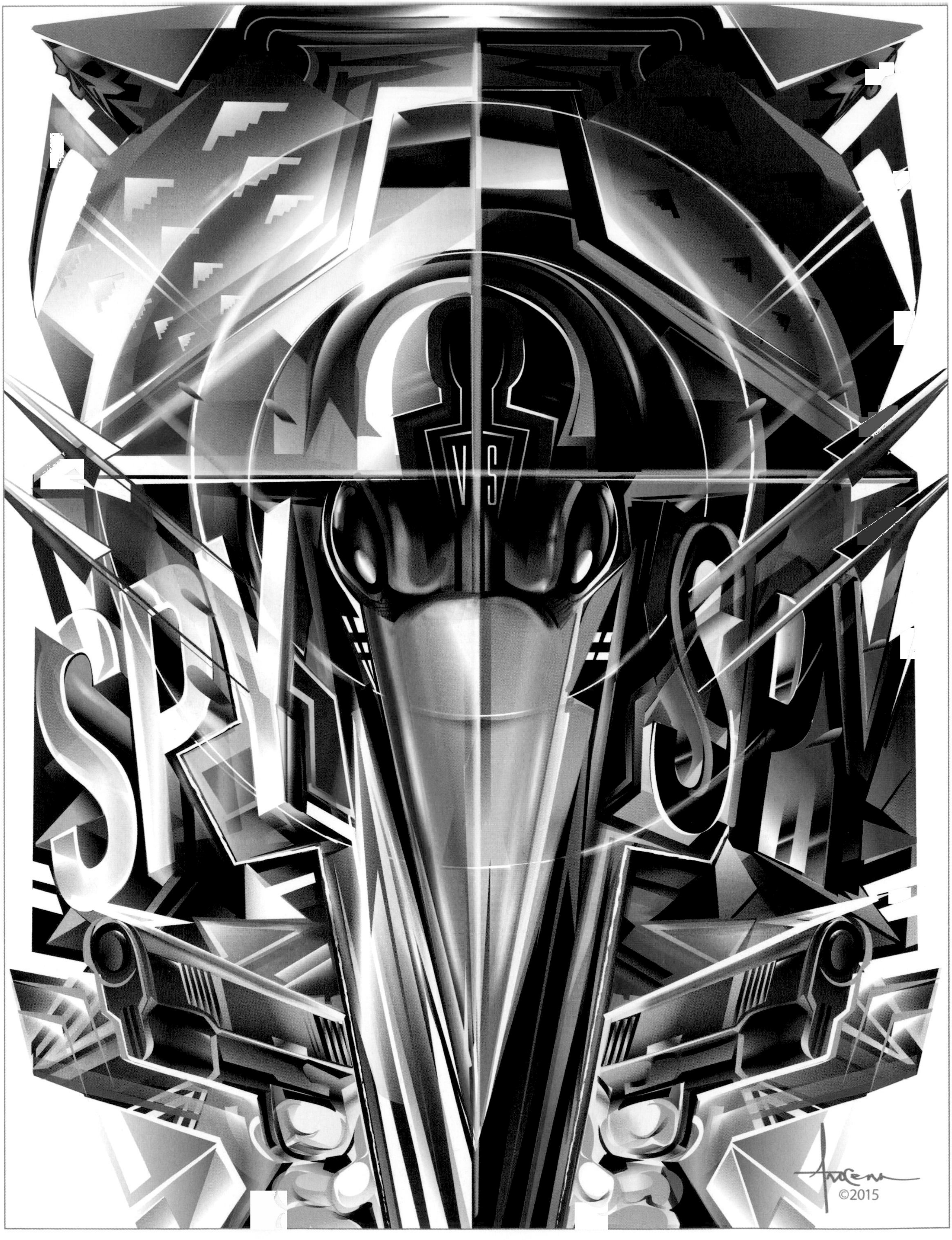

SPY
VS
SPY
©2015

Orlando Arocena

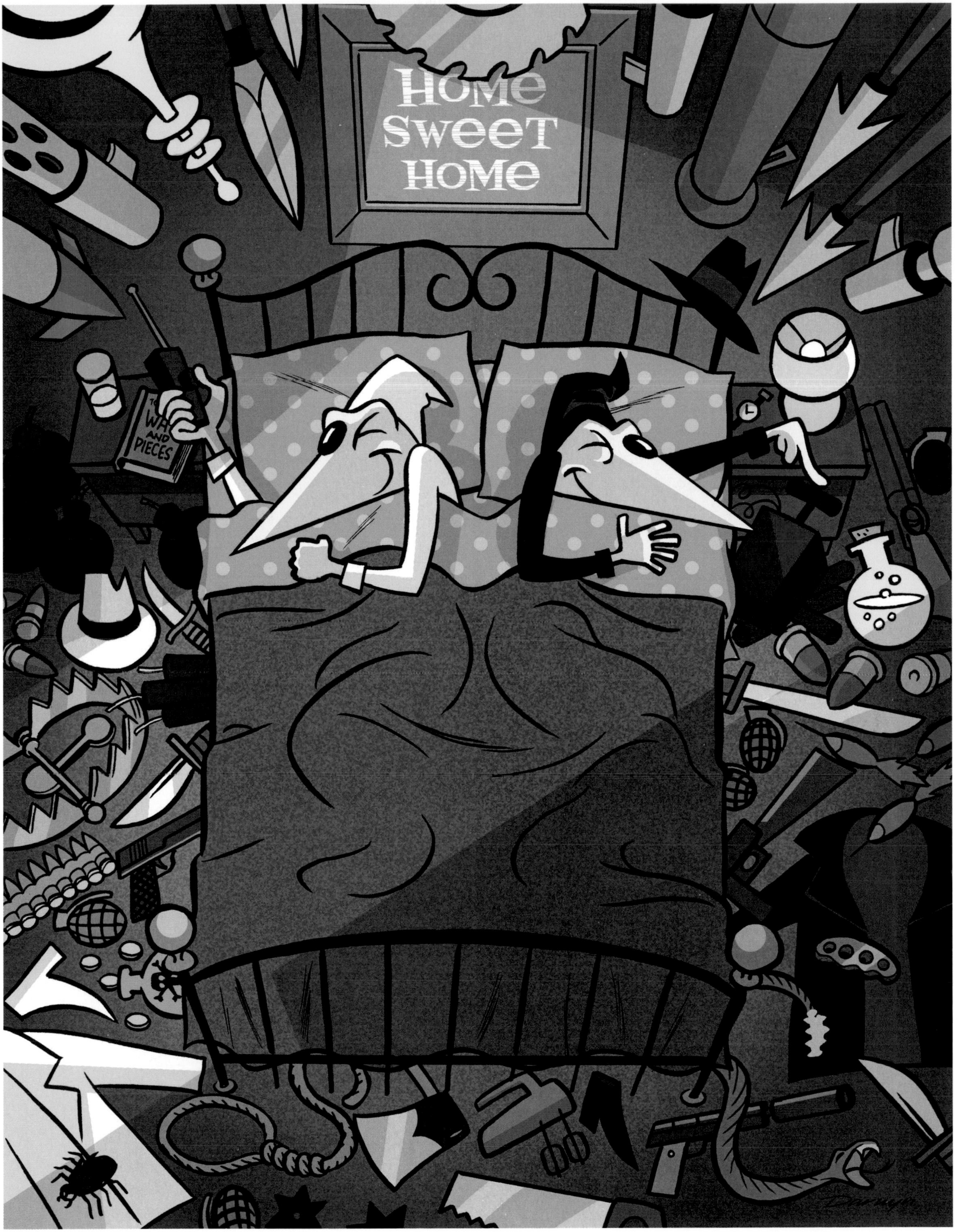
HOME SWEET HOME
WAR AND PIECES

Darwyn Cooke

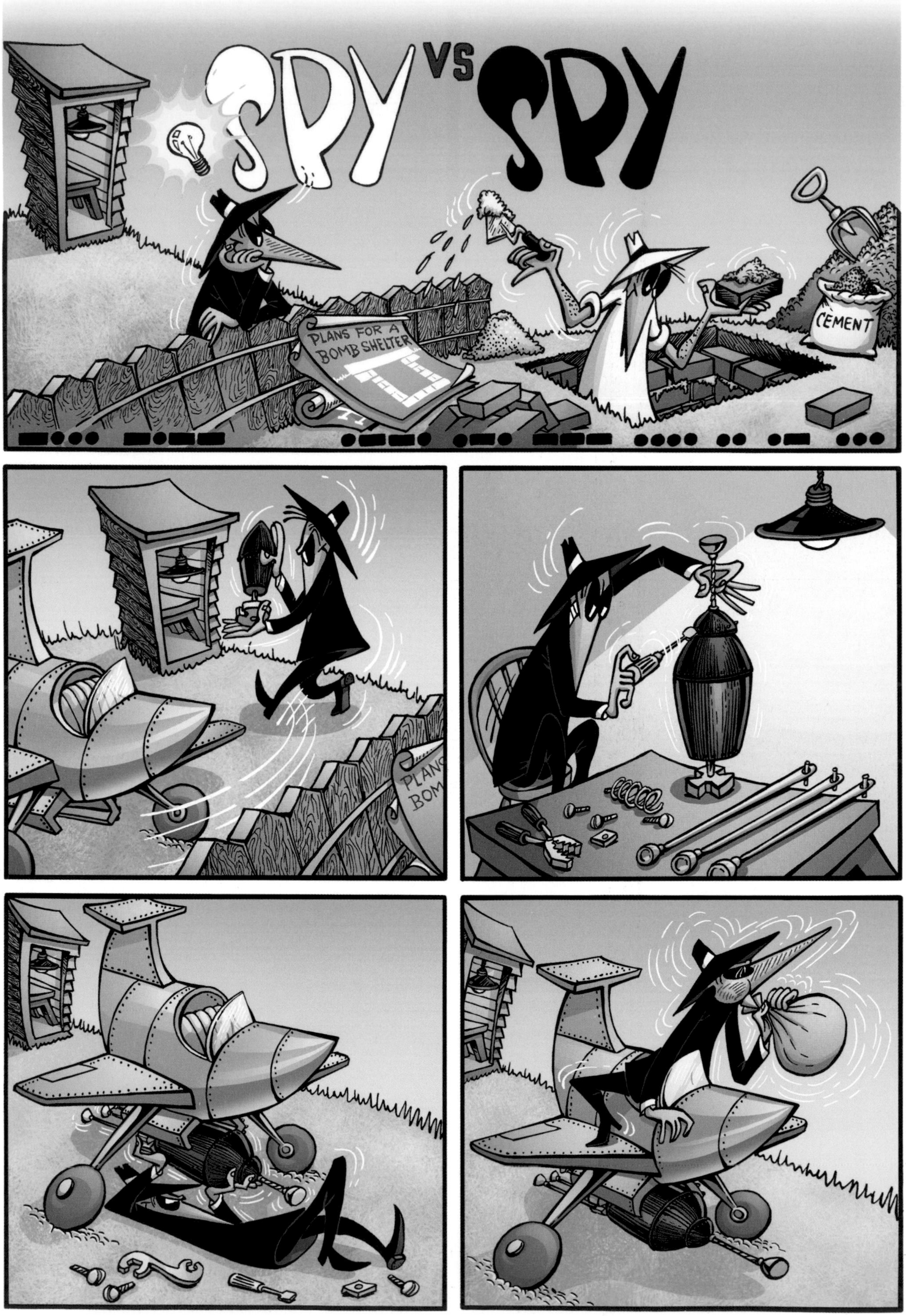
SPY vs SPY
PLANS FOR A BOMB SHELTER
CEMENT

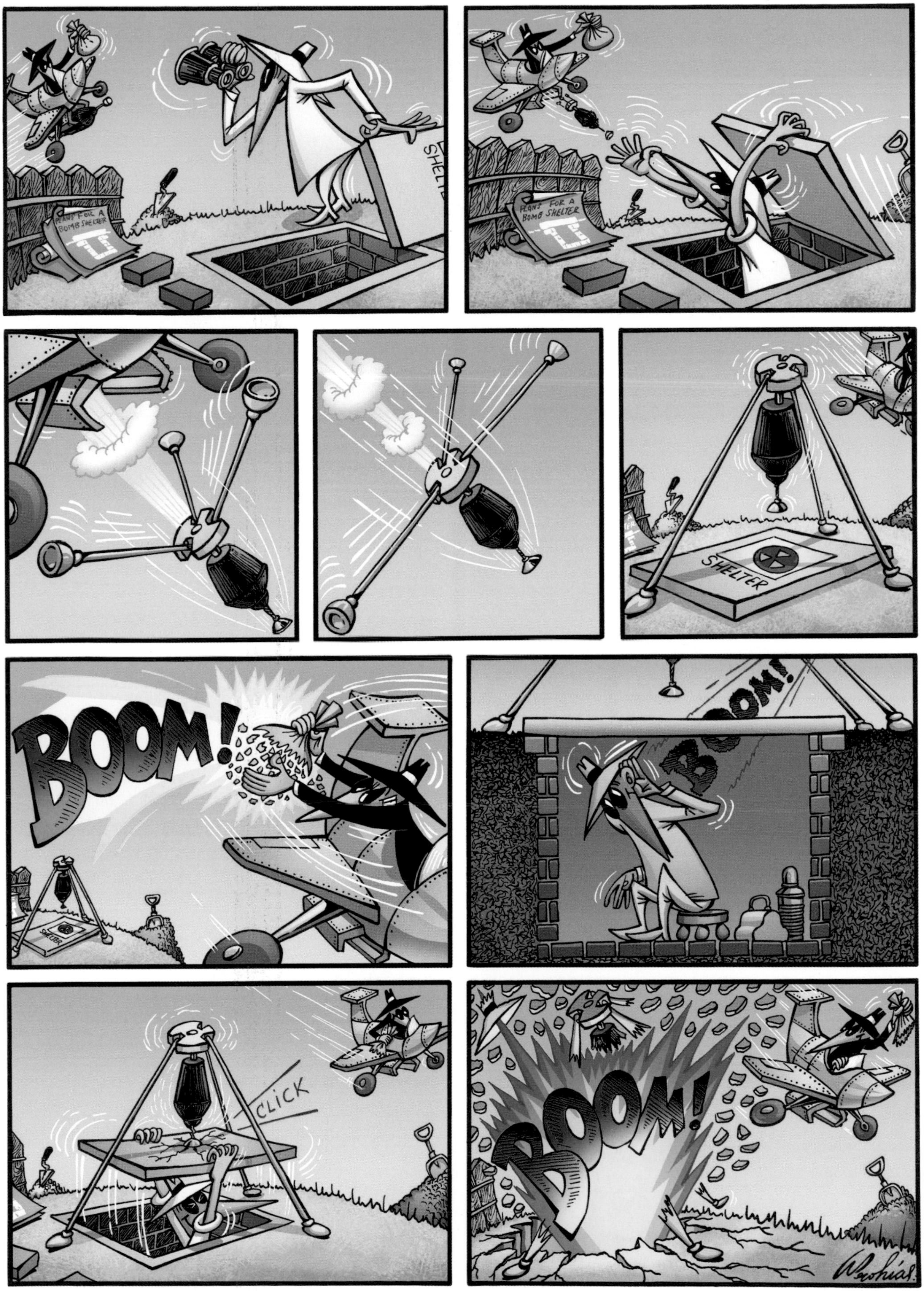

SHELTER
PLANS FOR A BOMB SHELTER
PLANS FOR A BOMB SHELTER
SHELTER
BOOM!
BOOM!
CLICK
SHELTER
BOOM!

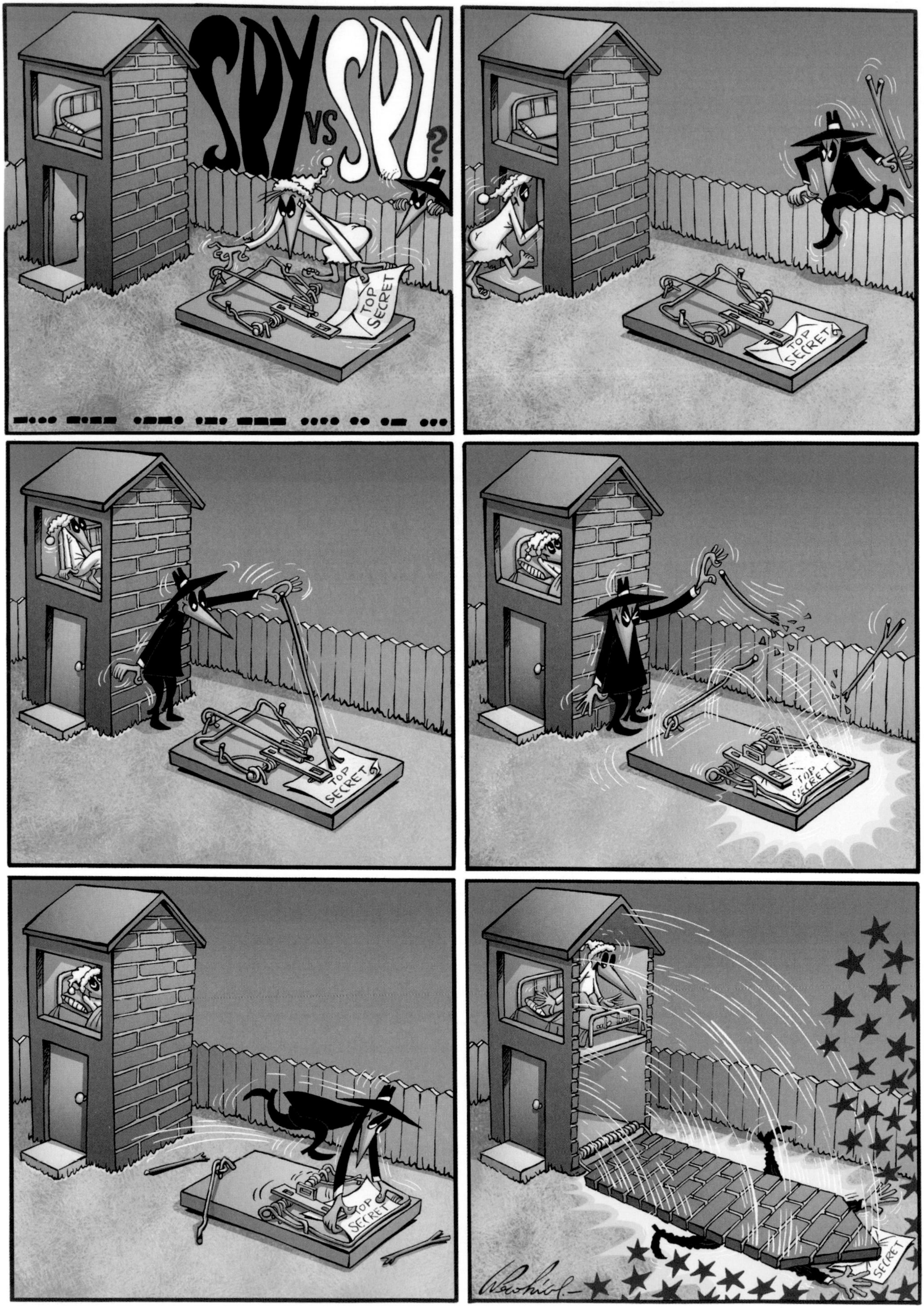
SPY vs SPY
TOP SECRET
TOP SECRET
TOP SECRET
TOP SECRET
TOP SECRET
SECRET

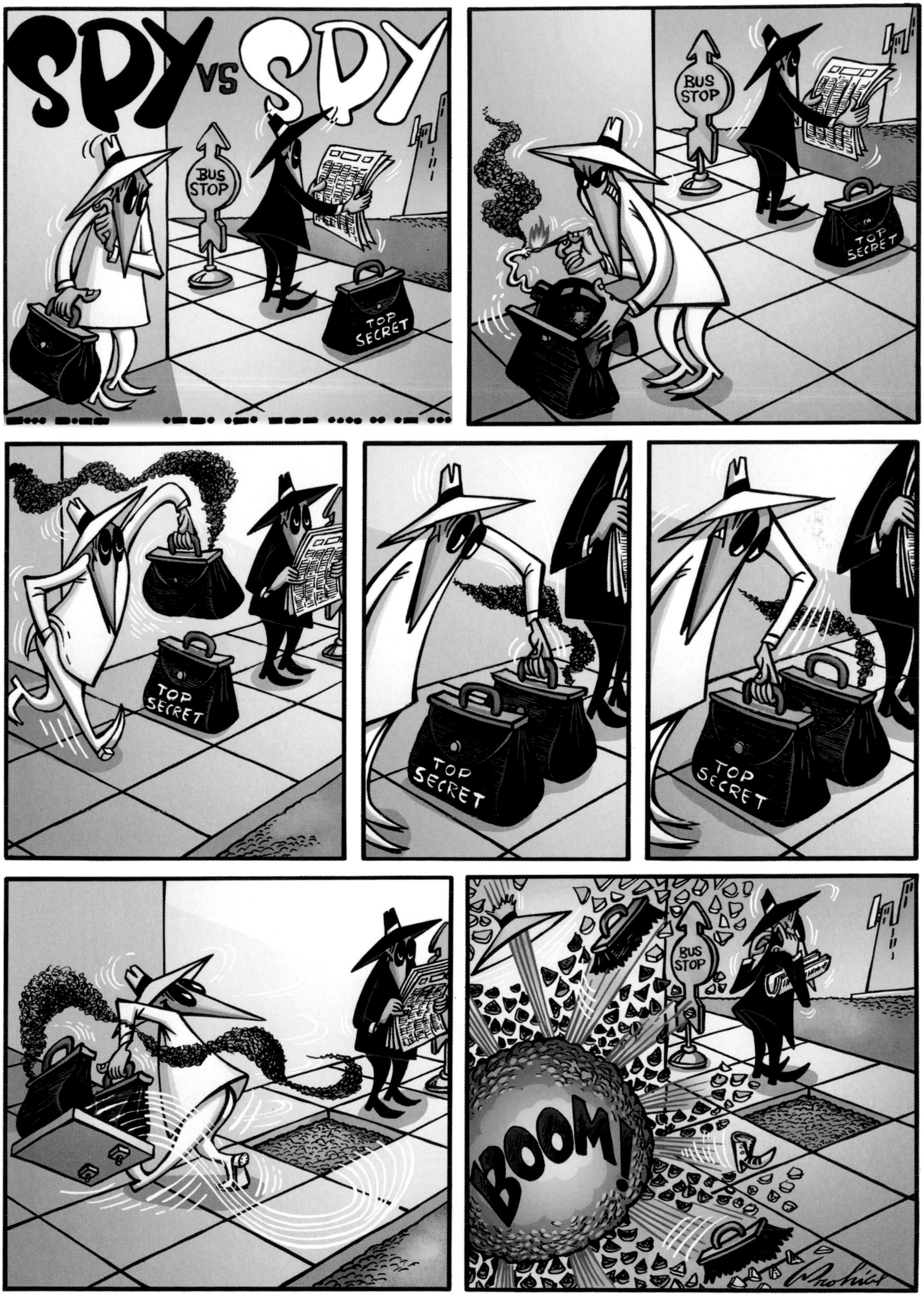
SPY VS SPY
BUS STOP
TOP SECRET
BUS STOP
TOP SECRET
TOP SECRET
TOP SECRET
TOP SECRET
BUS STOP
BOOM!

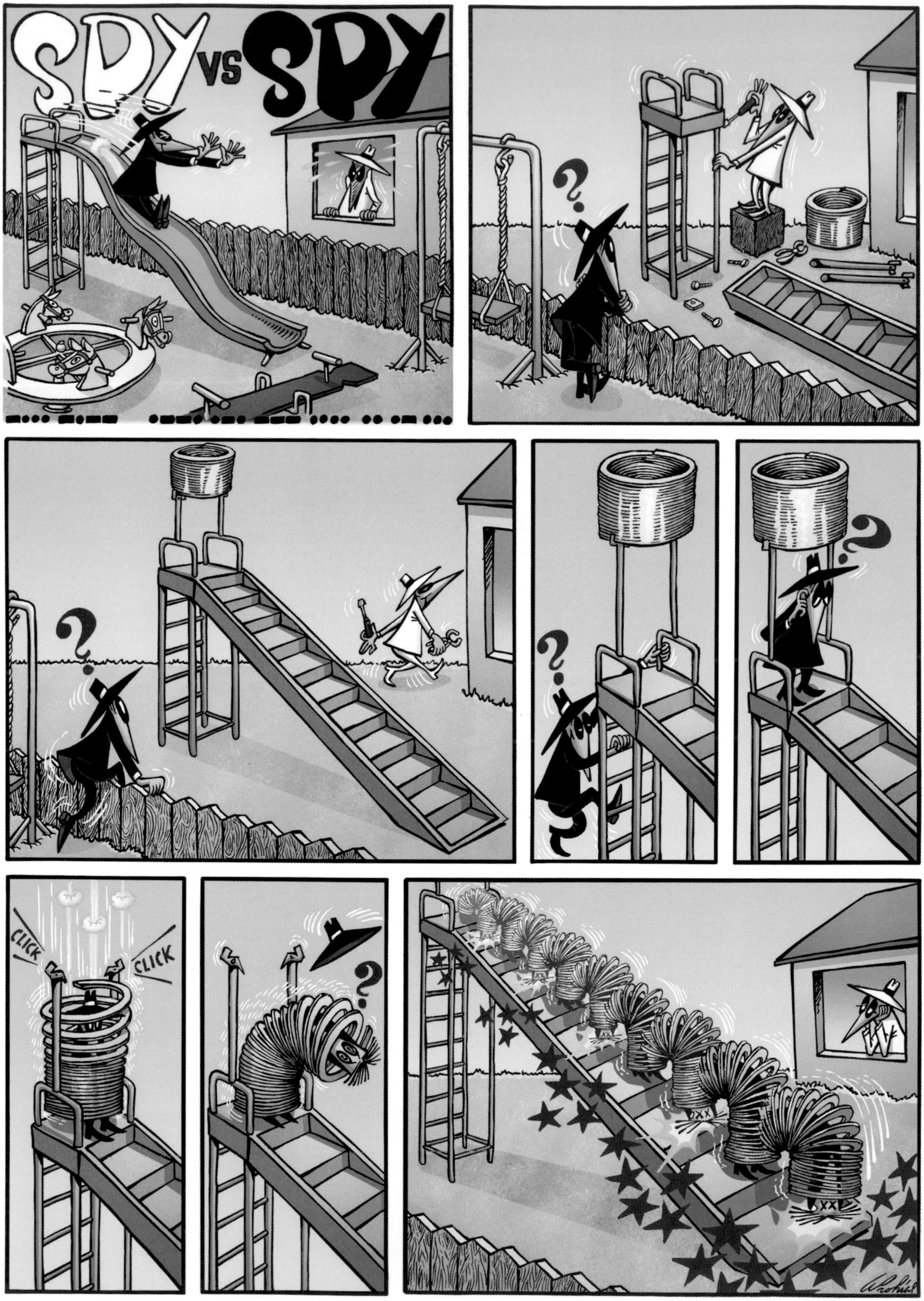
SPY vs SPY
CLICK
CLICK

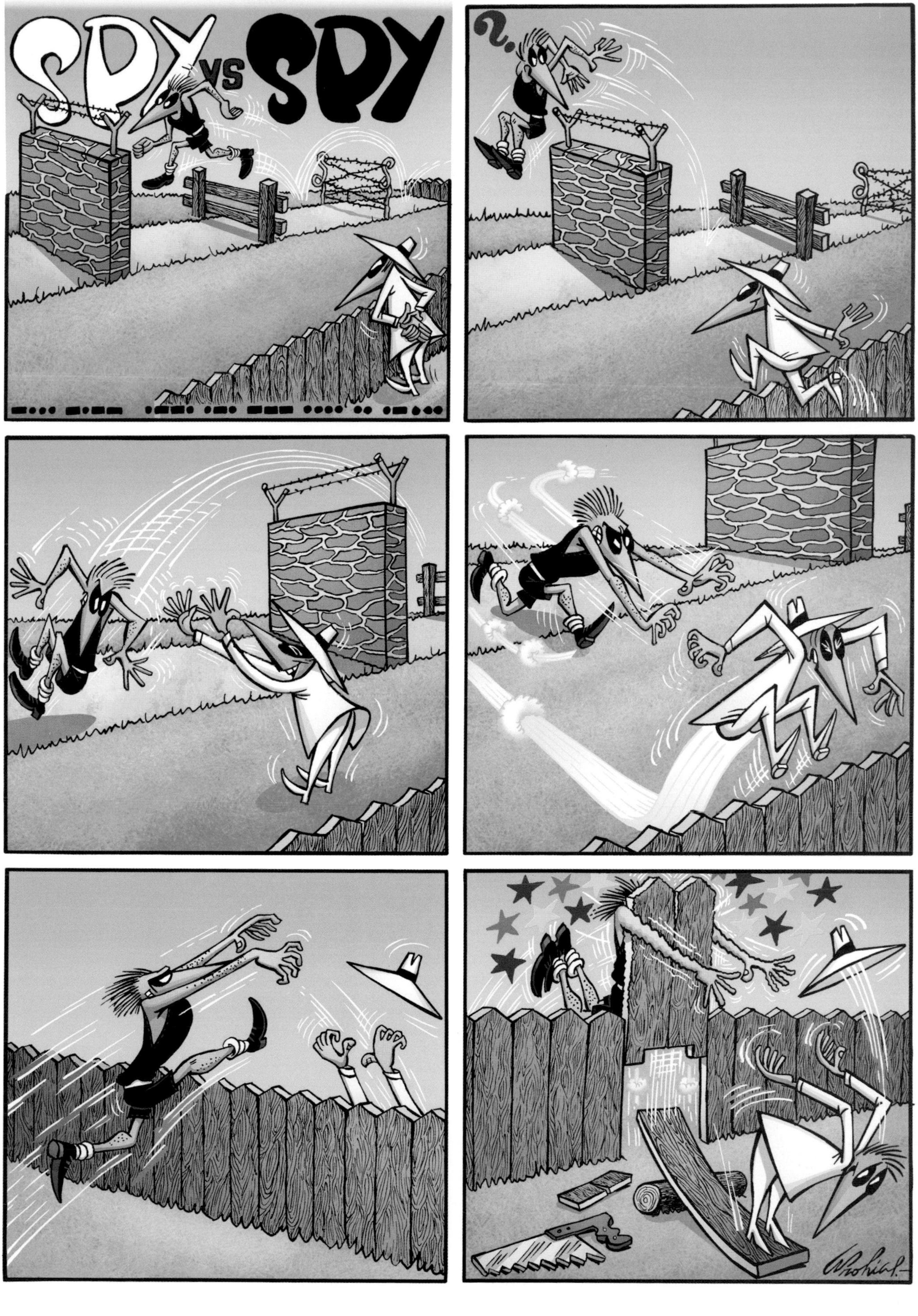
SPY vs SPY

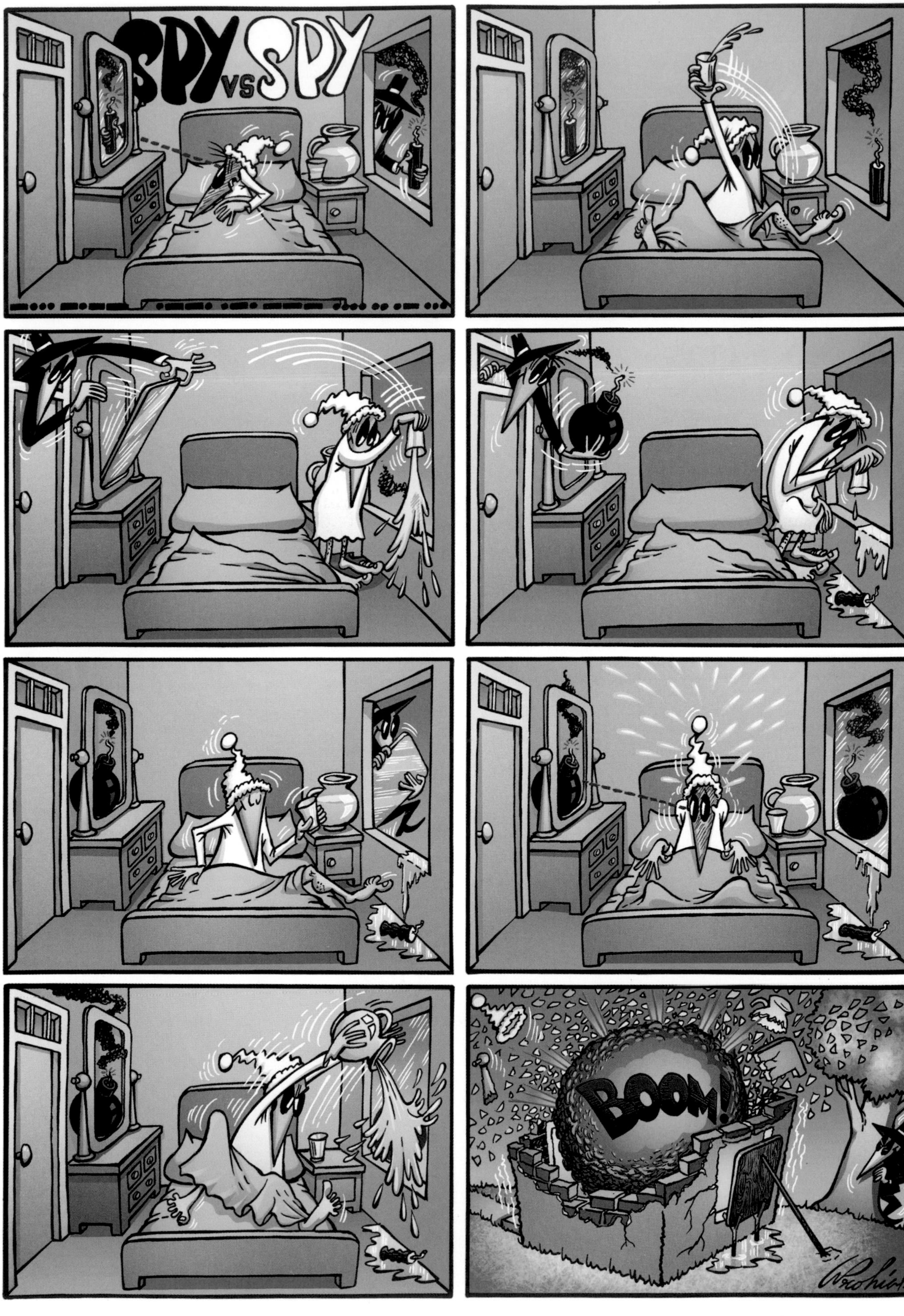
SPY vs SPY
BOOM!

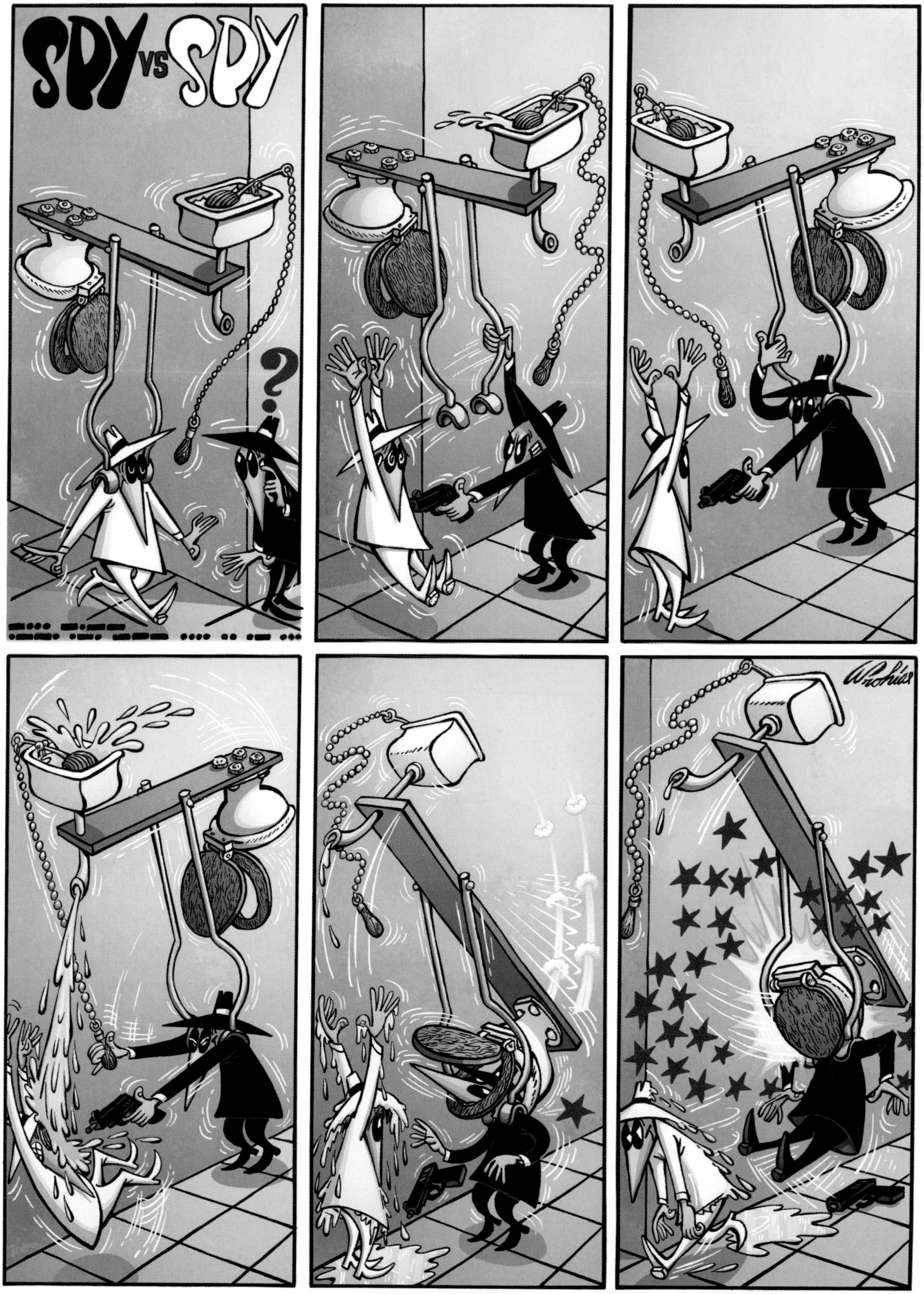
SPY vs SPY
?
Prohias

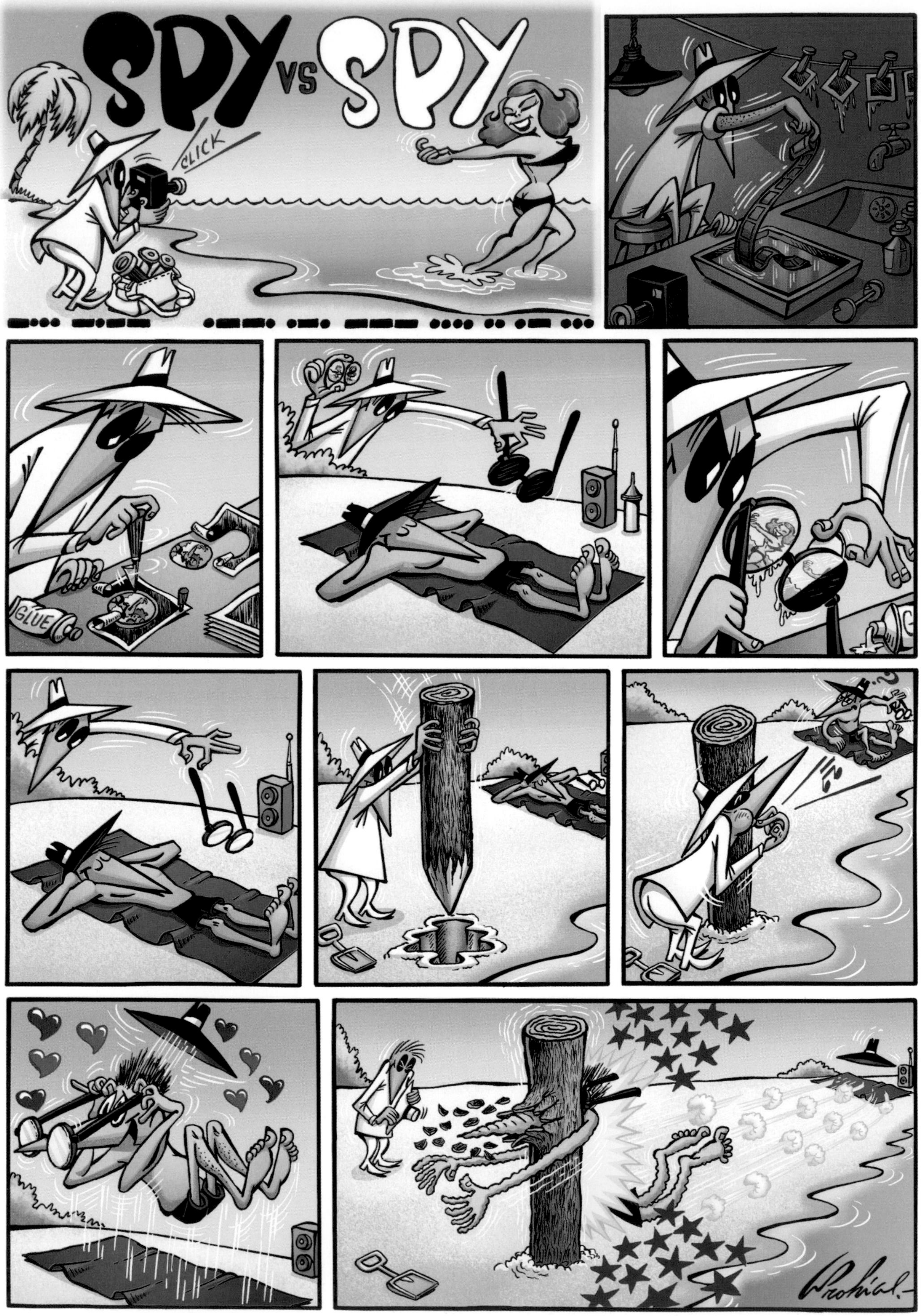
SPY vs SPY
CLICK
Prohías

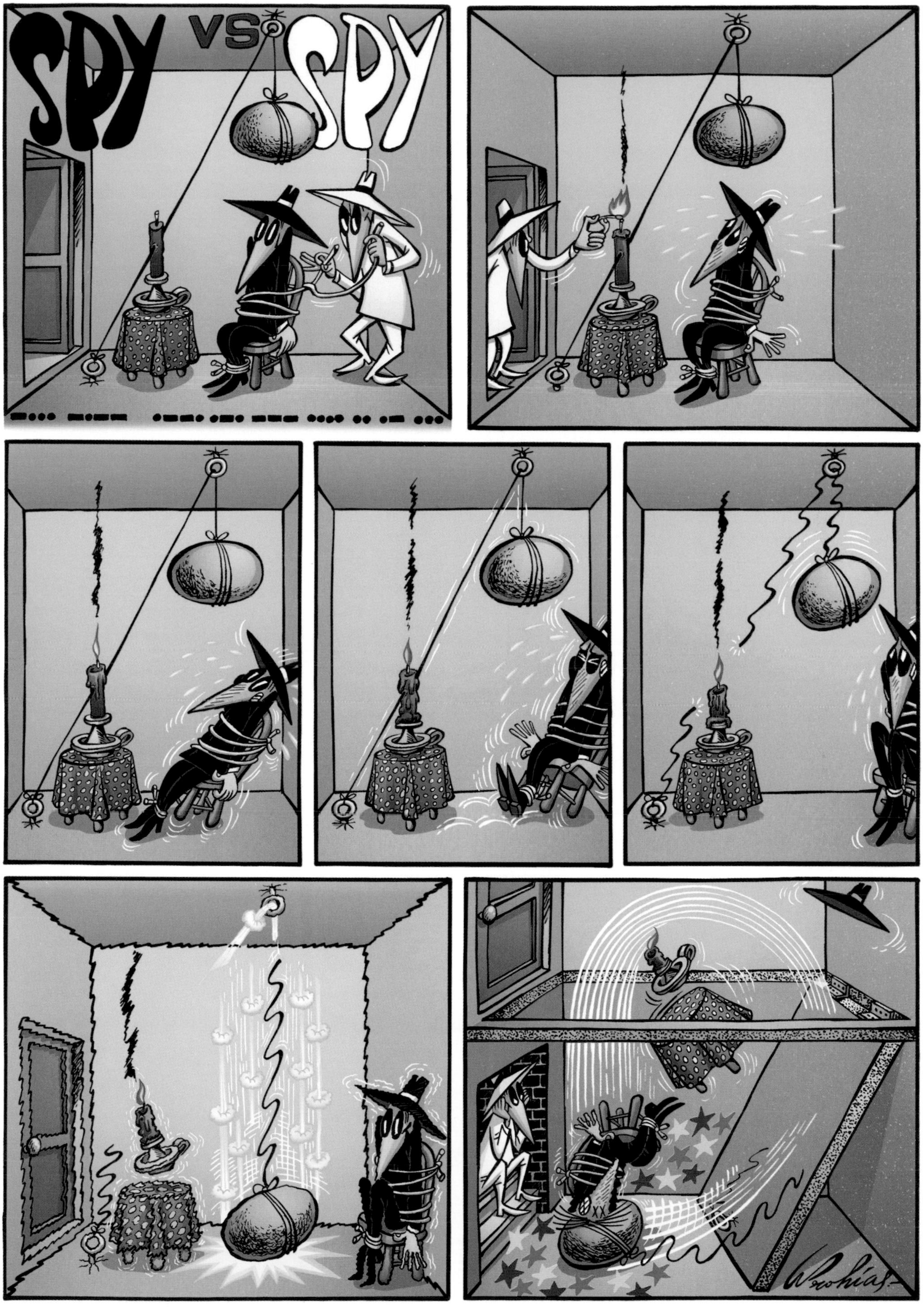

SPY VS SPY

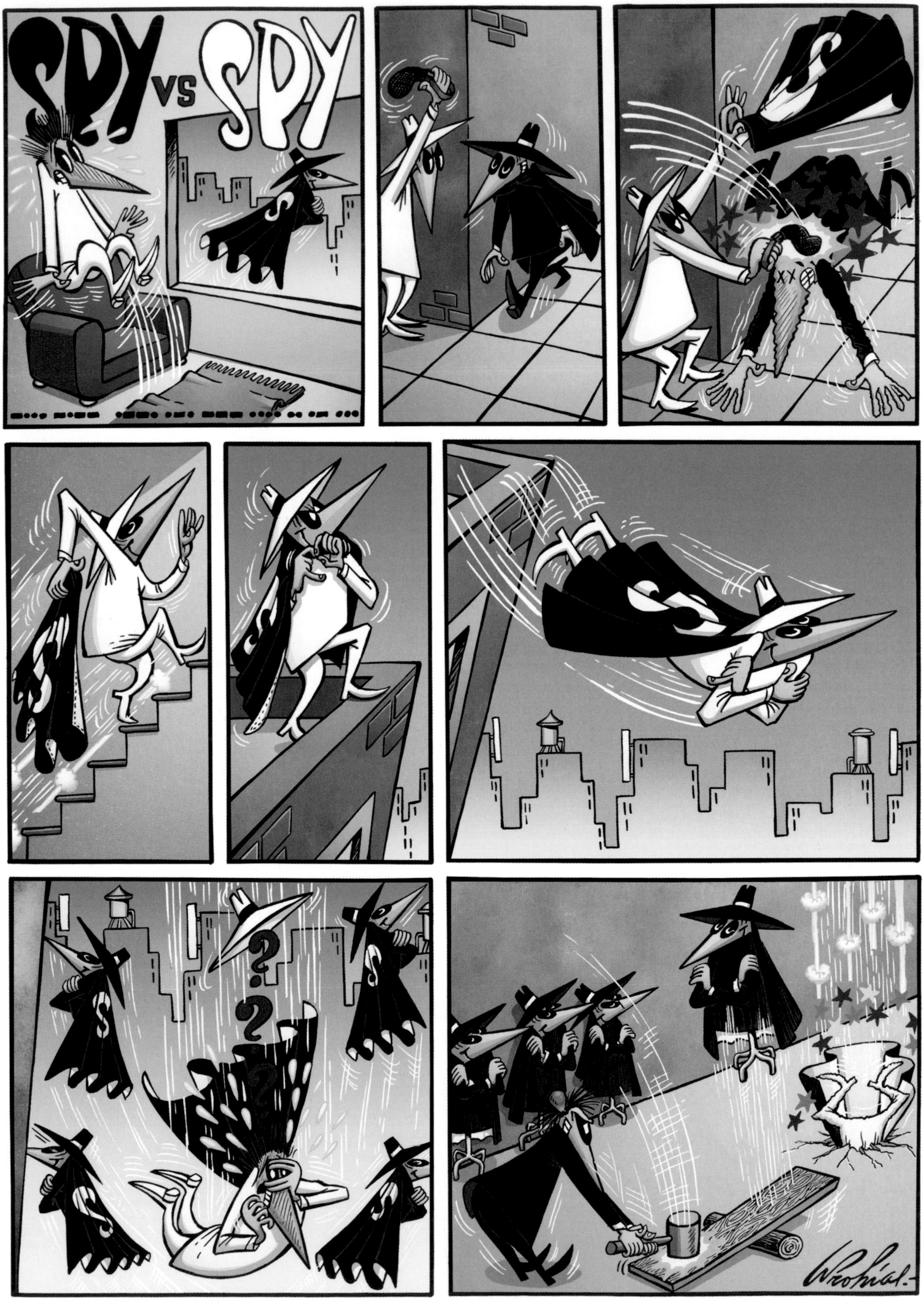
SPY vs SPY
Prohias

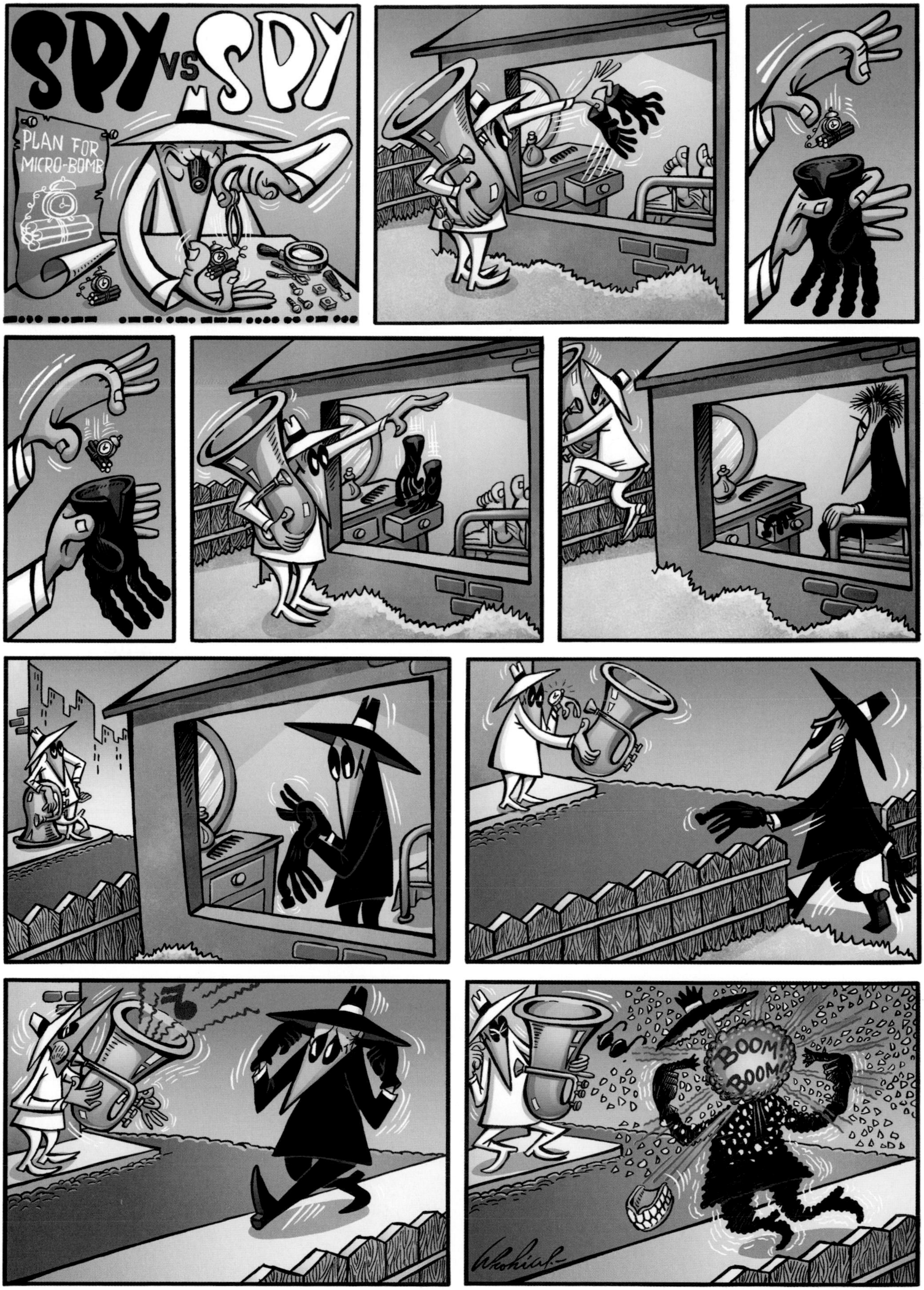
SPY vs SPY
PLAN FOR MICRO-BOMB
BOOM! BOOM!

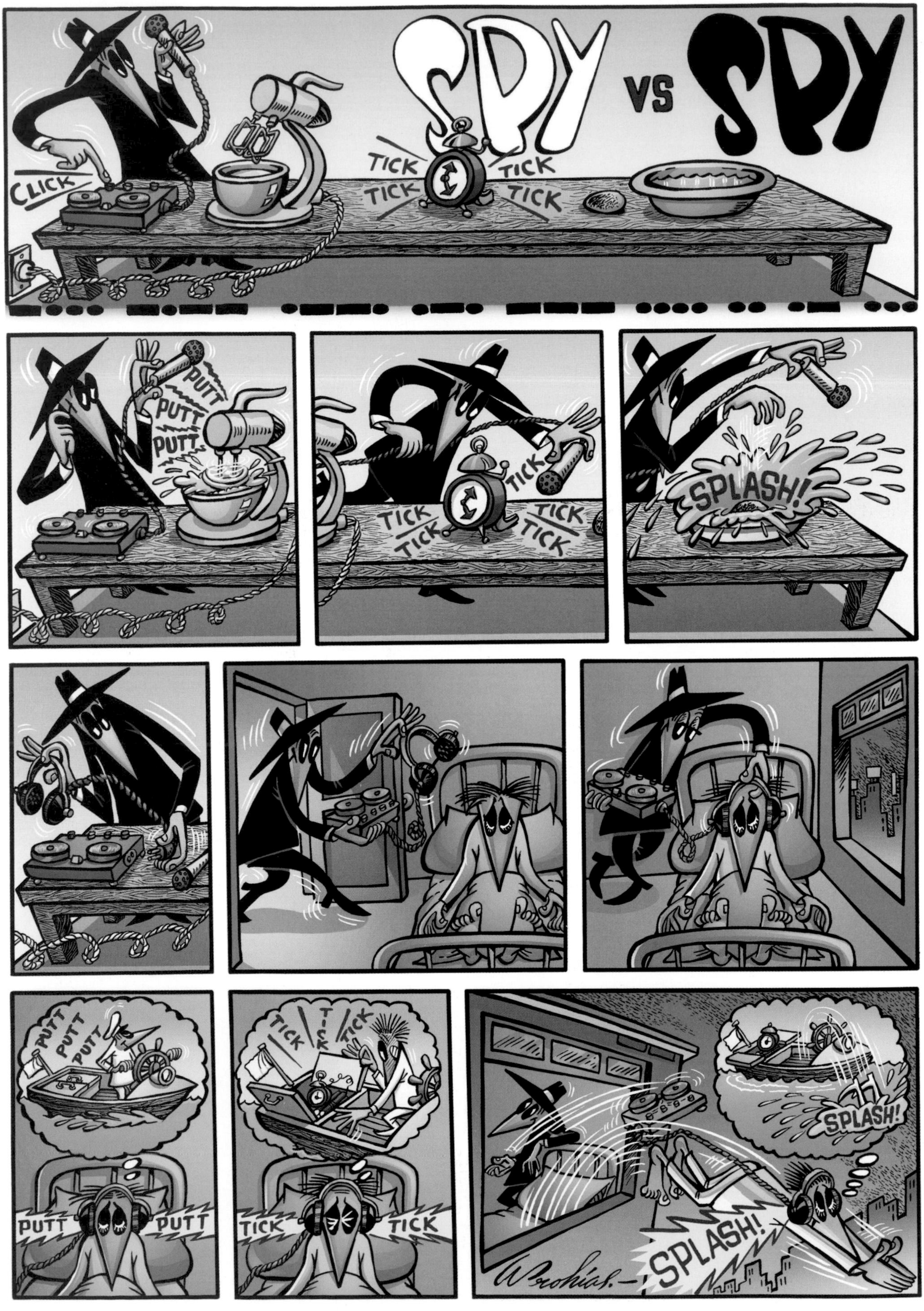
SPY vs SPY
CLICK
TICK
TICK
TICK
TICK
PUTT
PUTT
PUTT
TICK
TICK
TICK
TICK
TICK
SPLASH!
PUTT
PUTT
PUTT
PUTT
PUTT
TICK
TICK
TICK
TICK
TICK
SPLASH!
SPLASH!

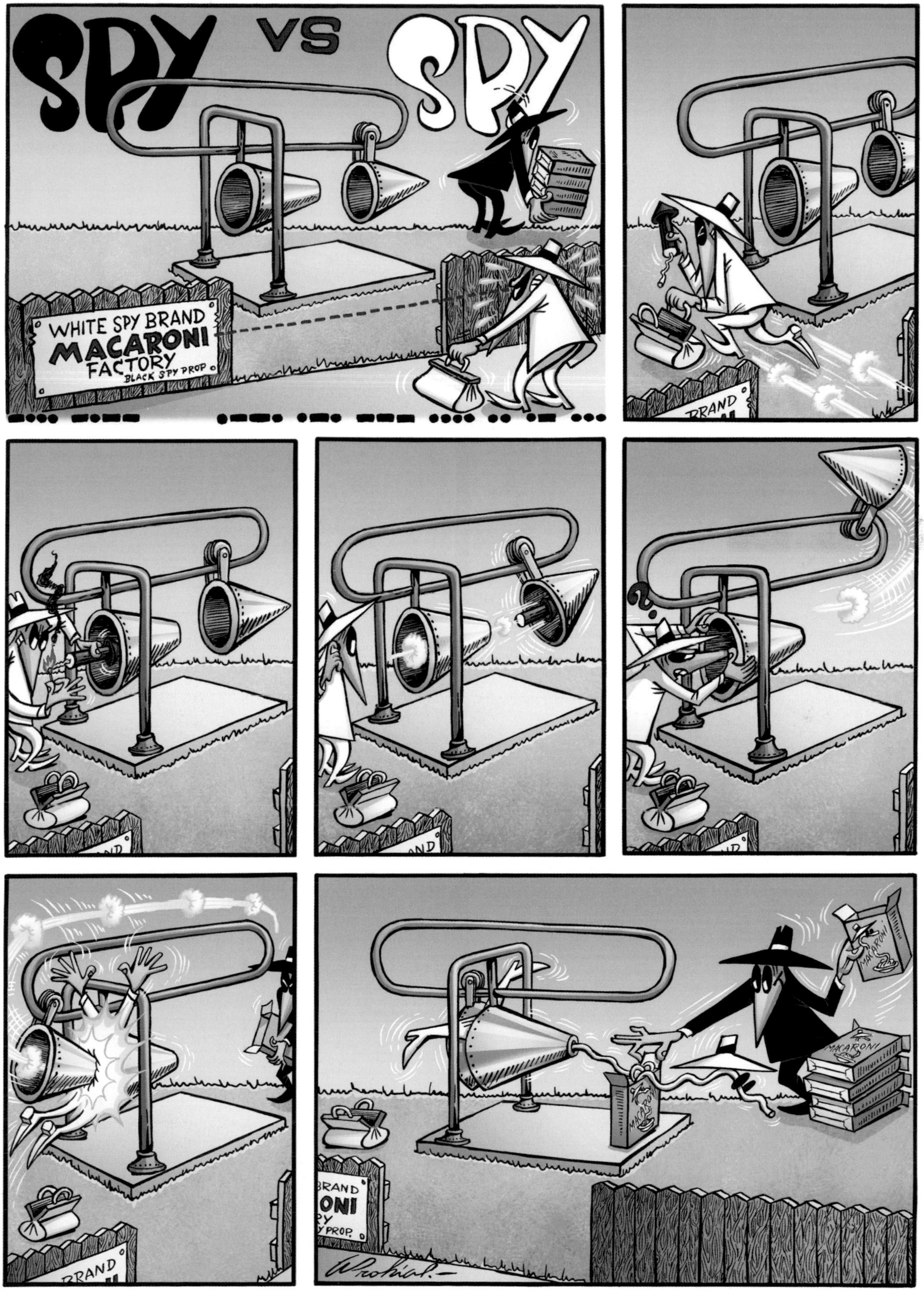
SPY vs SPY
WHITE SPY BRAND
MACARONI
FACTORY
BLACK SPY PROP
MACARONI
MACARONI

11 "Top Secret" satchels appeared

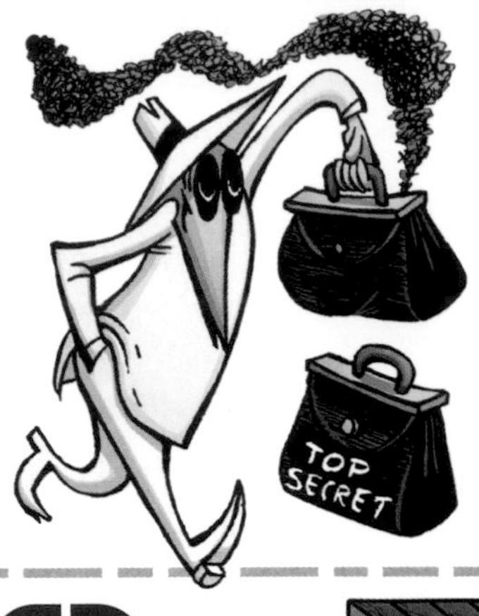
TOP SECRET

9% of strips showed a victorious Spy making the "V" sign

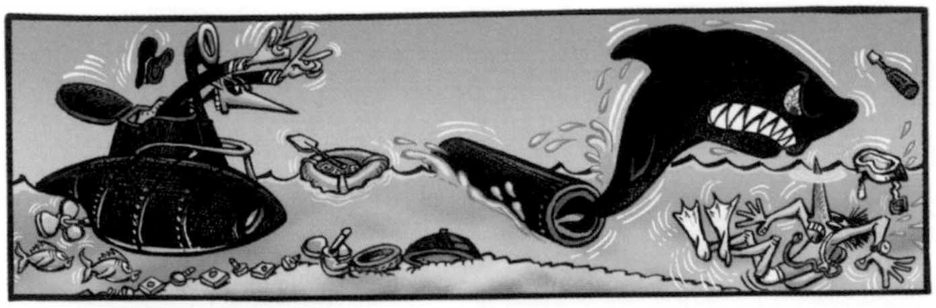

SPY VS. SPY: A DOSSIER

3 strips were set in the Old West

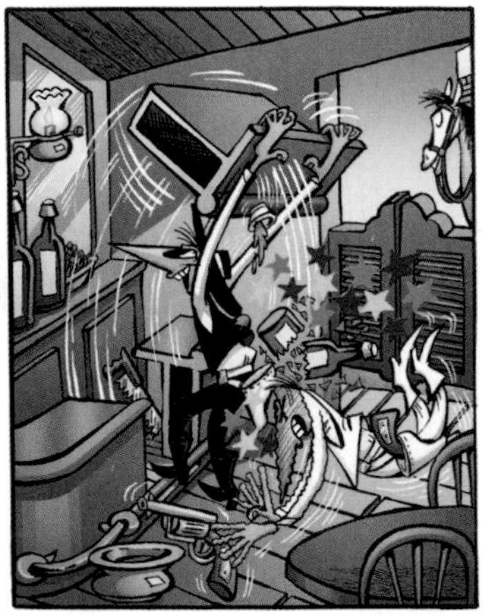

2 double-cannons were used fatally

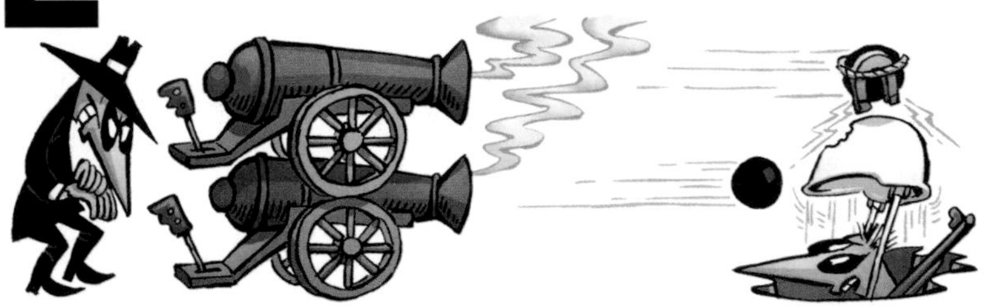

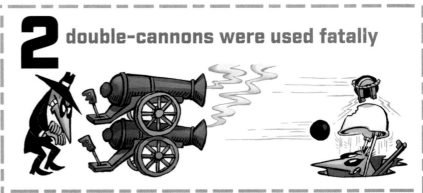

12 The average number of stars that appeared when the White Spy was hit in the head with a club

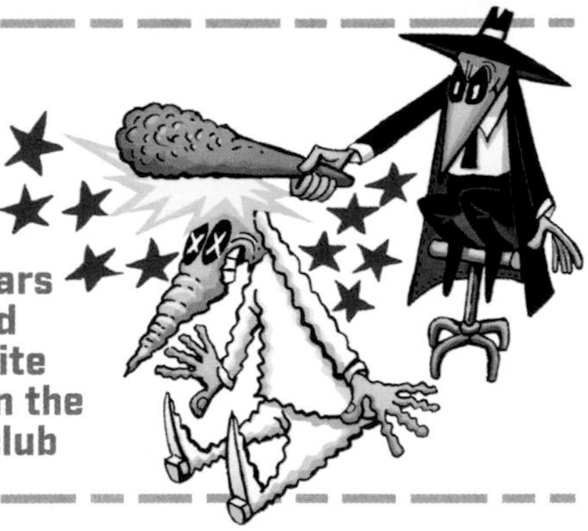

20 The average number of stars that appeared when the Black Spy was hit in the head with a club

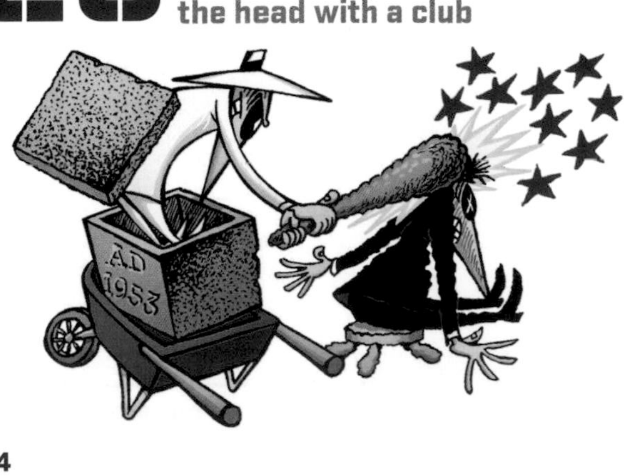
AD 1953

Types of sports involved in Spy killings:

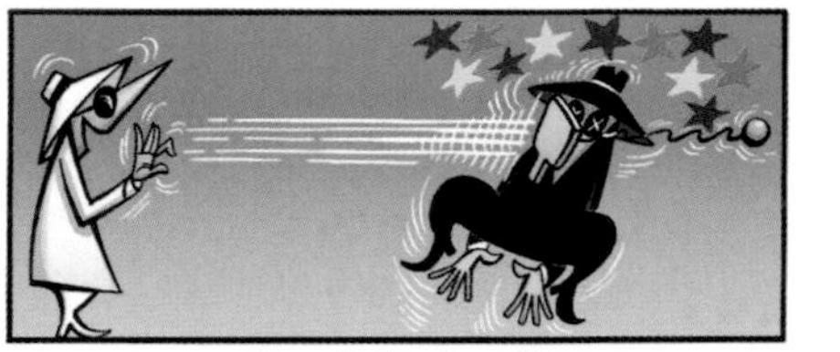

Paddleball

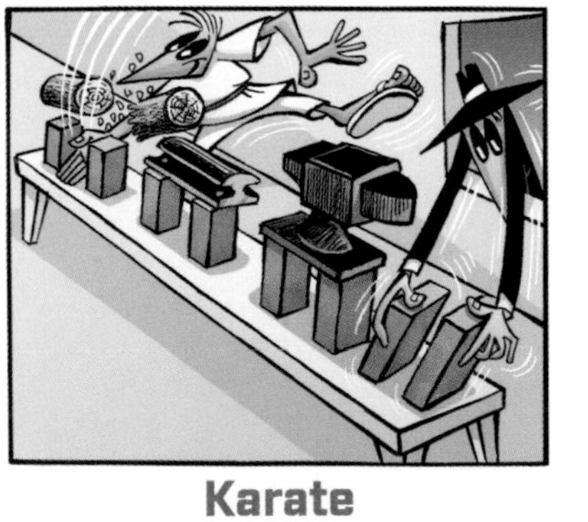

Karate

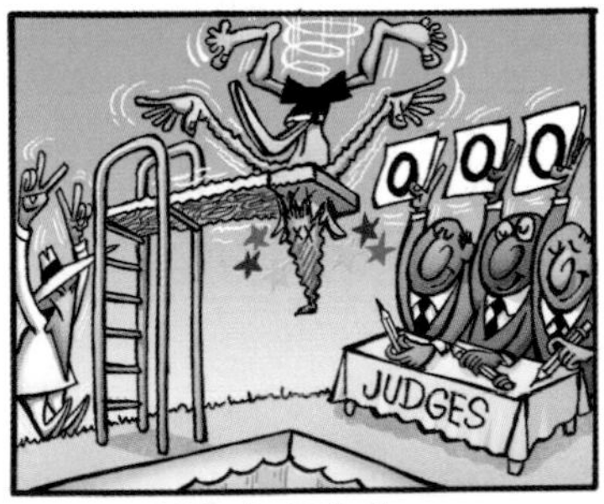
JUDGES

High Diving

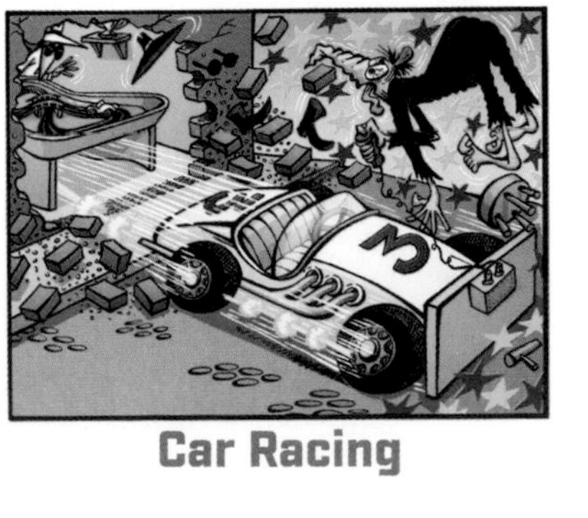

Car Racing

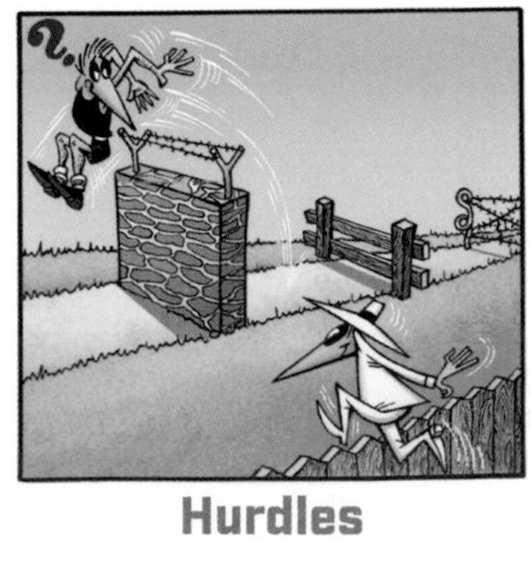

Hurdles

10%

of strips featured a shirtless Spy

3

giant mousetraps were used as weapons

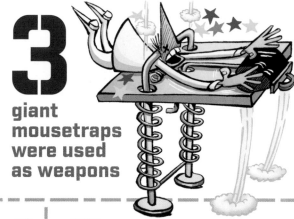

OF DEADLY FACTS

THE PROHIAS YEARS

Types of animals used as weapons:

Chicken ➡

⬅ Rattlesnake

Cross-bred Chickensnake ➡

2

waterfalls were involved in Spy fatalities

2

baby Spies appeared in strips

20

bumpy clubs were used as weapons

1

custom-built toilet was used to embarrass the White Spy

BLACK SPY FAN CLUB

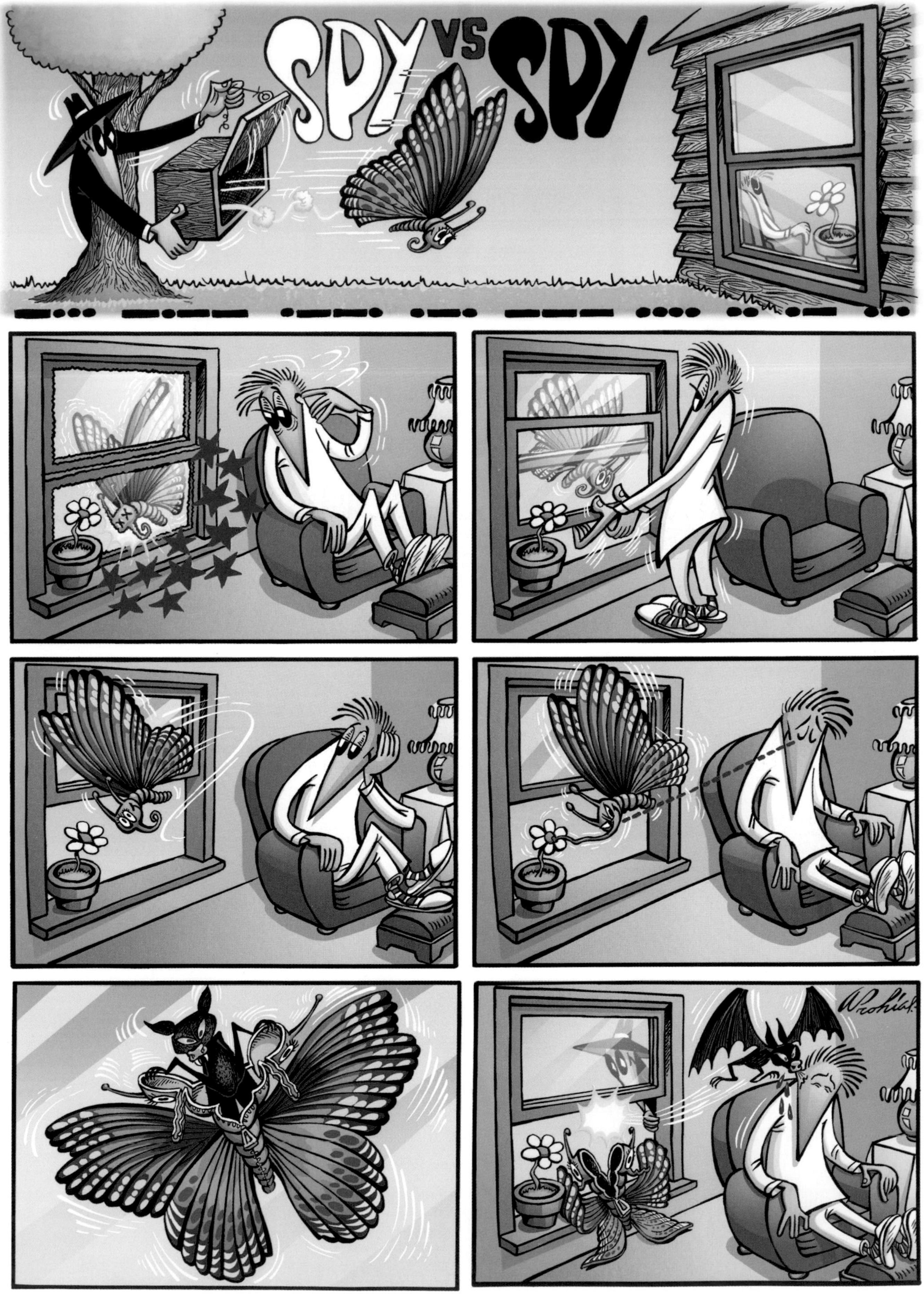
SPY VS SPY
Prohias

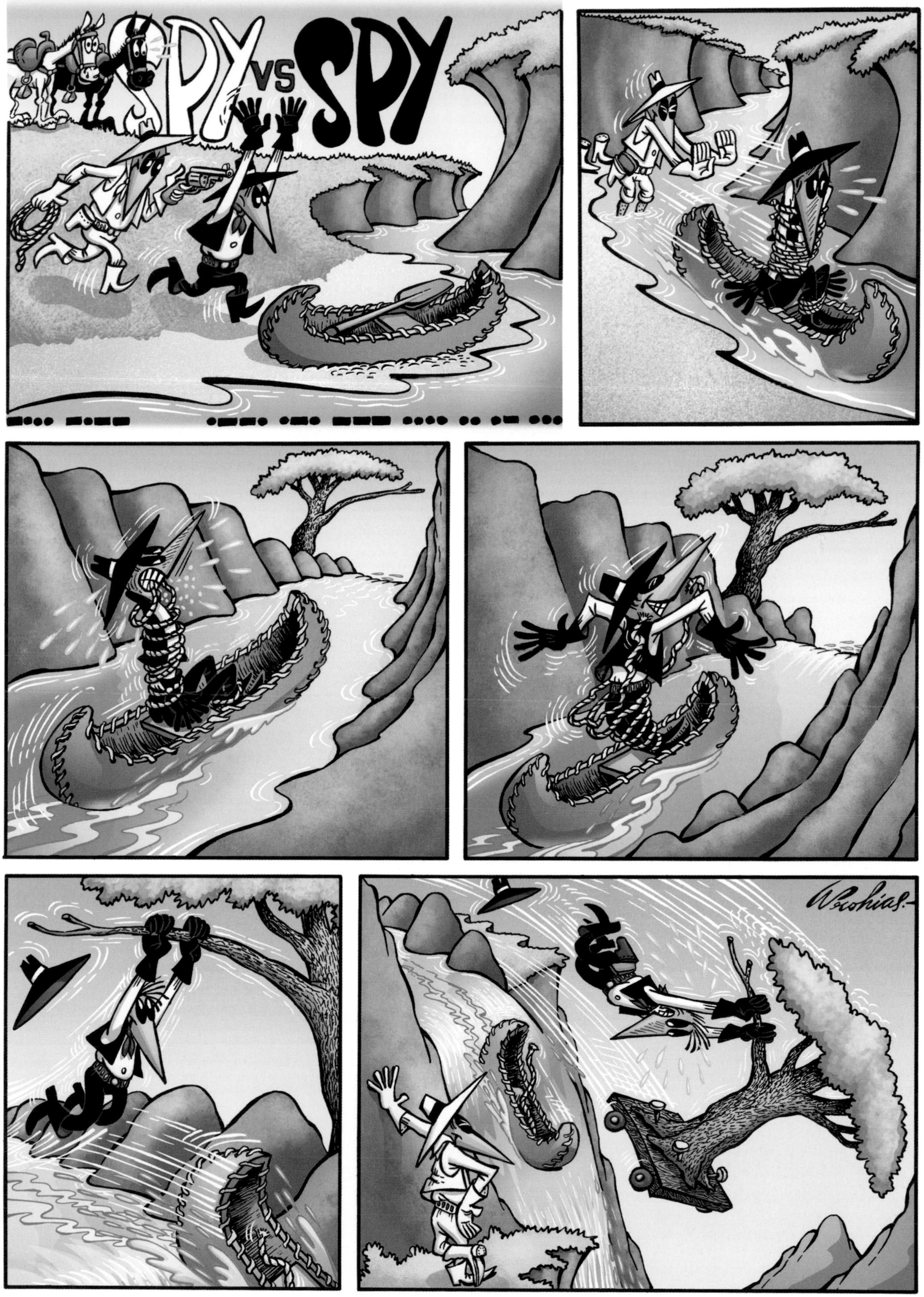
SPY VS SPY
Prohias

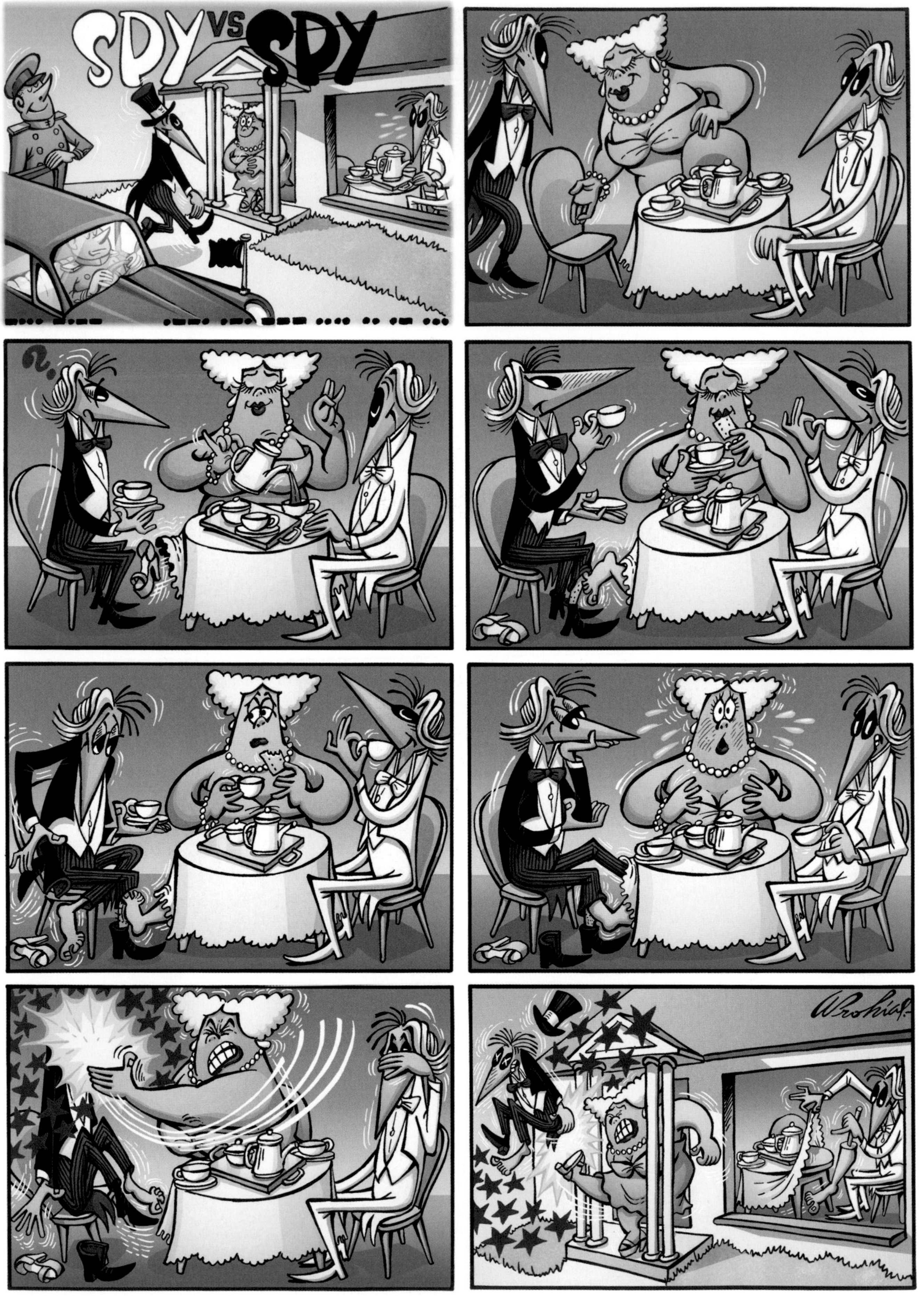
SPY VS SPY
?
Prohias

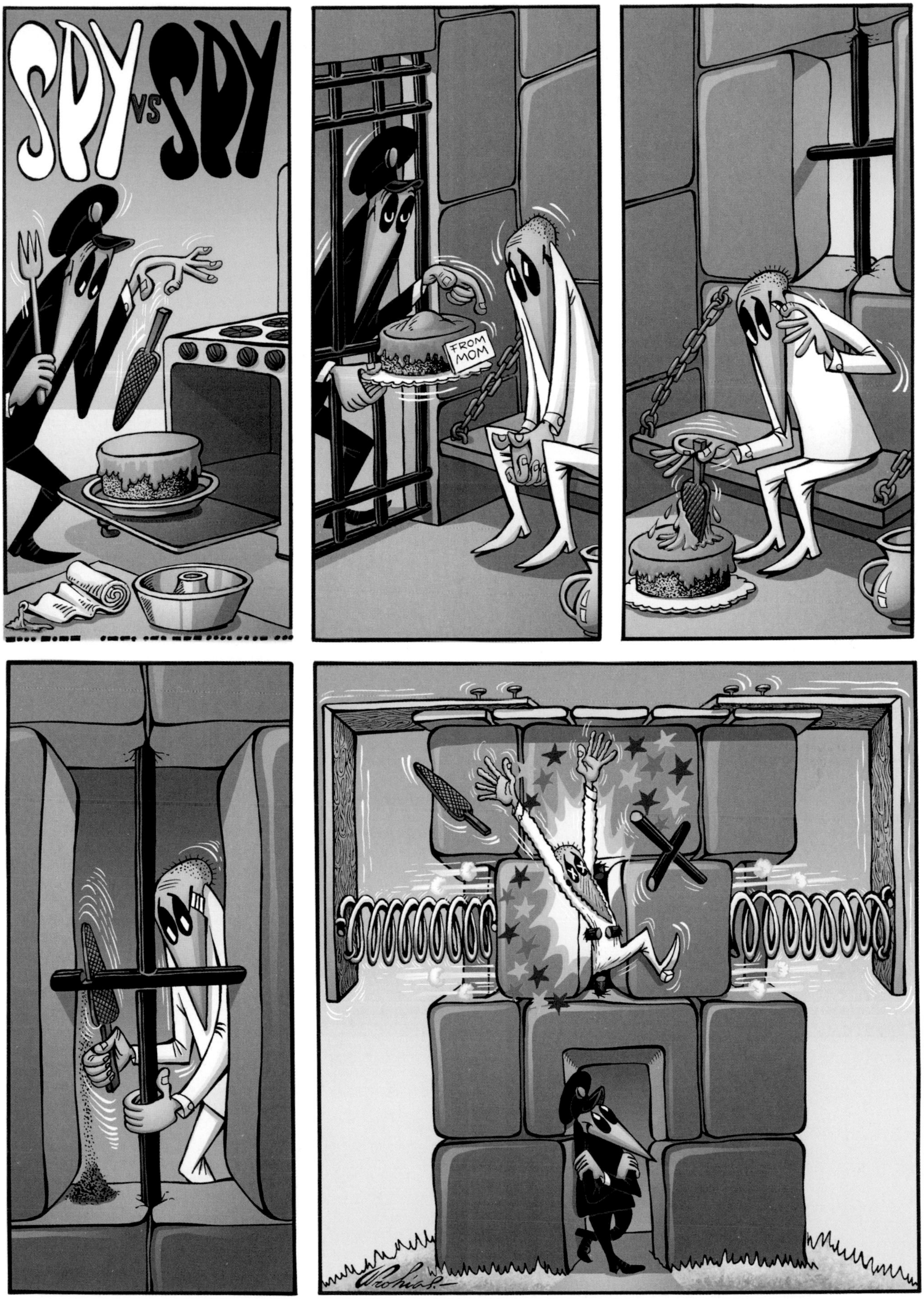
SPY vs SPY
FROM MOM

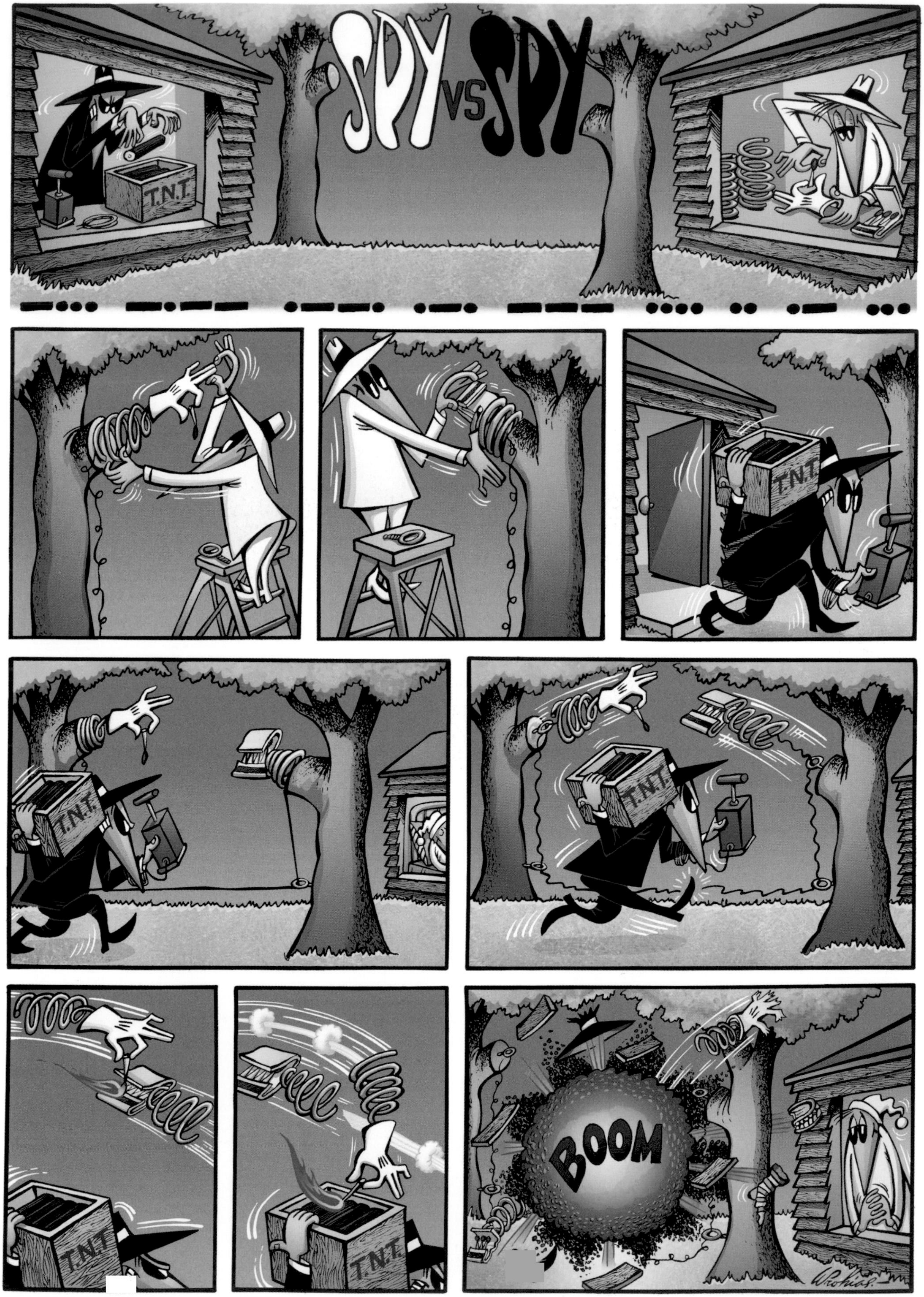
SPY vs SPY
T.N.T.
BOOM
Prohias

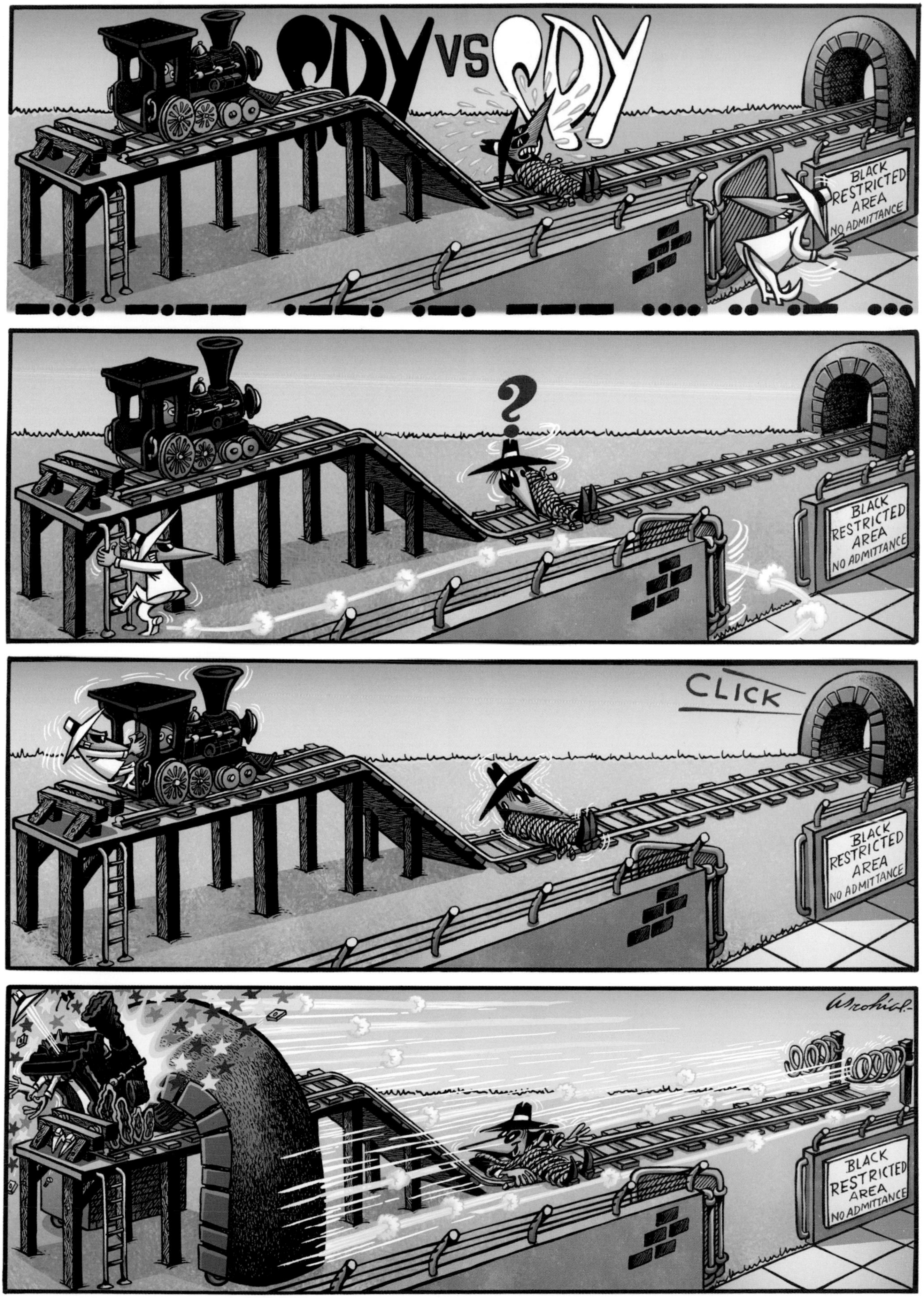
SPY VS SPY
BLACK RESTRICTED AREA NO ADMITTANCE
?
CLICK
Aragonés? Prohias

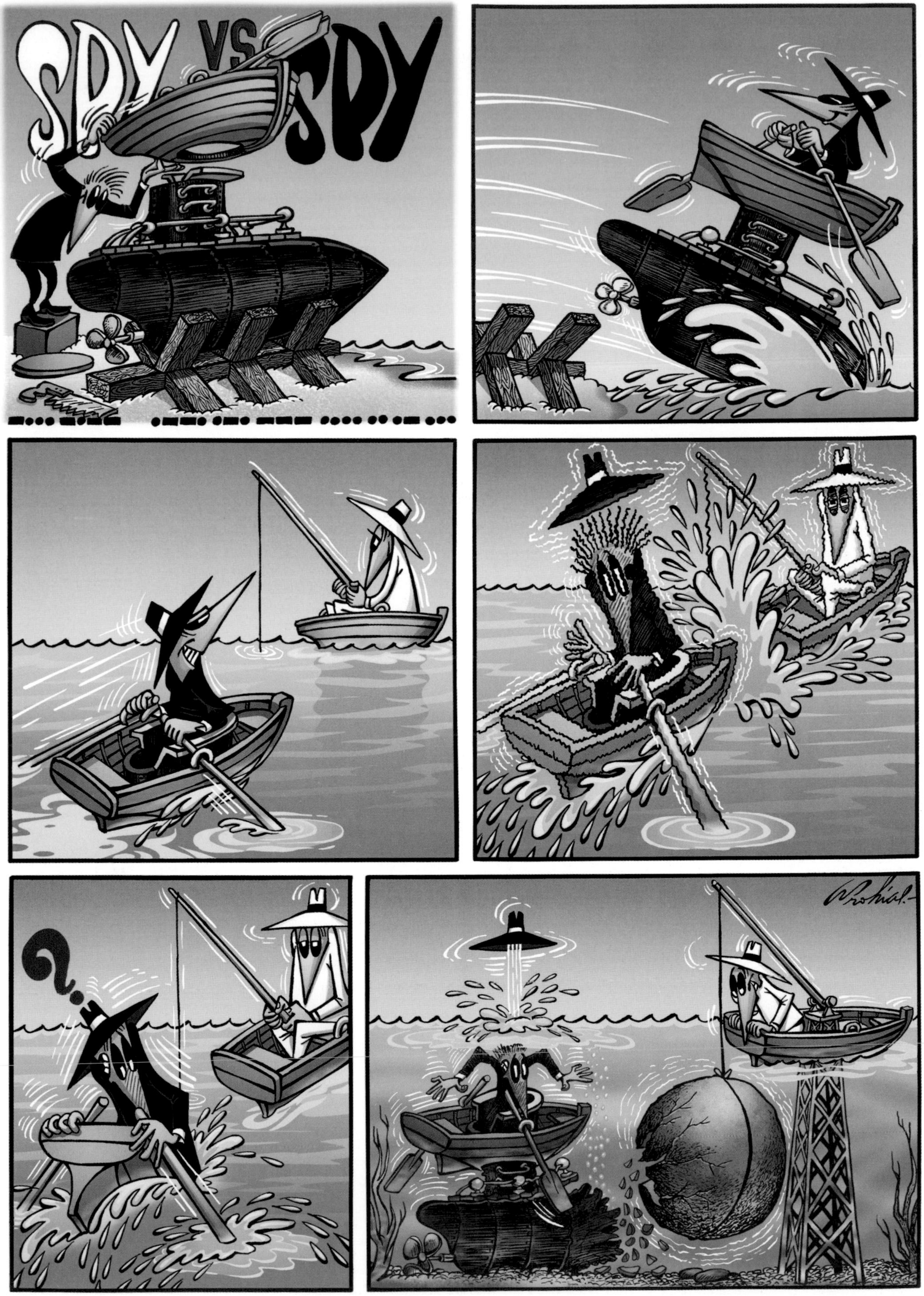
SPY vs SPY
Prohias

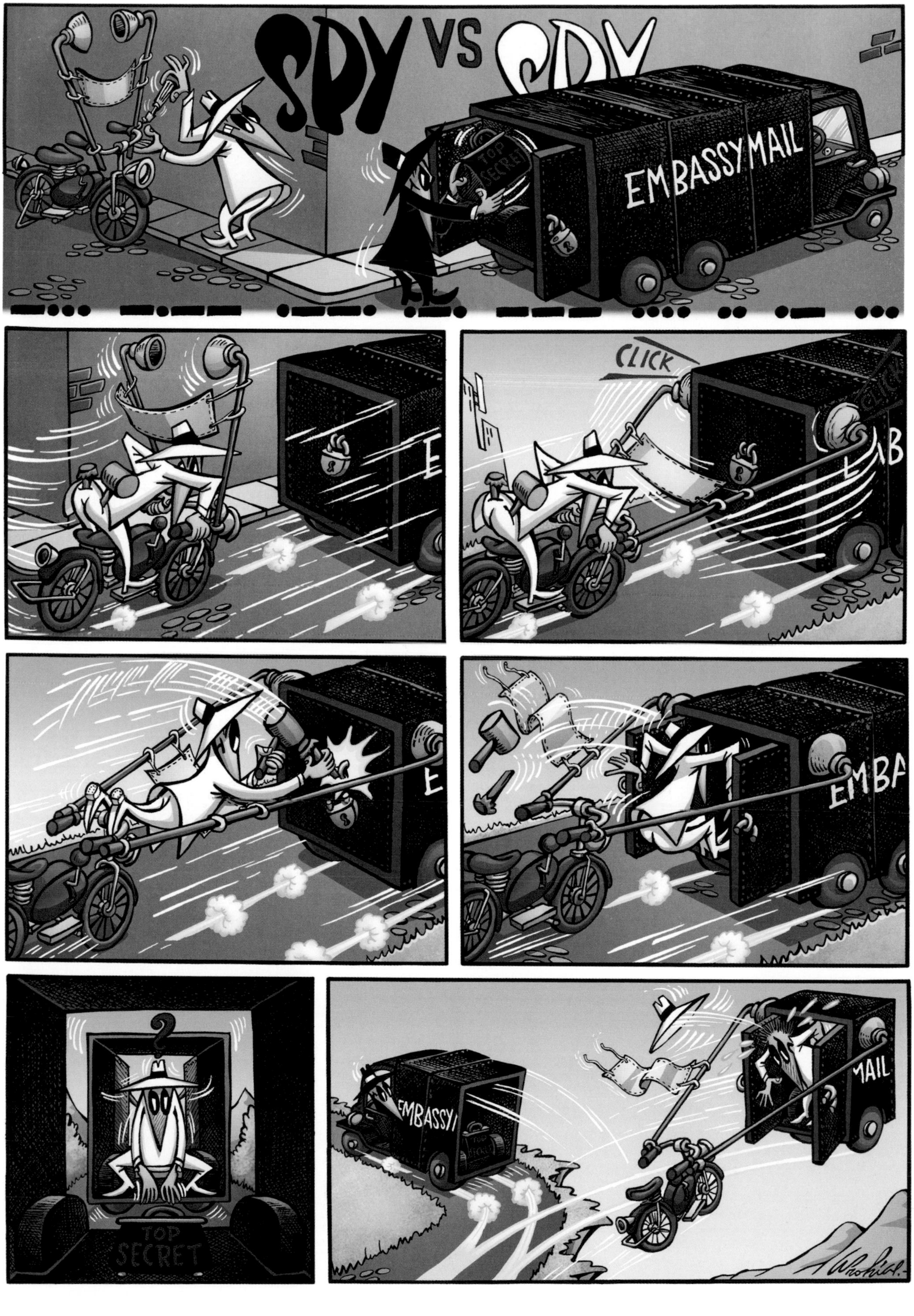
SPY VS SPY
TOP SECRET
EMBASSYMAIL
CLICK
EMBASSYMAIL
TOP SECRET
EMBASSY
MAIL

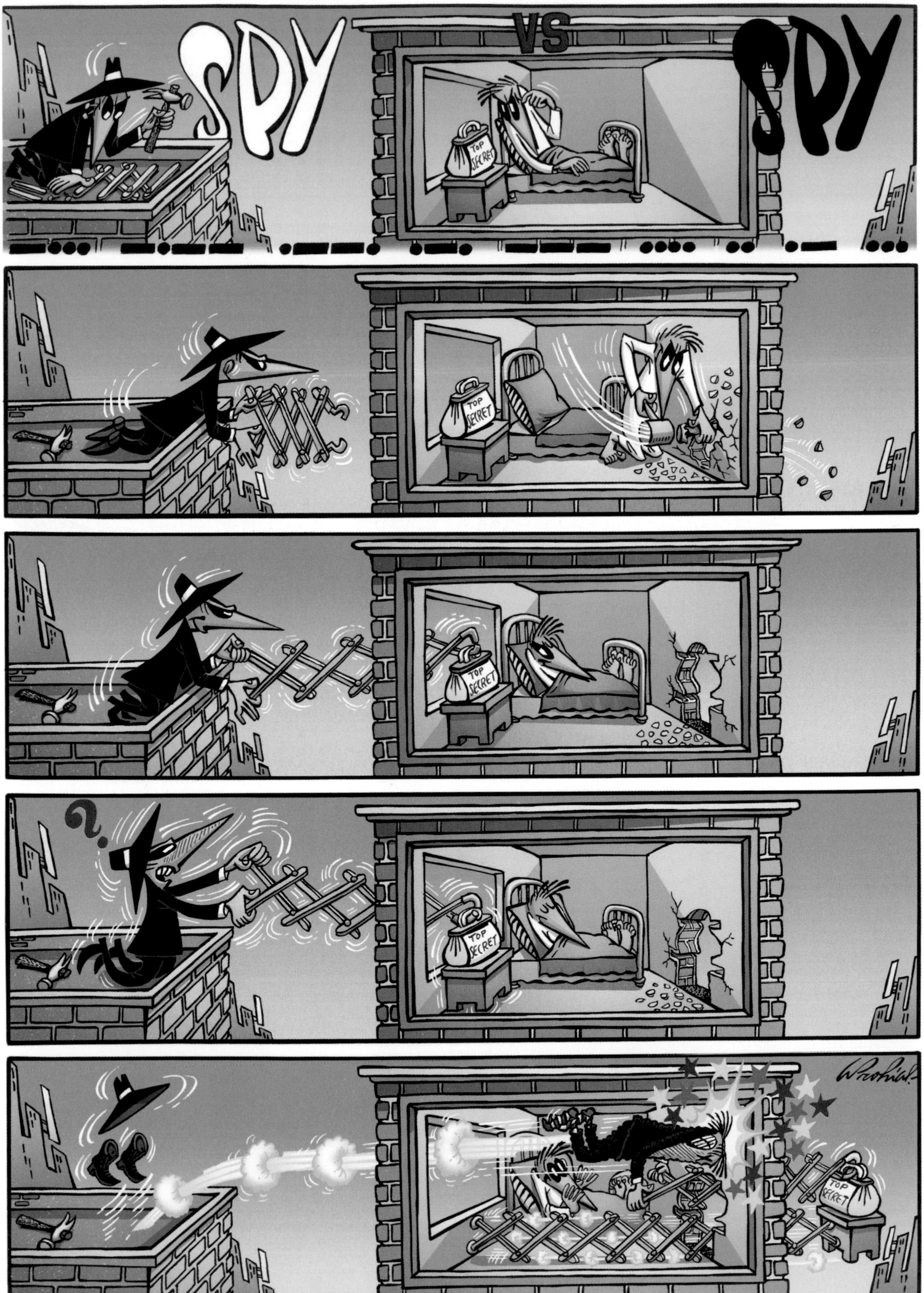
SPY
VS
SPY
TOP SECRET

SPY VS SPY
INSTANT CEMENT
WHITE EMBASSY

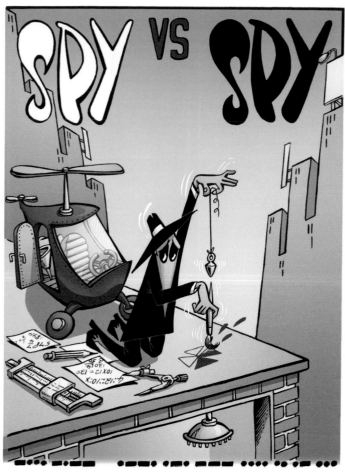

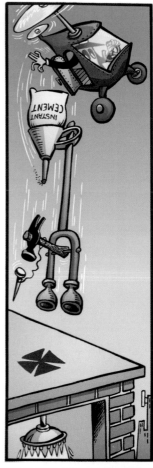

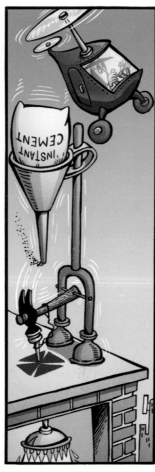

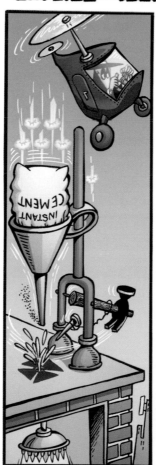

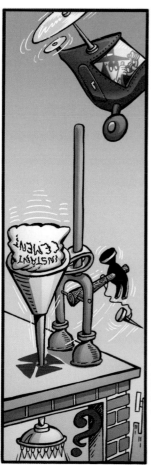

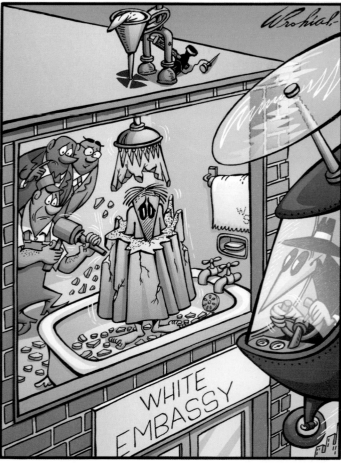

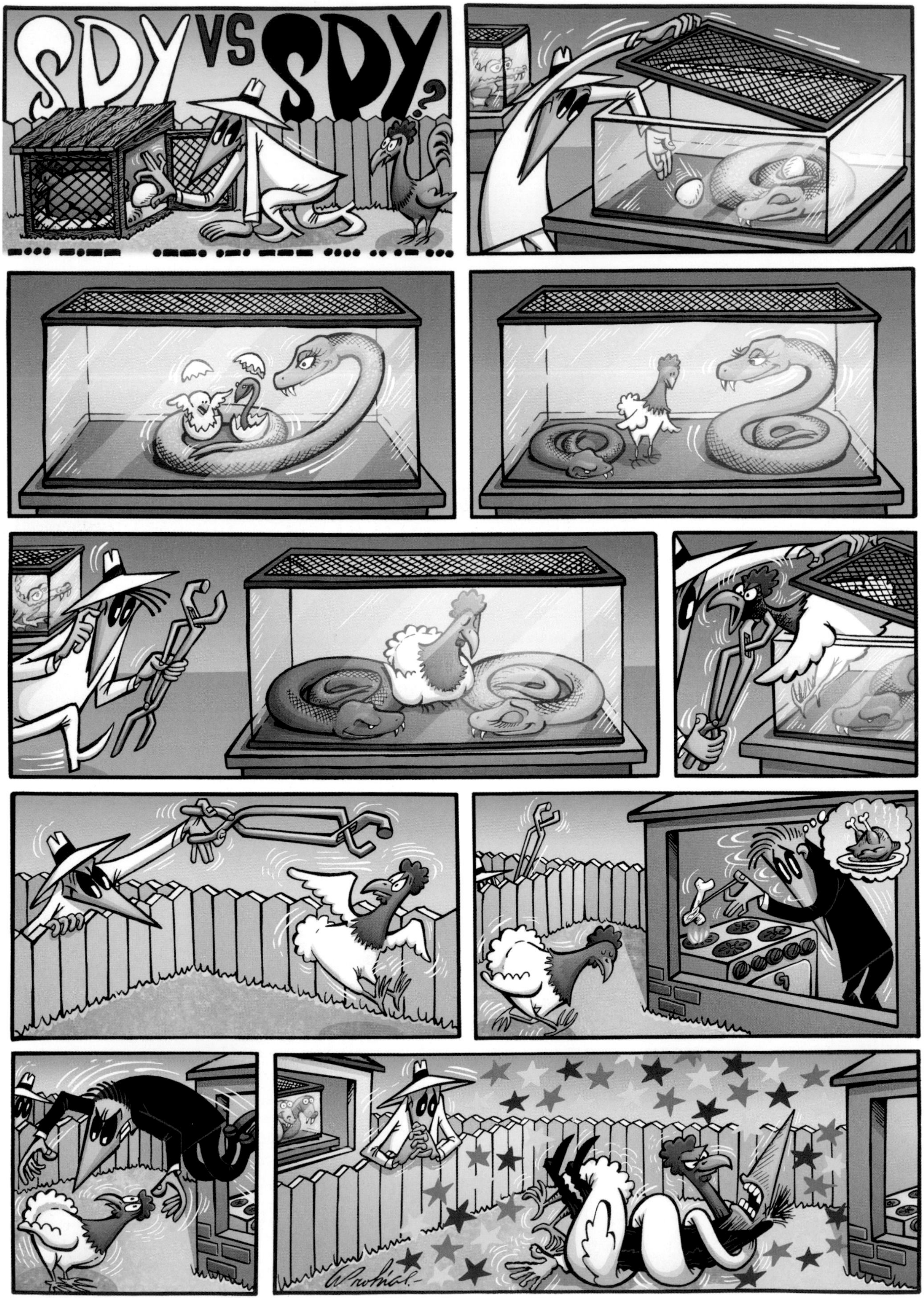
SPY VS SPY
Prohias

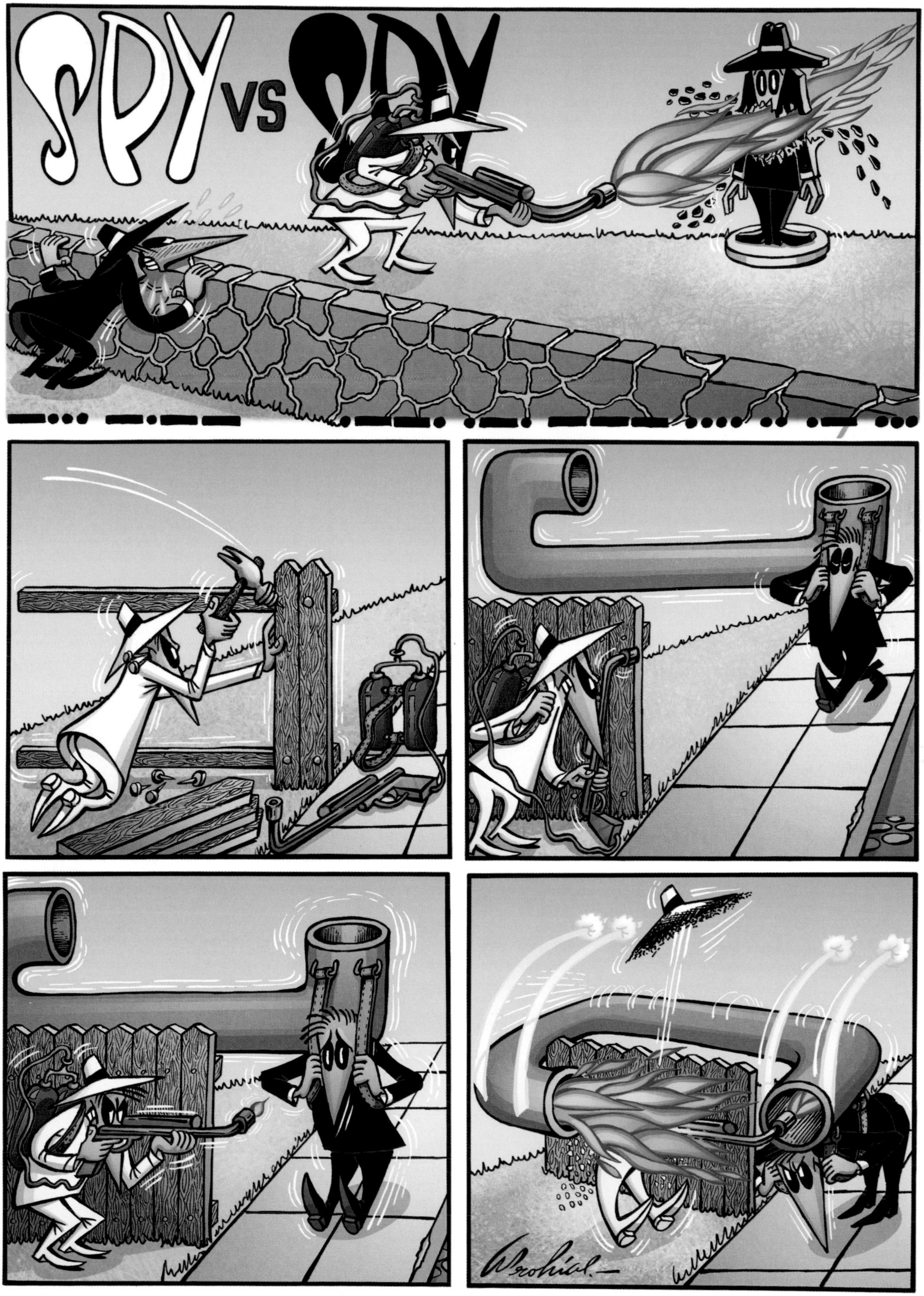
SPY vs SPY

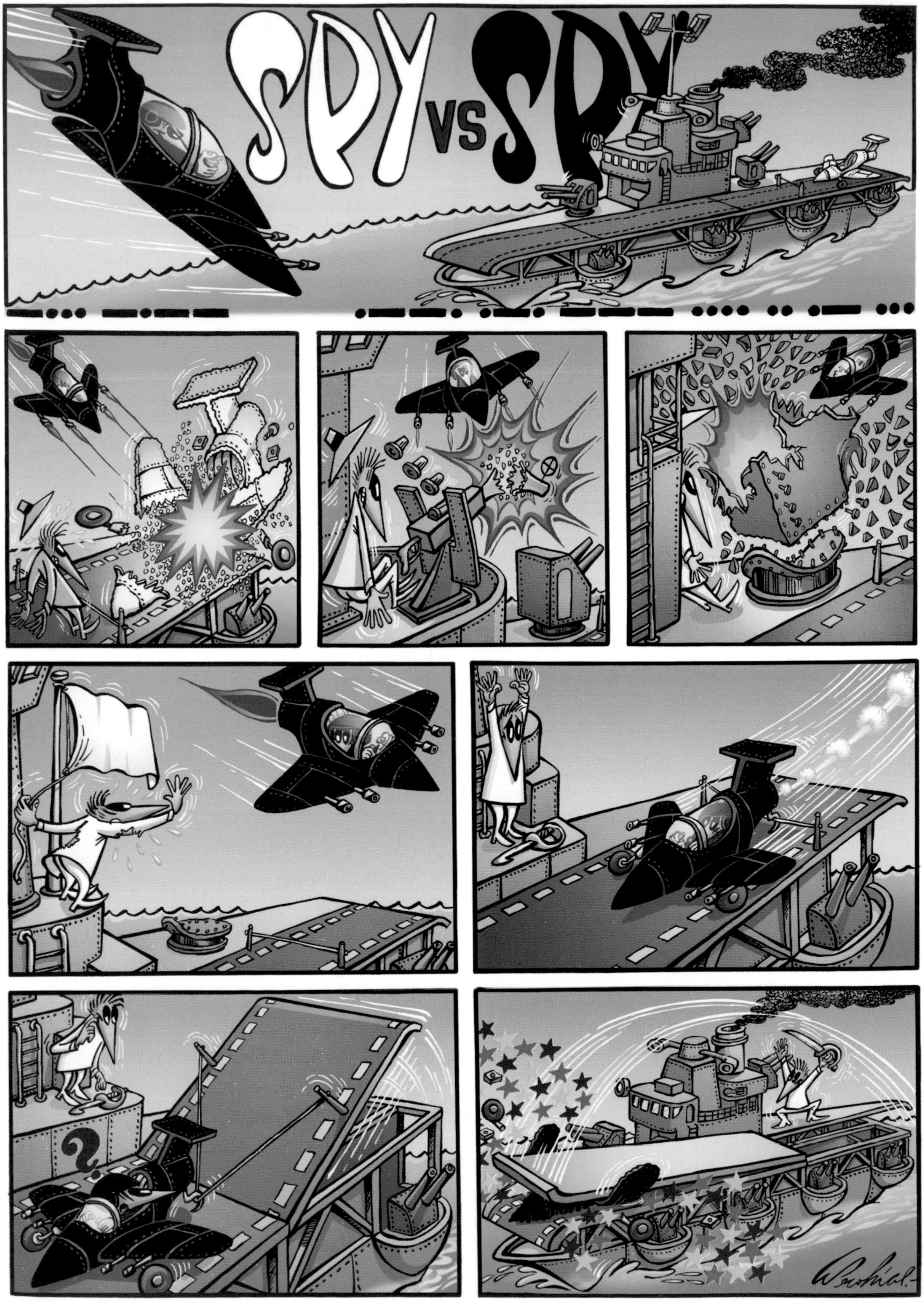
SPY vs SPY

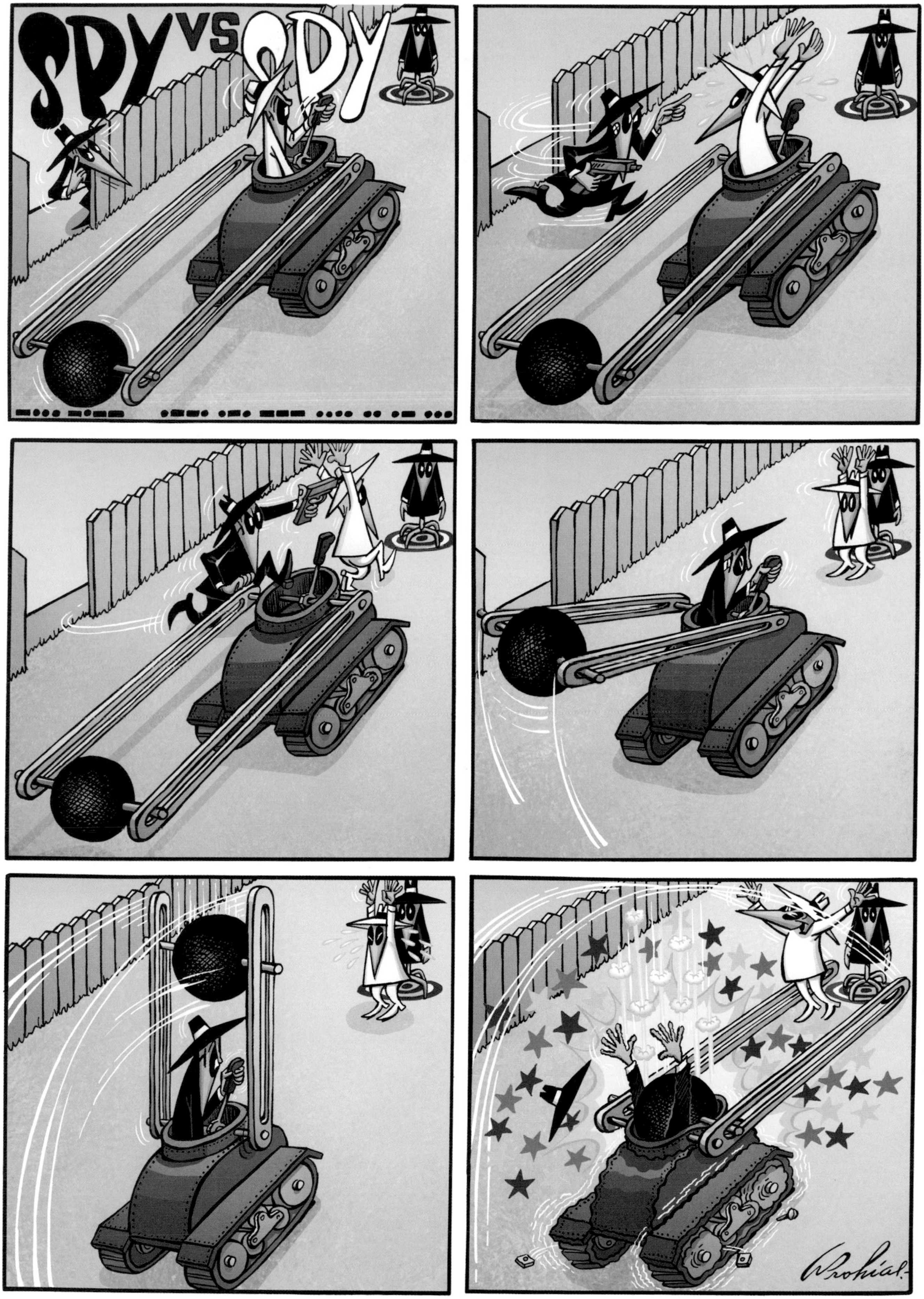
SPY vs SPY
Prohias

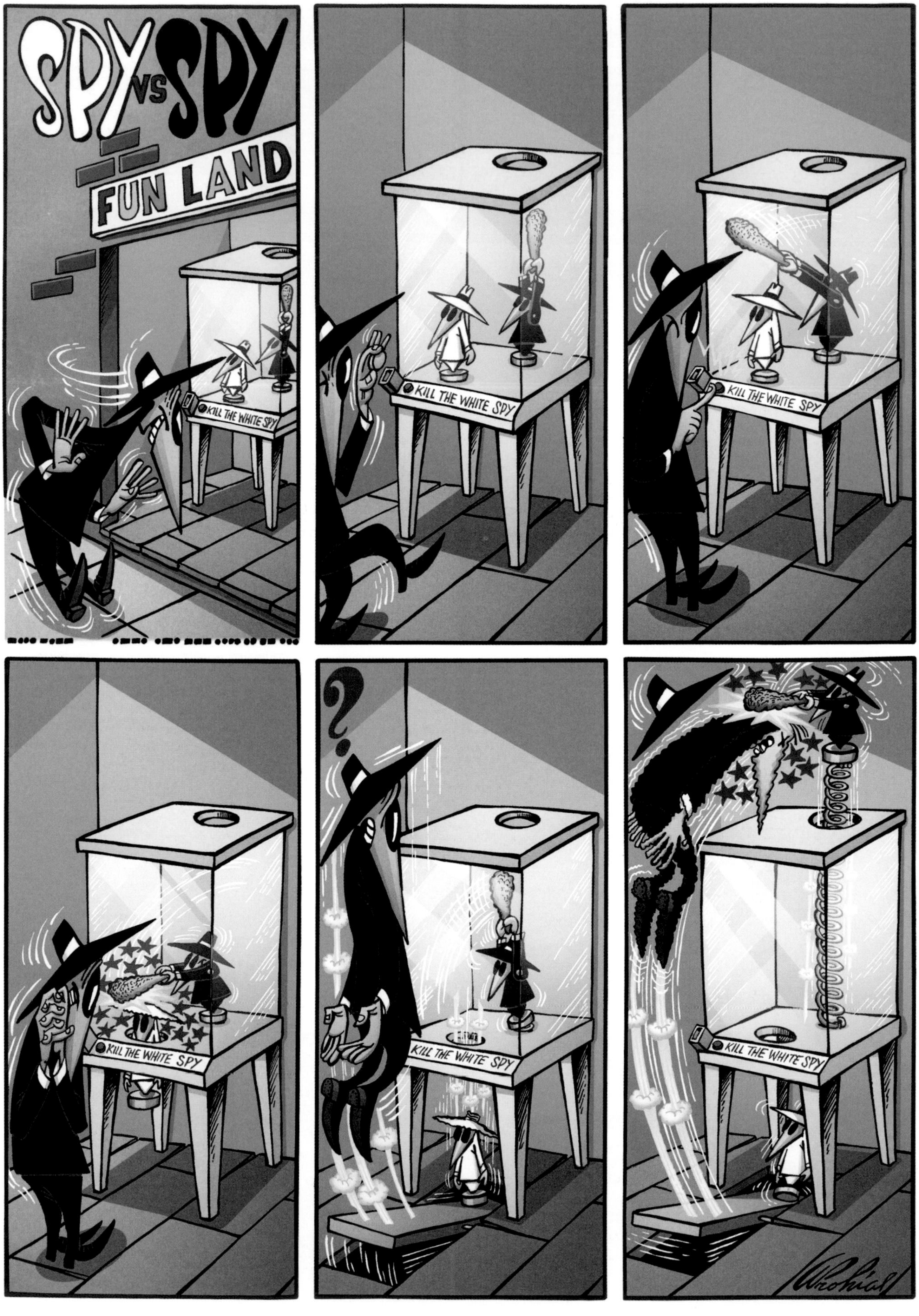
SPY vs SPY
FUN LAND
KILL THE WHITE SPY
KILL THE WHITE SPY
KILL THE WHITE SPY
KILL THE WHITE SPY
KILL THE WHITE SPY
KILL THE WHITE SPY

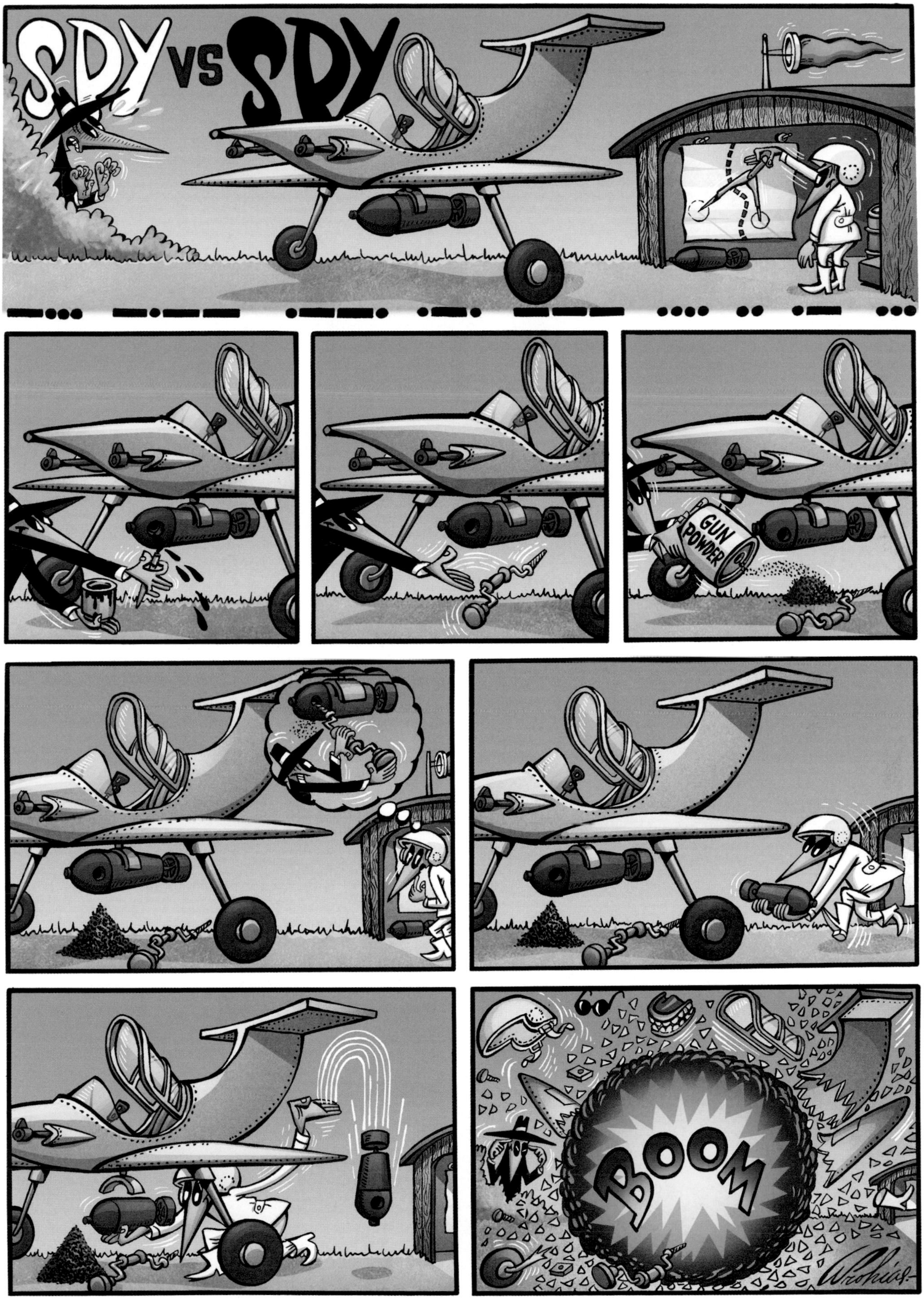
SPY vs SPY
GUN POWDER
BOOM

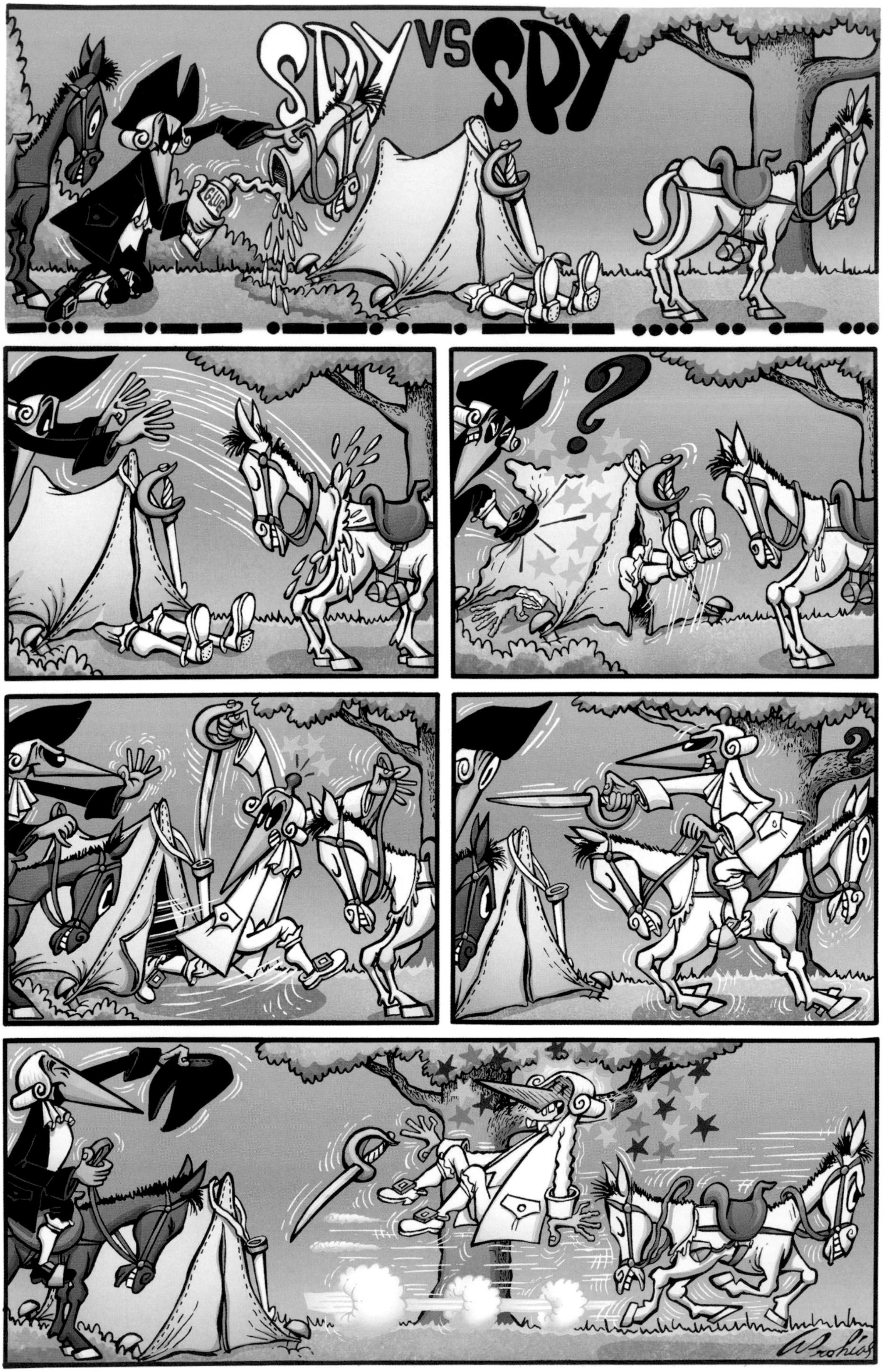
SPY VS SPY
GLUE
Prohias

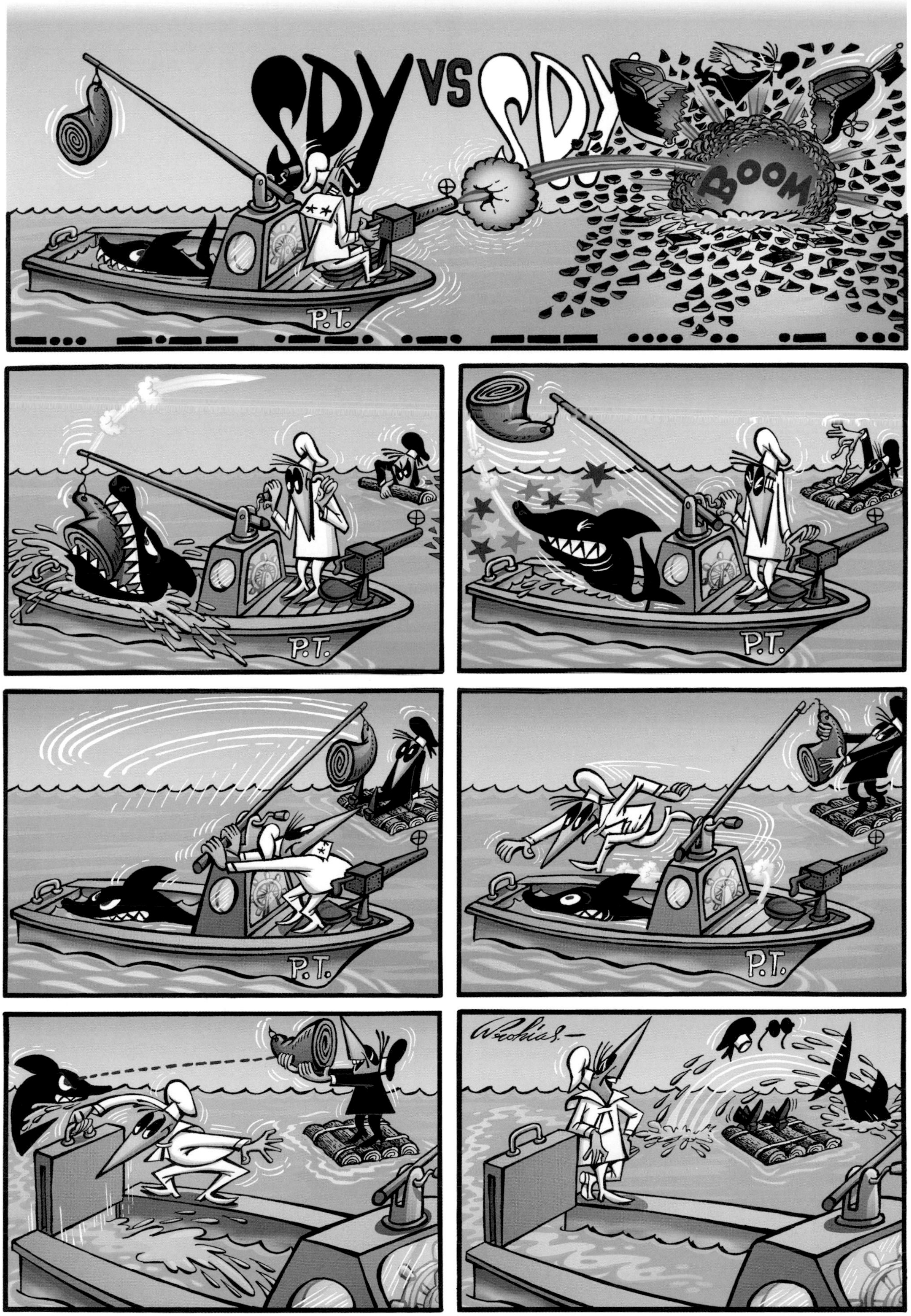
SPY vs SPY
BOOM
P.T.
P.T.
P.T.
P.T.
P.T.

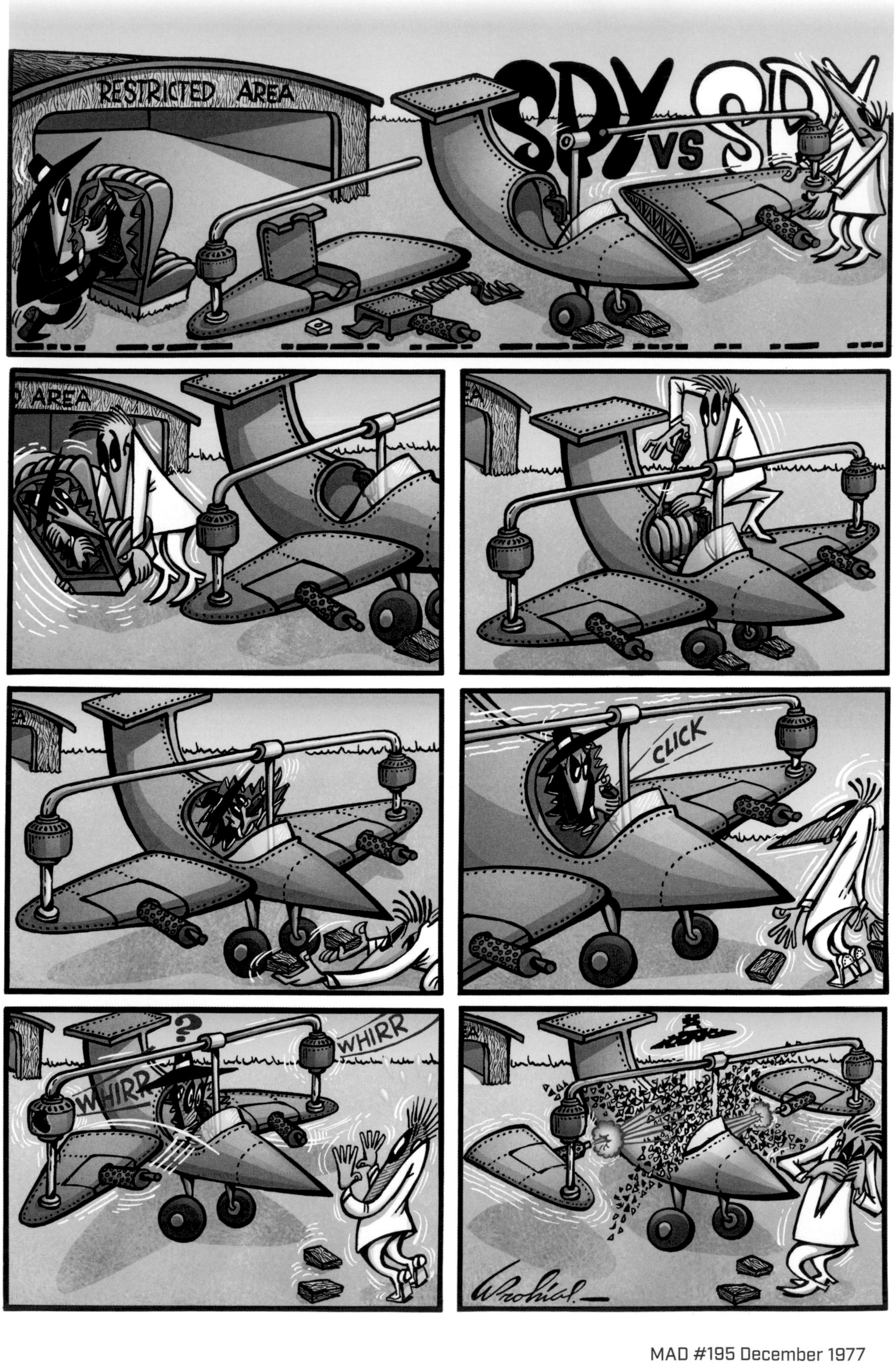
RESTRICTED AREA
SPY VS SPY
AREA
CLICK
?
WHIRR
WHIRR

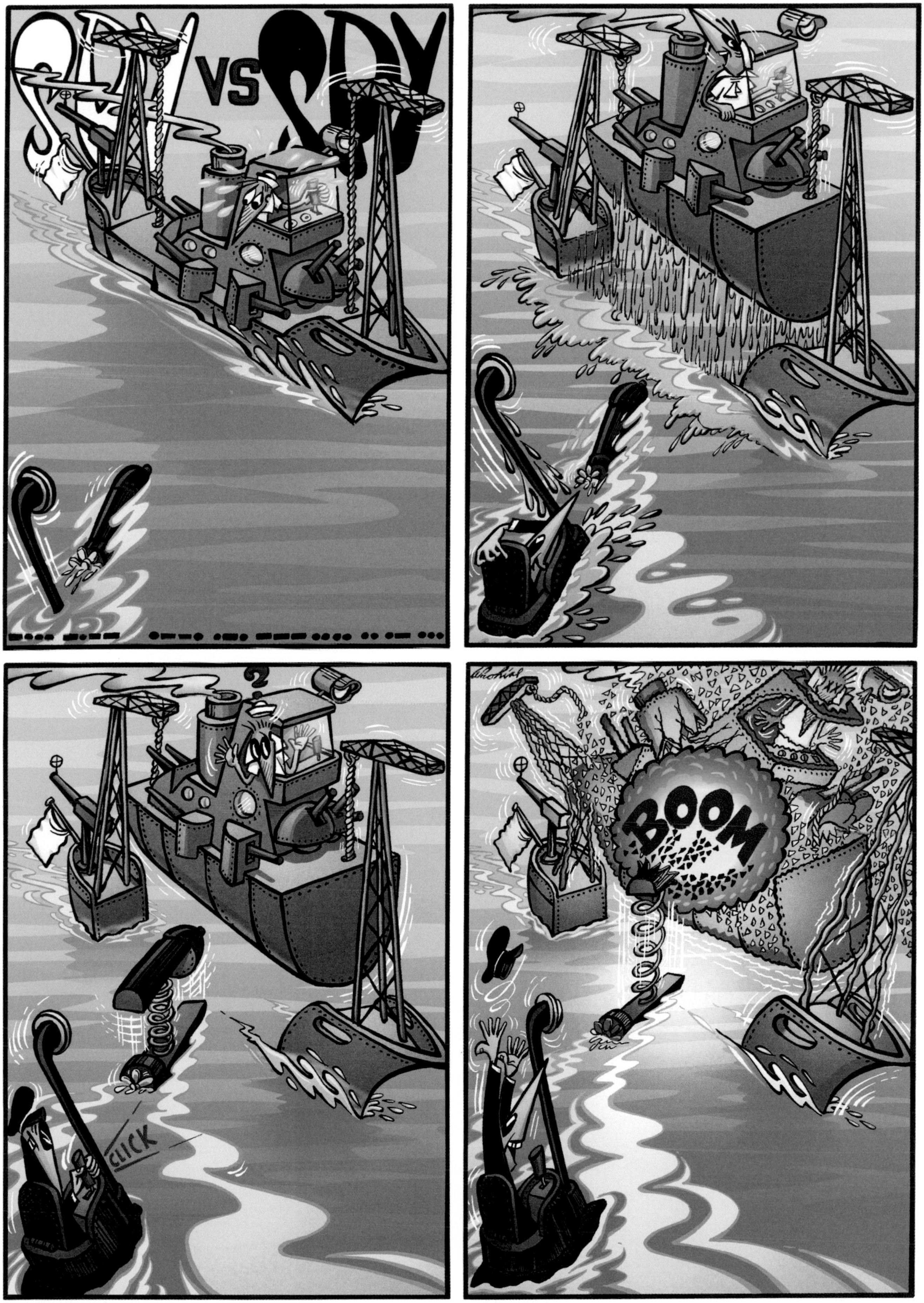
SPY vs SPY
CLICK
BOOM

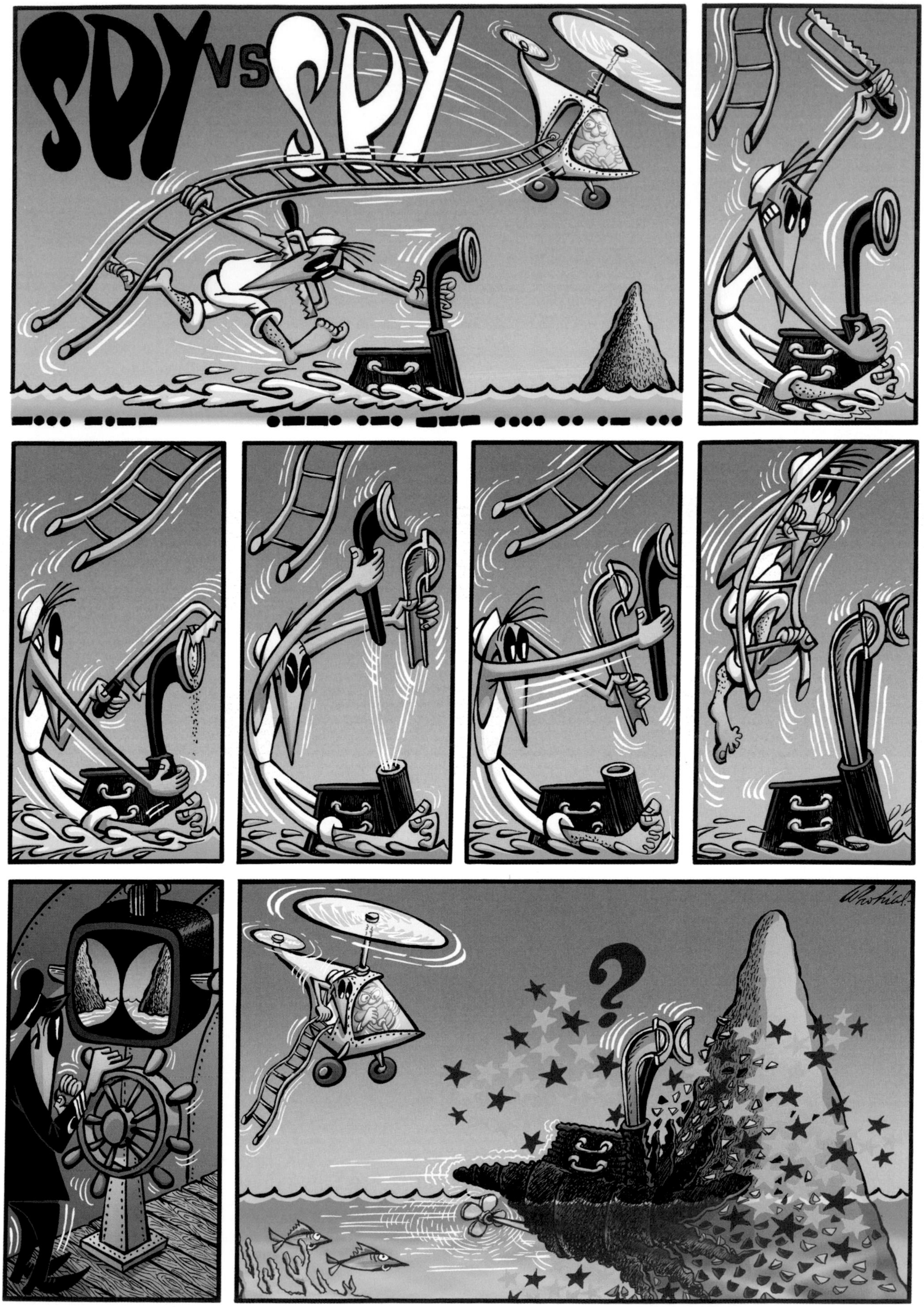
SPY vs SPY

The **Diabolical Duo** of **Double-Cross** and **Deceit** as **Depicted** by **Some** of the **World's Most Renowned Artists.**

THE SPY VS. SPY POSTER COLLECTION

GALLERY III

Bill Sienkiewicz

Yuko Shimizu

Peter Bagge

Nathan Sawaya

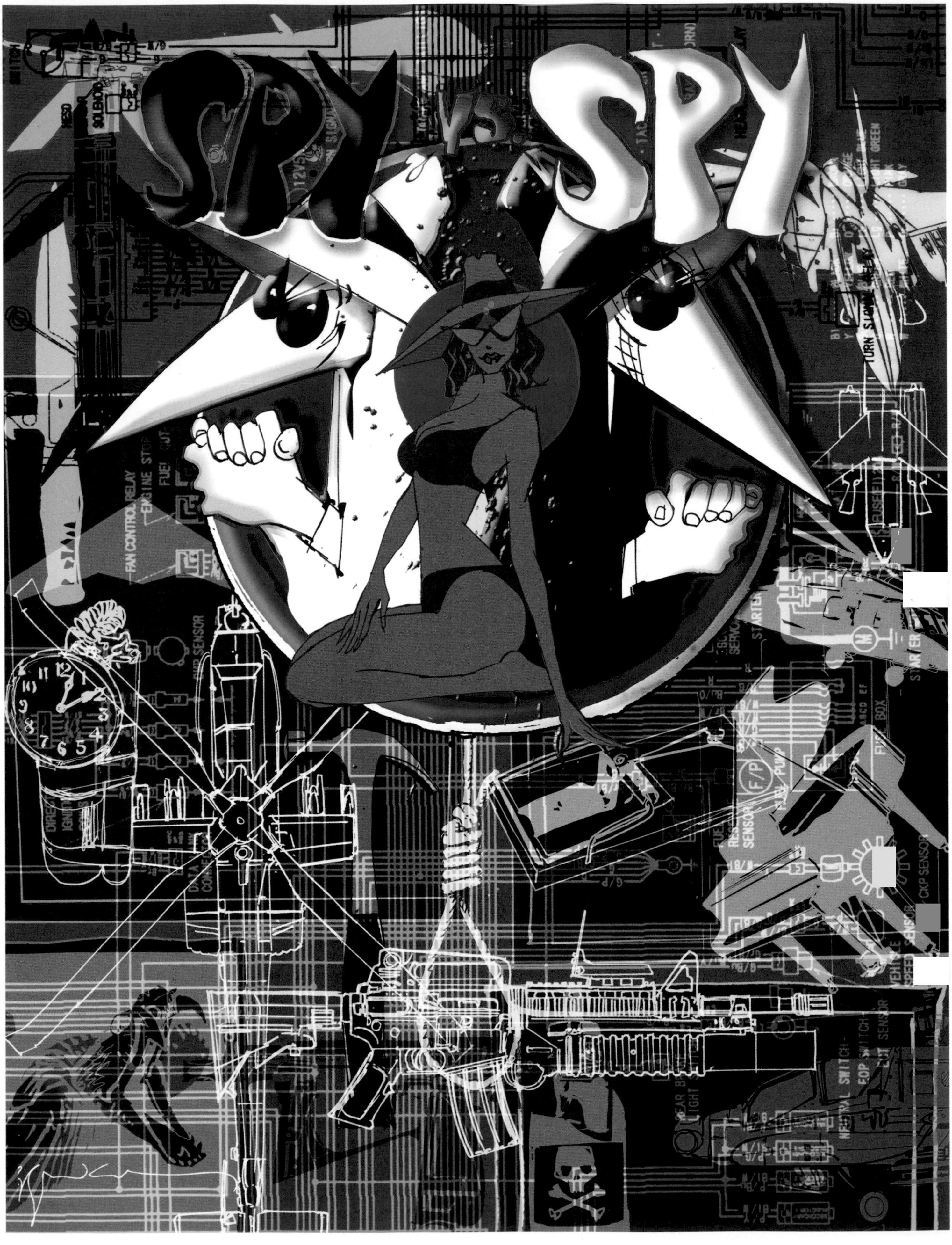
SPY vs SPY

Bill Sienkiewicz

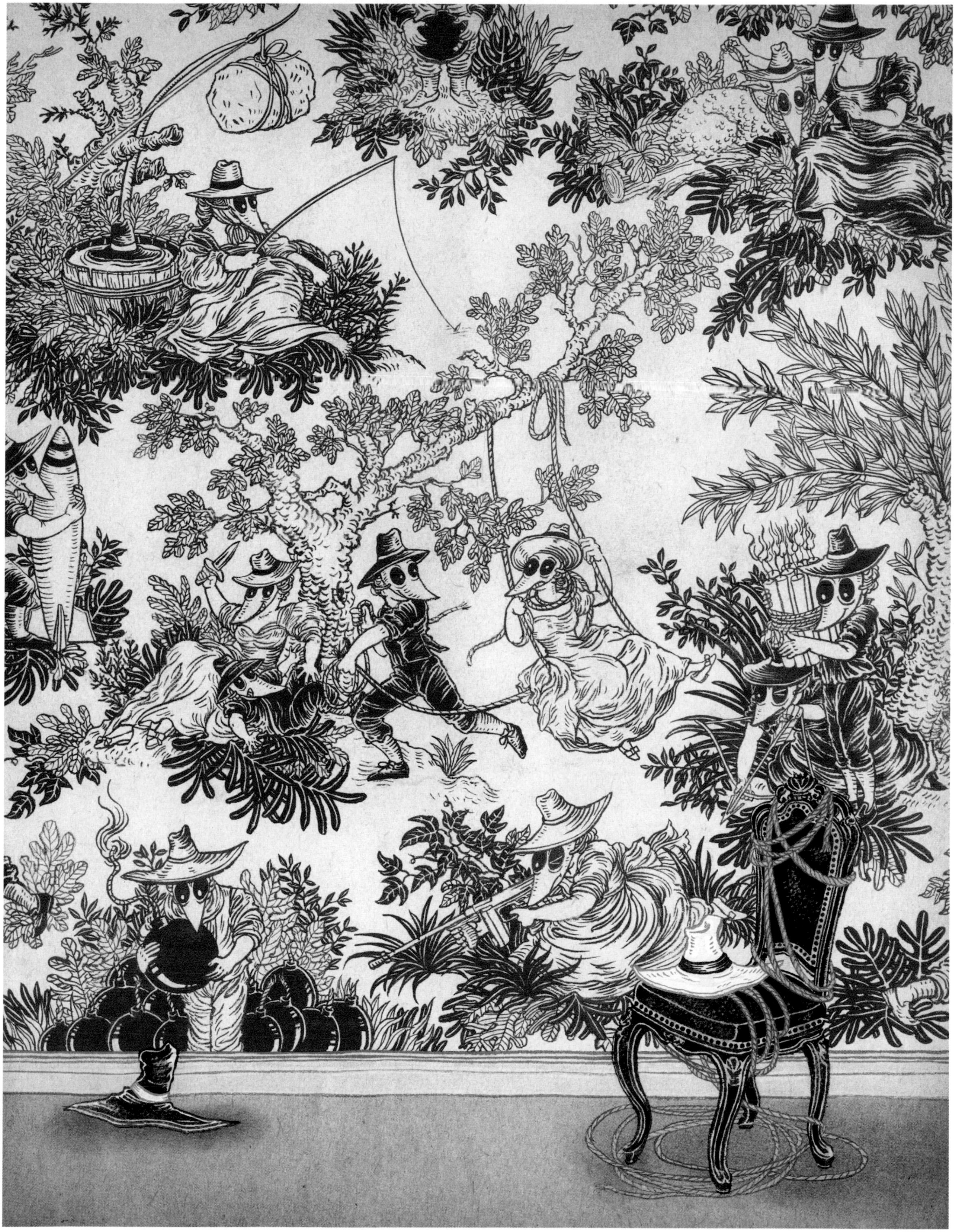

Yuko Shimizu

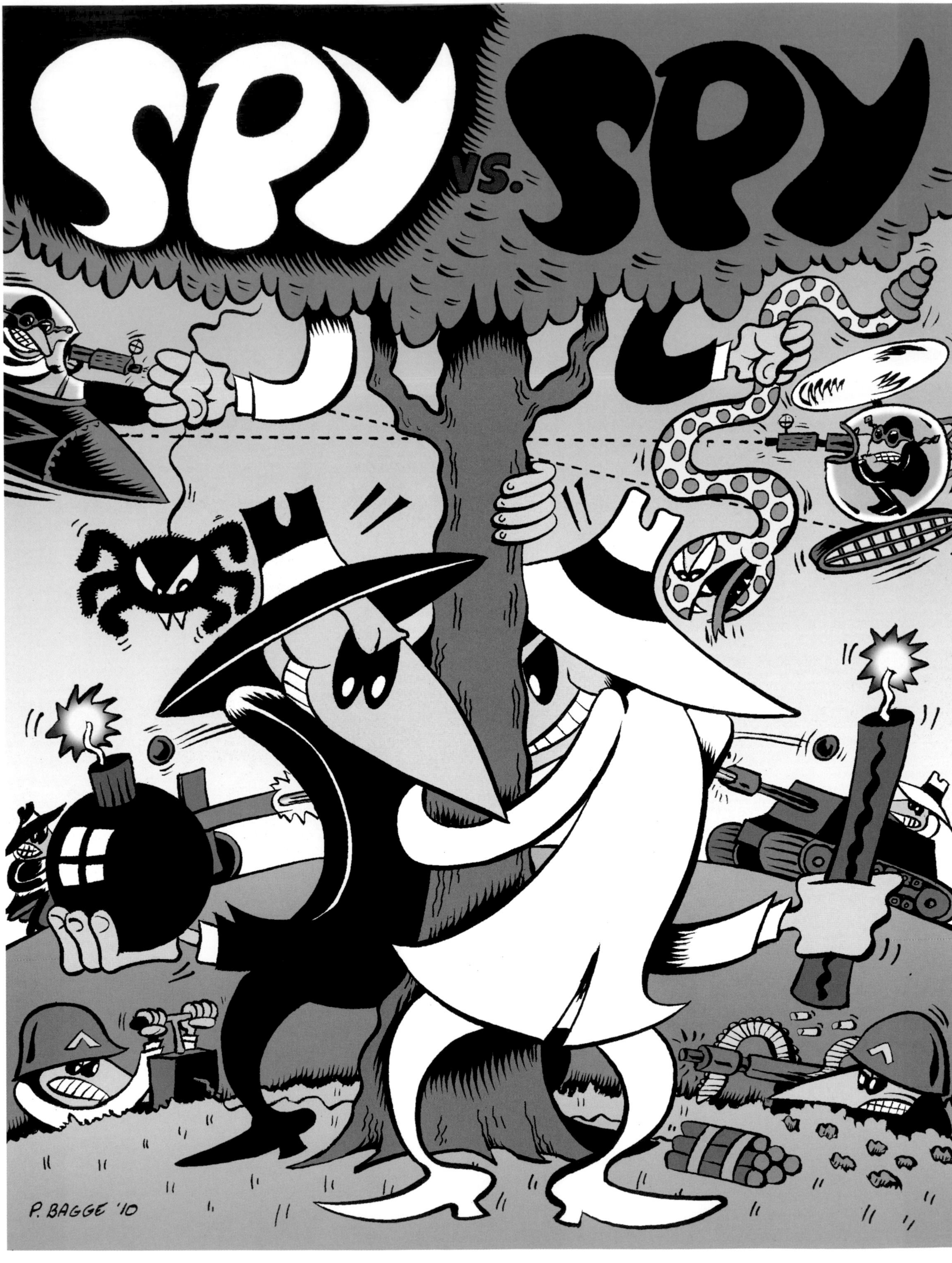
SPY vs. SPY
P. BAGGE '10

Peter Bagge

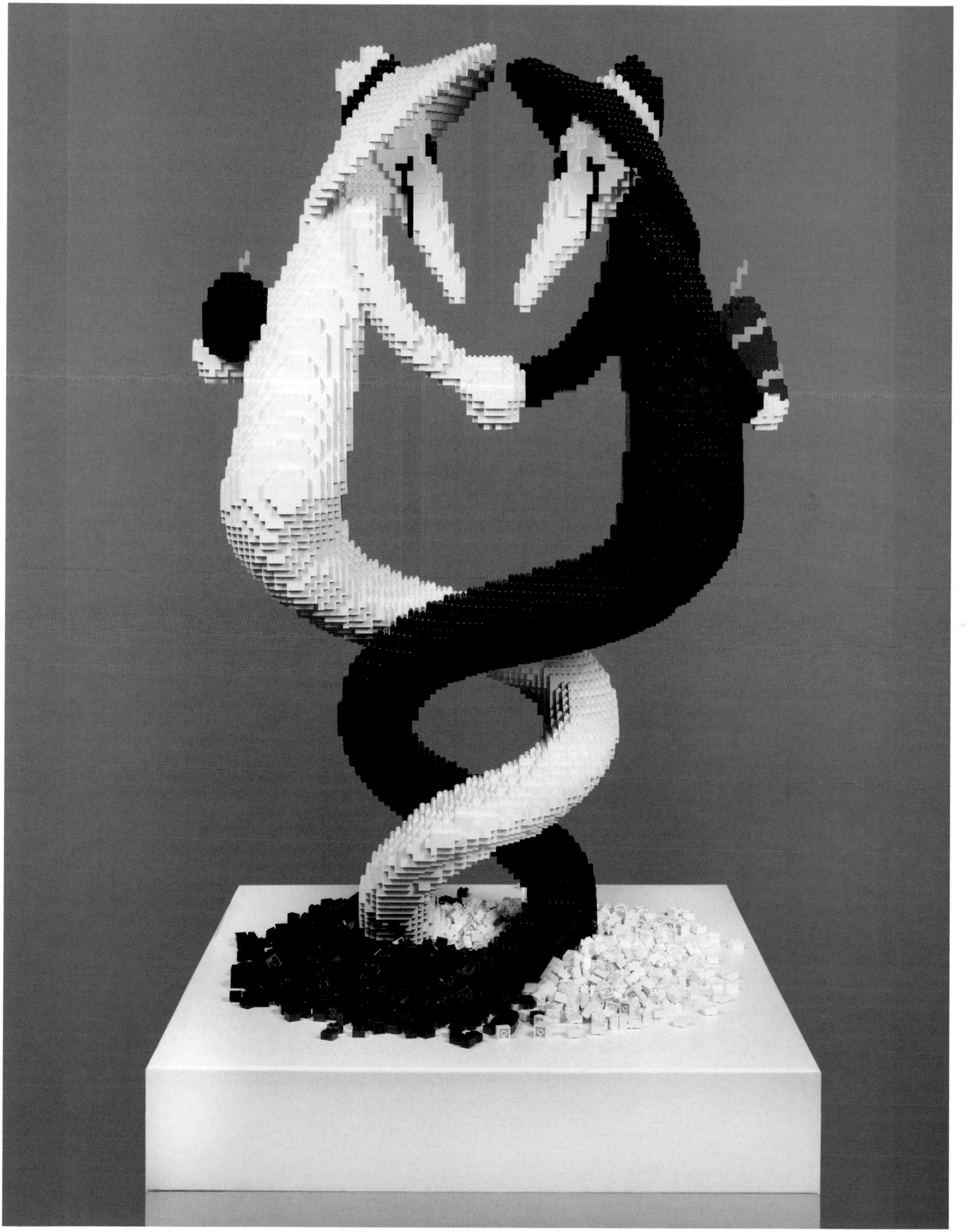

Nathan Sawaya

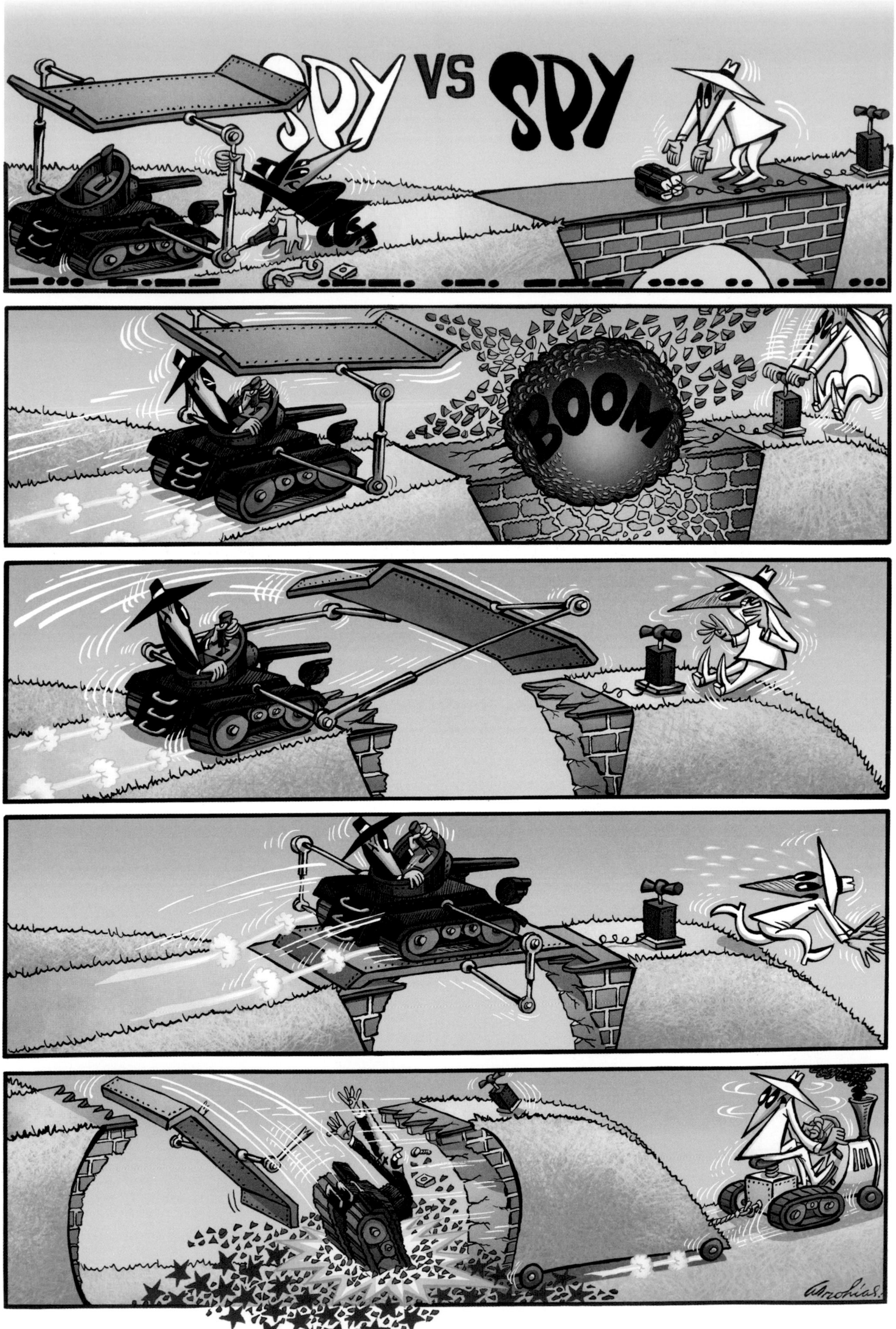
SPY vs SPY
BOOM

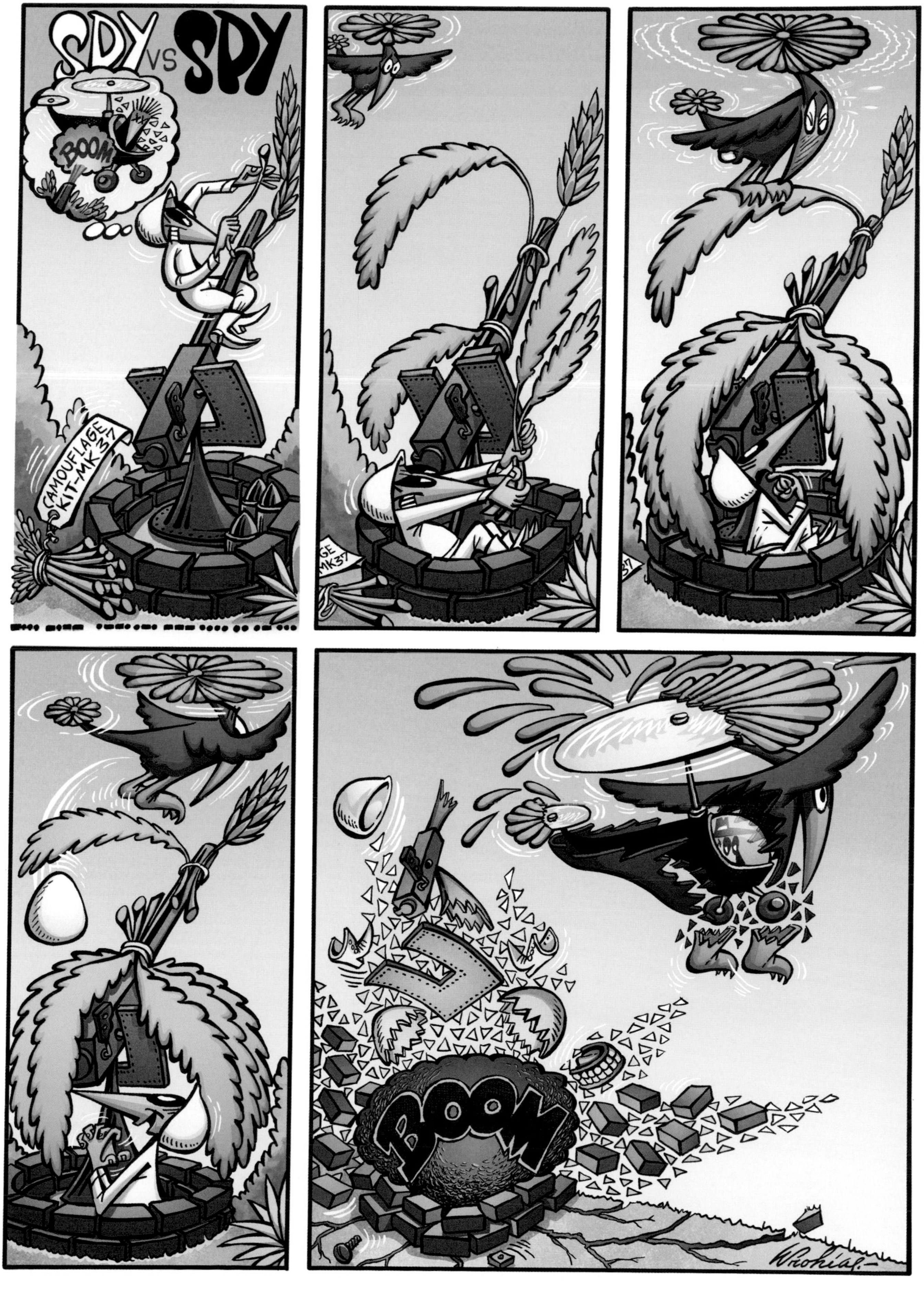
SPY VS SPY
BOOM
CAMOUFLAGE KIT-MK 37
BOOM

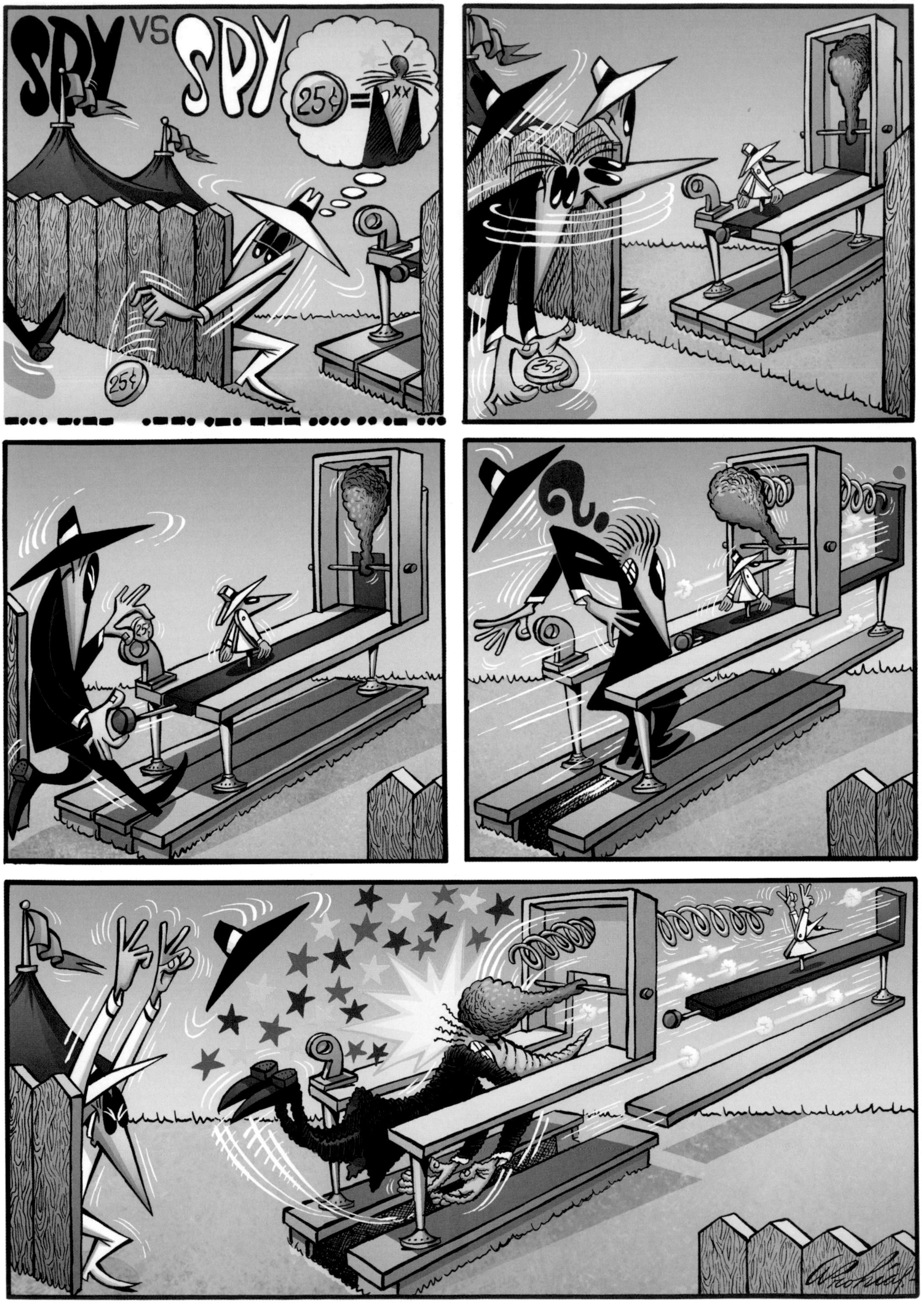
SPY VS SPY
25¢ =
25¢
25¢
25¢
Prohias

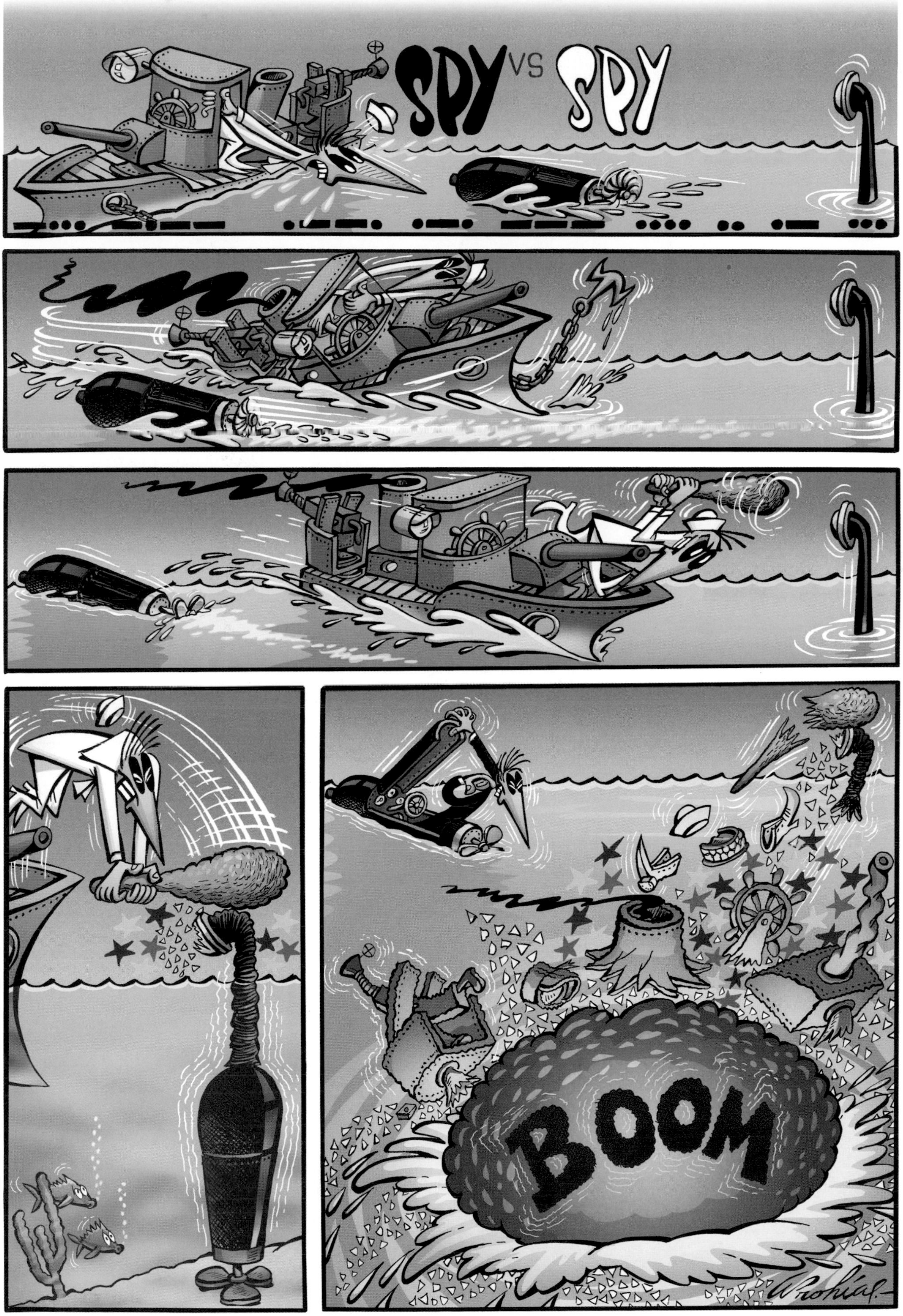
SPY vs SPY
BOOM
Prohias

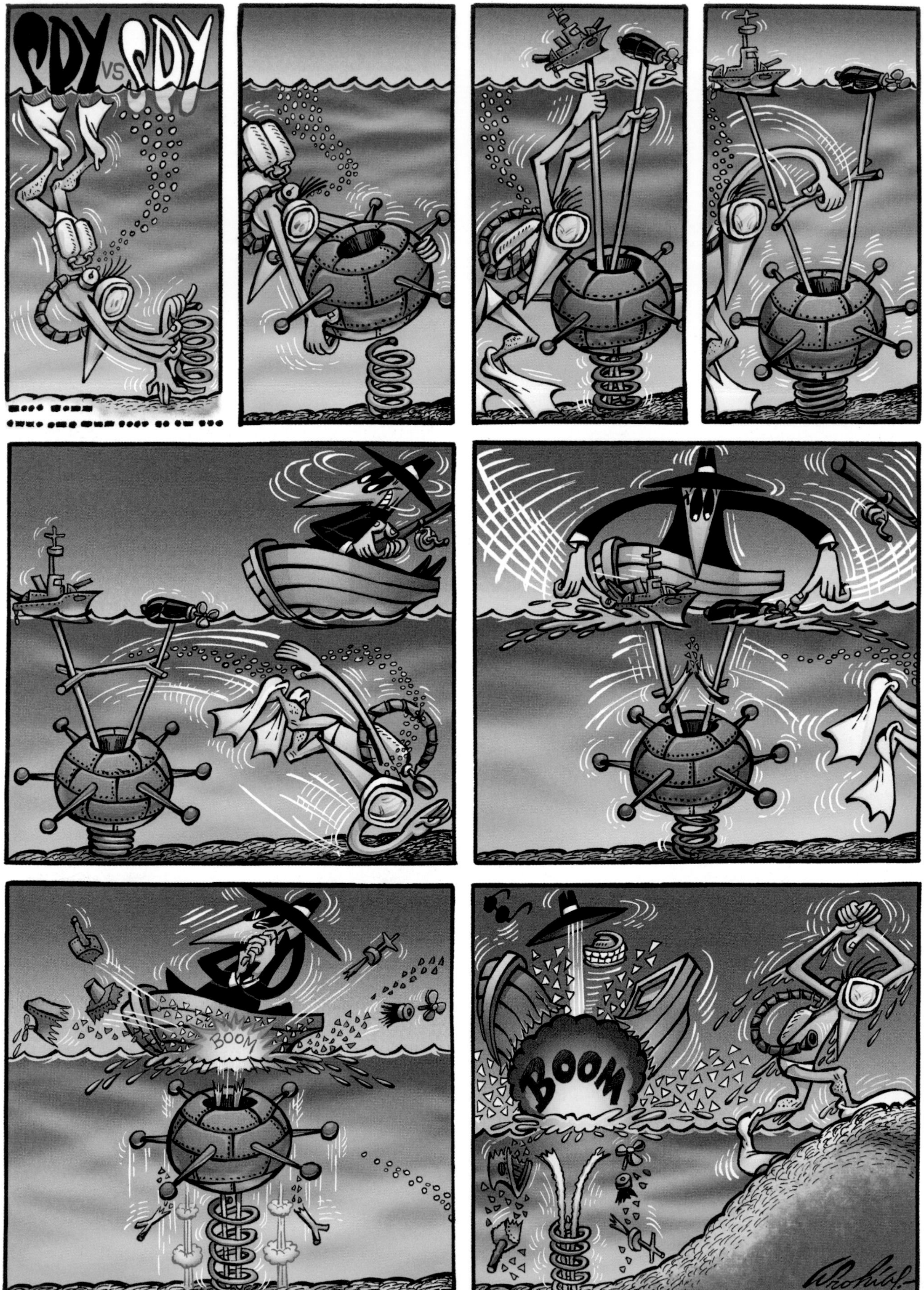
SPY VS SPY
BOOM
BOOM

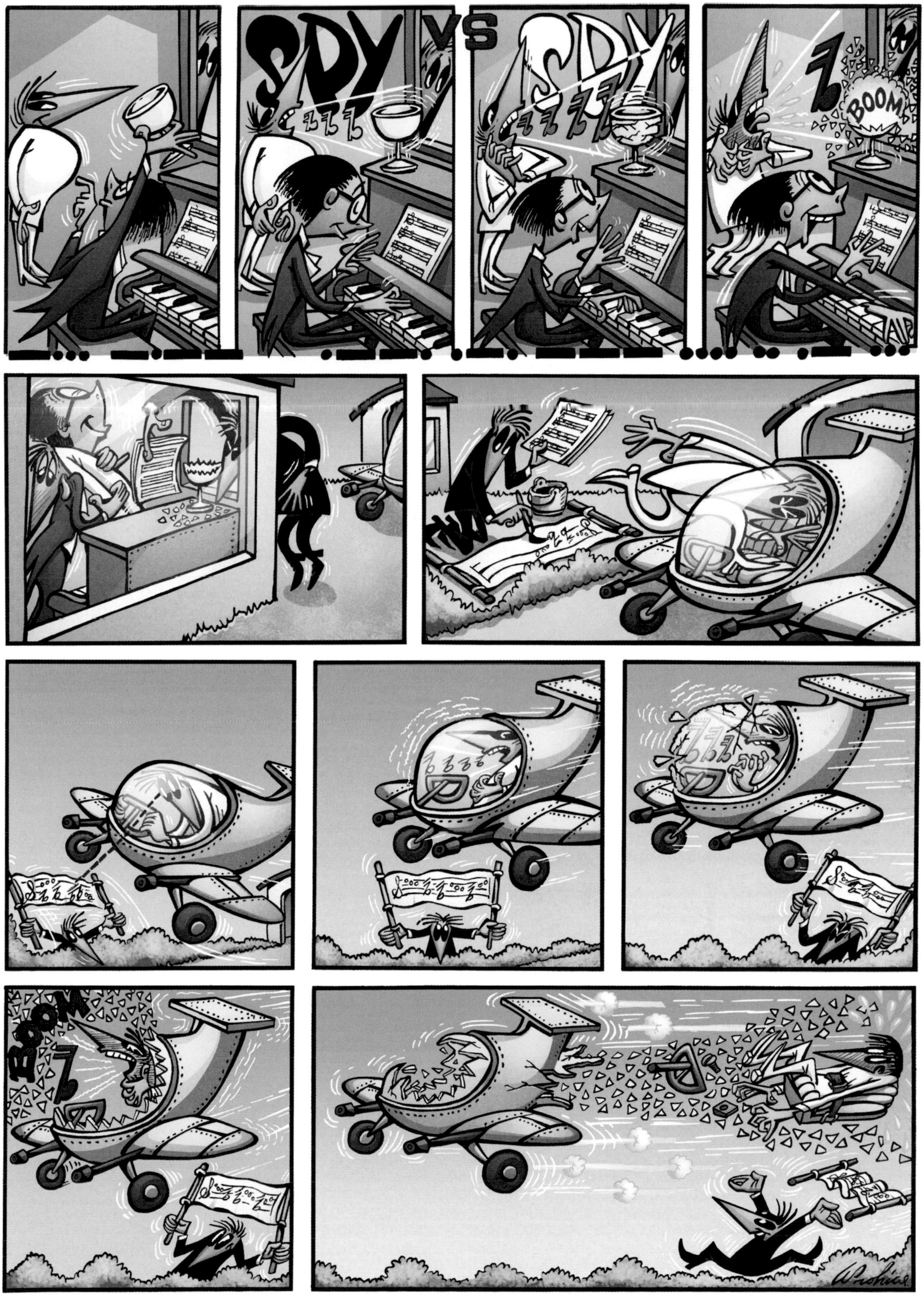
SPY vs SPY
BOOM
BOOM

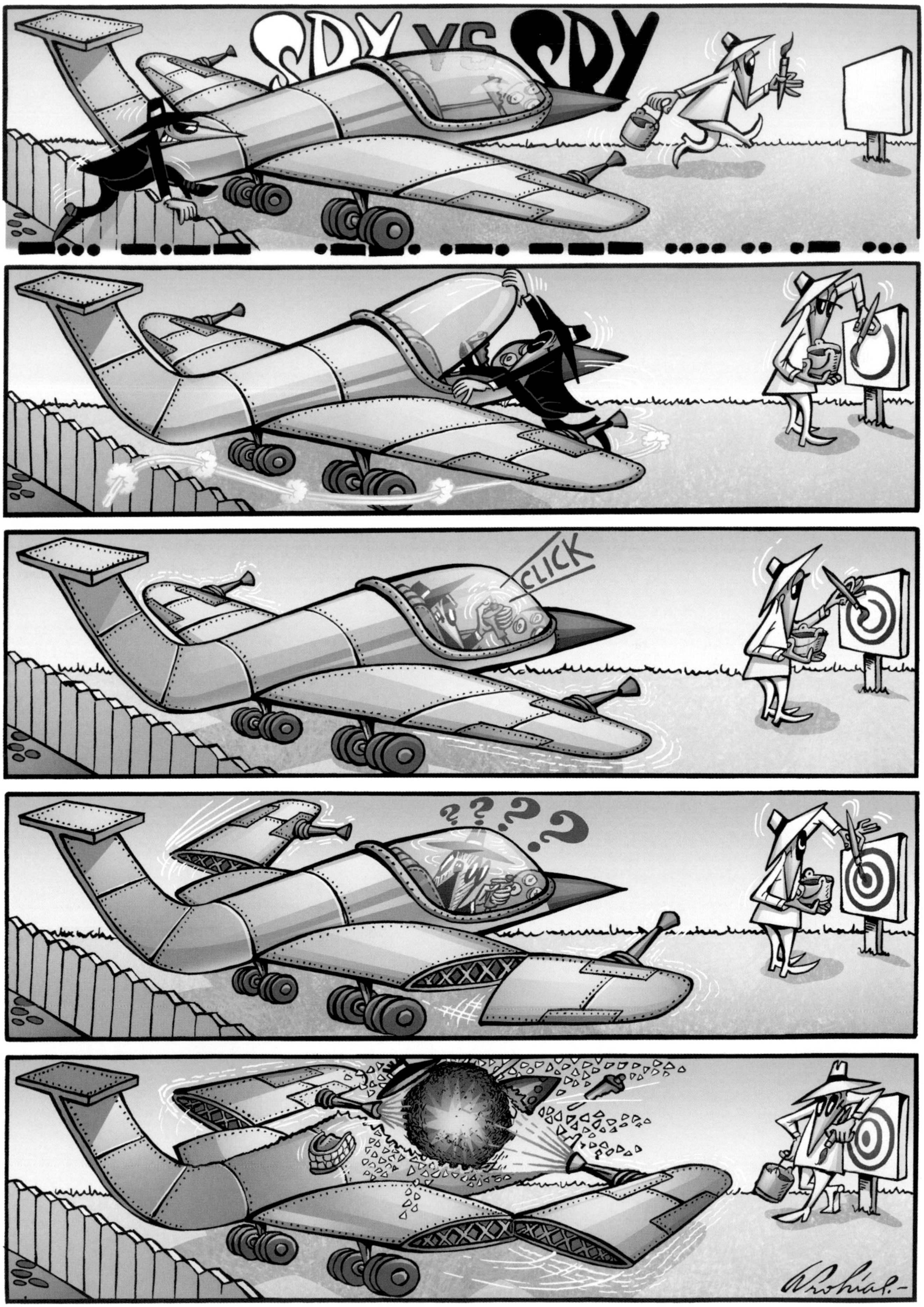
SPY vs SPY
CLICK
? ? ? ?
Prohias

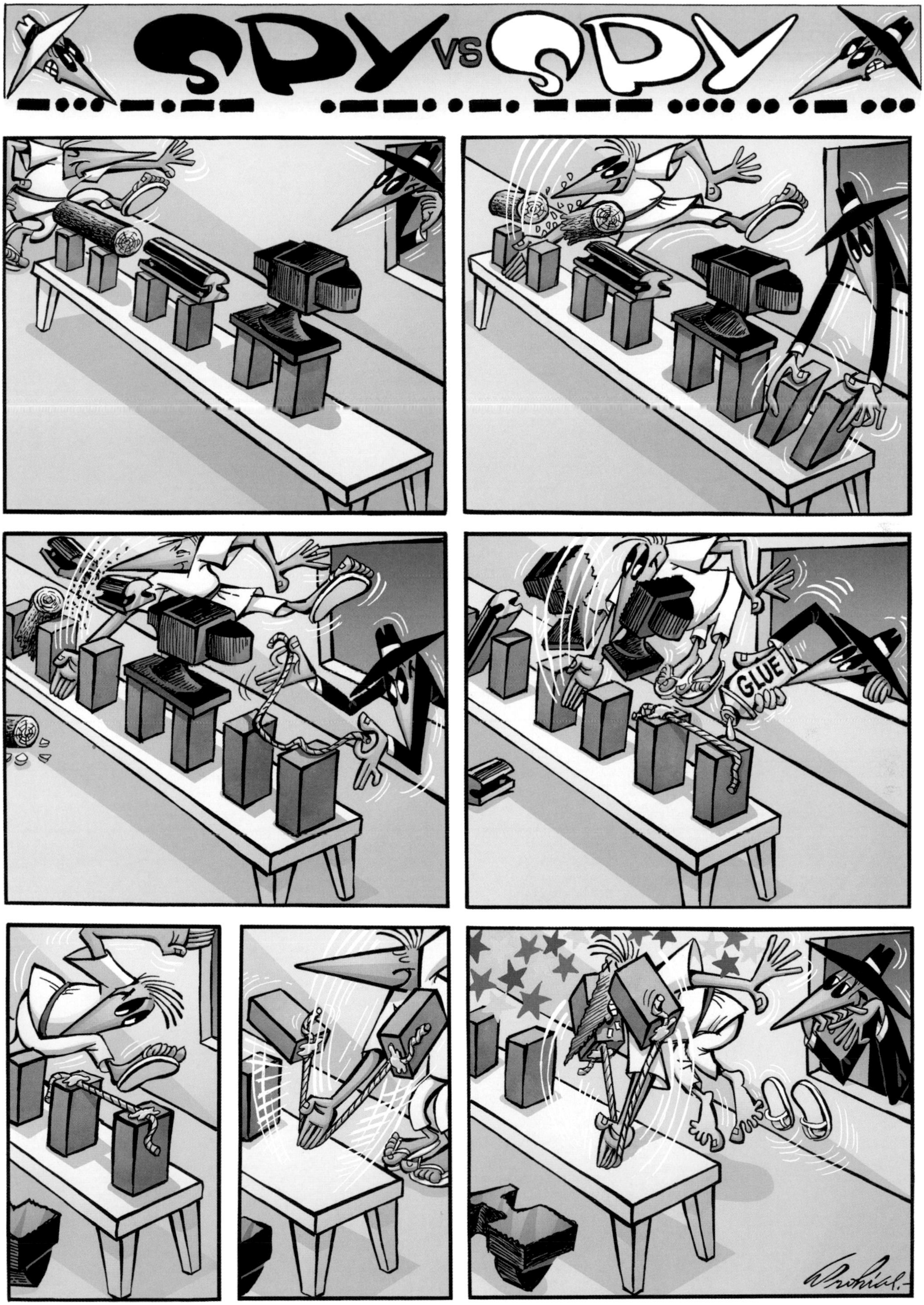
SPY vs SPY
GLUE

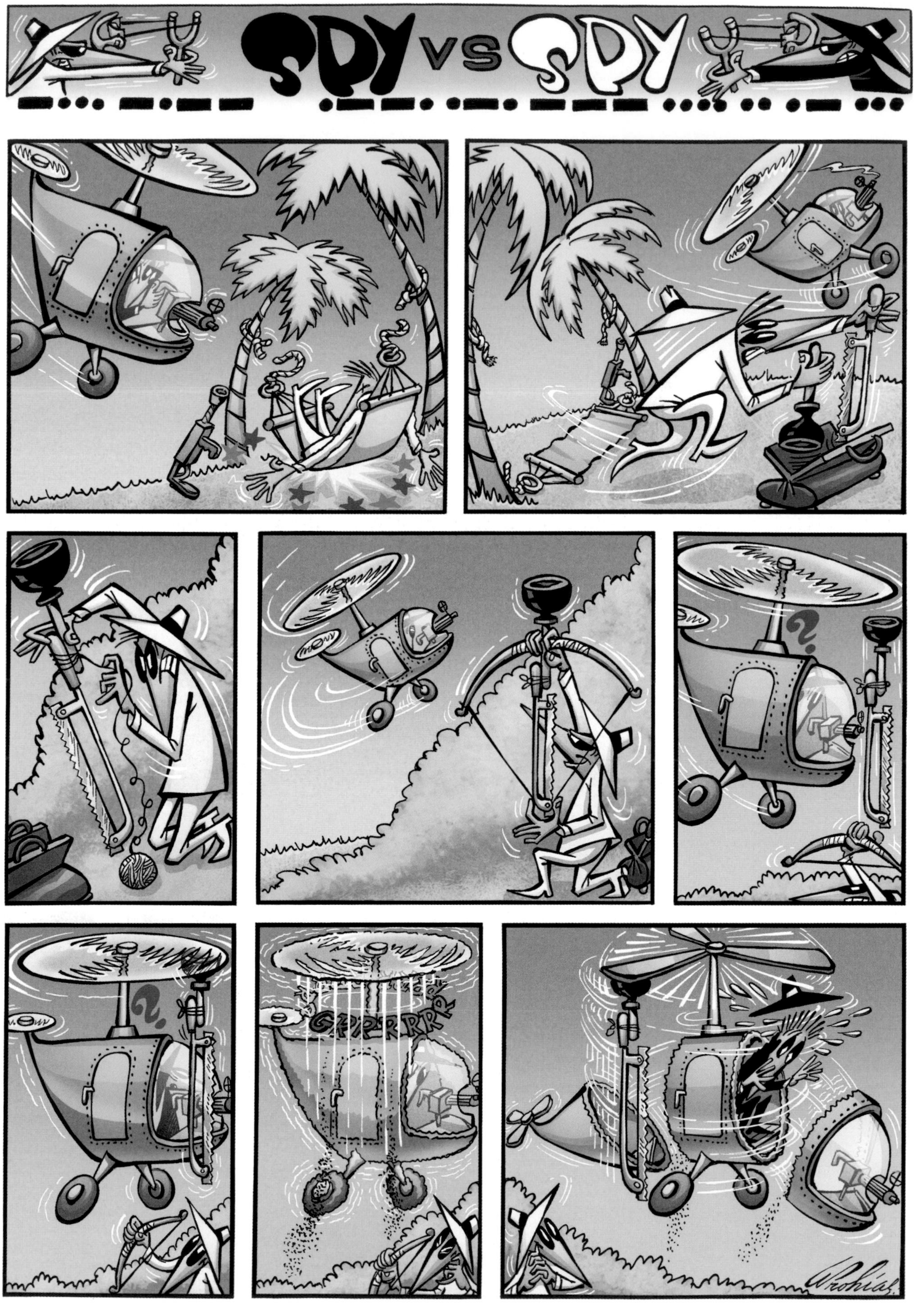
SPY vs SPY
GRRRRRR

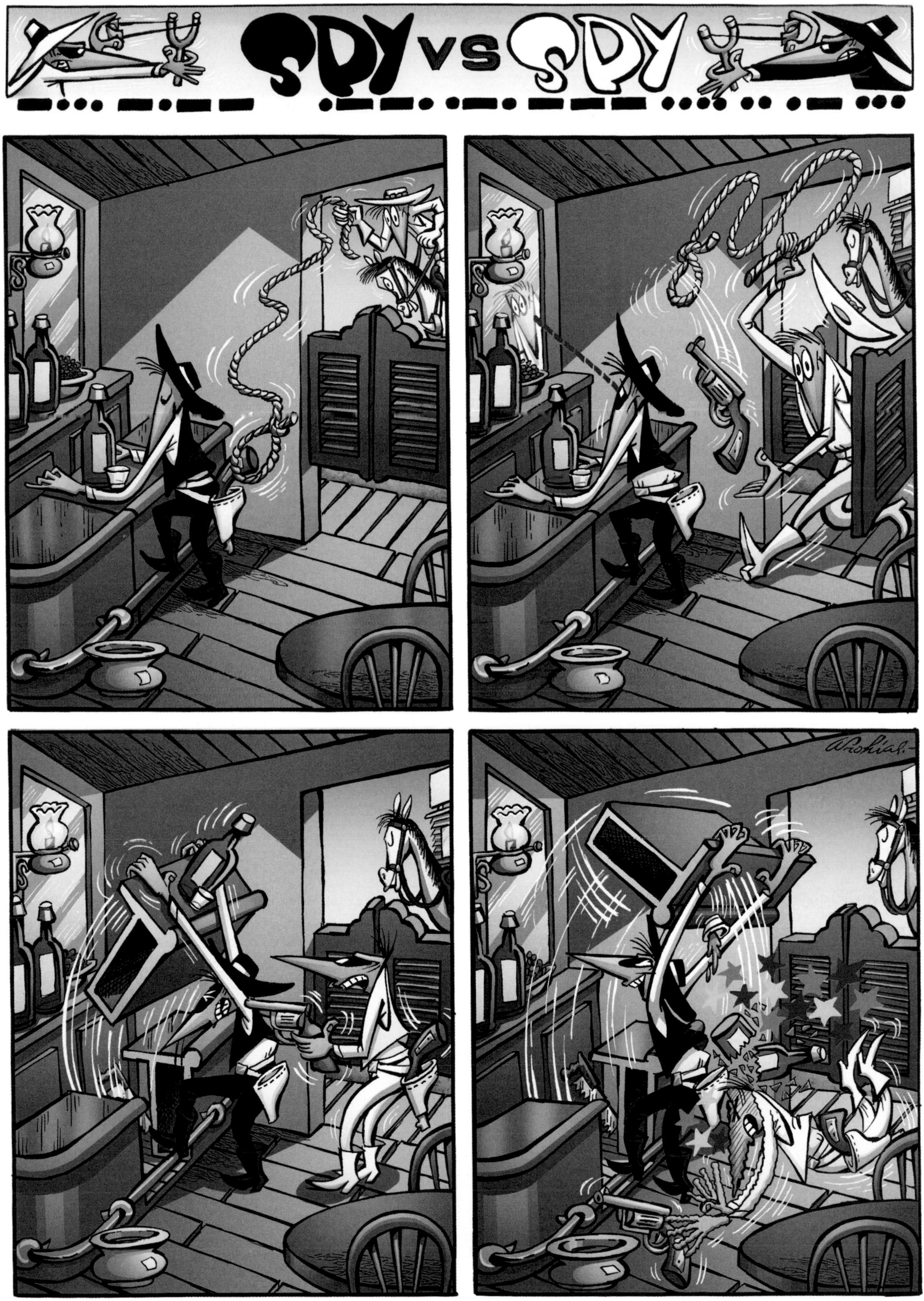
SPY vs SPY

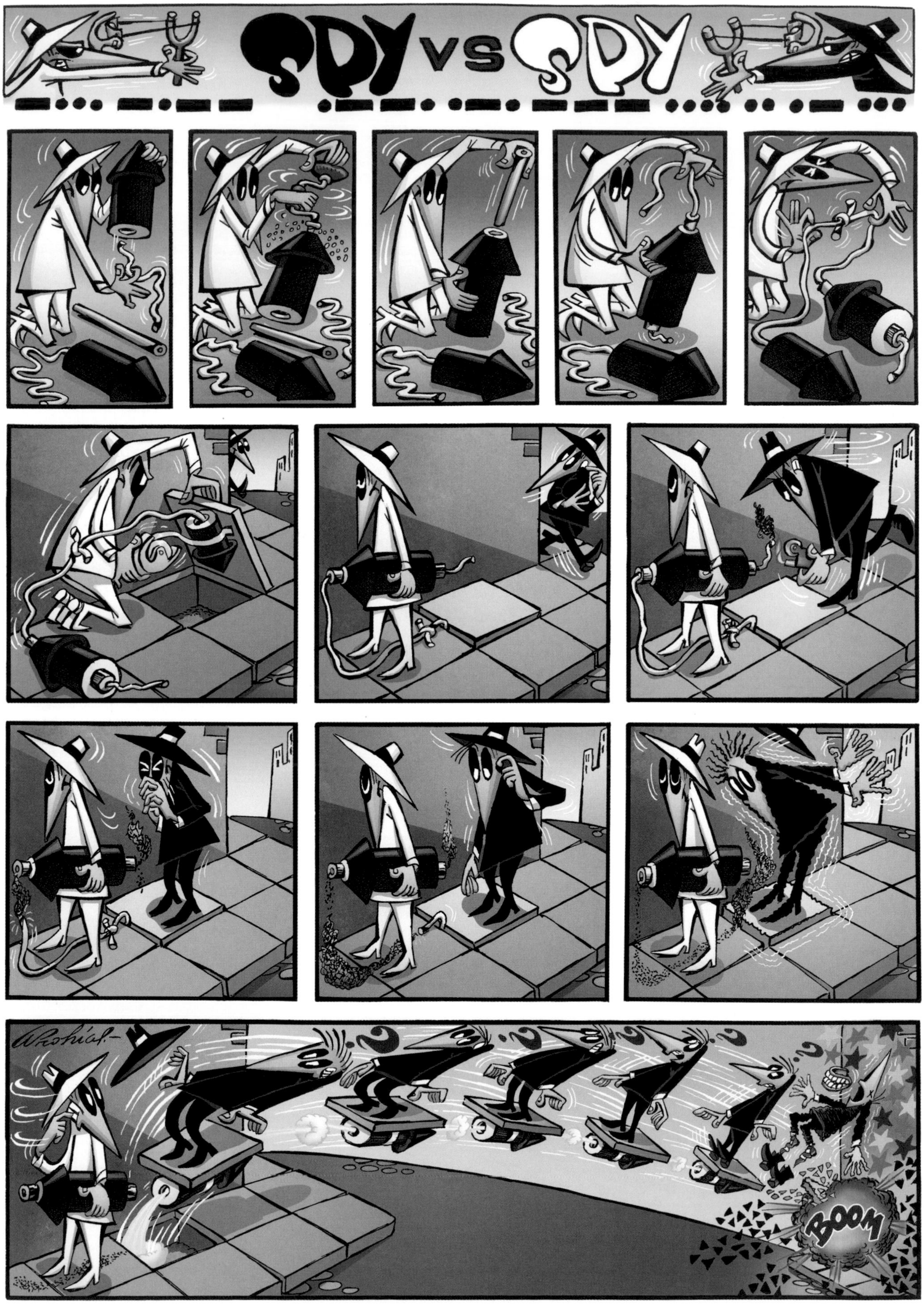
SPY vs SPY
BOOM

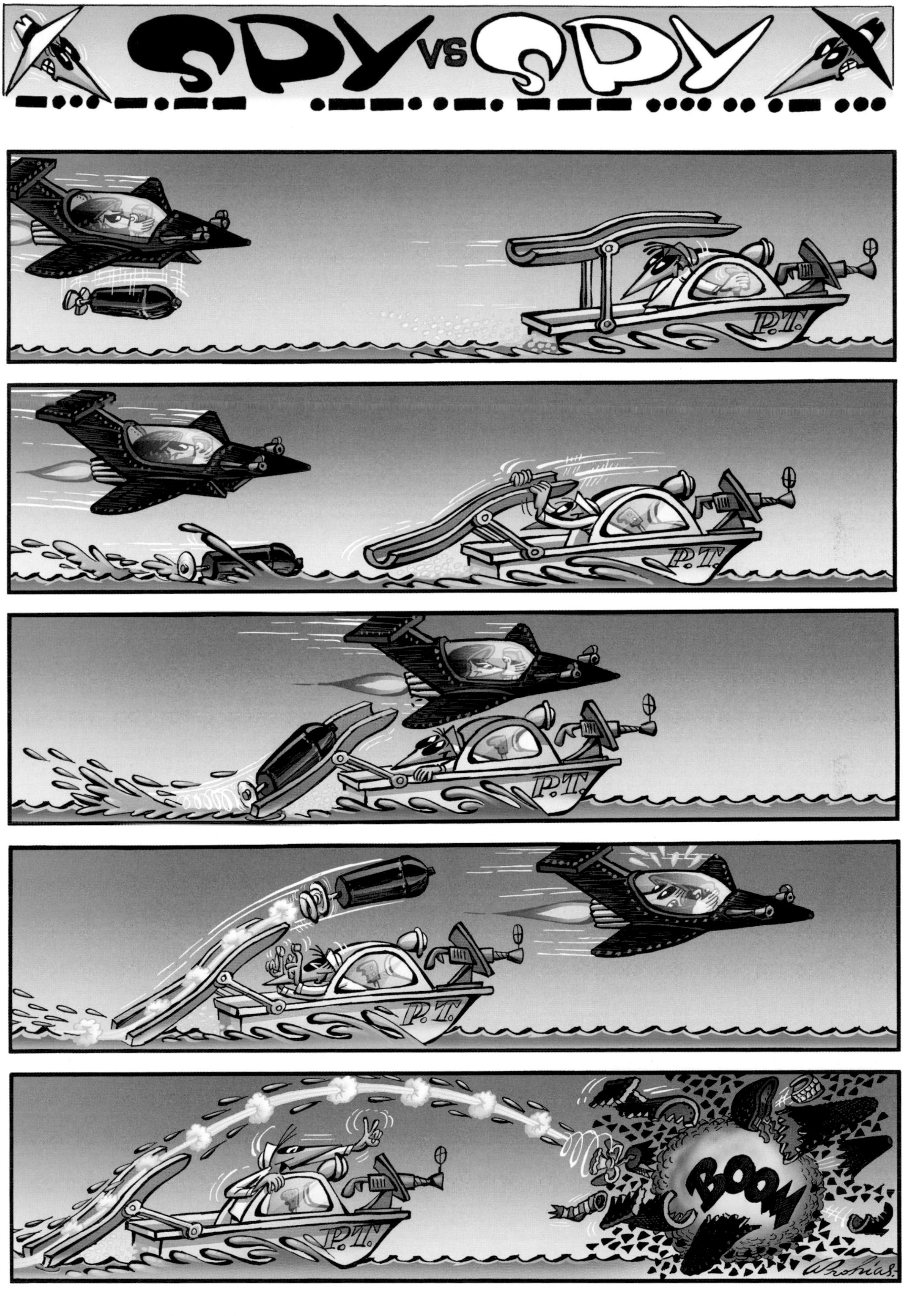
SPY VS SPY
P.T.
P.T.
P.T.
P.T.
P.T.
BOOM
Prohias

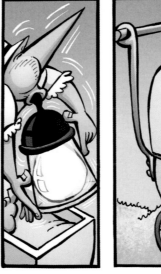

MAD #229 March 1982

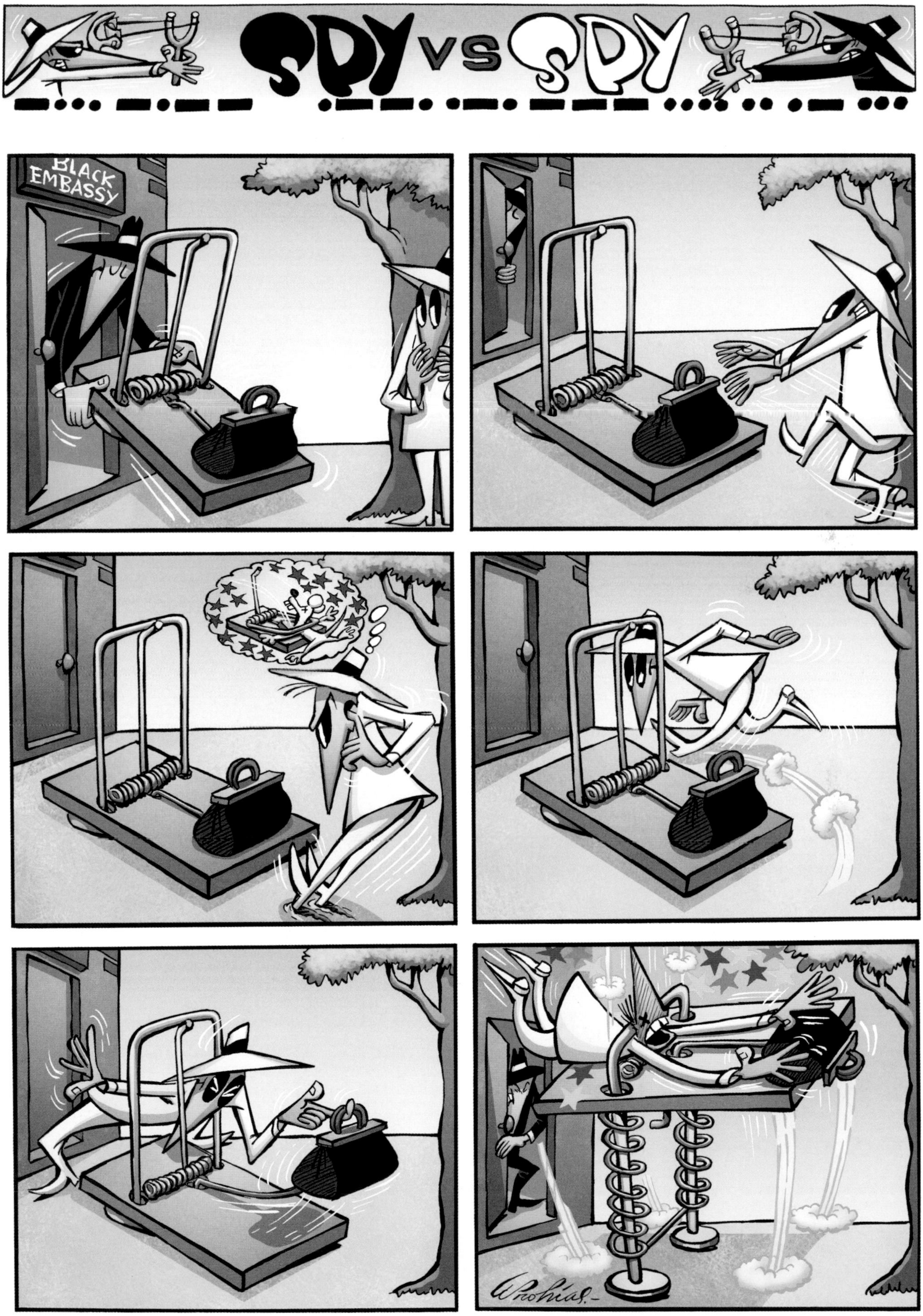
SPY vs SPY
BLACK EMBASSY
Prohías

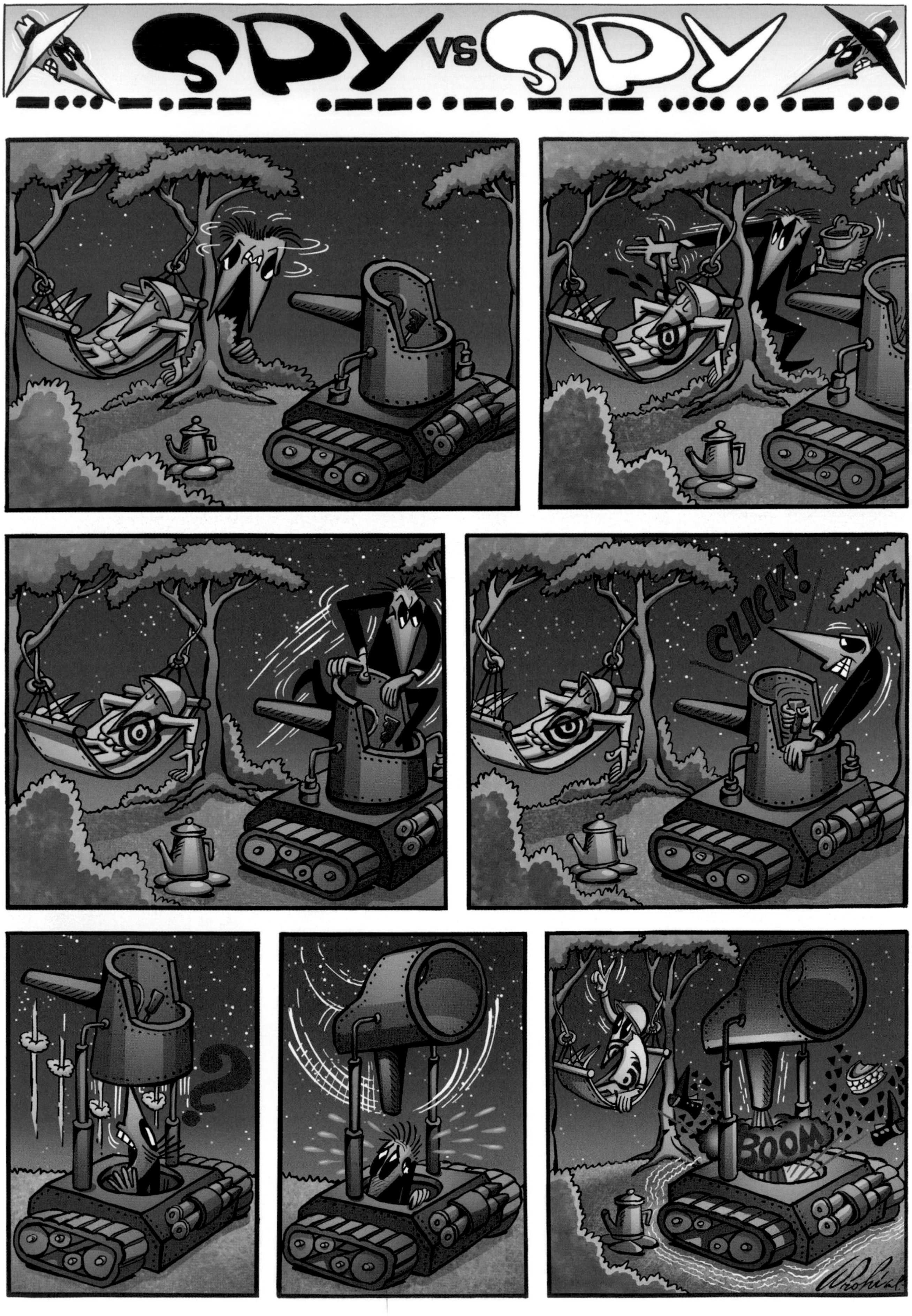
SPY vs SPY
CLICK!
?
BOOM

SPY vs SPY
CLICK
BOOM
BOOM
CLICK
BOOM
BOOM

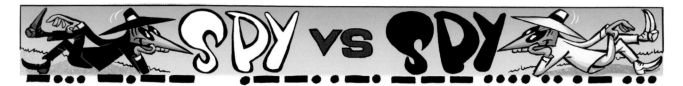

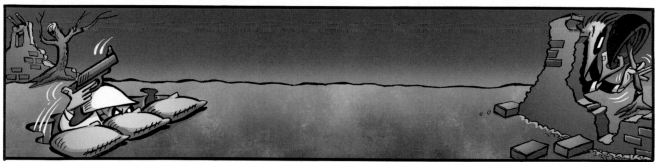

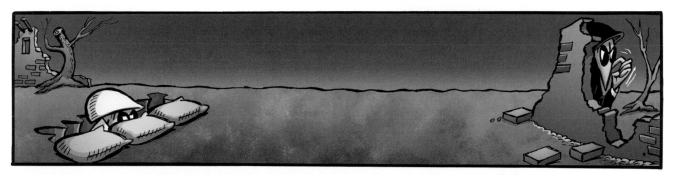

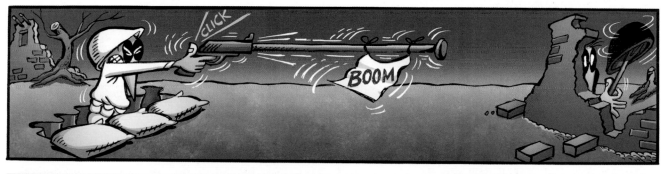

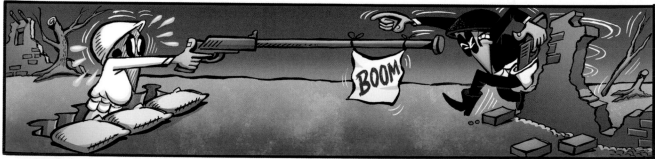

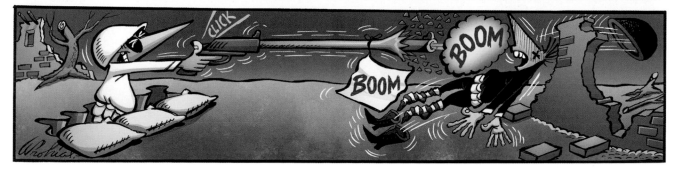

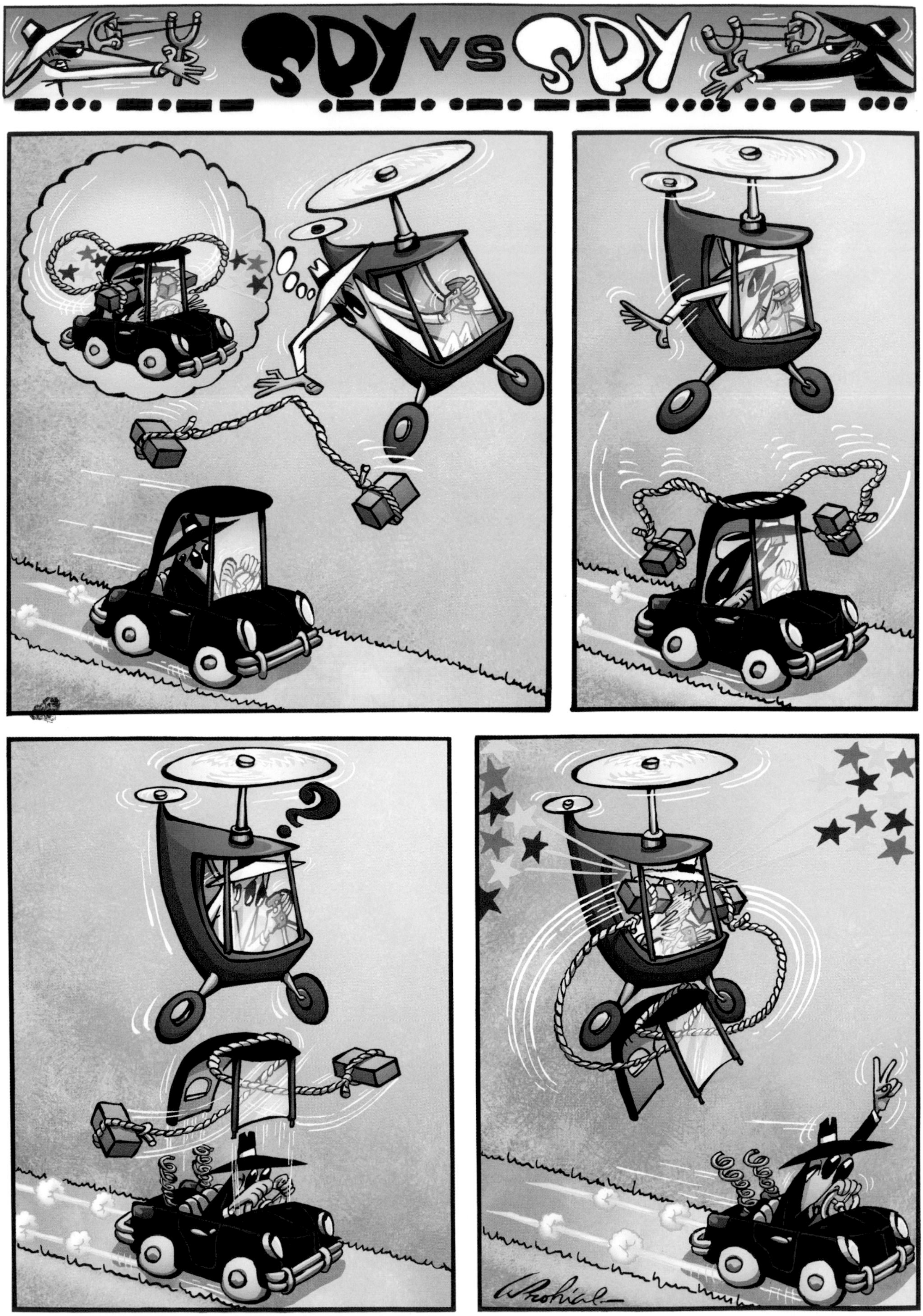
SPY vs SPY

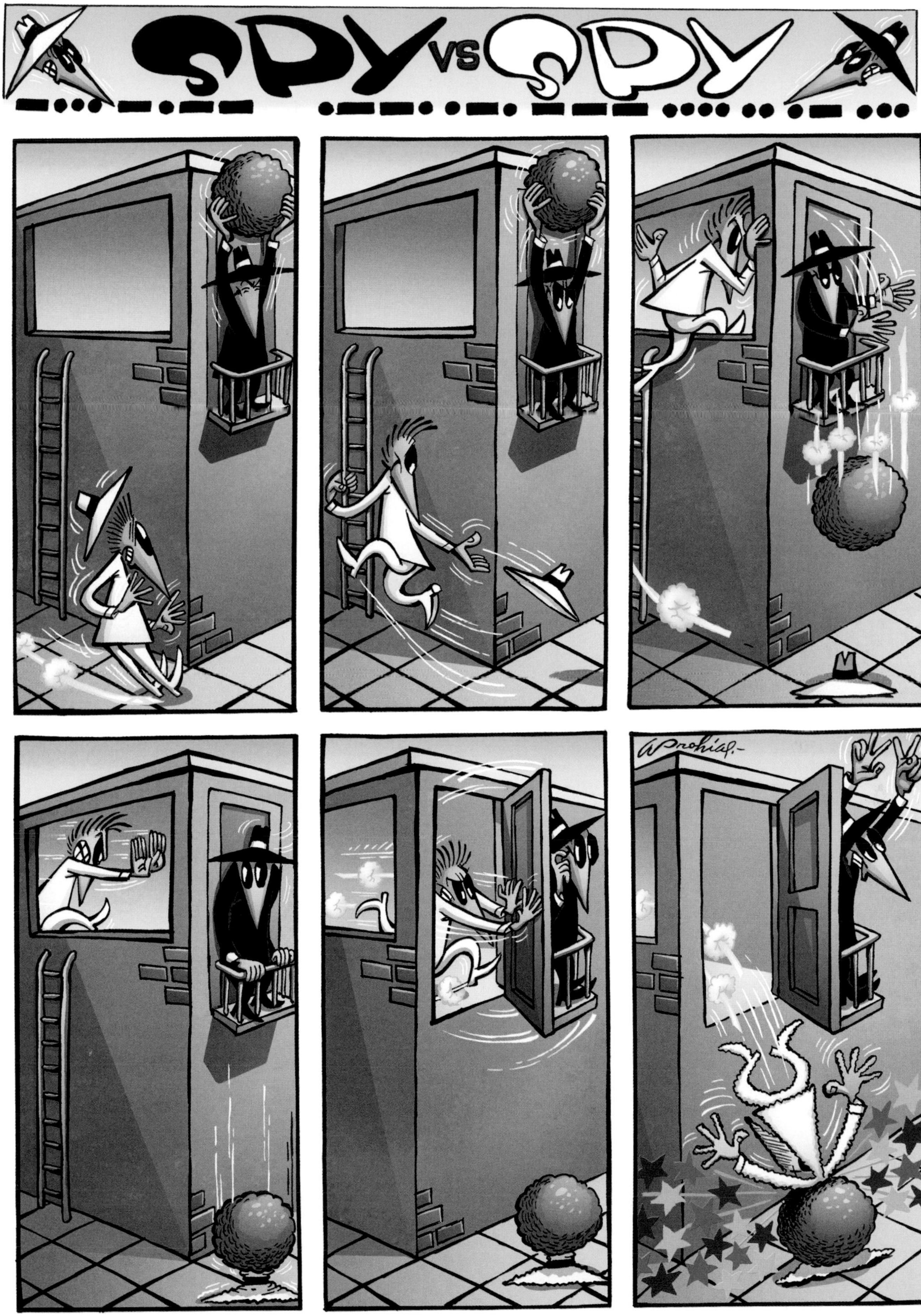
SPY vs SPY

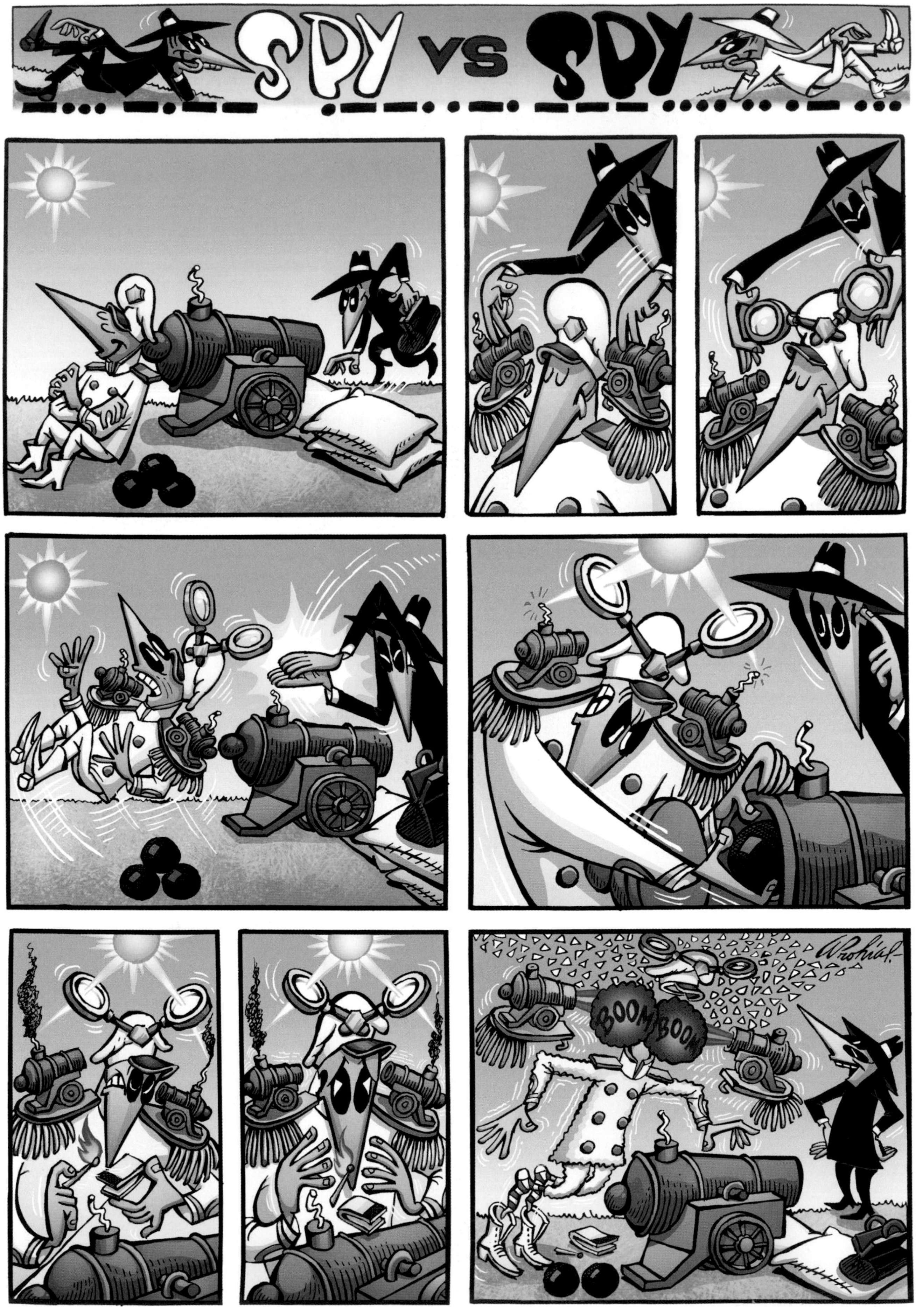
SPY vs SPY
BOOM
BOOM
Prohías

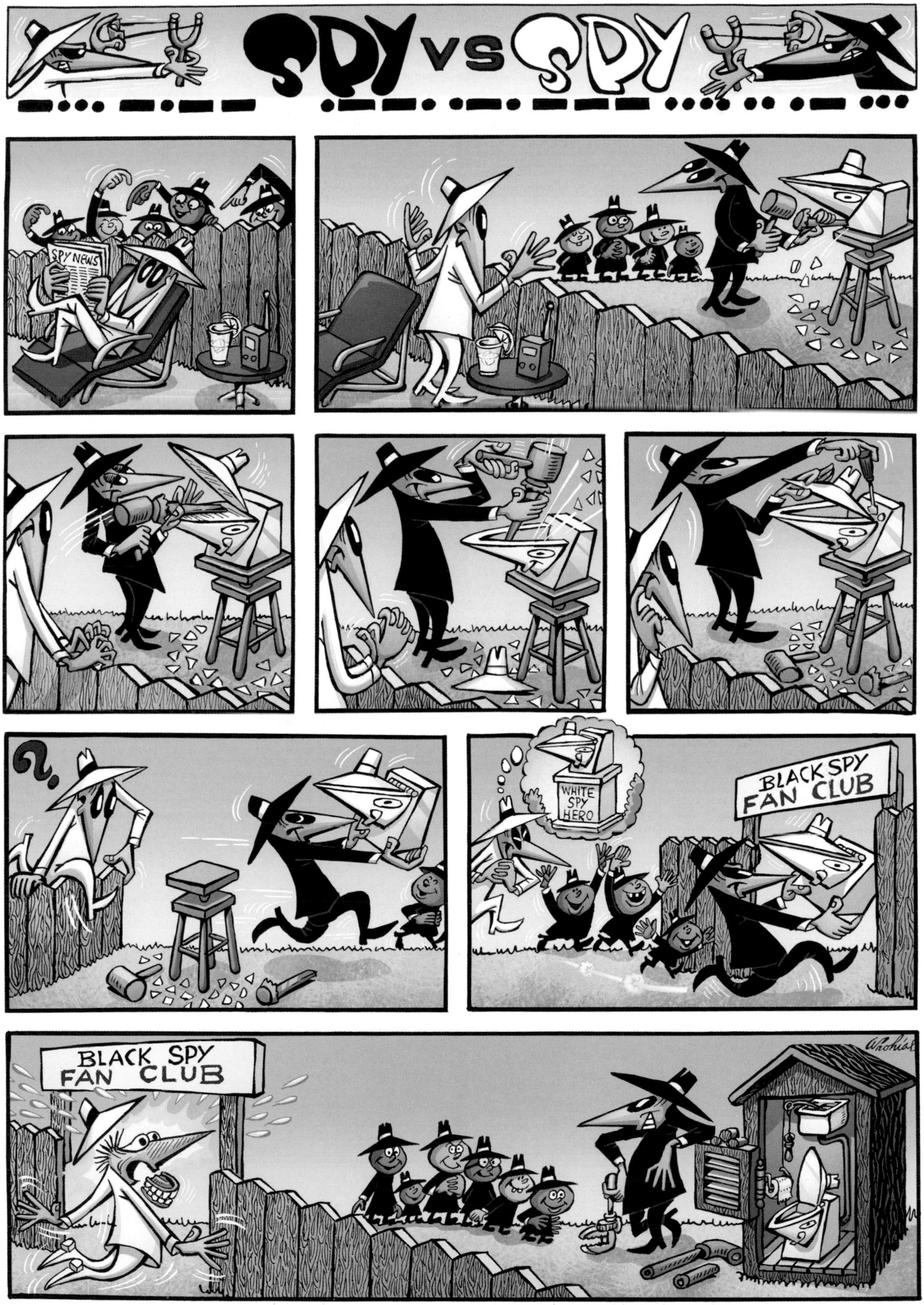
SPY vs SPY
SPY NEWS
WHITE SPY HERO
BLACK SPY FAN CLUB
BLACK SPY FAN CLUB

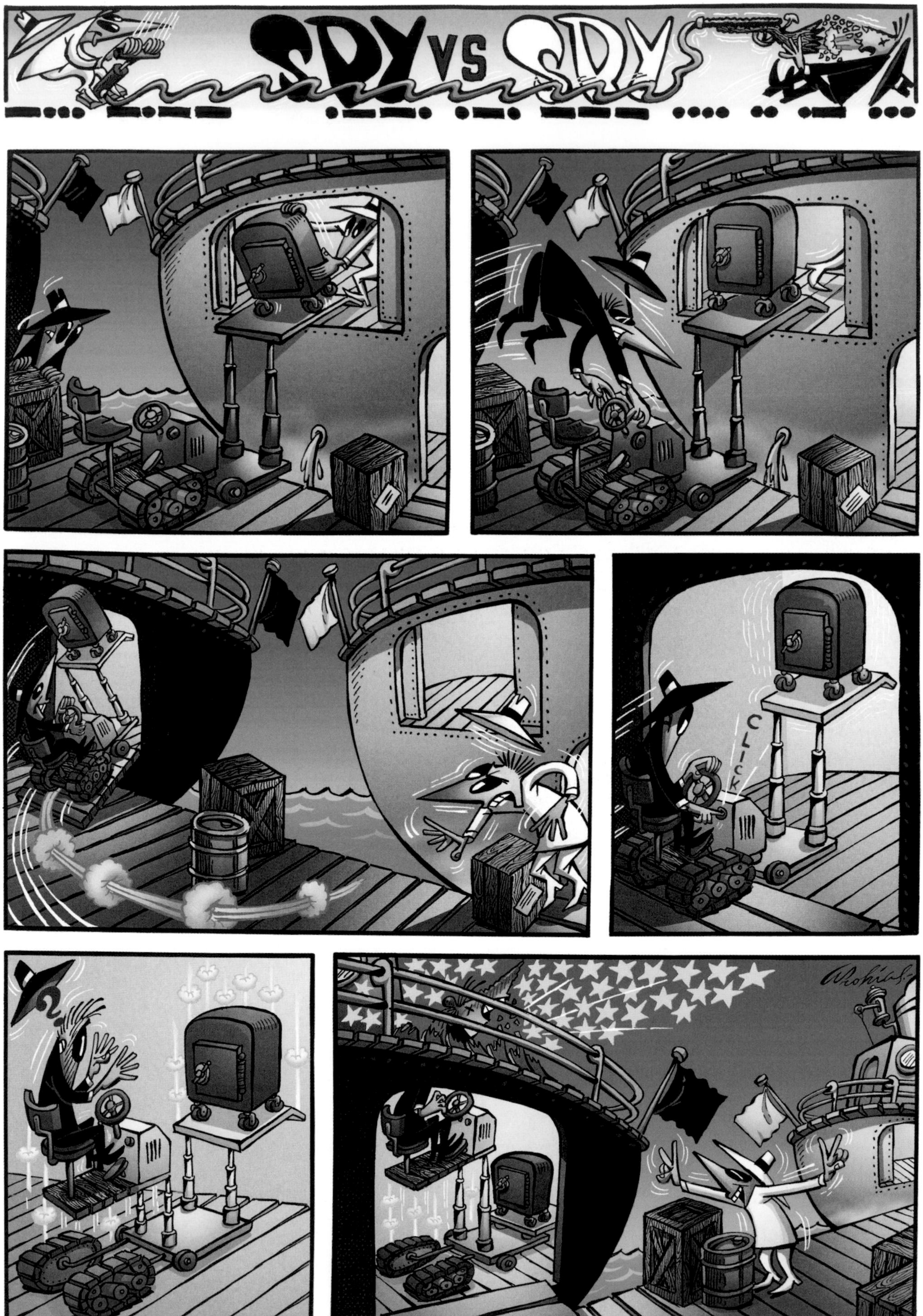
SPY VS SPY
CLICK
Prohias

SPY VS SPY

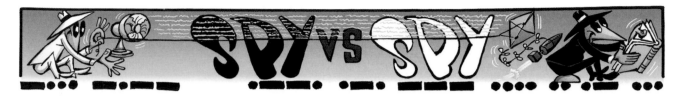

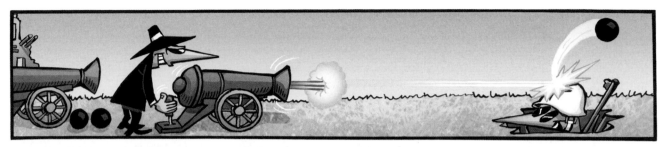

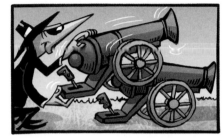

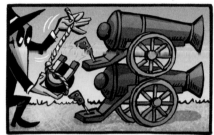

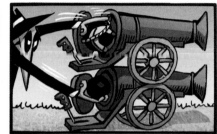

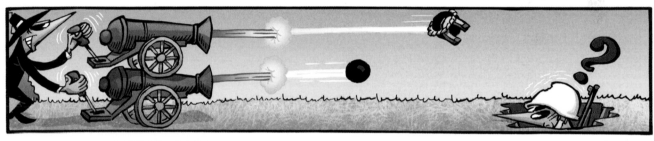

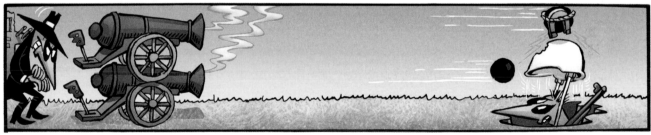

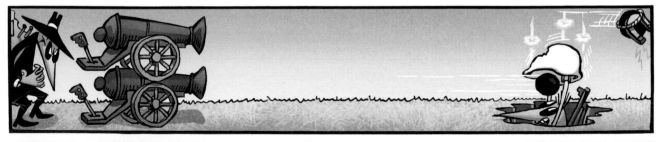

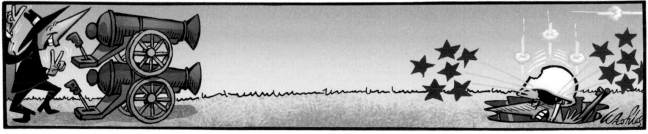

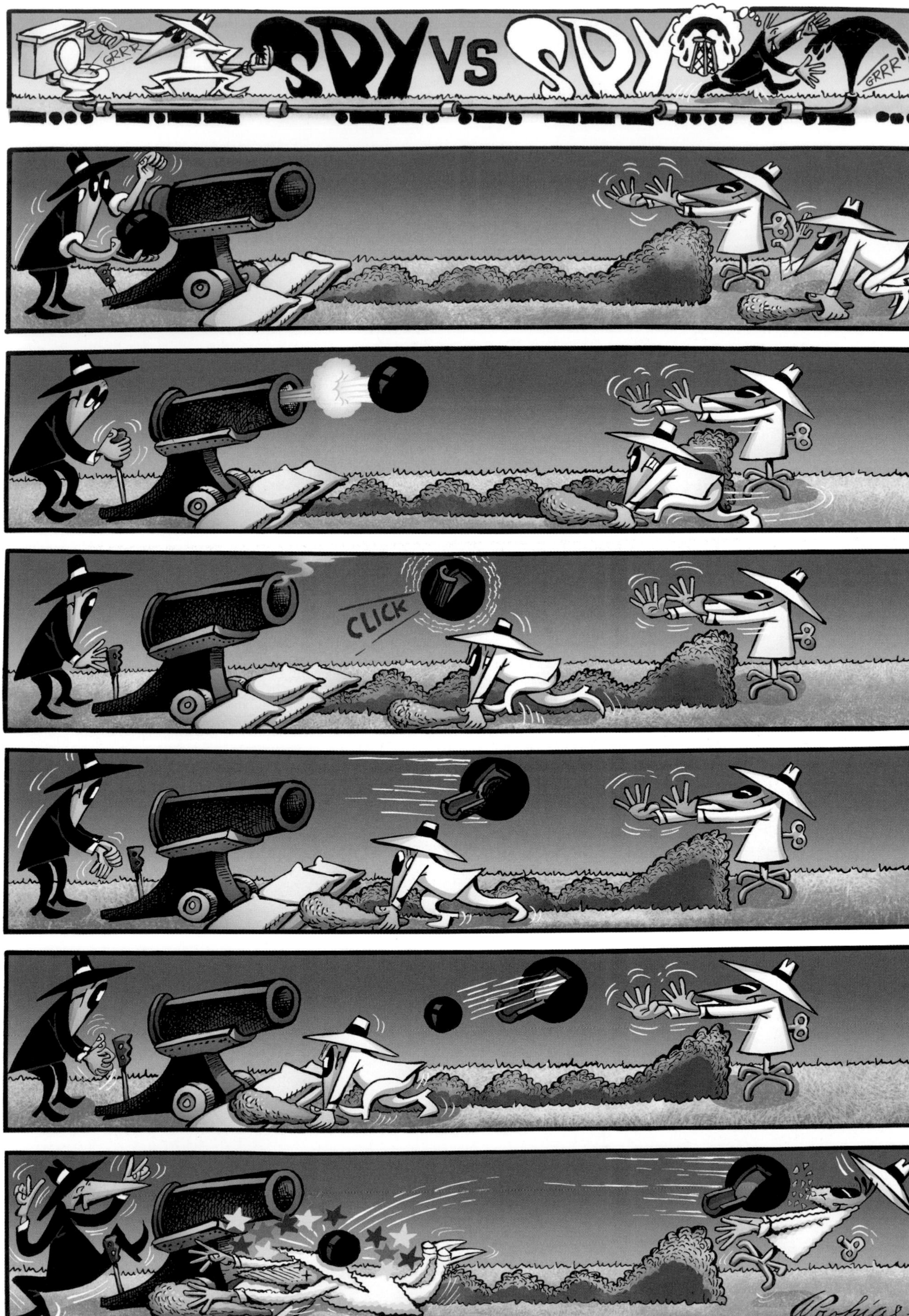
GRRR
SPY VS SPY
GRRR
CLICK
Prohías

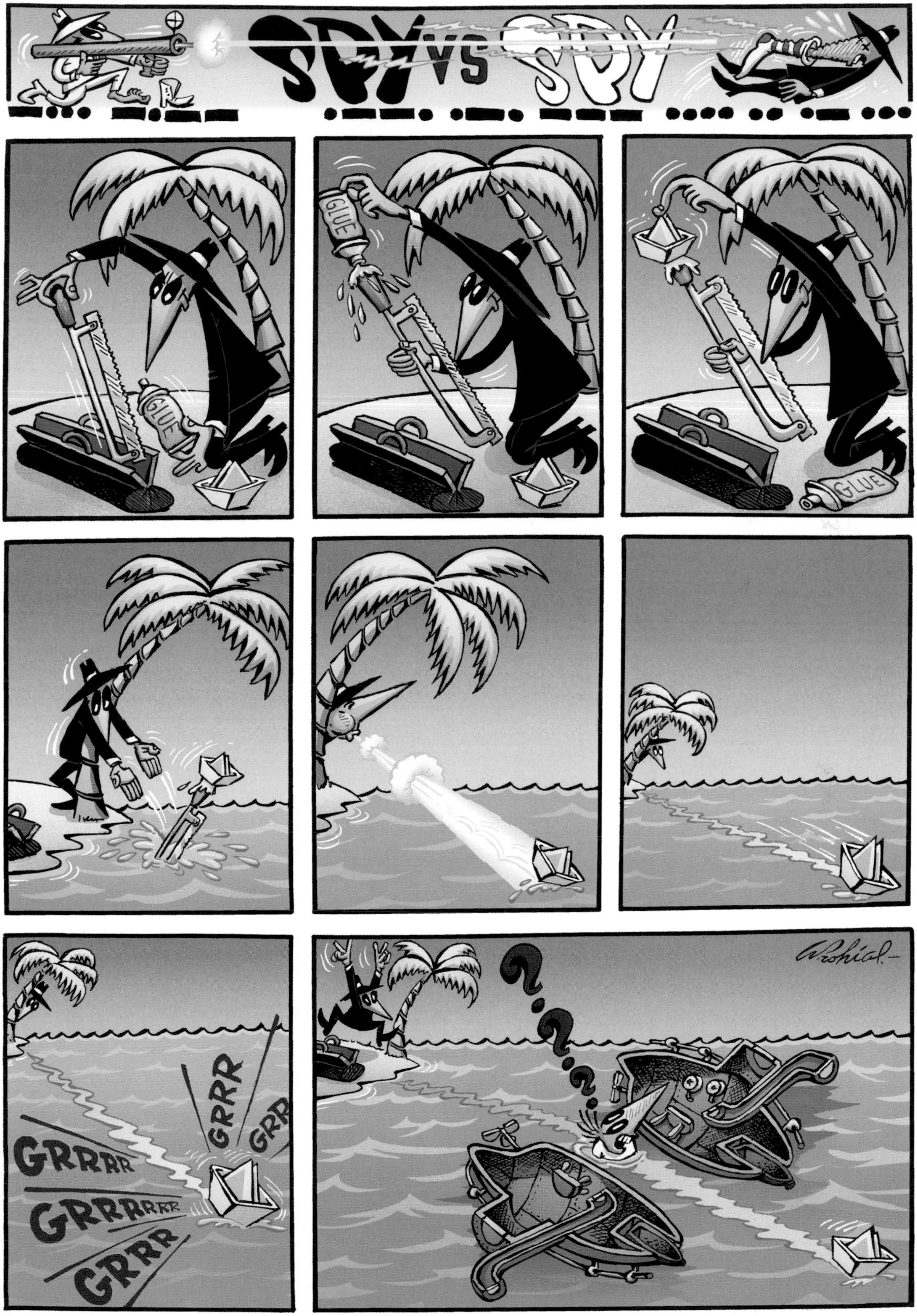
SPY vs SPY
GLUE
GLUE
GLUE
GRRRR
GRR
GRRRRR
GRRRRRRR
GRRR
???

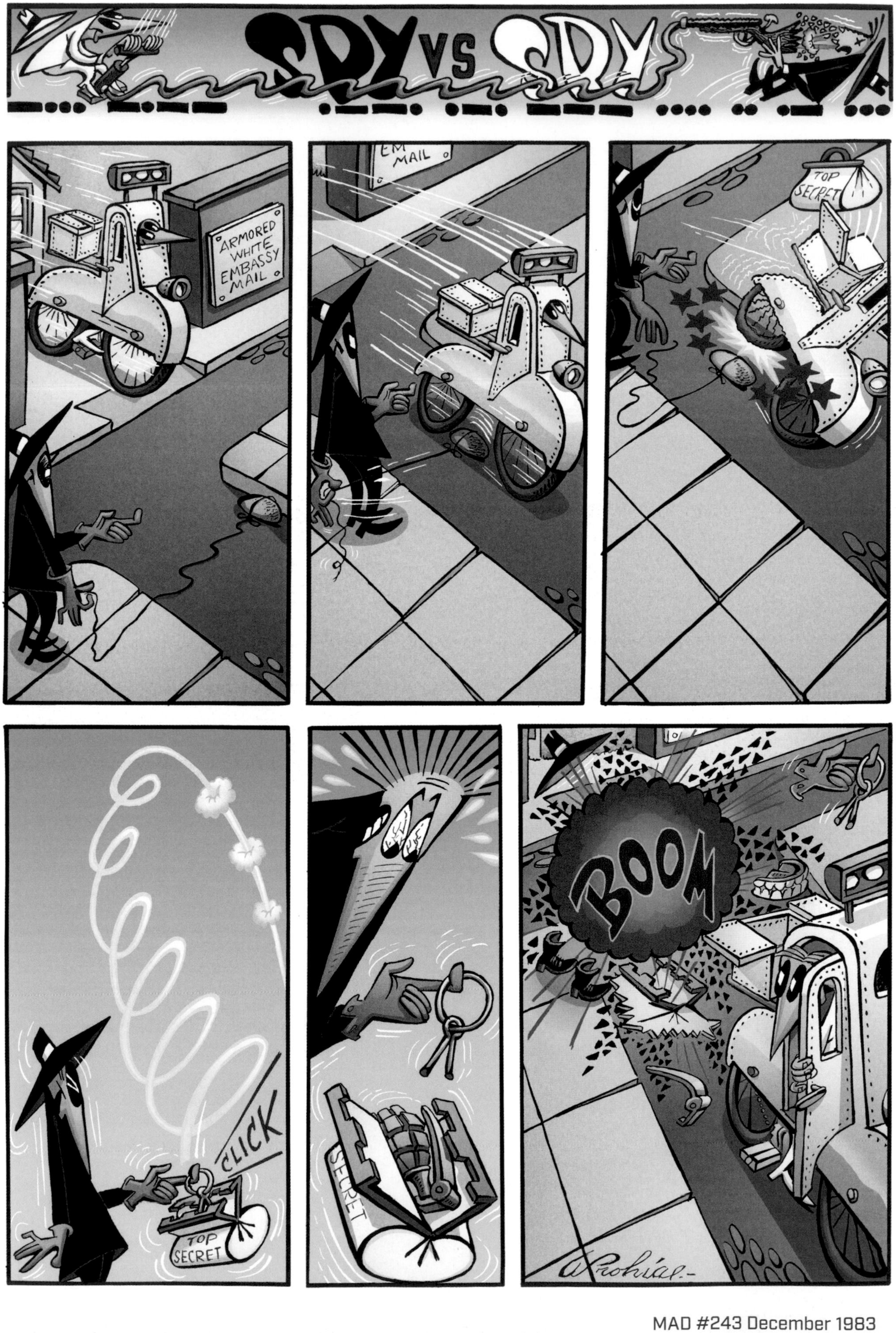
SPY VS SPY
ARMORED WHITE EMBASSY MAIL
MAIL
TOP SECRET
CLICK
TOP SECRET
SECRET
BOOM
A. Prohías

The **Diabolical Duo** of **Double-Cross** and **Deceit** as **Depicted** by **Some** of the **World's Most Renowned Artists**.

THE SPY VS. SPY POSTER COLLECTION

GALLERY IV

Rich Webber

André Carrilho

Tom Bunk

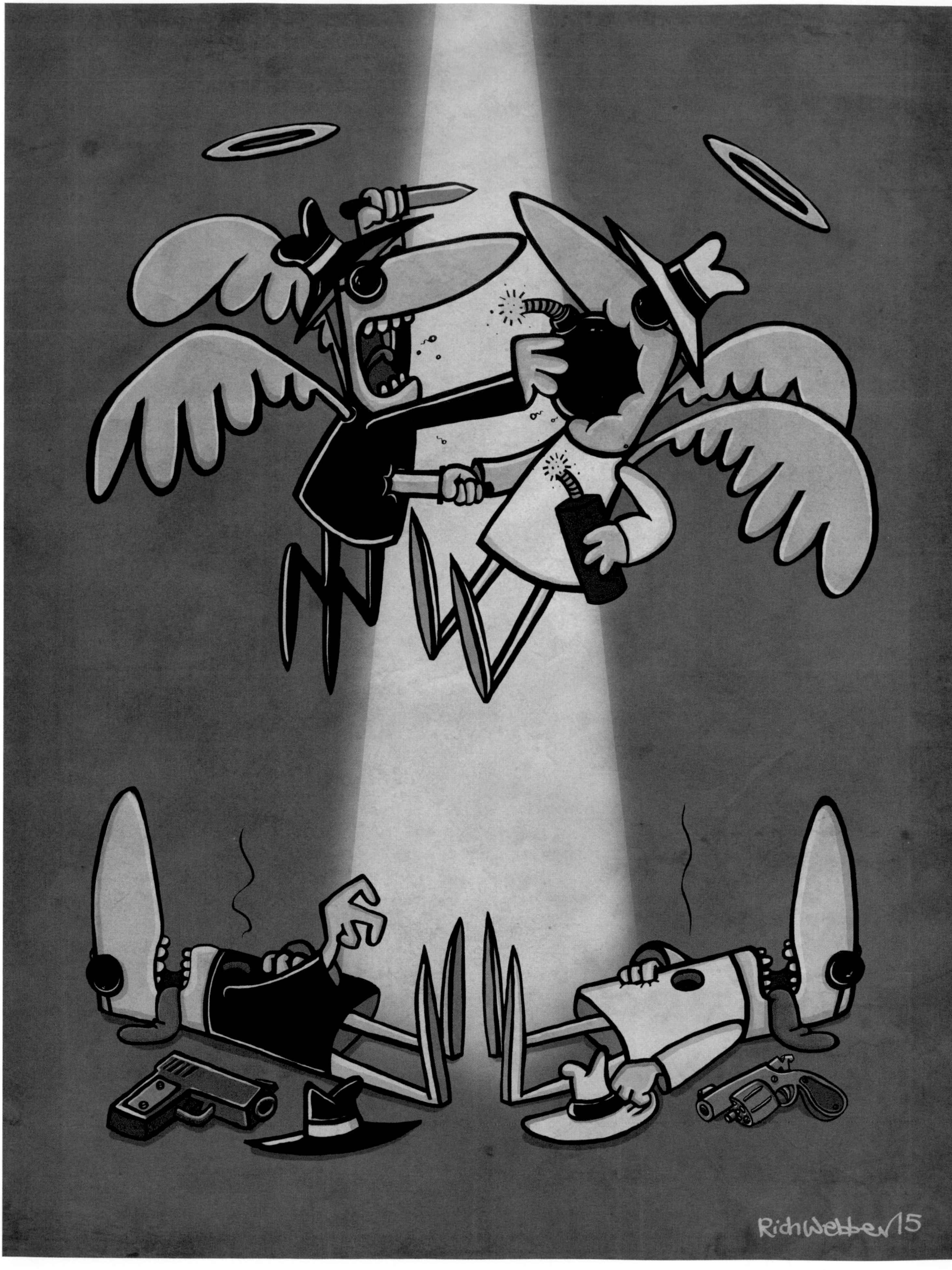
RichWebber/15

Rich Webber

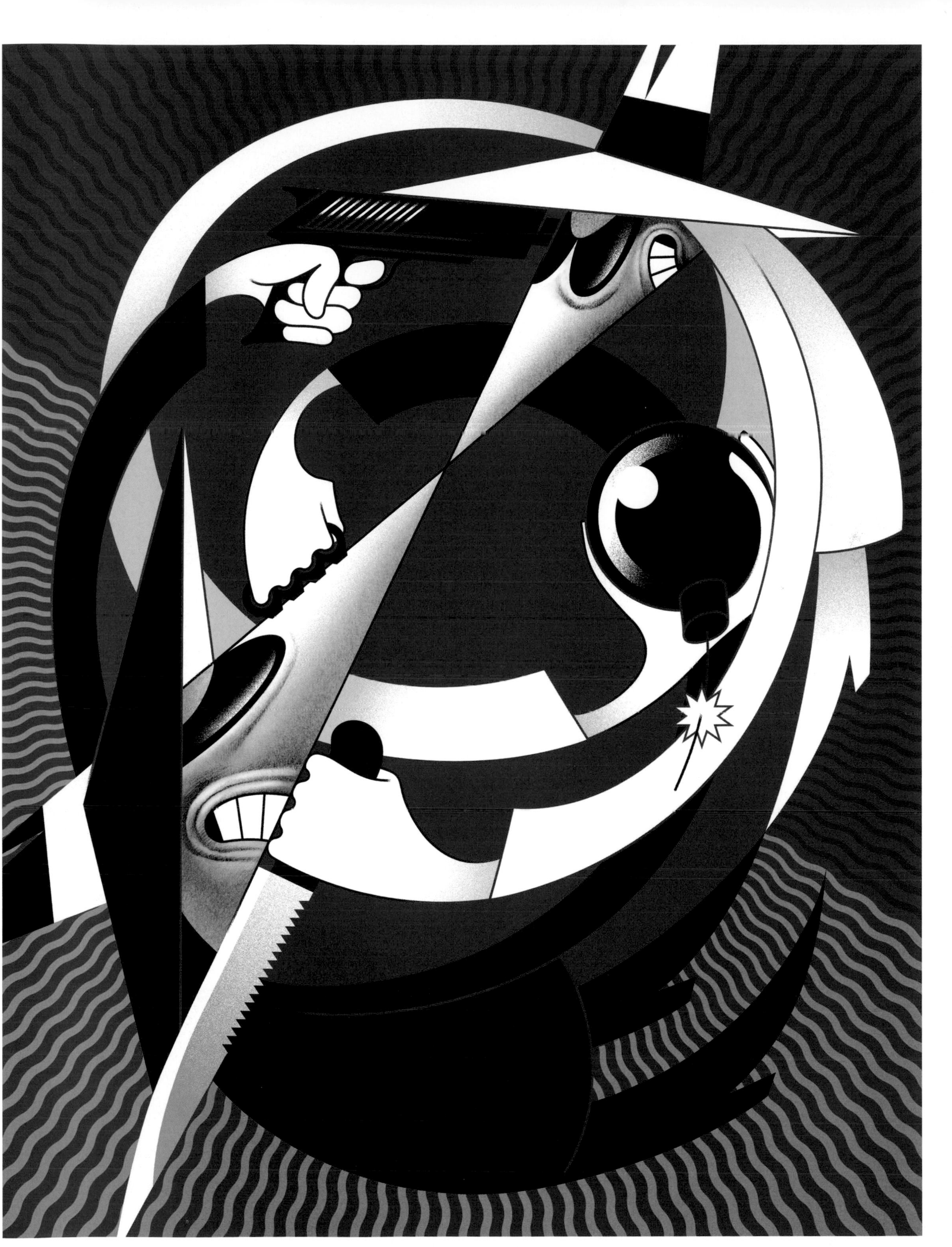

André Carrilho

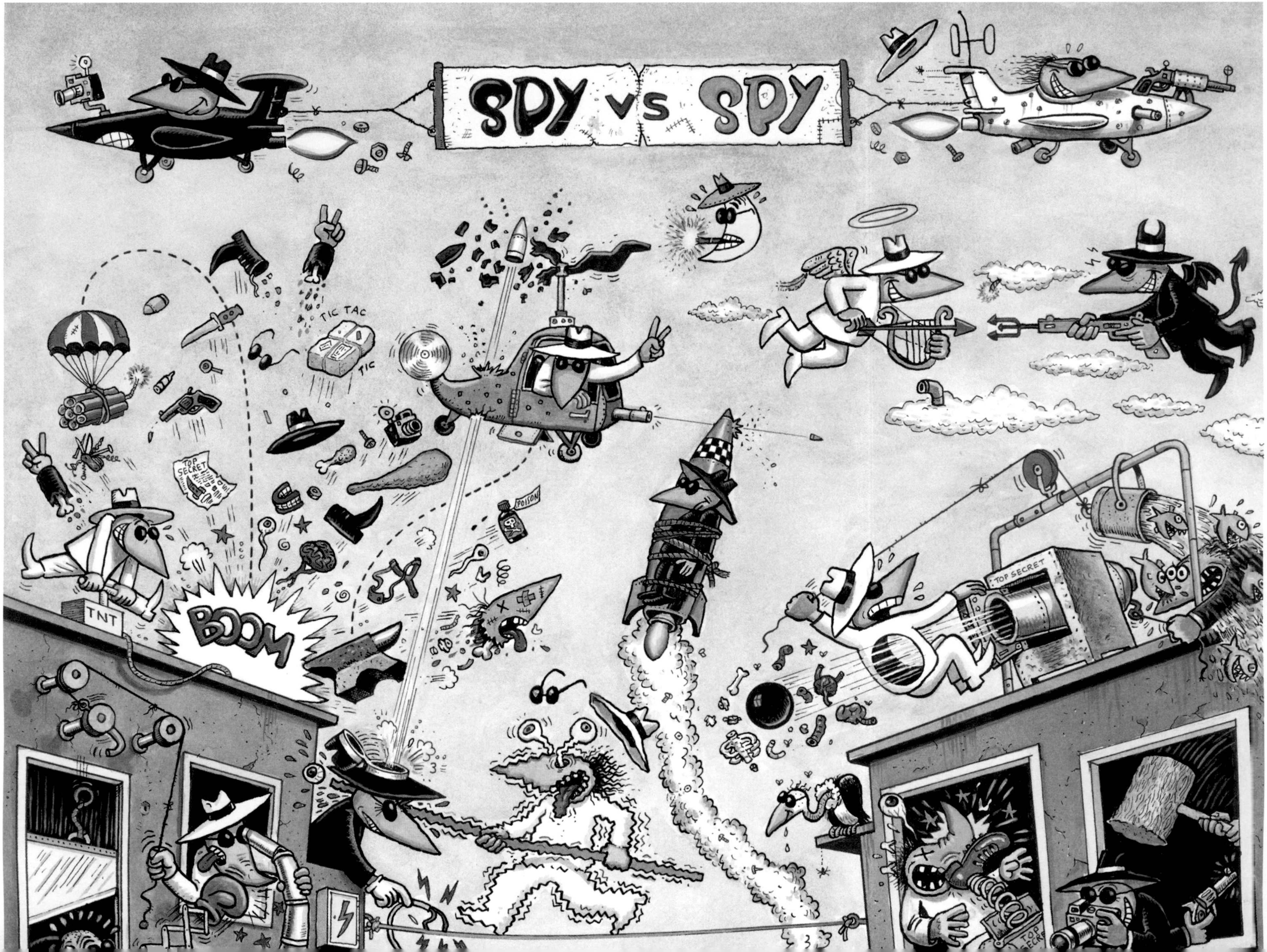

SPY vs SPY
TIC TAC
TIC
TOP SECRET
POISON
TNT
BOOM
TOP SECRET
TOP SECRET

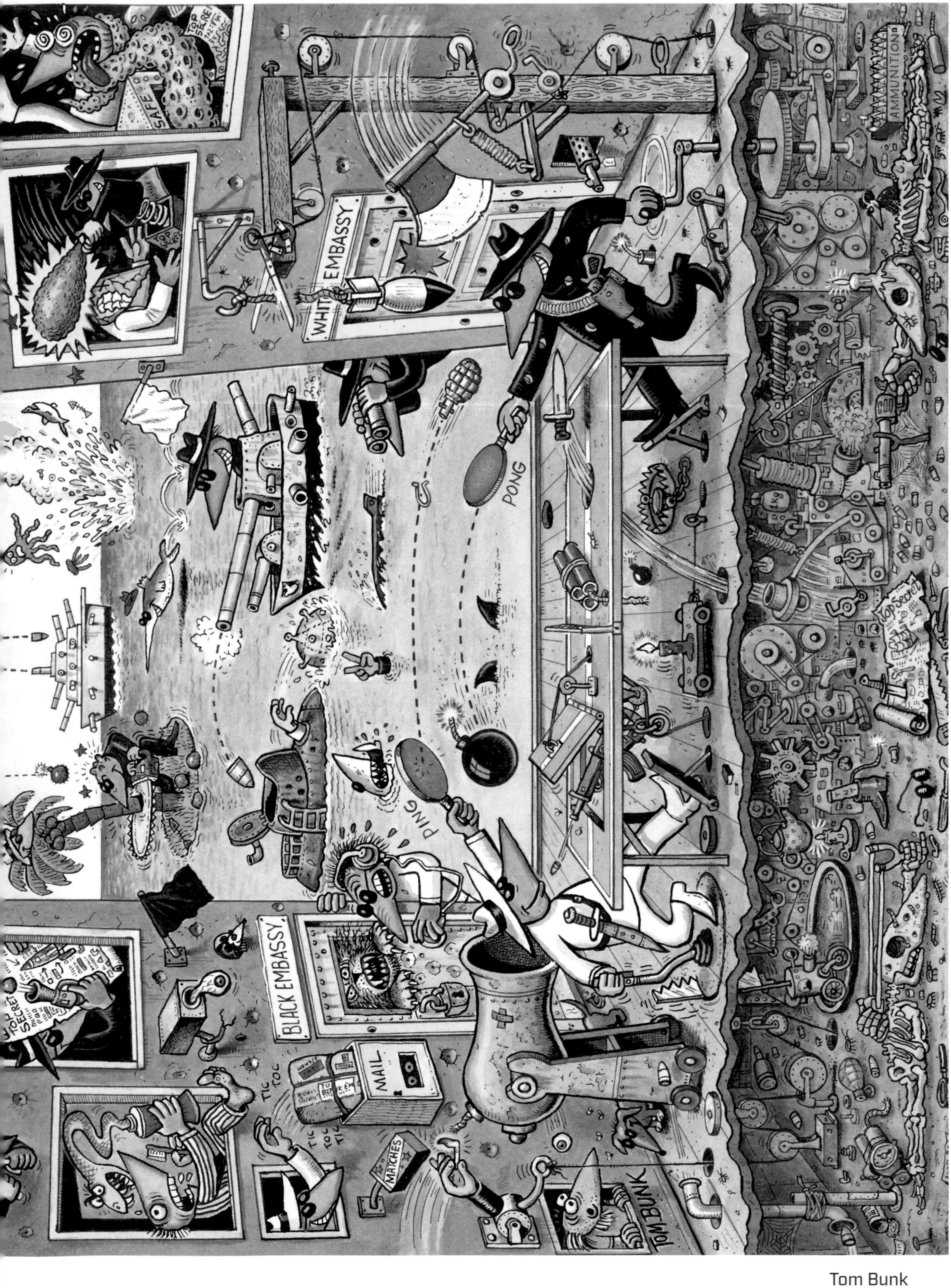
SAFE
TOP SECRET
WHITE EMBASSY
AMMUNITION
PONG
PING
BLACK EMBASSY
TOP SECRET
MAIL
TIC TOC
TIC TOC
MATCHES
TOM BUNK

Tom Bunk

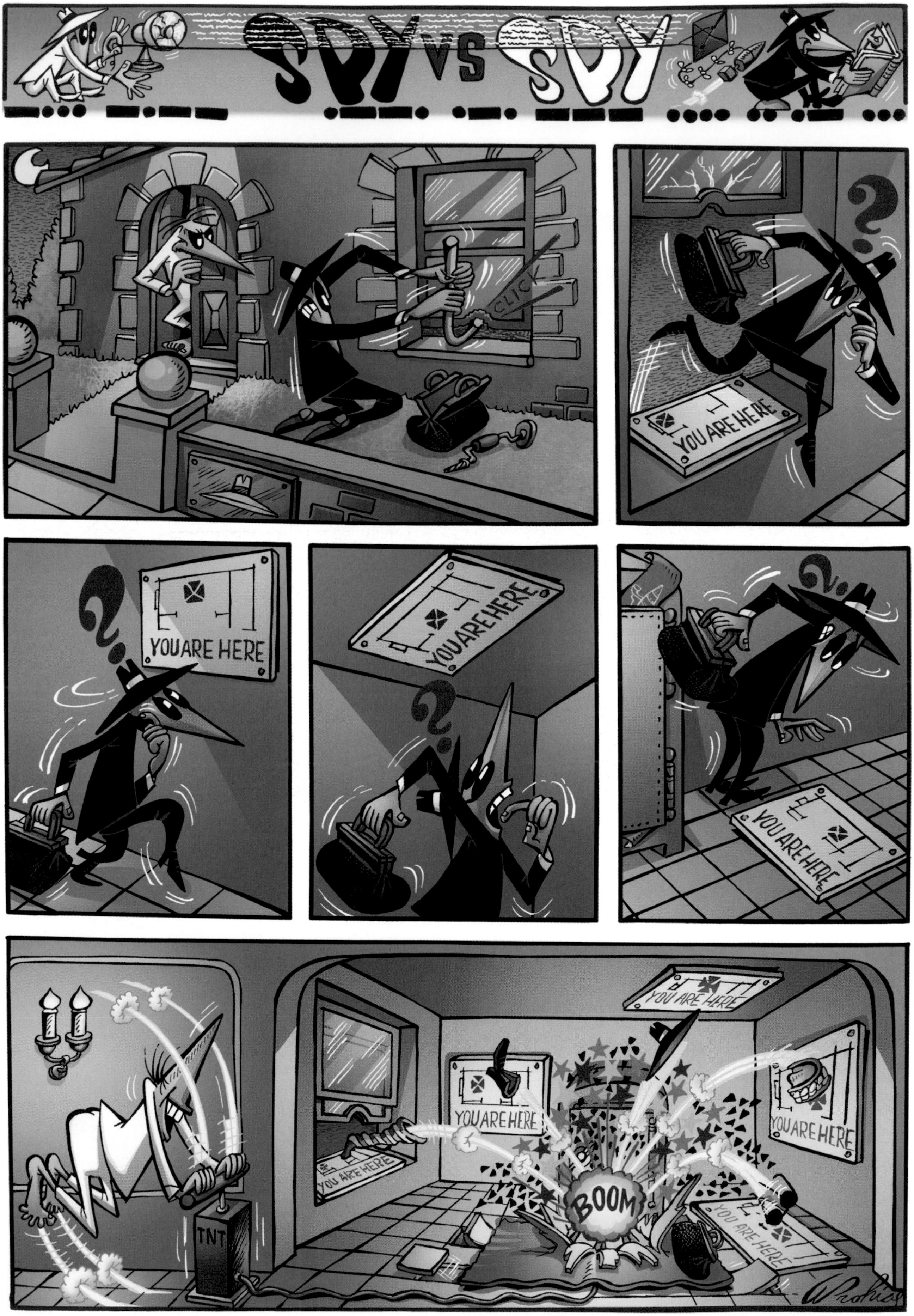
SPY VS SPY
CLICK
YOU ARE HERE
YOU ARE HERE
YOU ARE HERE
YOU ARE HERE
TNT
YOU ARE HERE
YOU ARE HERE
YOU ARE HERE
YOU ARE HERE
YOU ARE HERE
BOOM

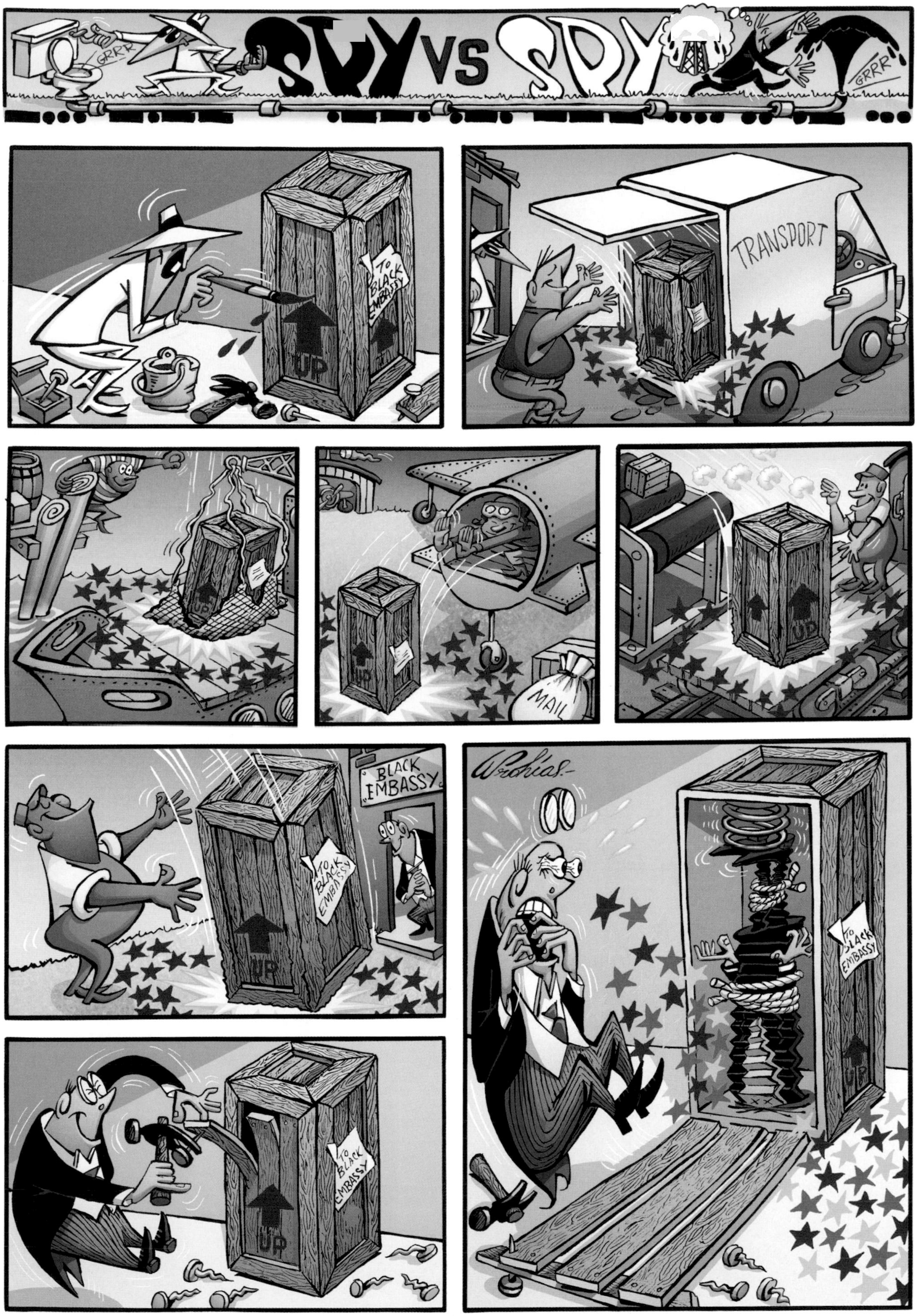
GRRR
VS SPY
GRRR
TO BLACK EMBASSY
UP
TRANSPORT
MAIL
BLACK EMBASSY
Prohias

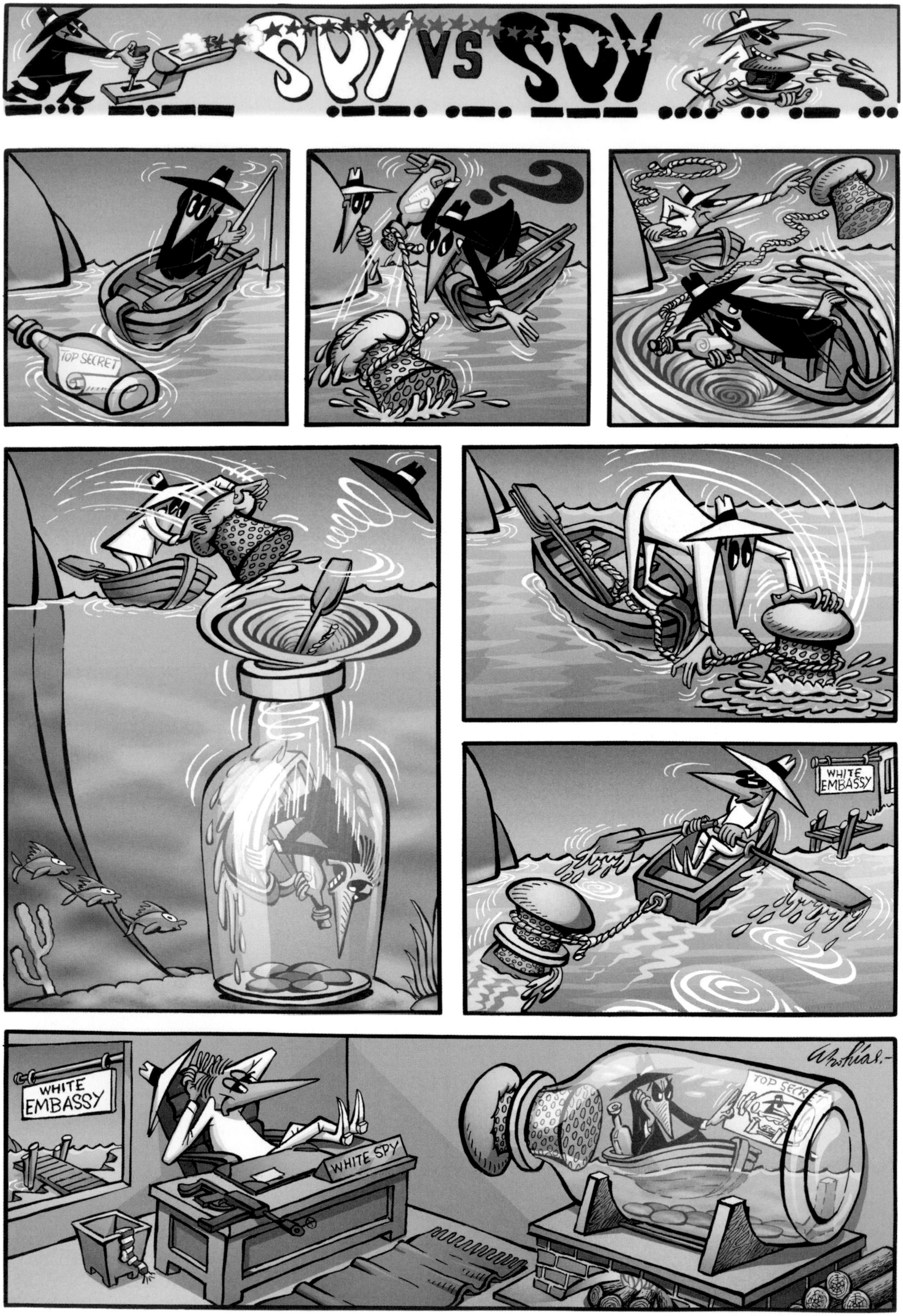
SPY VS SPY
TOP SECRET
WHITE EMBASSY
WHITE EMBASSY
WHITE SPY
TOP SECRET

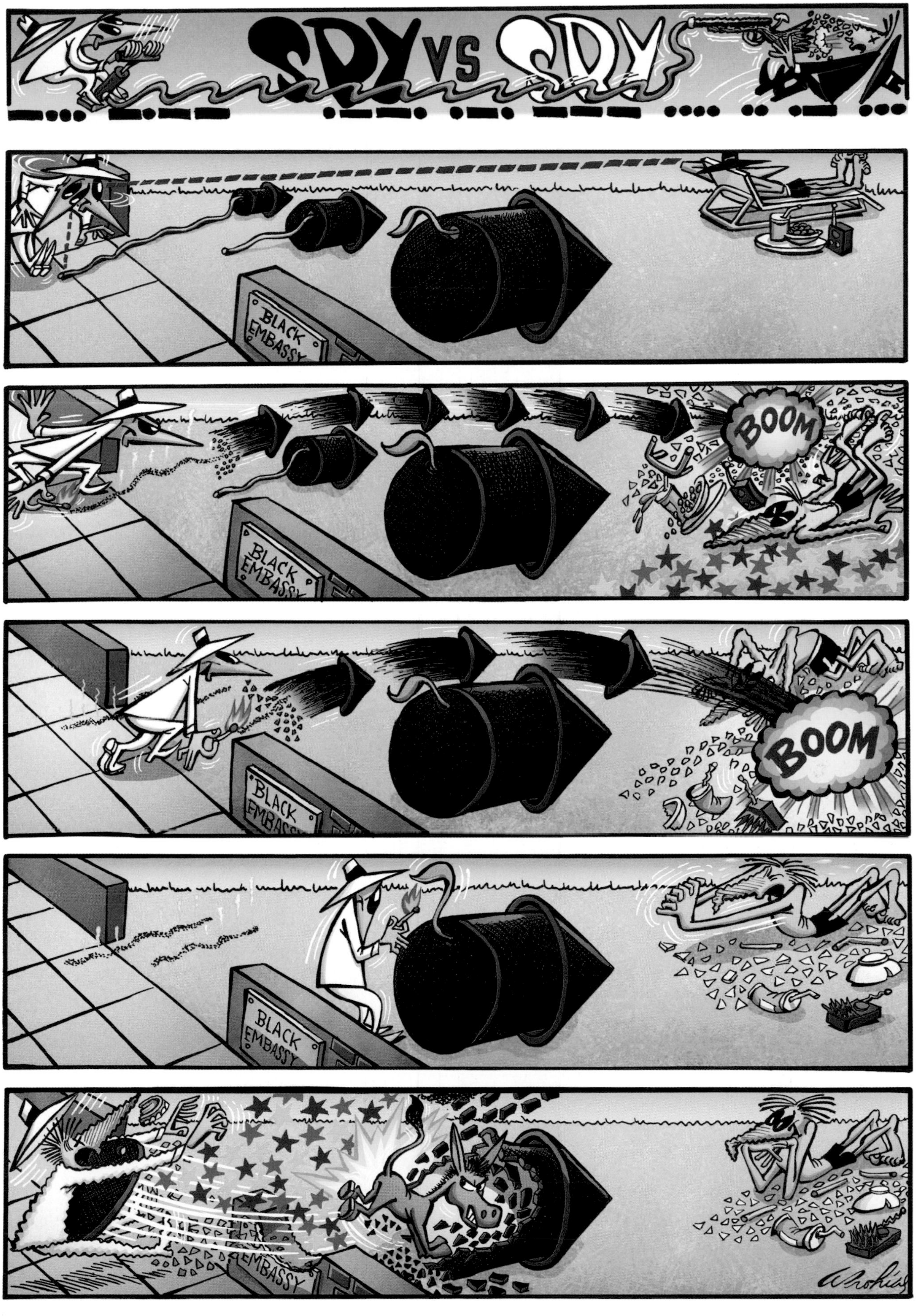
SPY vs SPY
BLACK EMBASSY
BOOM
BLACK EMBASSY
BOOM
BLACK EMBASSY
BLACK EMBASSY
EMBASSY

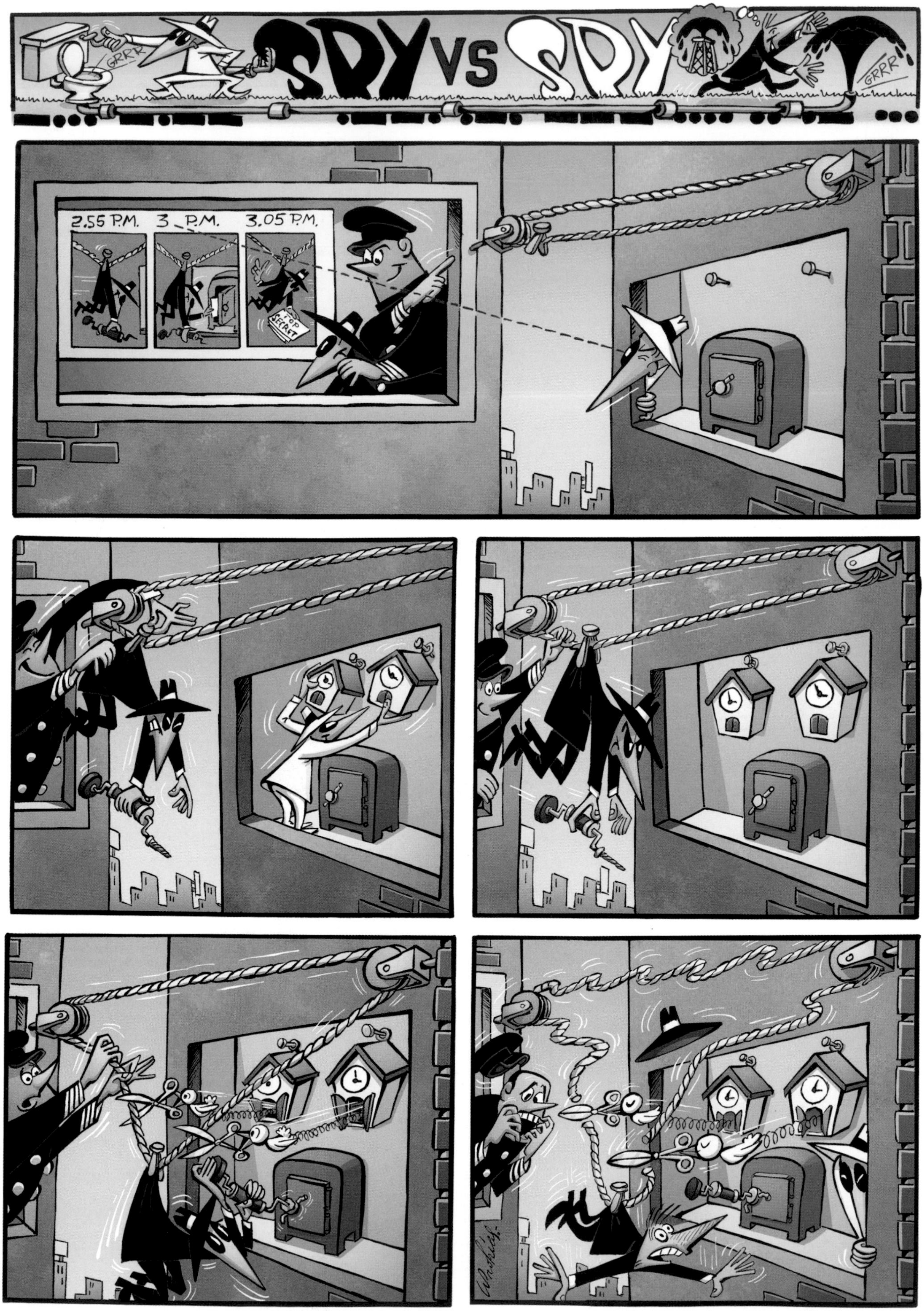
SPY VS SPY
GRRR
GRRR
2.55 P.M.
3 P.M.
3.05 P.M.
TOP SECRET

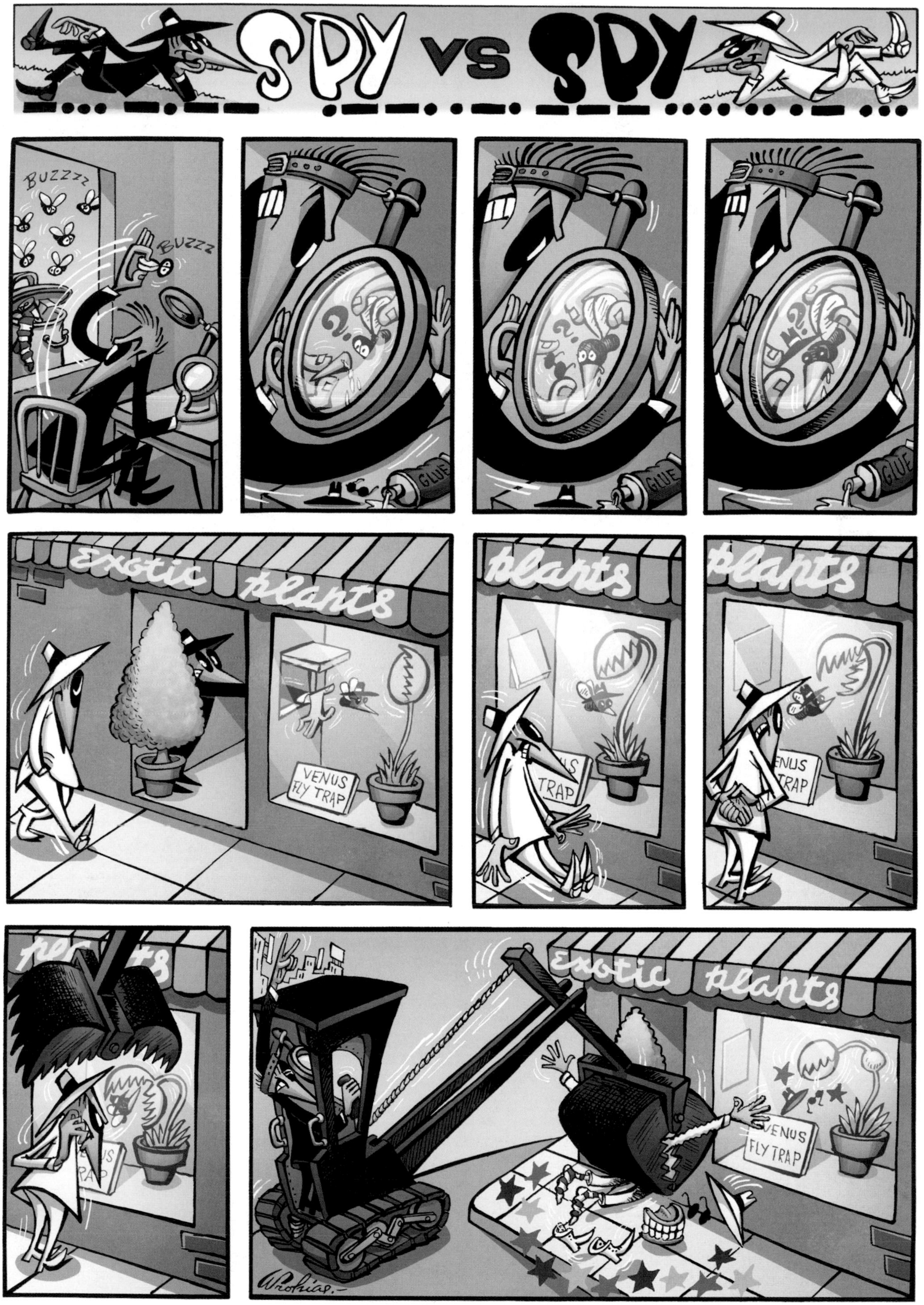
SPY vs SPY
BUZZZZ
BUZZZ
GLUE
GLUE
GLUE
Exotic plants
VENUS FLY TRAP
plants
VENUS FLY TRAP
plants
VENUS FLY TRAP
Exotic plants
VENUS FLY TRAP
Prohias

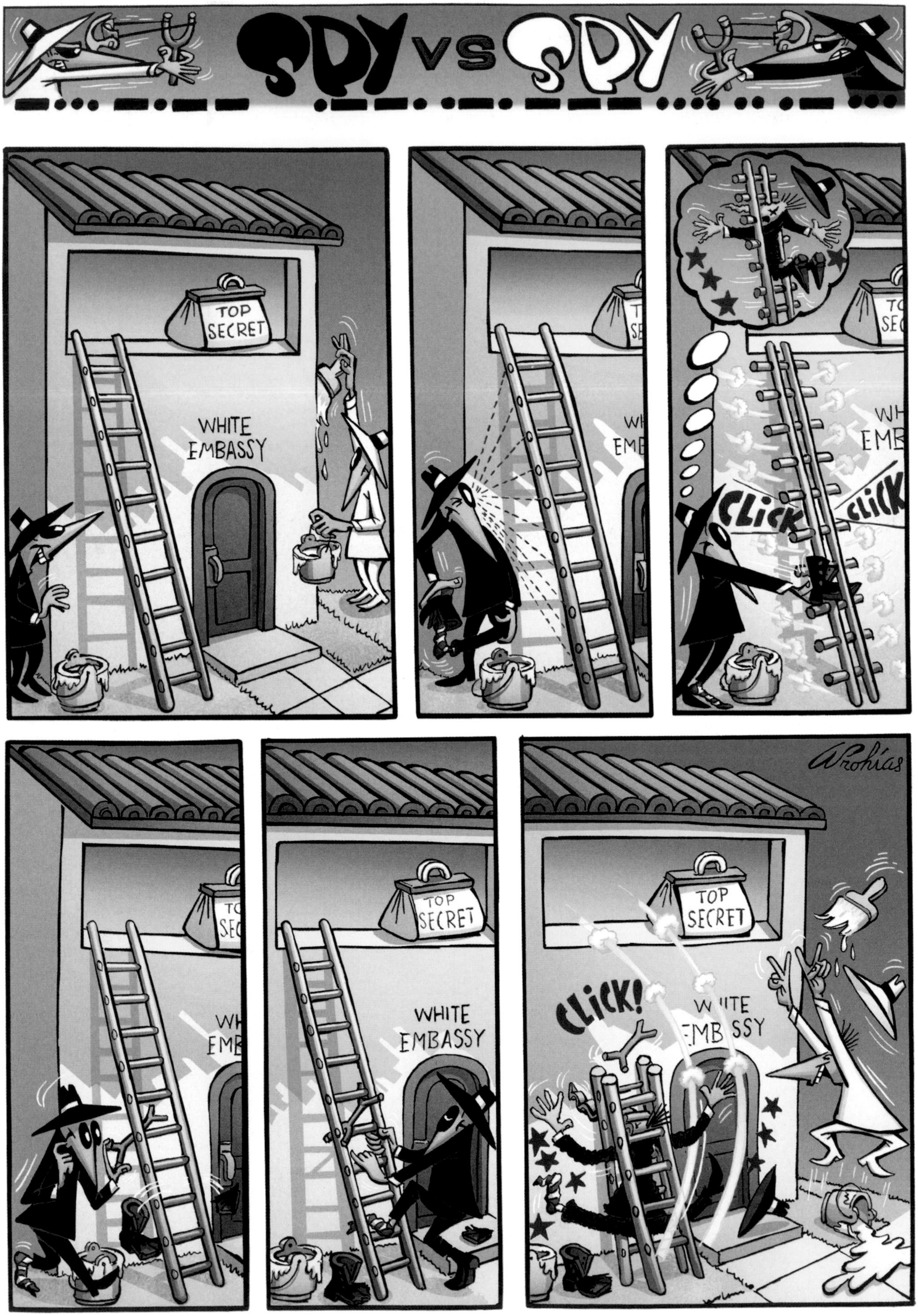
SPY vs SPY
TOP SECRET
WHITE EMBASSY
CLICK
CLICK
CLICK!
Prohías

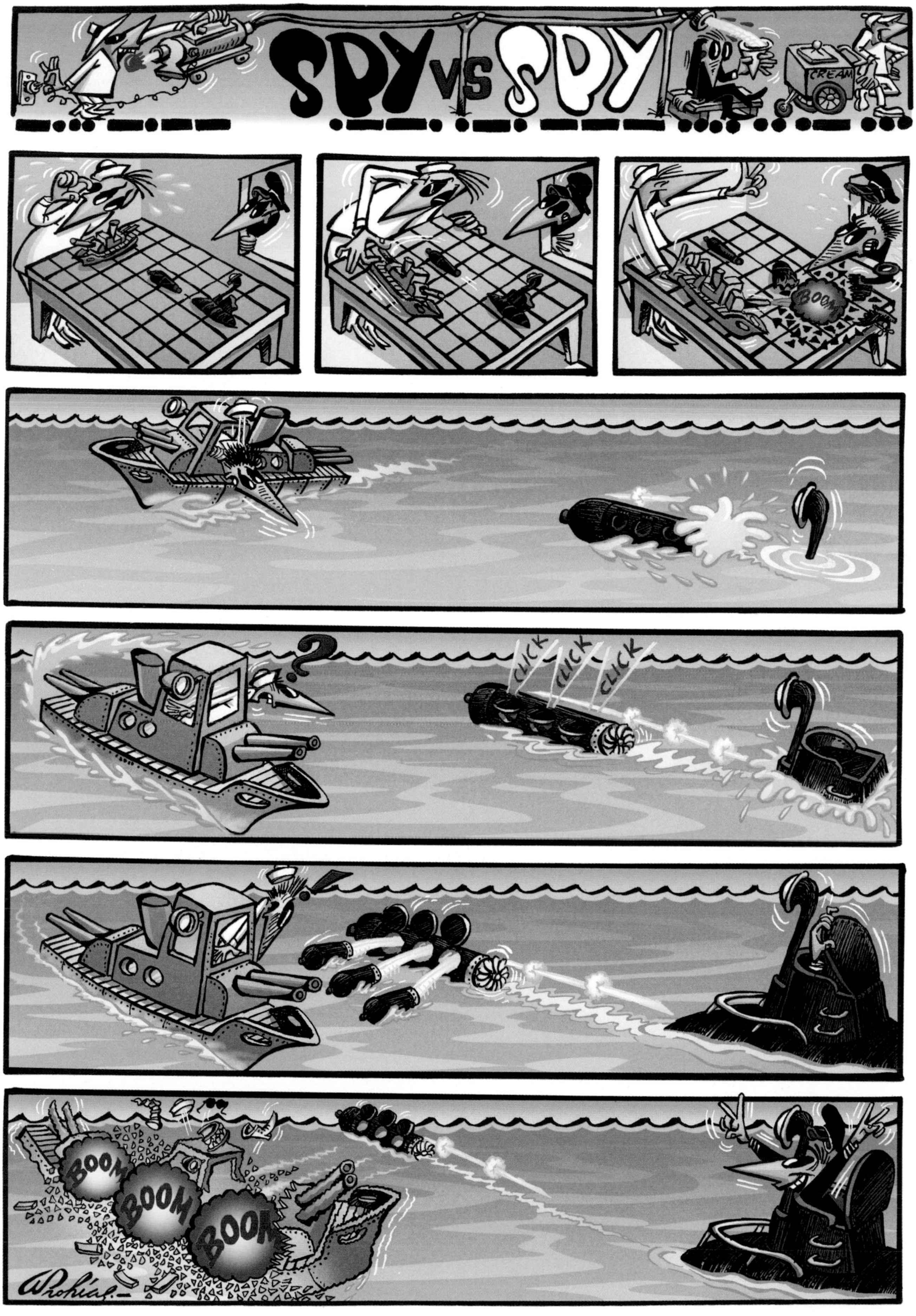
SPY vs SPY
CREAM
BOOM
CLICK
CLICK
CLICK
BOOM
BOOM
BOOM

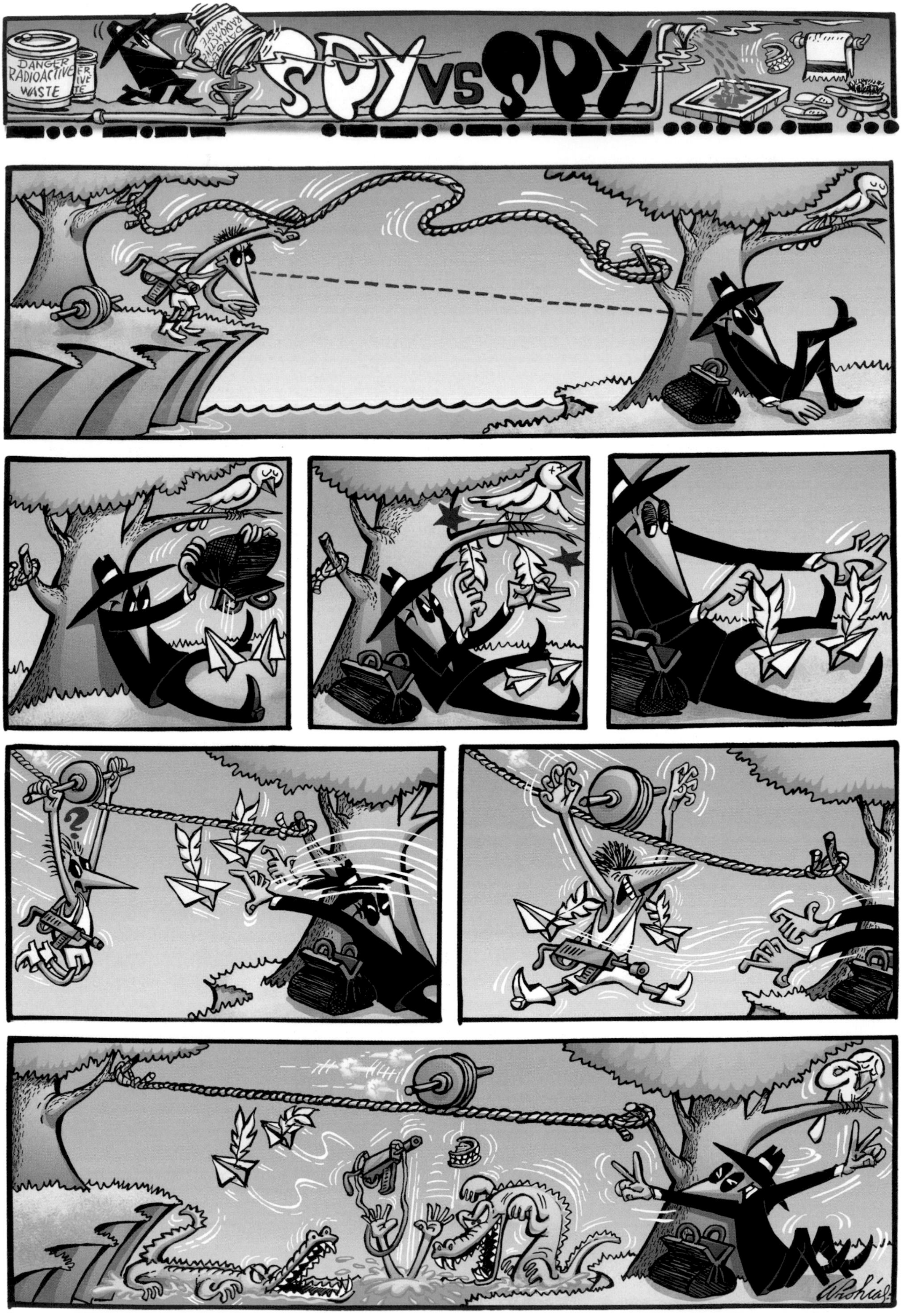
SPY vs SPY
DANGER RADIOACTIVE WASTE
DANGER RADIOACTIVE WASTE

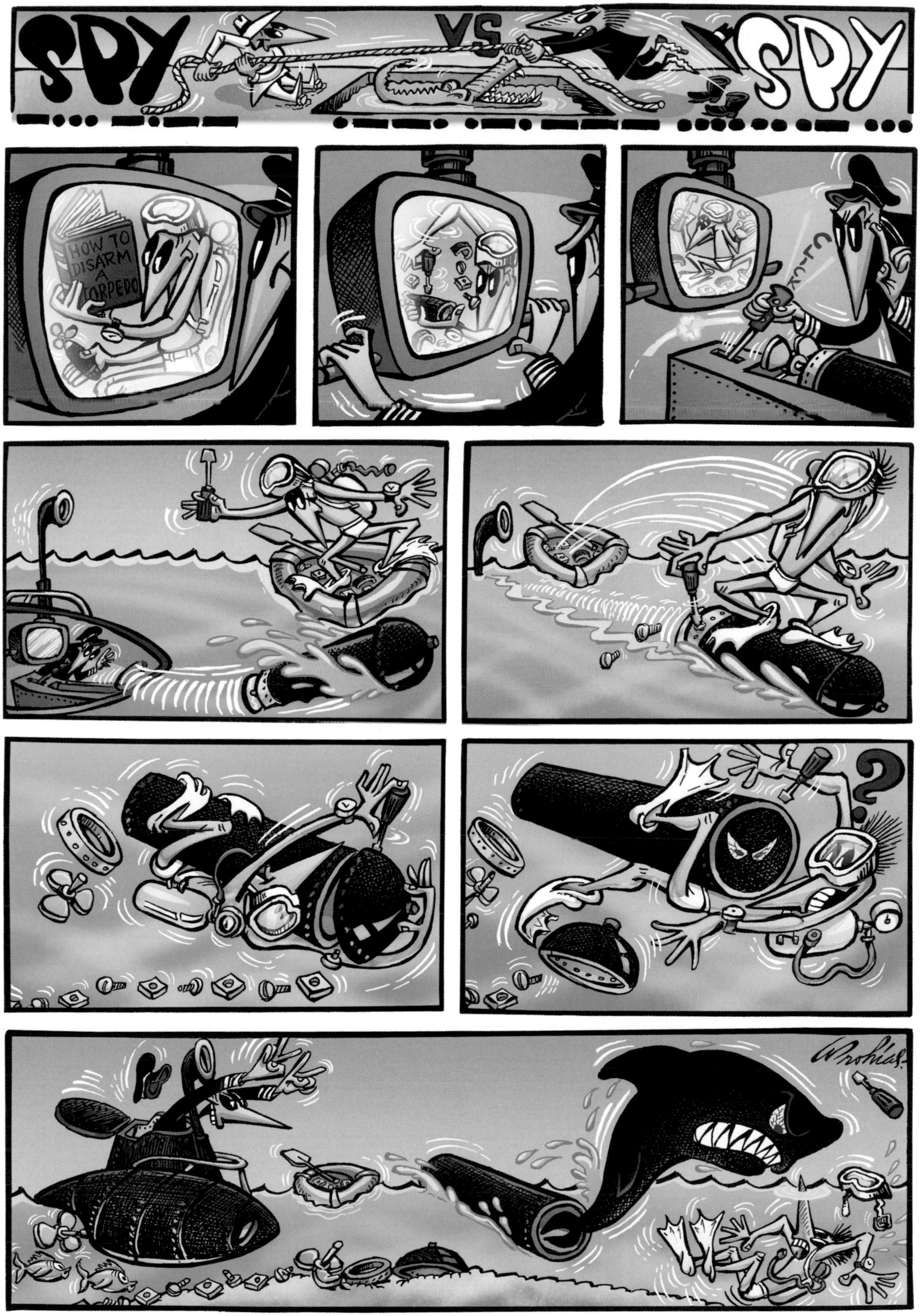
SPY VS SPY
HOW TO DISARM A TORPEDO
CLICK
?

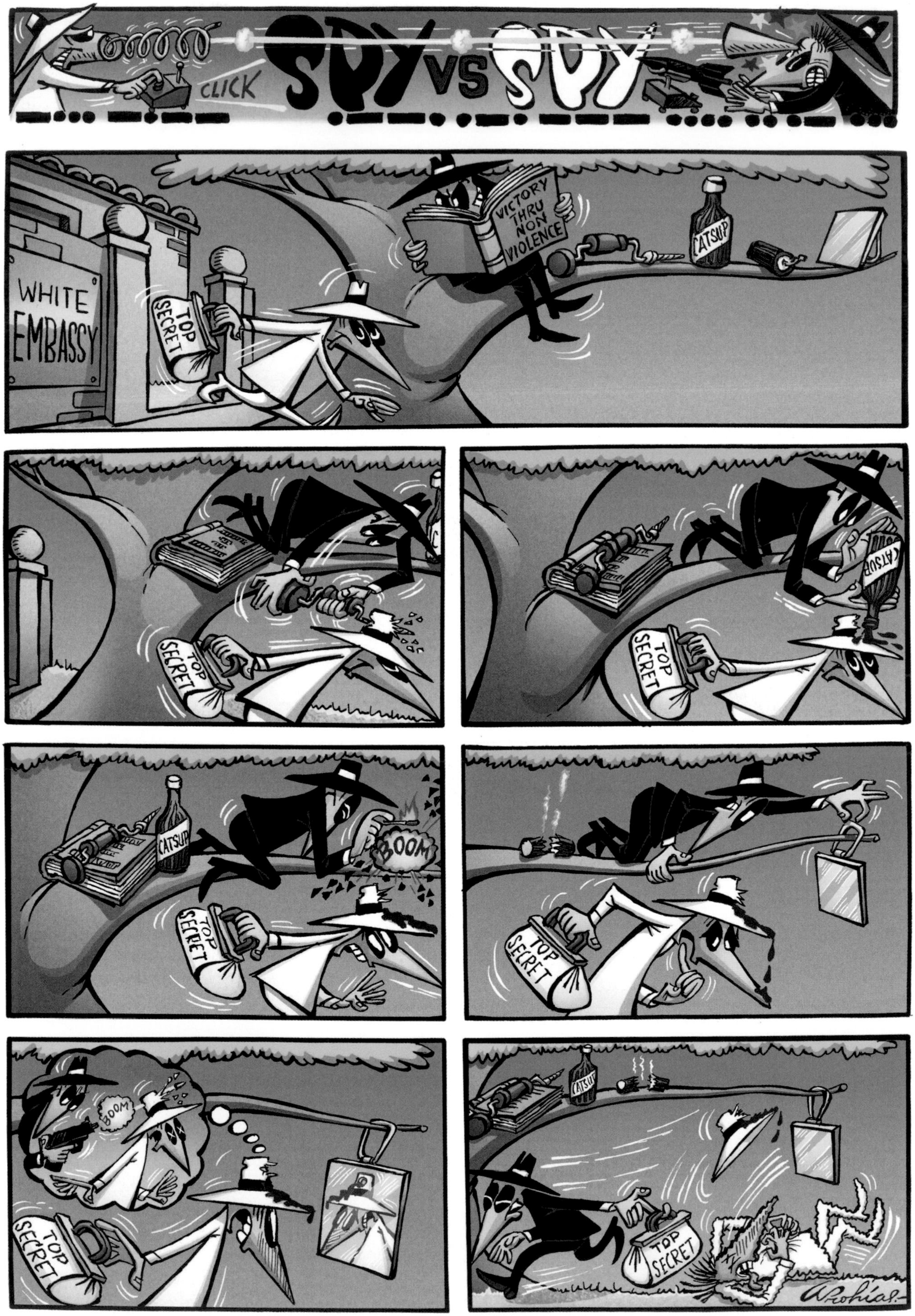
CLICK
SPY vs SPY
WHITE EMBASSY
TOP SECRET
VICTORY THRU NON VIOLENCE
CATSUP
TOP SECRET
TOP SECRET
CATSUP
CATSUP
BOOM
TOP SECRET
TOP SECRET
BOOM
TOP SECRET
CATSUP
TOP SECRET
Prohias

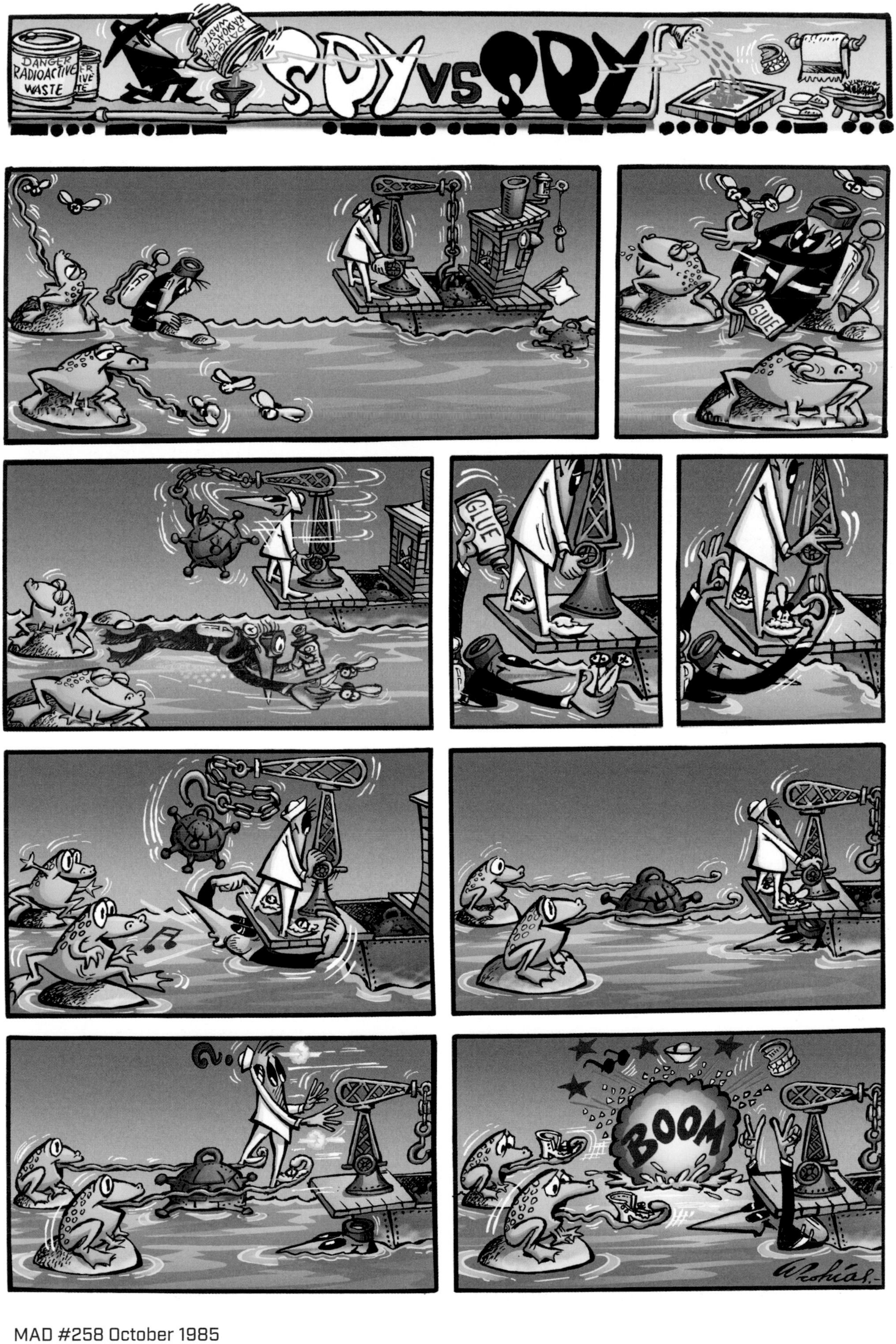
SPY VS SPY
DANGER RADIOACTIVE WASTE
GLUE
GLUE
BOOM
Prohias

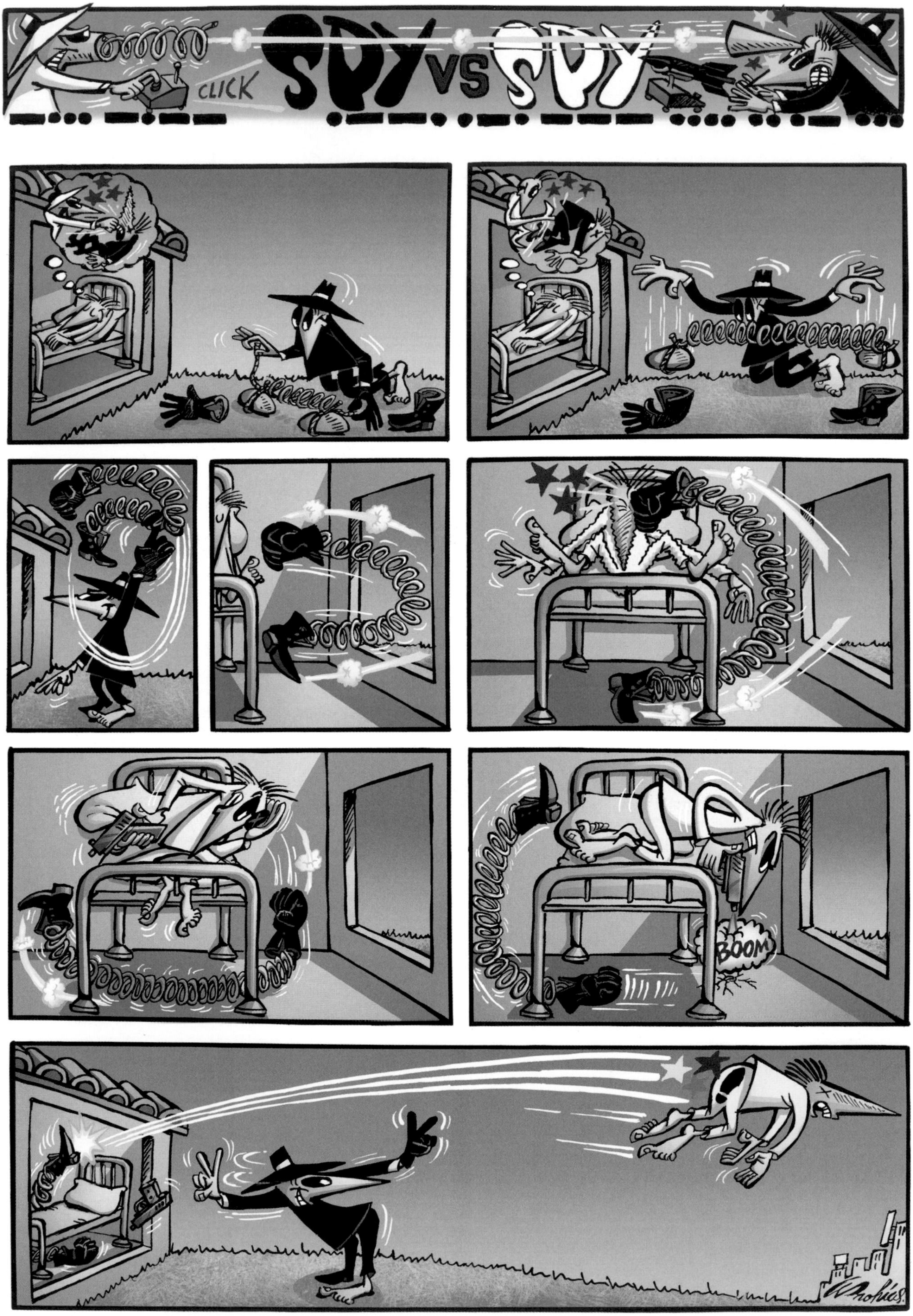
CLICK
SPY VS SPY
BOOM
Prohías

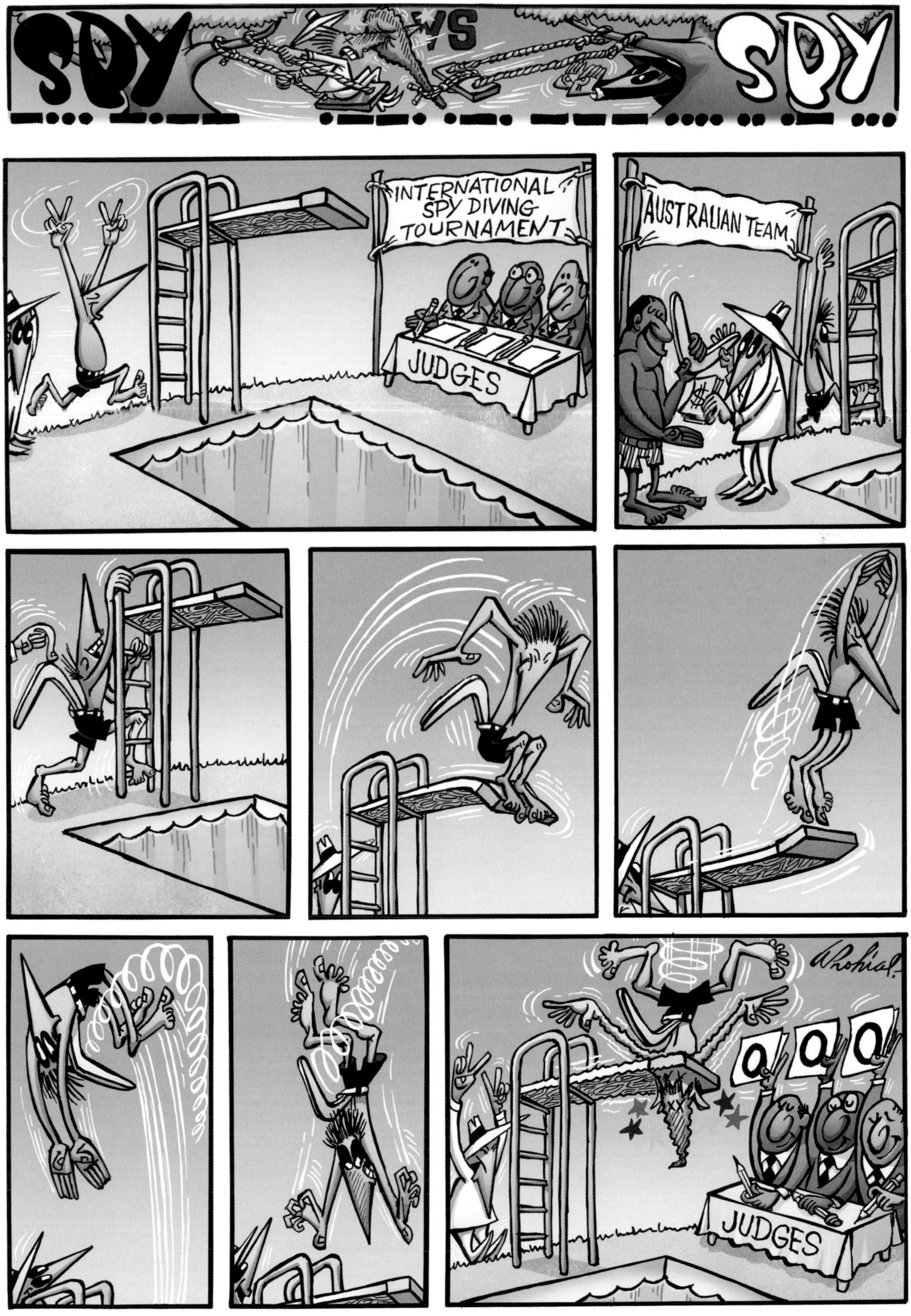
SPY vs SPY
INTERNATIONAL SPY DIVING TOURNAMENT
JUDGES
AUSTRALIAN TEAM
JUDGES
0 0 0

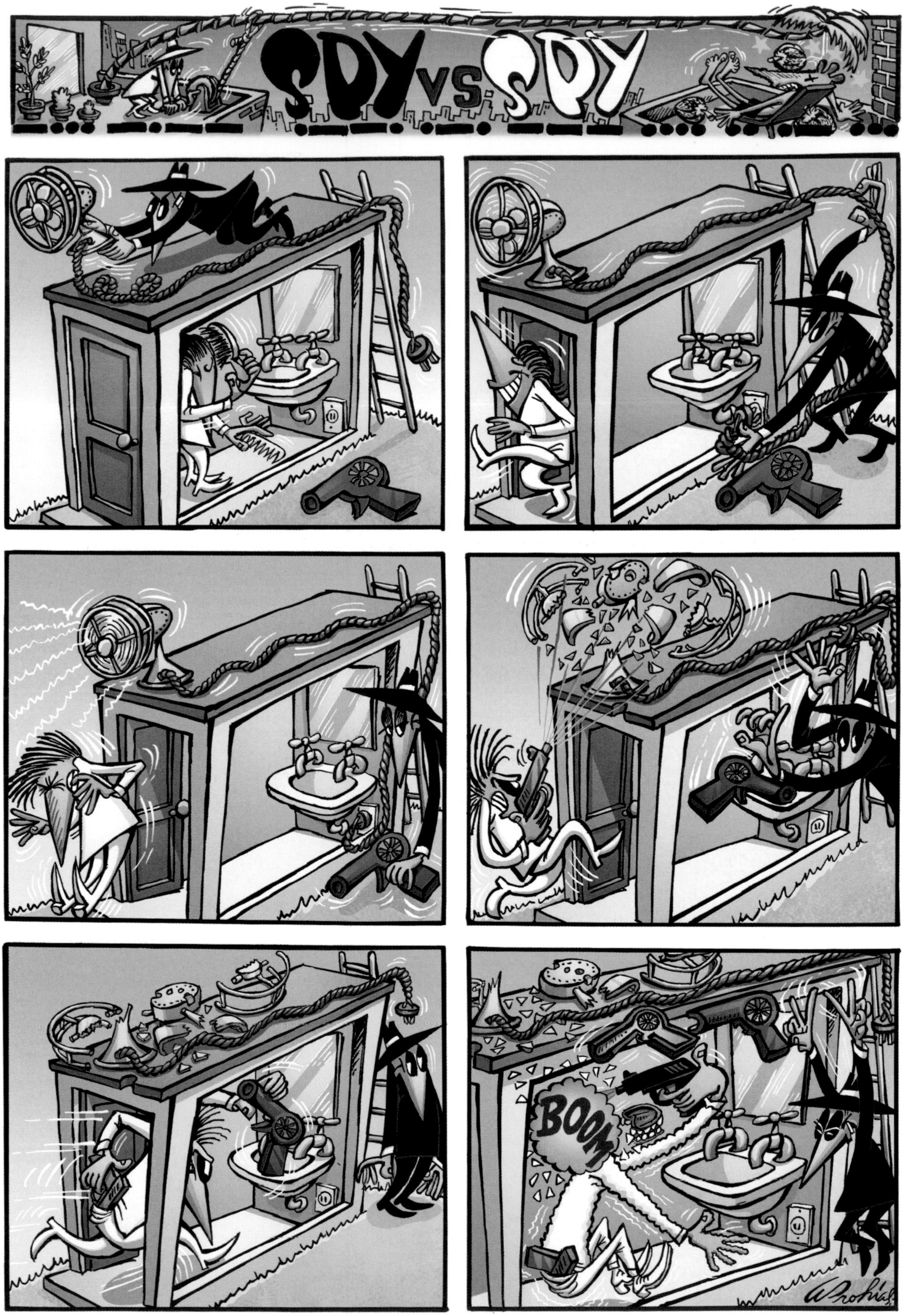
SPY vs SPY
BOOM

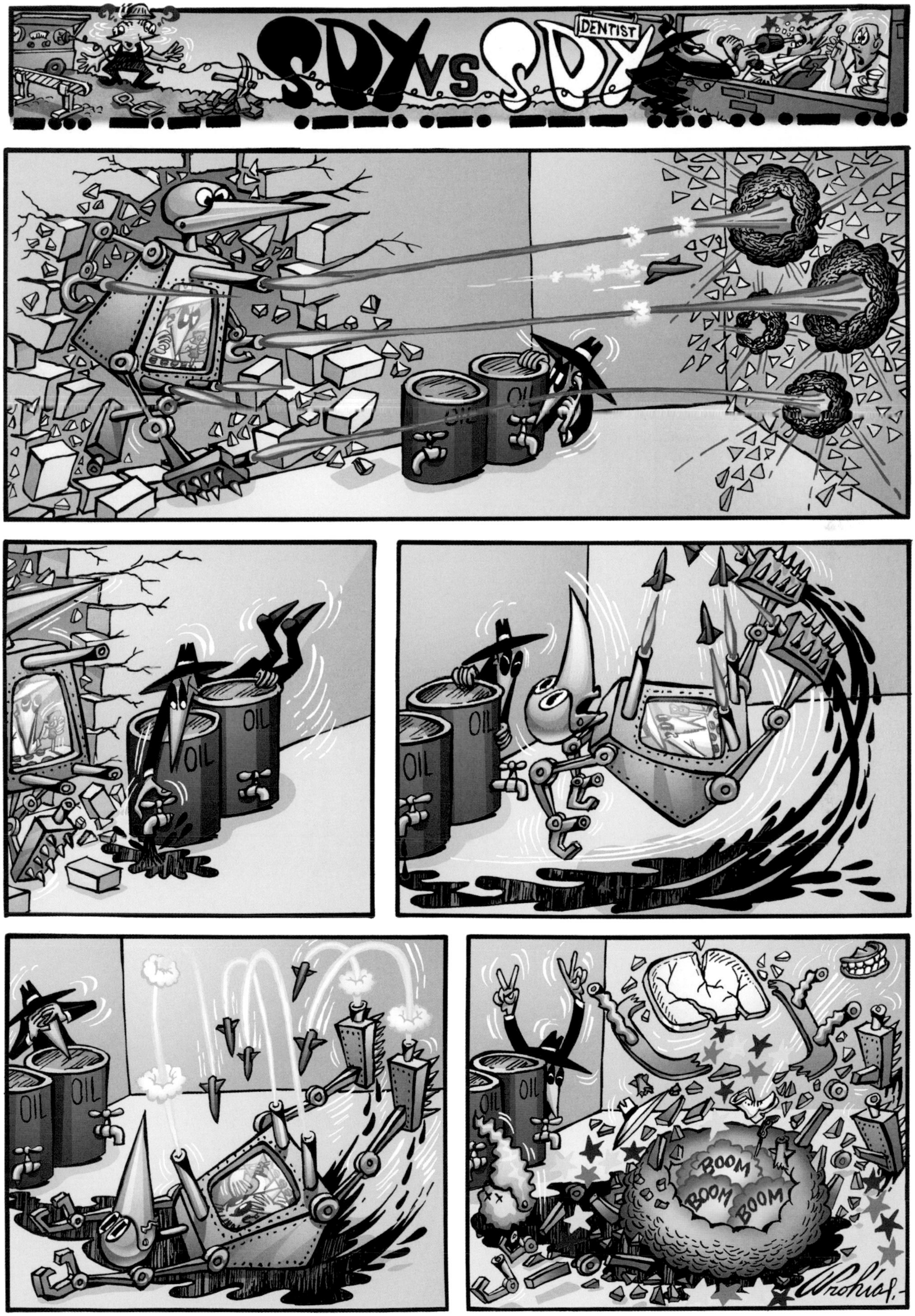
SPY vs SPY
DENTIST
OIL
OIL
BOOM
BOOM
BOOM
Prohías

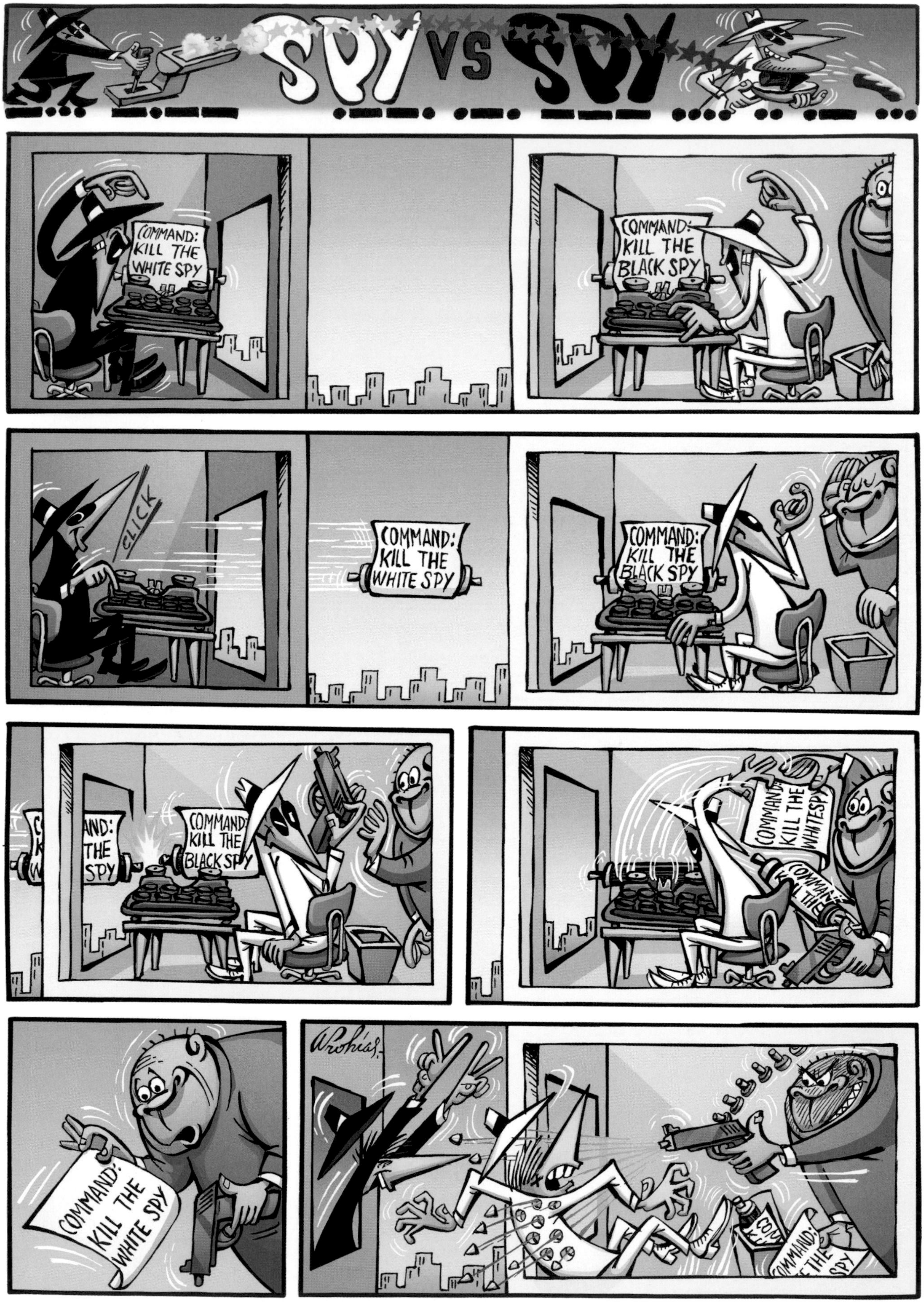
SPY VS SPY
COMMAND: KILL THE WHITE SPY
COMMAND: KILL THE BLACK SPY
CLICK
COMMAND: KILL THE WHITE SPY
COMMAND: KILL THE BLACK SPY
COMMAND: KILL THE BLACK SPY
COMMAND: KILL THE WHITESPY
COMMAND: KILL THE WHITE SPY
Prohias

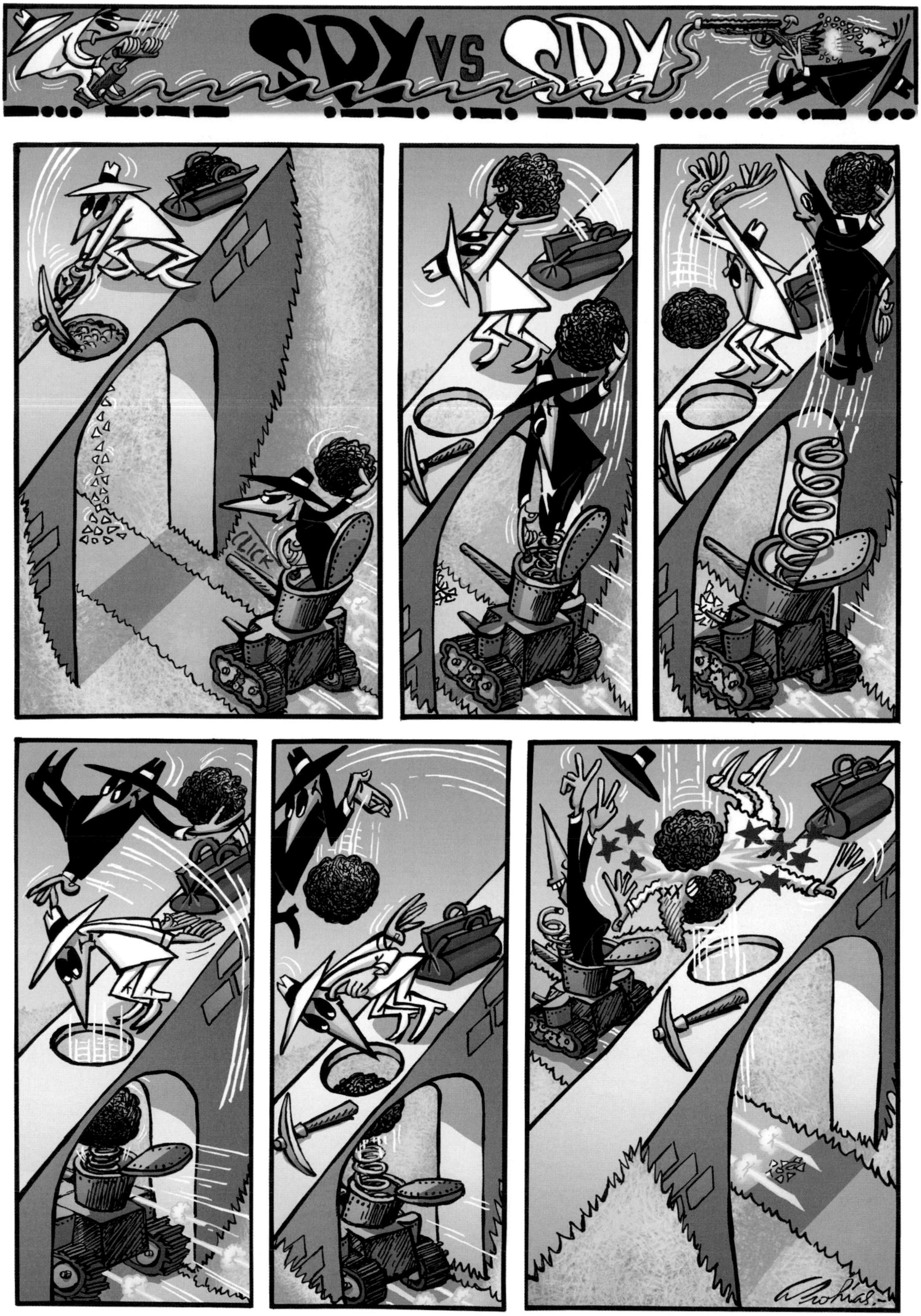
SPY vs SPY
CLICK
Prohias

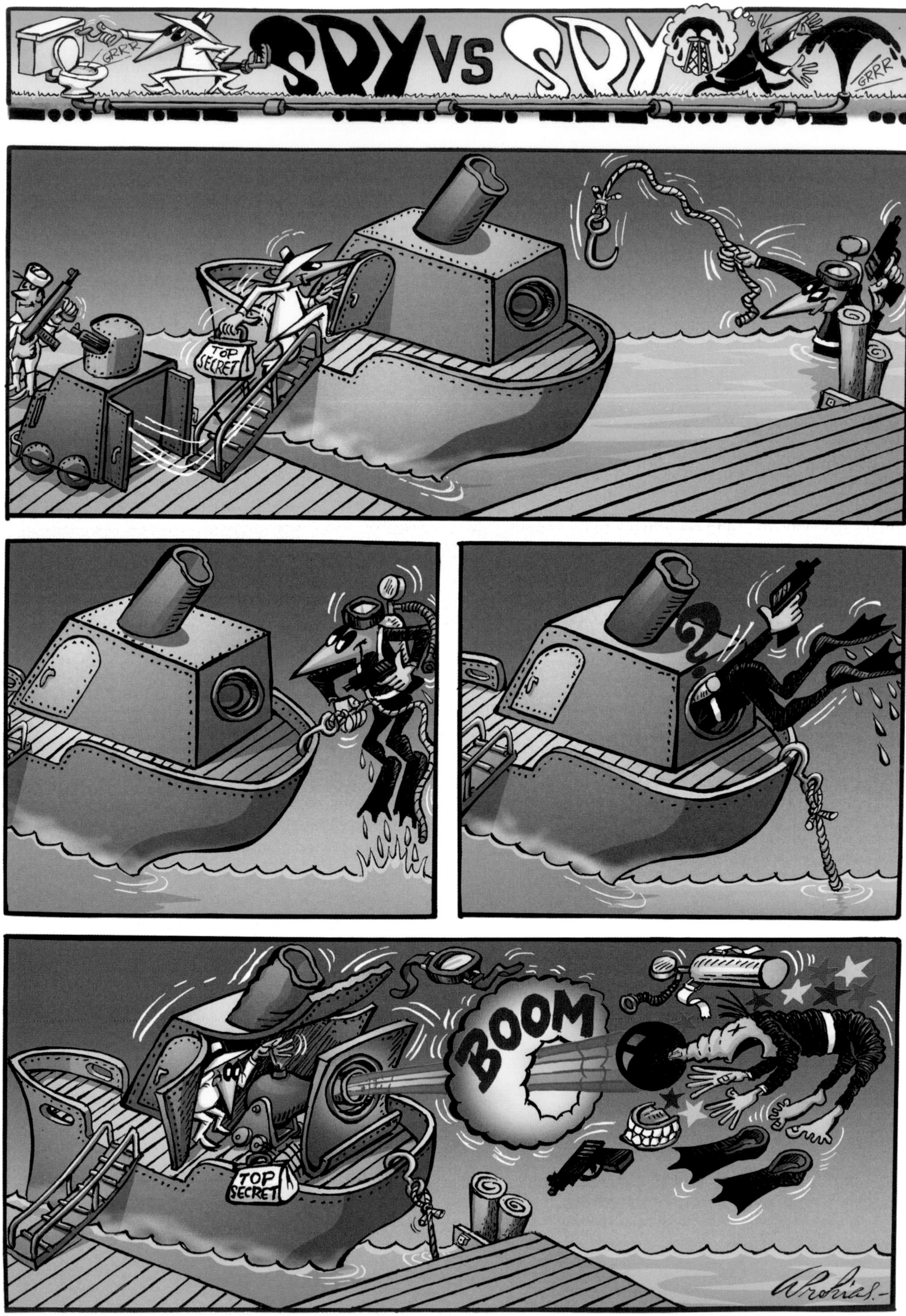
SPY VS SPY
GRRR
GRRR
TOP SECRET
BOOM
TOP SECRET

Is Peter Kuper a SPY?

I ask this question not because of Peter's habit of wearing all black clothing, from head to toe, 365 days a year. And not because of his tendency to jet away to exotic locales — Africa, Mexico, Harvard University — at a moment's notice. No, not even because of his status as the prime suspect in a devastating string of bathroom stall booby traps that have traumatized the MAD offices for well over a decade.

Why, then, am I accusing the man who's written and drawn *Spy vs. Spy* for the last 18 years of covert behavior and subterfuge? Allow me to explain.

Peter spent his teenage years in Cleveland palling around with Harvey Pekar and convincing Robert Crumb to trade artwork for old records. He went on to co-found the highly respected political comics anthology *World War 3 Illustrated*, pen a number of critically acclaimed graphic novels, and create comics and illustrations for elite publications like *The New York Times.* The stencil-and-spray paint style he employed in these endeavors became his hallmark, allowing his artwork to be immediately recognizable. Peter won numerous awards, his career flourished and his name rose in prominence.

Despite all of that, he agreed to work for MAD.

In 1997, Peter was given the opportunity to re-imagine *Spy vs. Spy*. His initial reaction was to turn down the offer. And who would blame him? Why would a man gifted with Peter's creative powers, who had achieved his level of highbrow success, choose to join the "Usual Gang of Idiots"? Well, like the clandestine deeds of the Black Spy and White Spy themselves, Peter's entire career is a testament to the thrill of sabotaging expectations. He clearly saw an advantage, and began his infiltration.

First drawing the Spies' adventures with a rotation of writers, and eventually taking over the reins completely, Peter set about reinventing *Spy vs. Spy* for our modern age. From drone attacks to Swiss Army cars to rocket-launching tubas, Peter is consistently finding new ways to confound MAD's readers with narrative trickery. That stunning black and white paint spatter effect of his, which helped solidify Peter's *Spy vs. Spy* as something truly different from its predecessor, became even more eye-catching when MAD began running the strip in full color. More recently, the spatter gave way to two tools of which Peter remains a master — the ink brush and its inverse, the notoriously difficult scratchboard — while still exploiting his surreal sense of color. All the while, the strips' layouts and panel shapes break all comic conventions, and when Peter added a second gag strip to the regular feature, he opted to literally force the reader to turn the magazine upside down in order to read it. Even in his presentation, Peter keeps us guessing.

Clearly I admire this man's talents, but that comes with a healthy dose of suspicion. Why does Peter Kuper continue down this path, giving it his all? What does he have to gain? (It sure ain't the money — this *is* MAD, remember.) Peter is no fool, yet here he has been, almost twenty years amongst the Idiots, awing us with the ingenuity he brings to each new installment of *Spy vs. Spy*.

There are just too many questions to take the whole thing at face value. What does Peter really want? What are his end goals? Who is he working for?

And what — dear heavens, WHAT — will he do next?

— Ryan Flanders, Associate Art Director

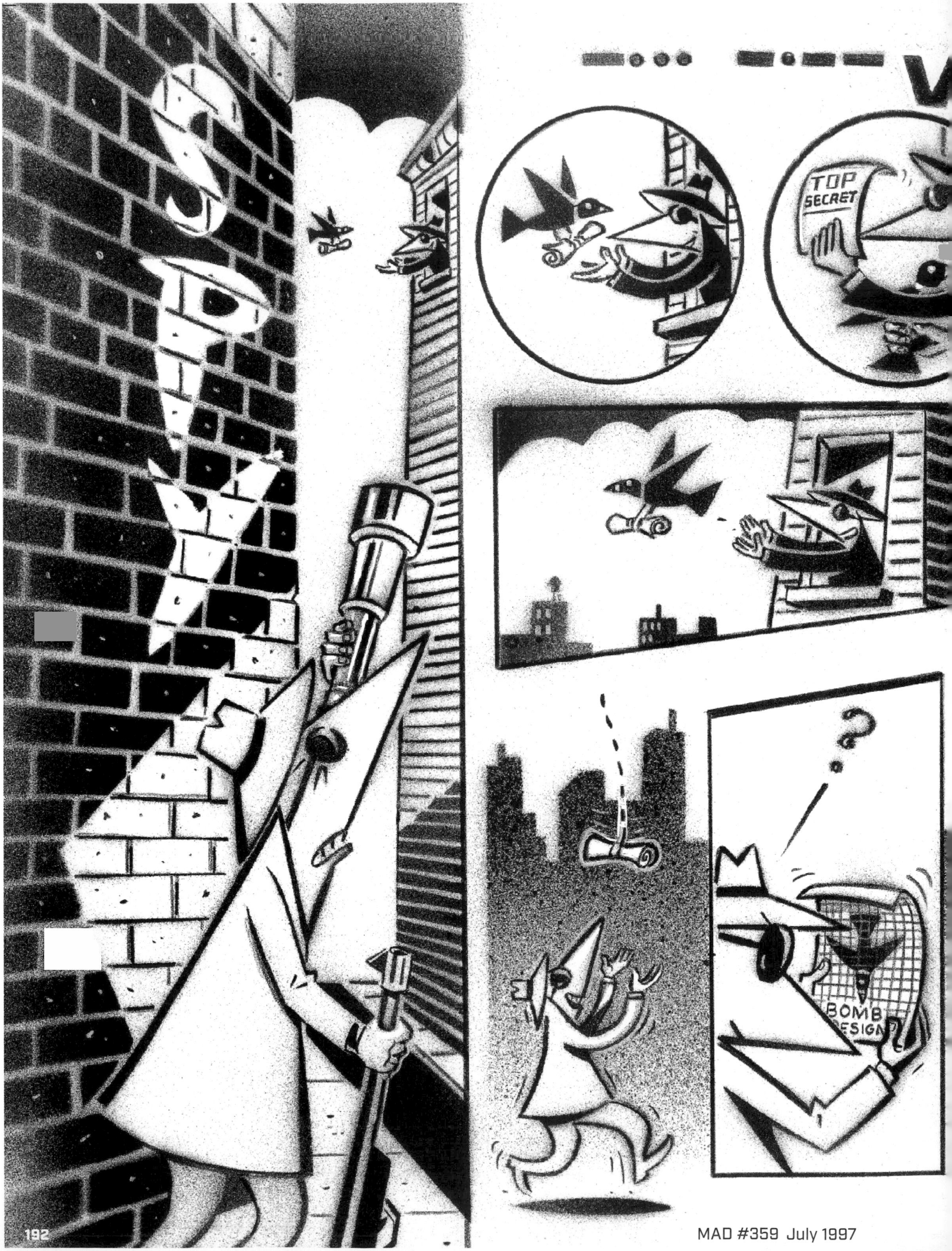
TOP SECRET
BOMB

MAD #359 July 1997

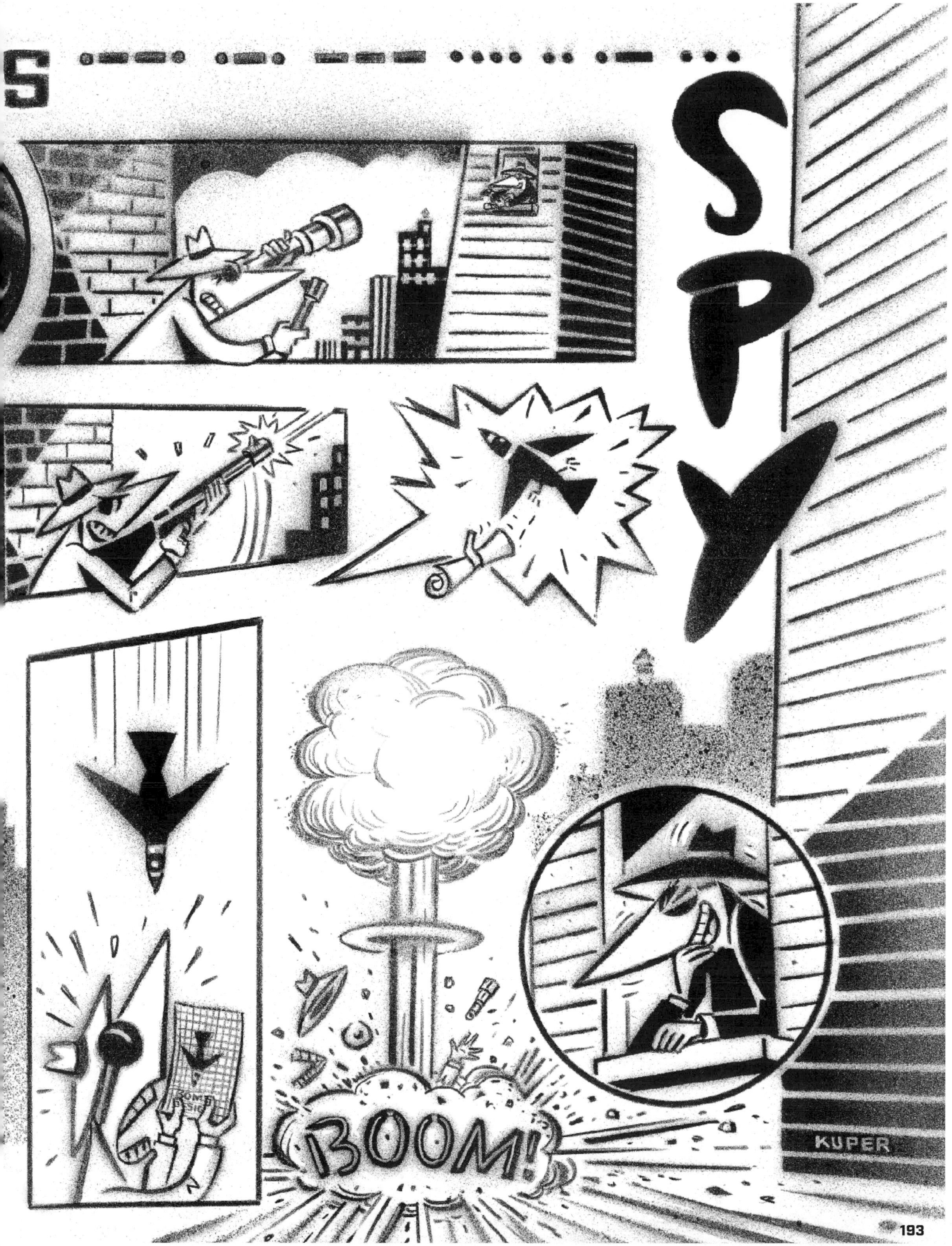
S
SPY
BOOM!
KUPER

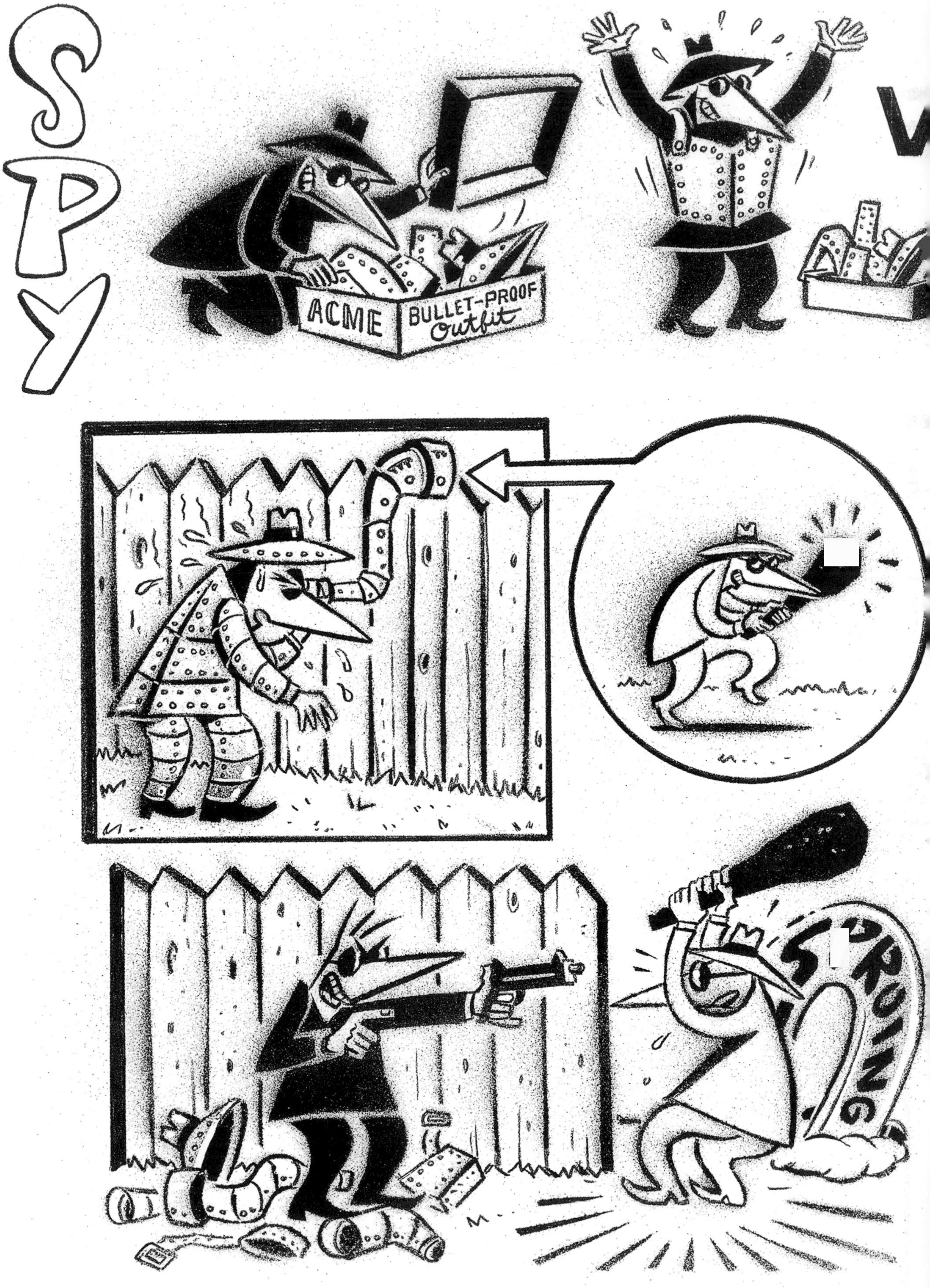
SPY
ACME
BULLET-PROOF Outfit
SPROING

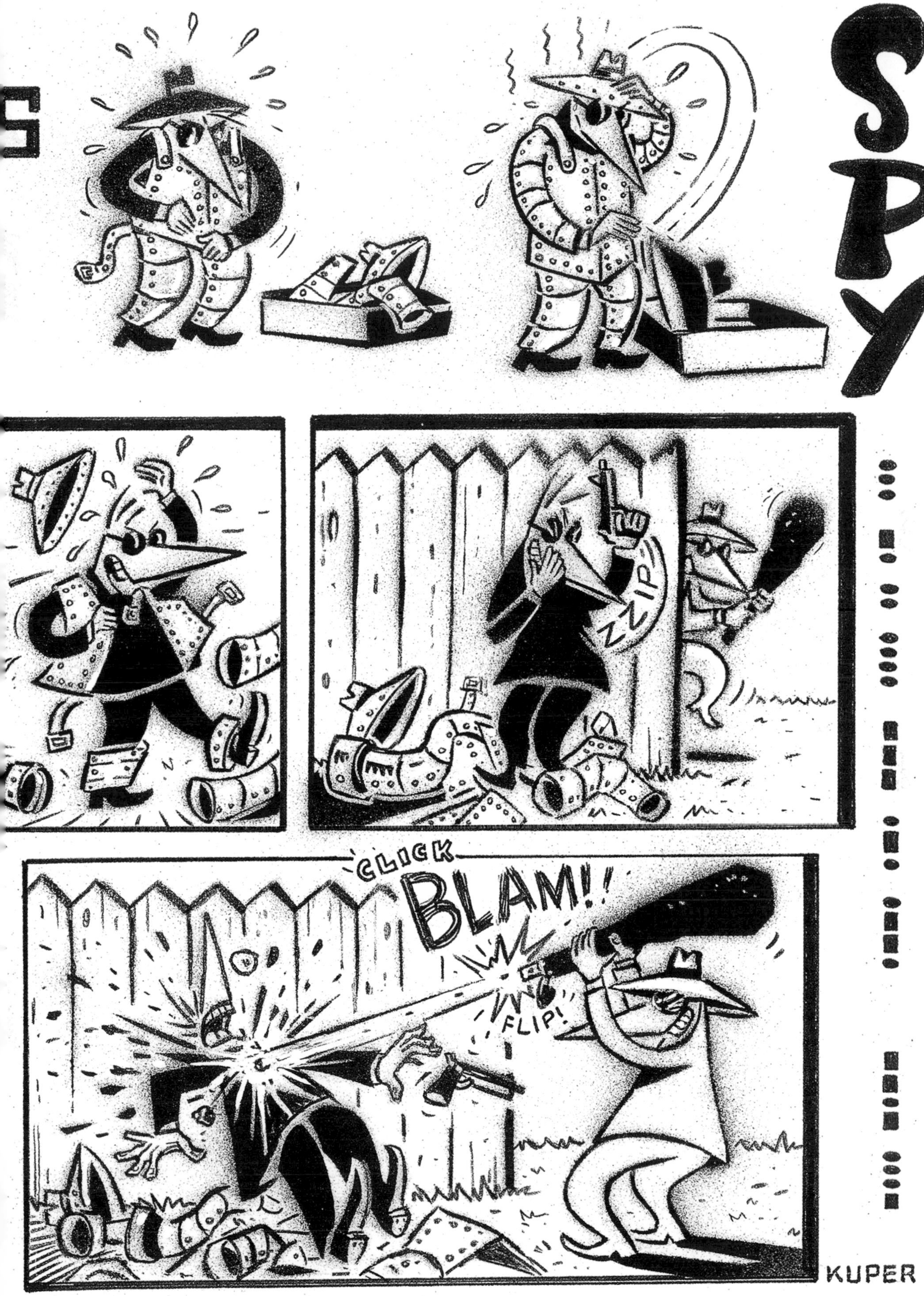

SPY
ZZIP
CLICK
BLAM!!
FLIP!
KUPER

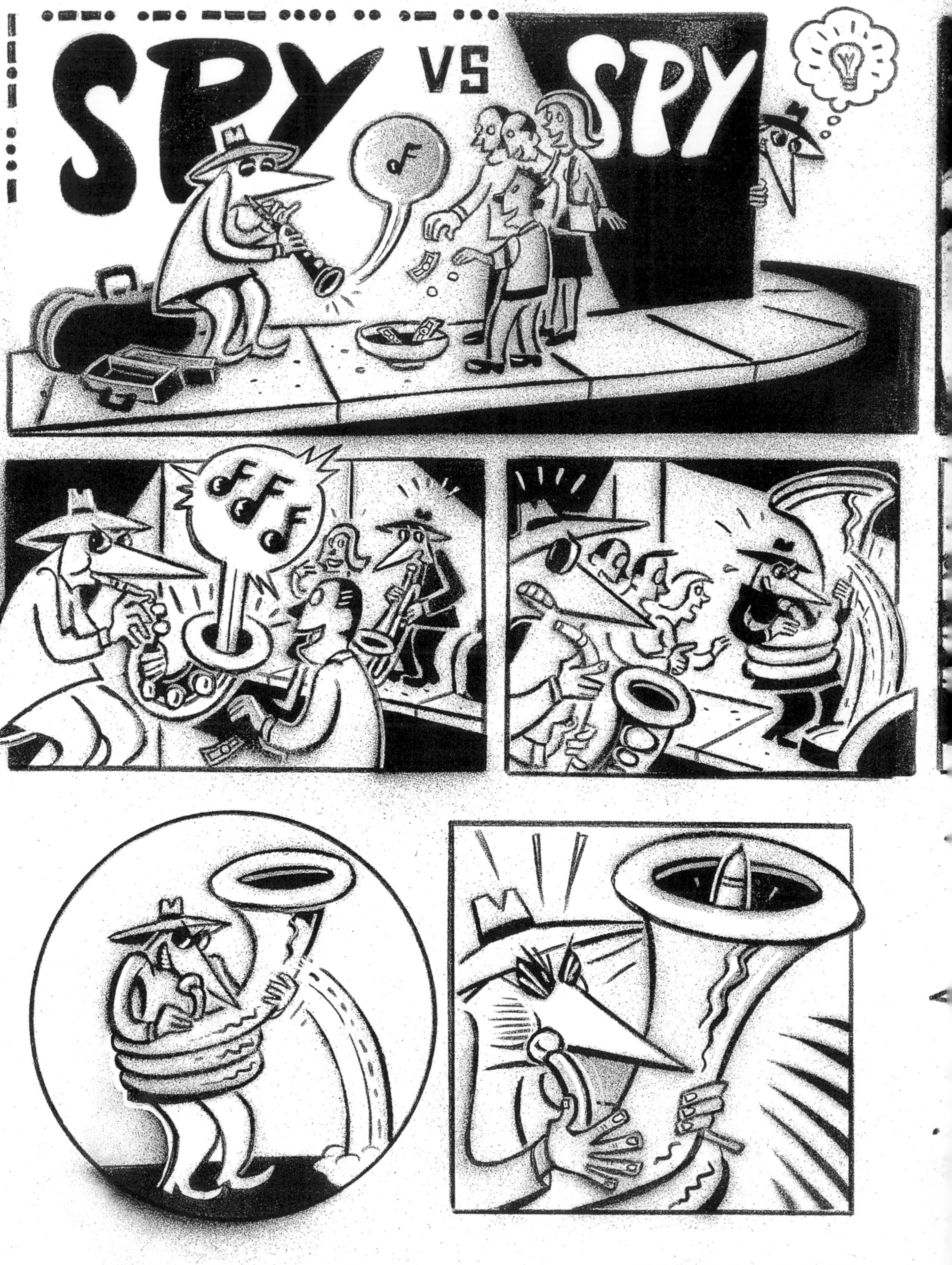
SPY VS SPY

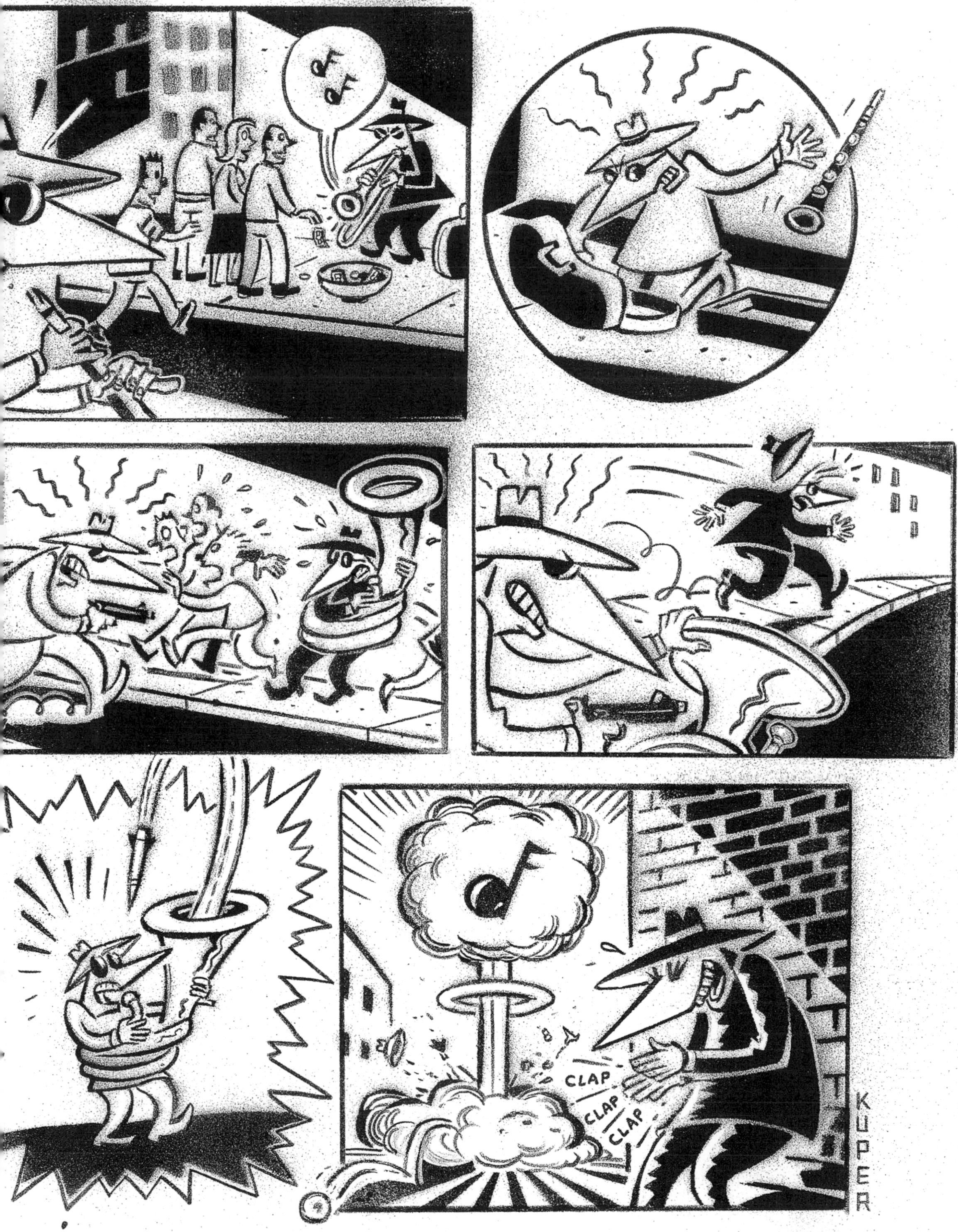
CLAP
CLAP
CLAP
KUPER

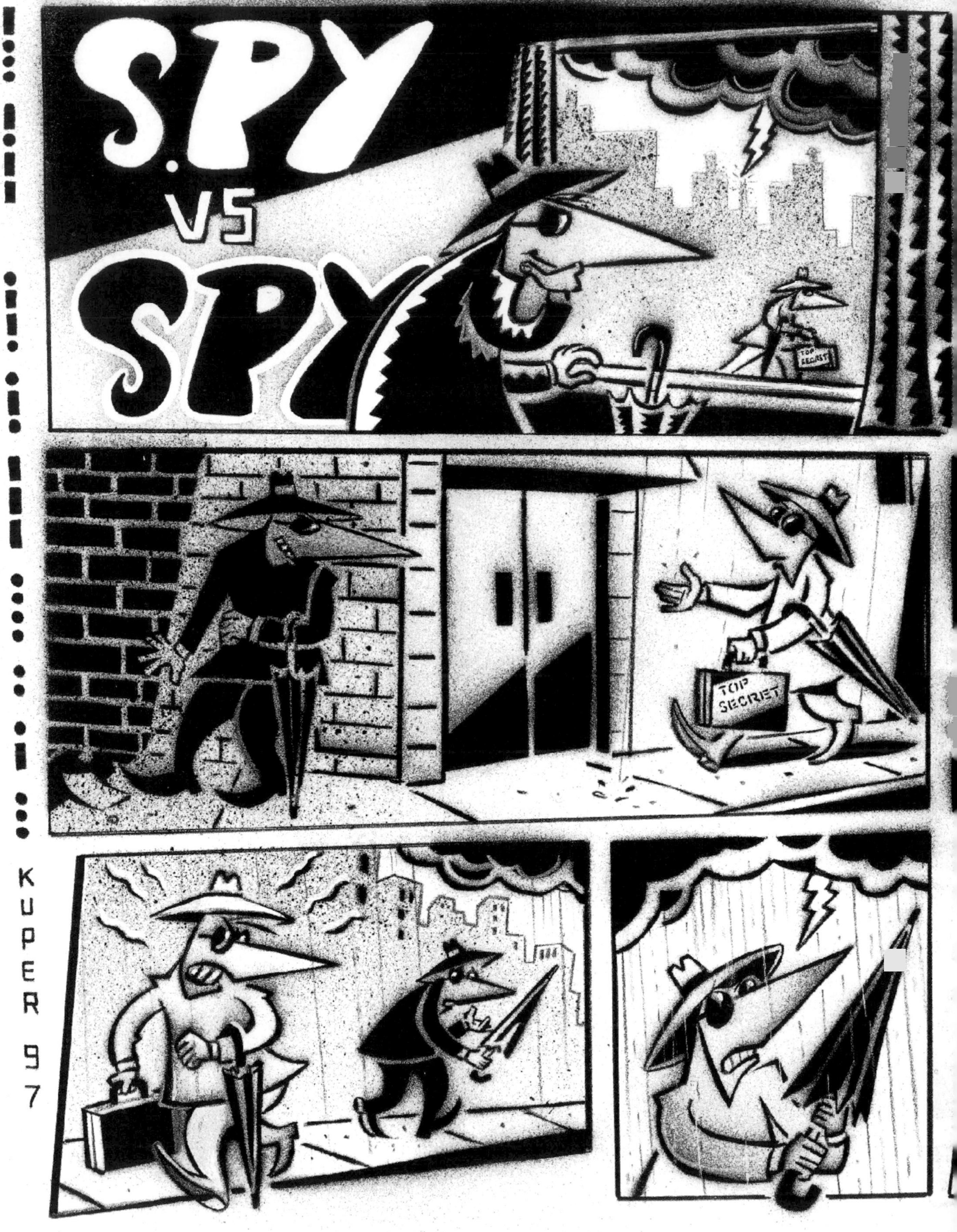
SPY VS SPY
TOP SECRET
TOP SECRET
KUPER 97

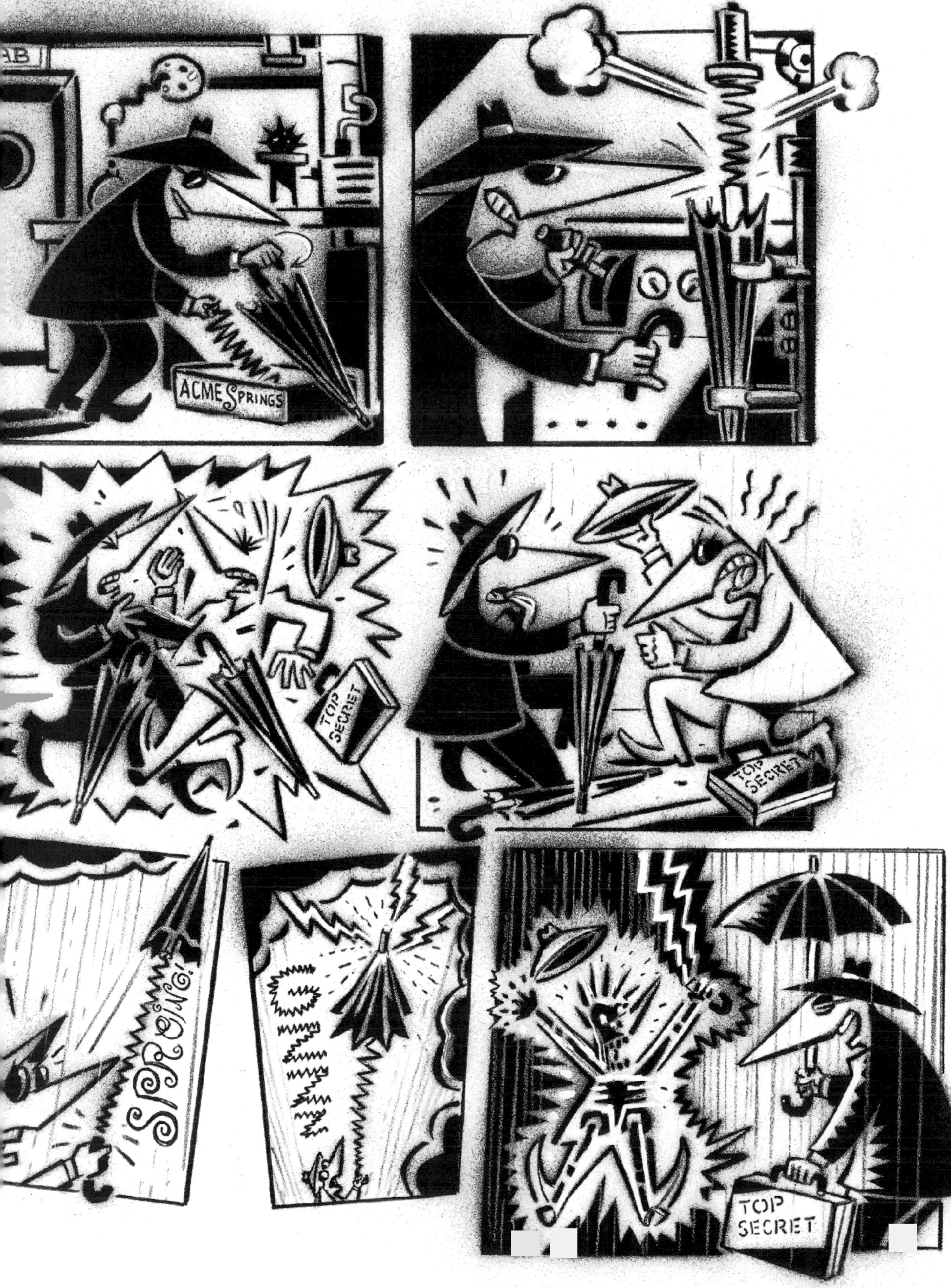
ACME SPRINGS
TOP SECRET
TOP SECRET
SPROING!
TOP SECRET

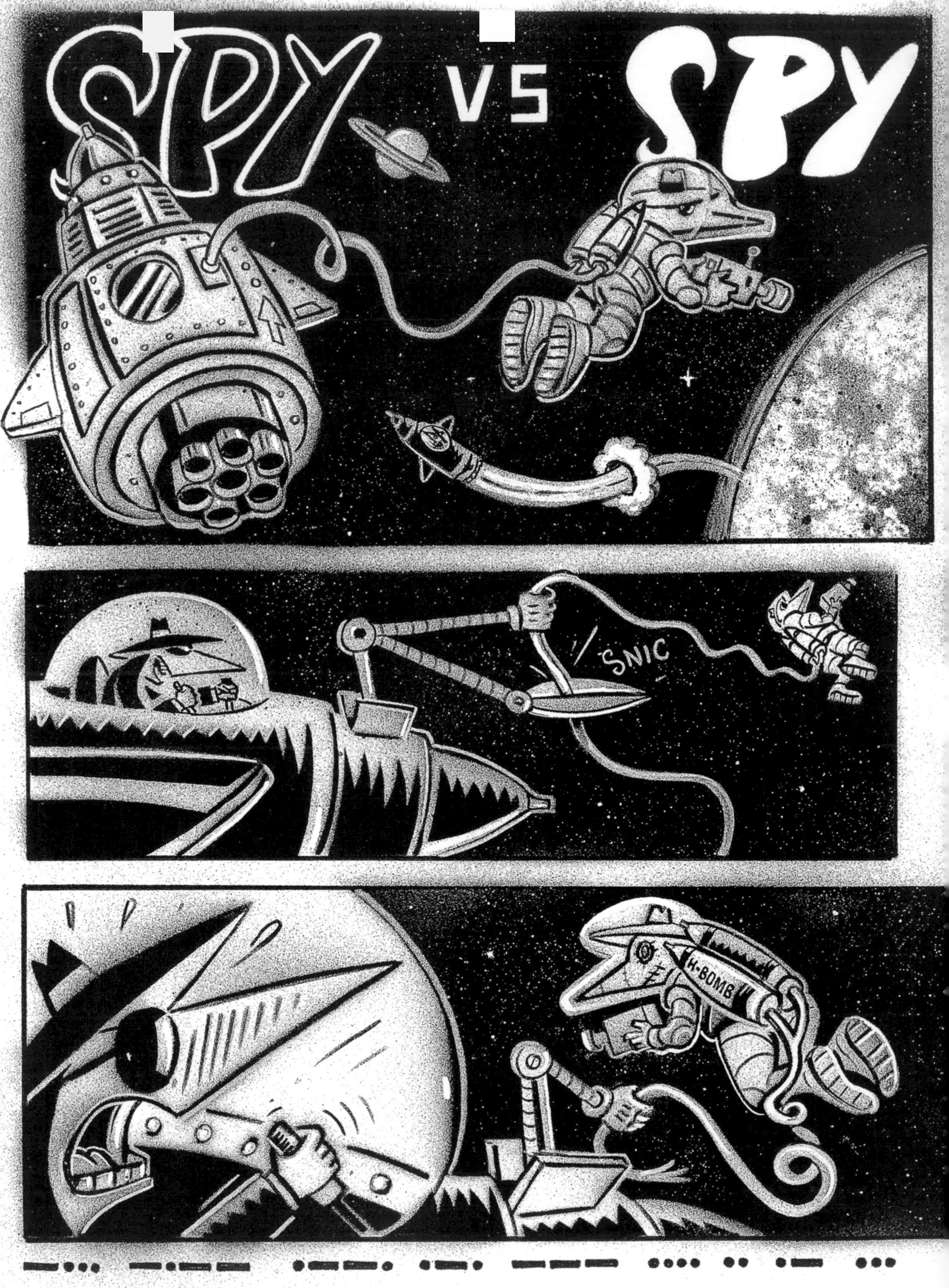
SPY VS SPY
SNIC
H-BOMB

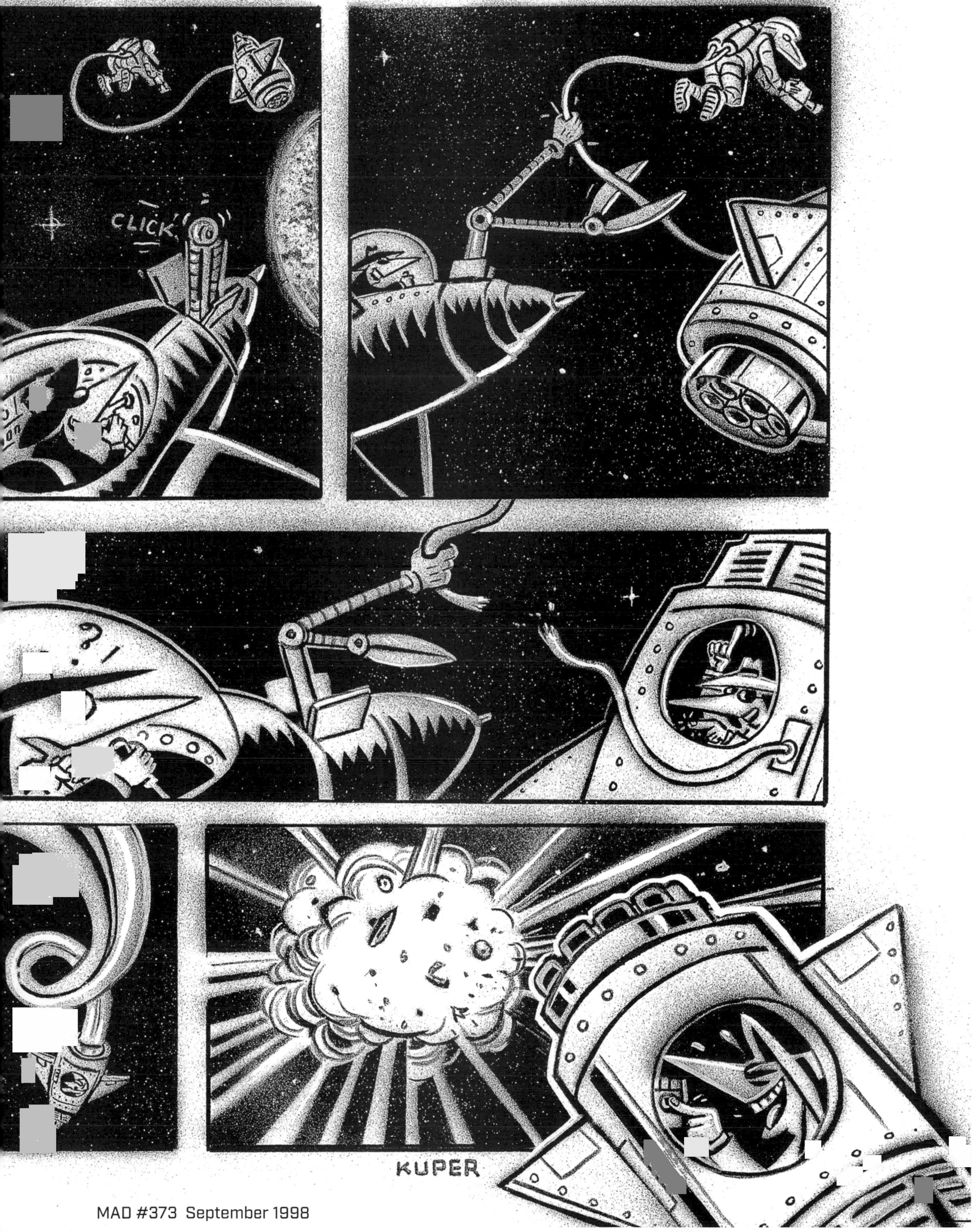
CLICK
?!
KUPER

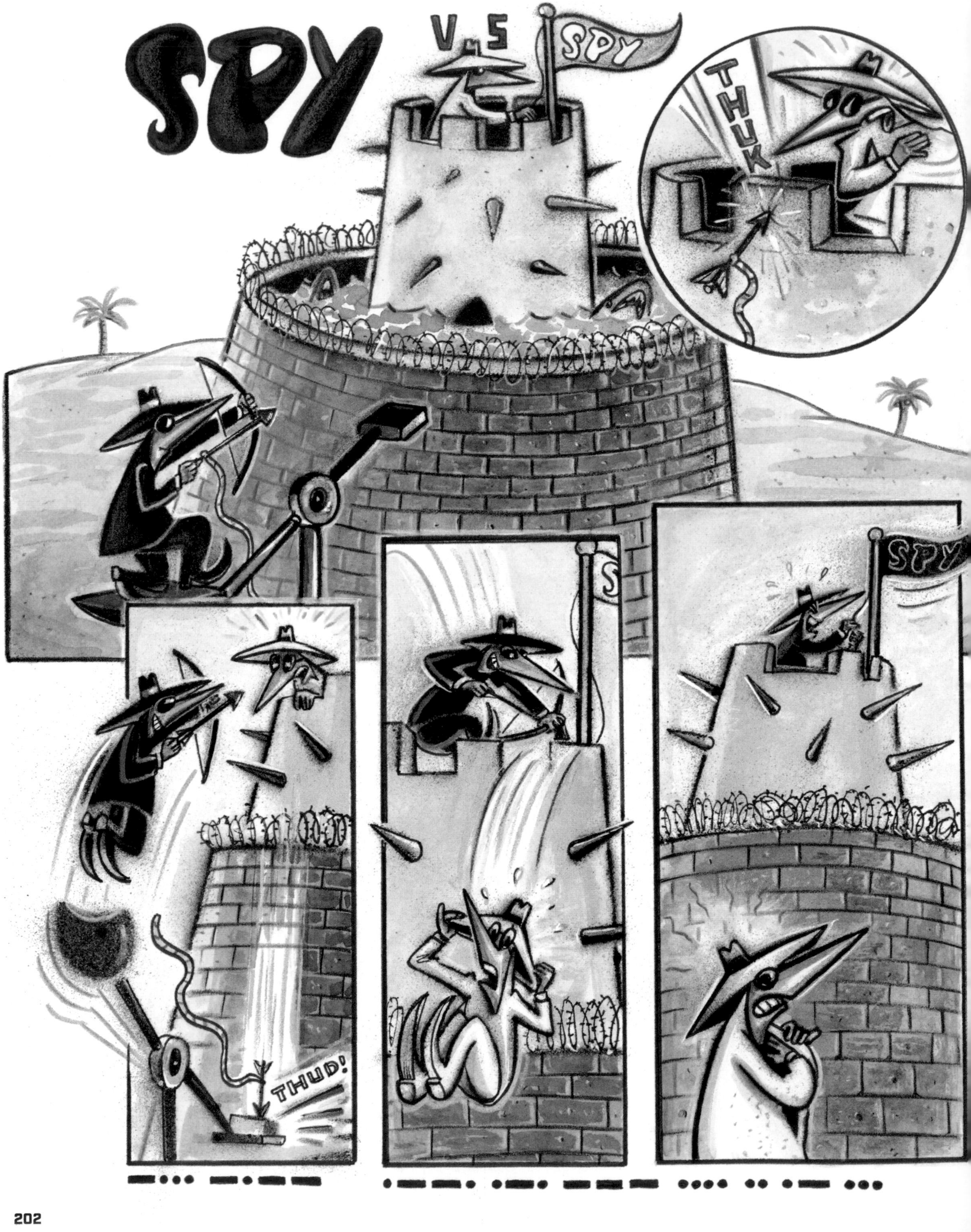
SPY VS
SPY
THUK
THUD!
S
SPY

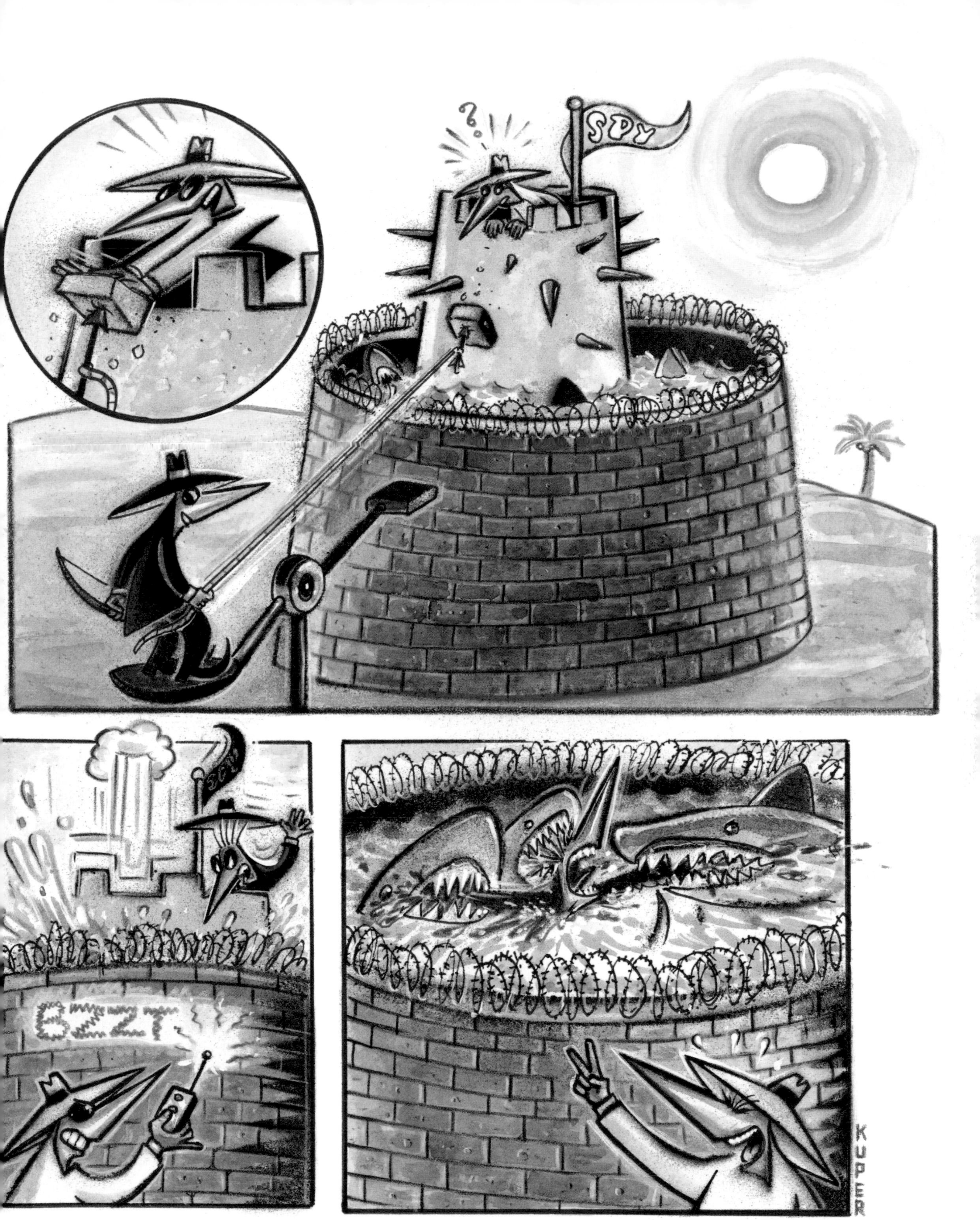

SPY
?
BZZT
KUPER

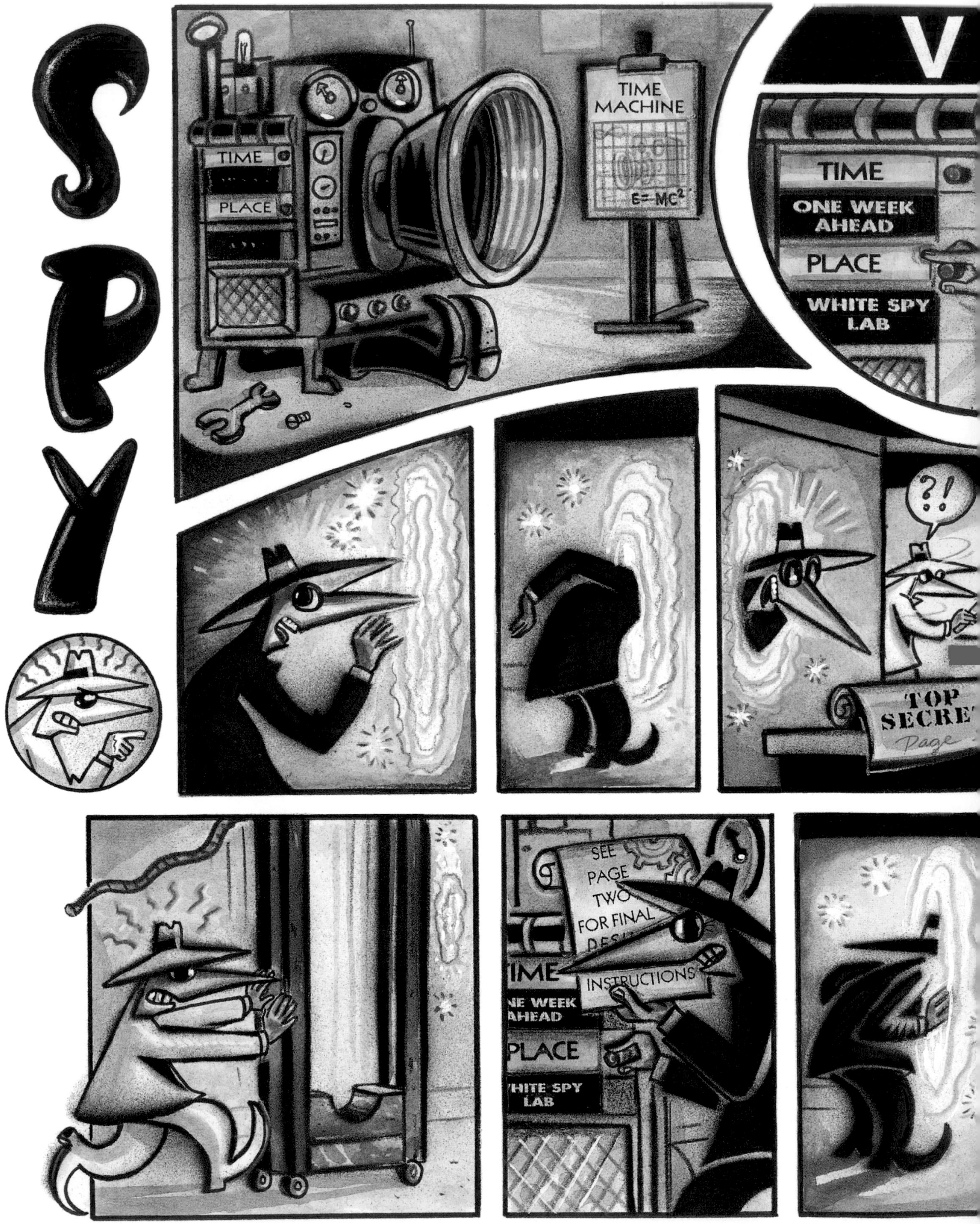
SPY
V
TIME
PLACE
TIME MACHINE
E=MC²
TIME
ONE WEEK AHEAD
PLACE
WHITE SPY LAB
?!
TOP
SECRE
SEE PAGE TWO FOR FINAL
INSTRUCTIONS
TIME
NE WEEK AHEAD
PLACE
HITE SPY LAB

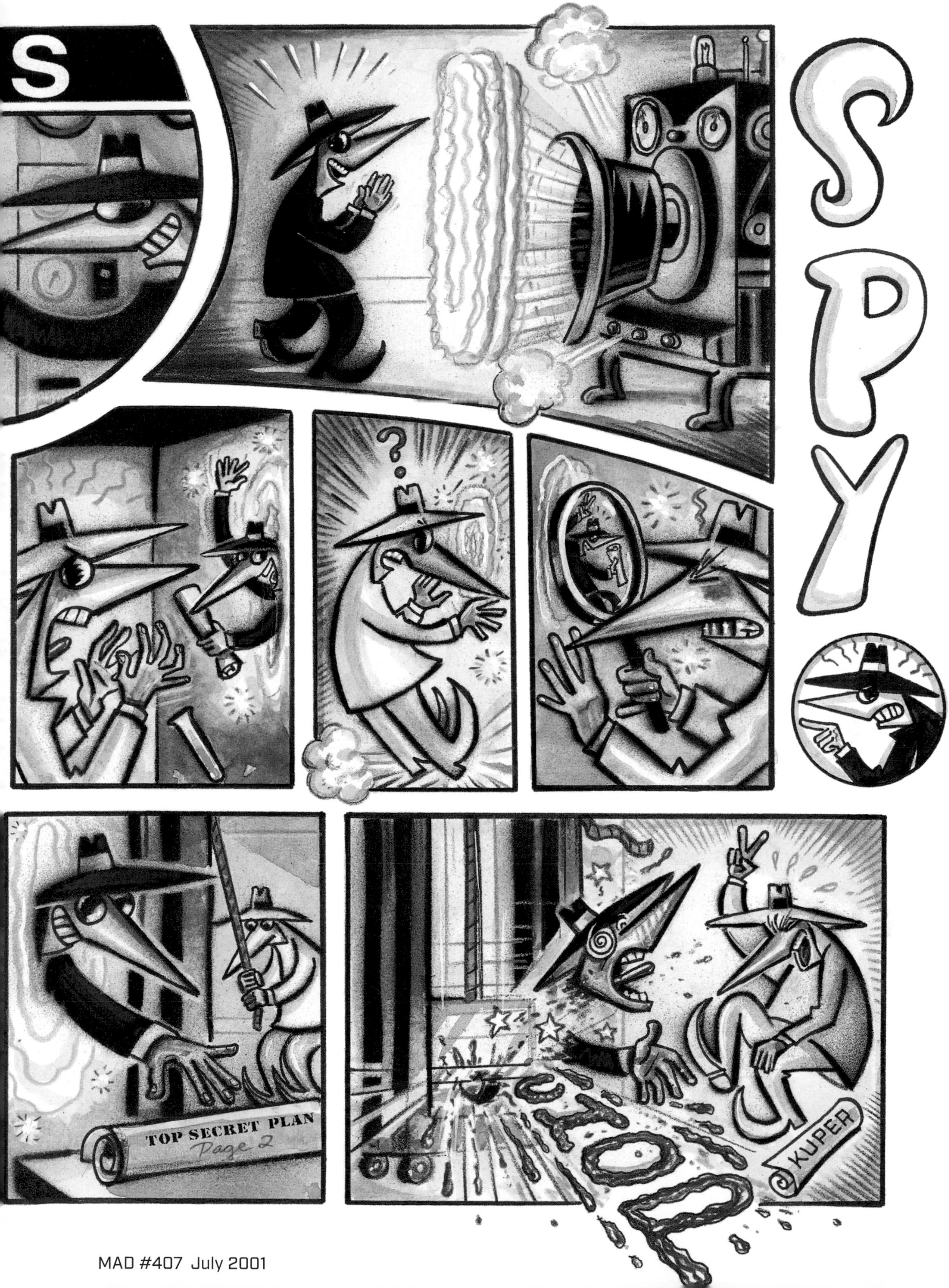
S
SPY
TOP SECRET PLAN
Page 2
KUPER

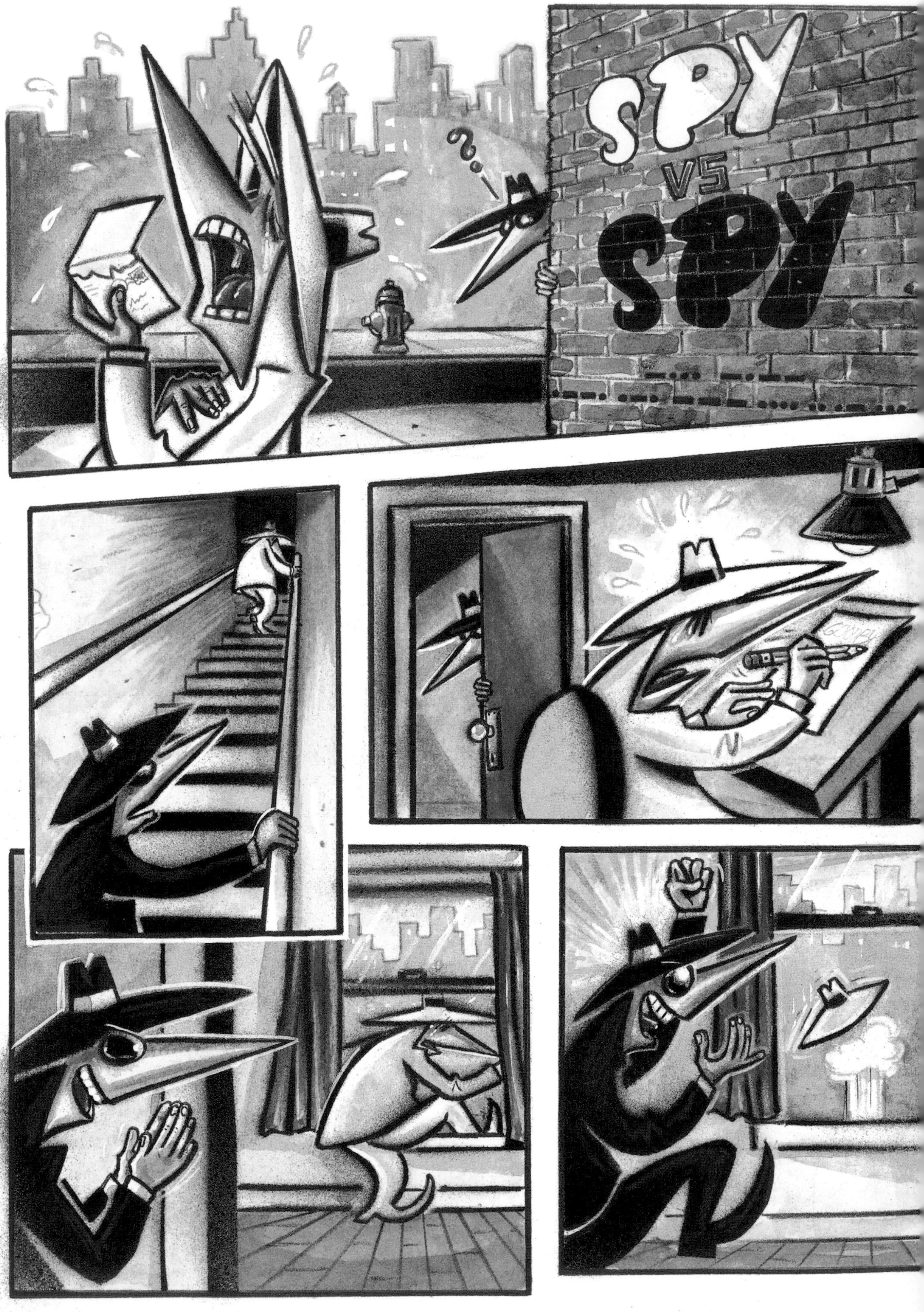
SPY
VS
SPY

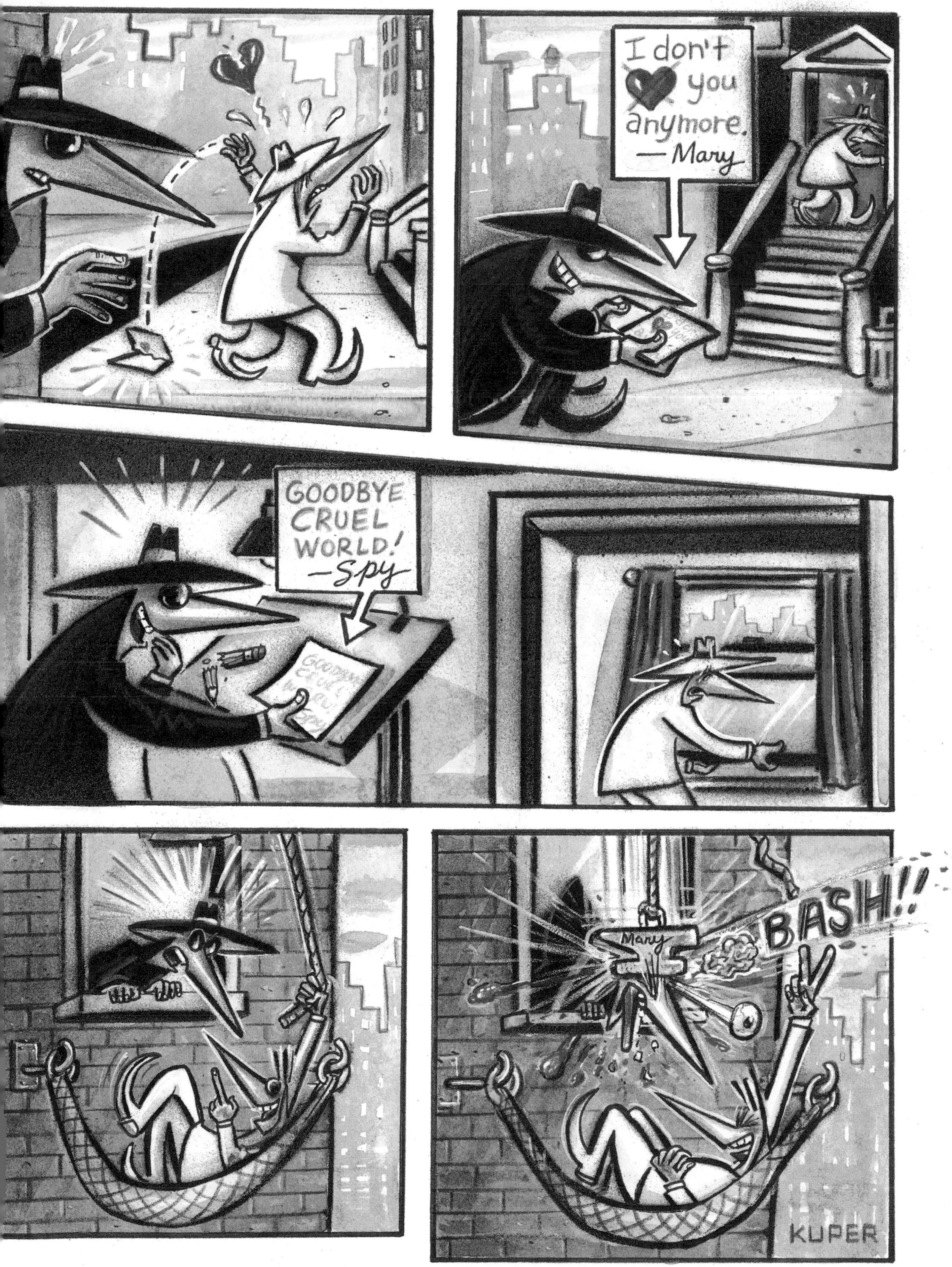
I don't you anymore. —Mary
GOODBYE CRUEL WORLD! —Spy
Mary
BASH!!
KUPER

SPY VS SPY
?
SPROING!!
WACK!
ZZIP
DING!!

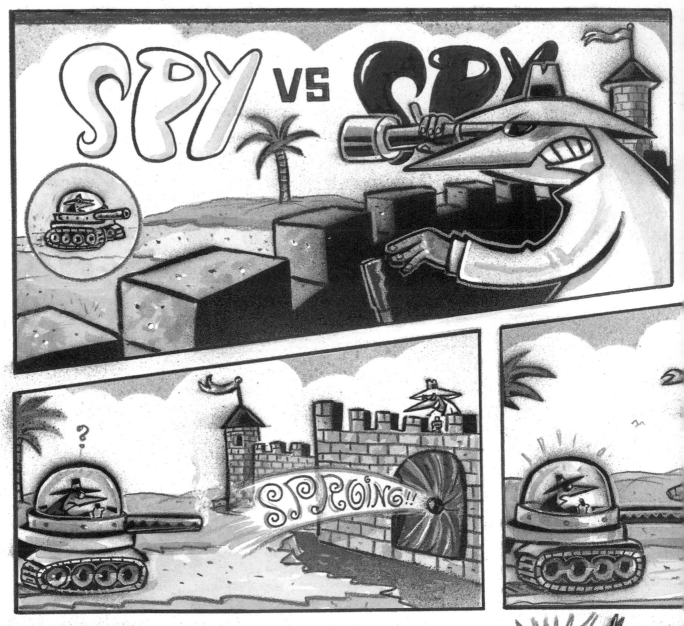

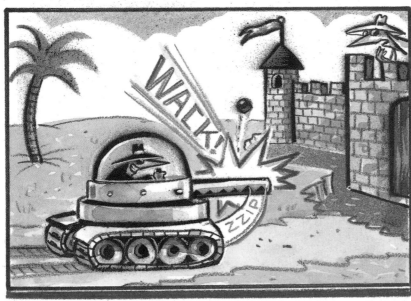

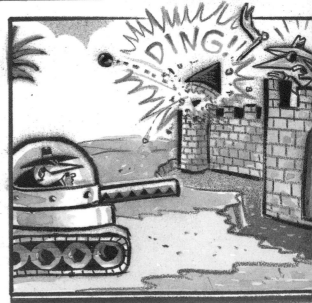

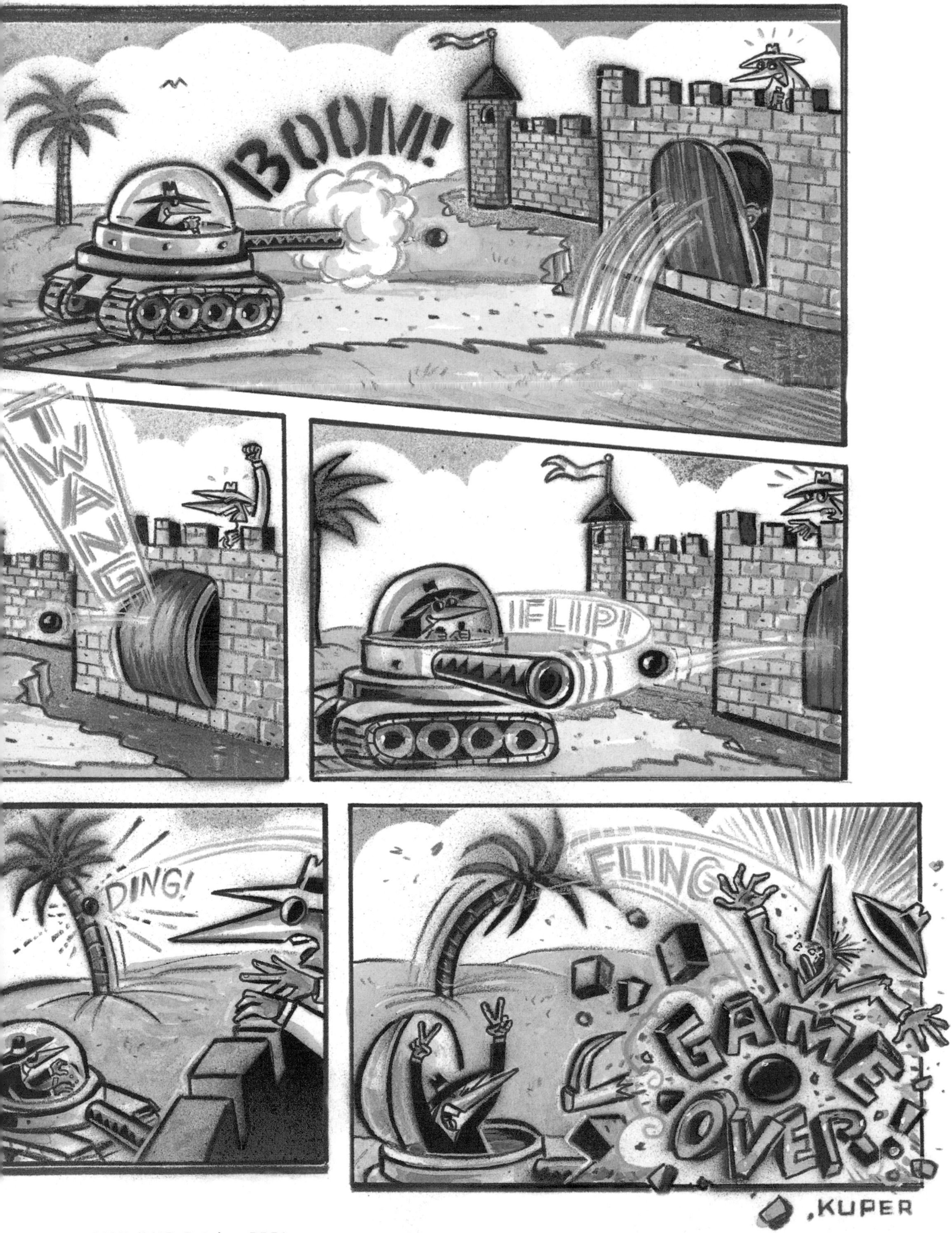
BOOM!
TWANG
FLIP!
DING!
FLING
GAME OVER!
KUPER

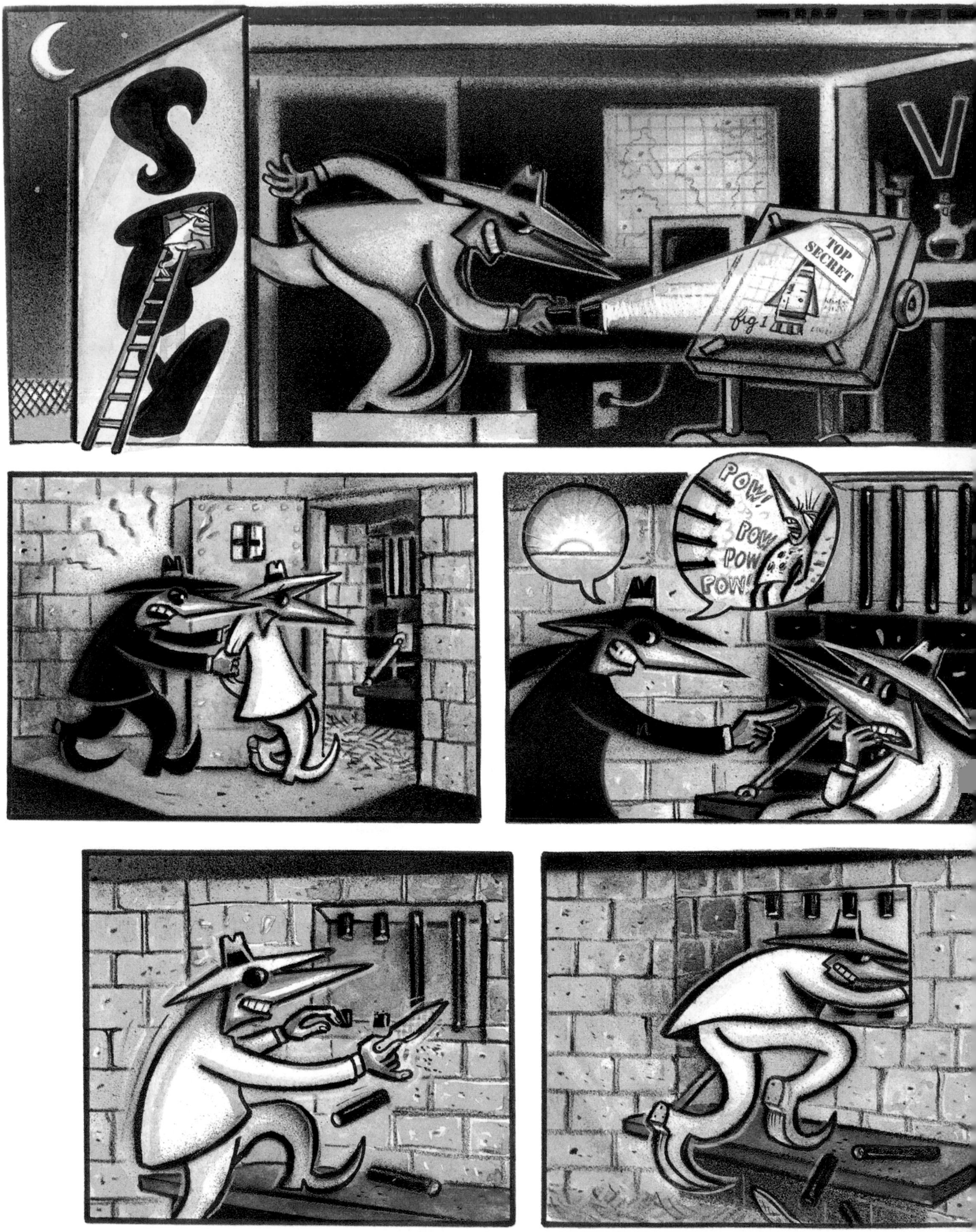
TOP SECRET
fig 1
POW!
POW
POW
POW!

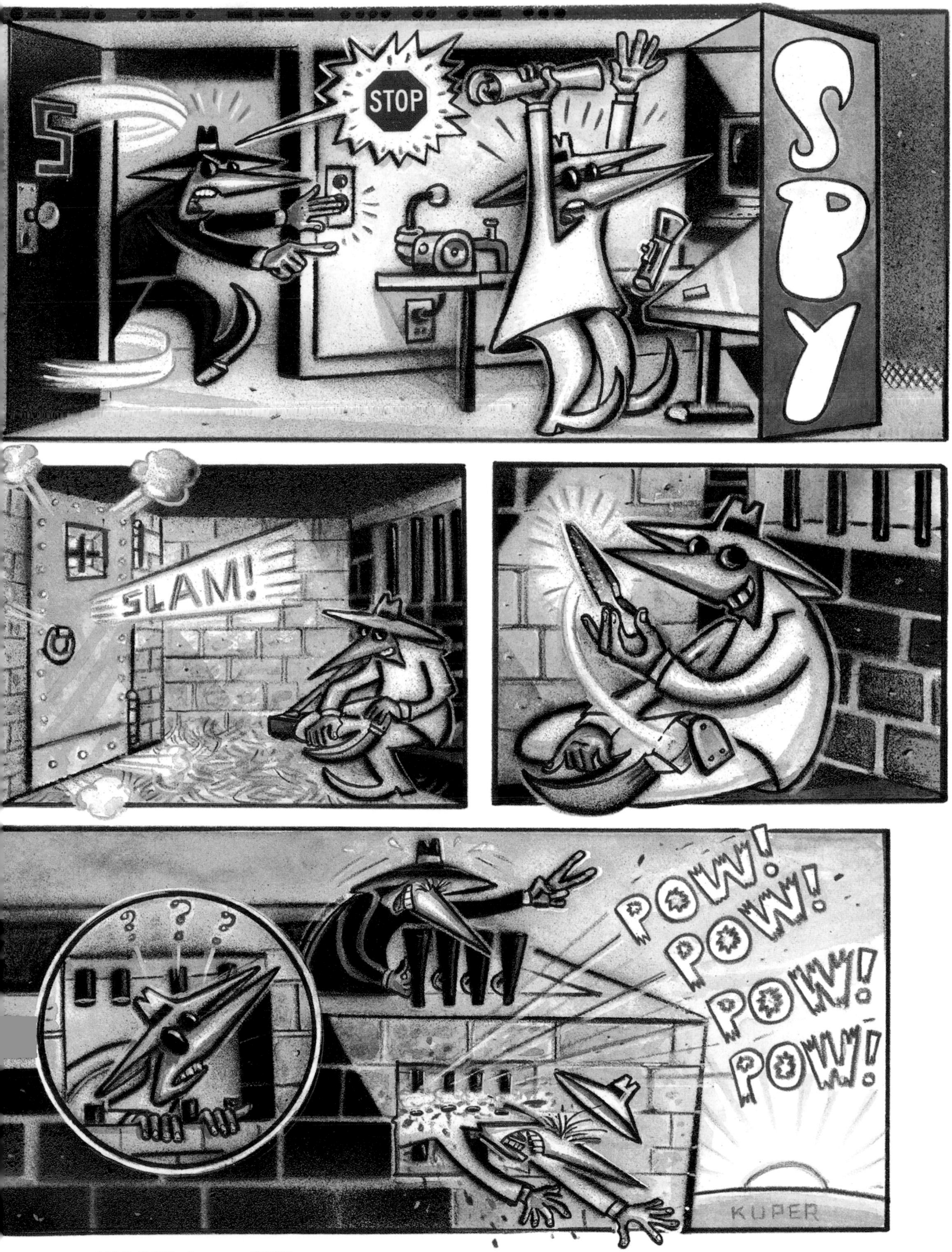
STOP
SPY
SLAM!
POW!
POW!
POW!
POW!
KUPER

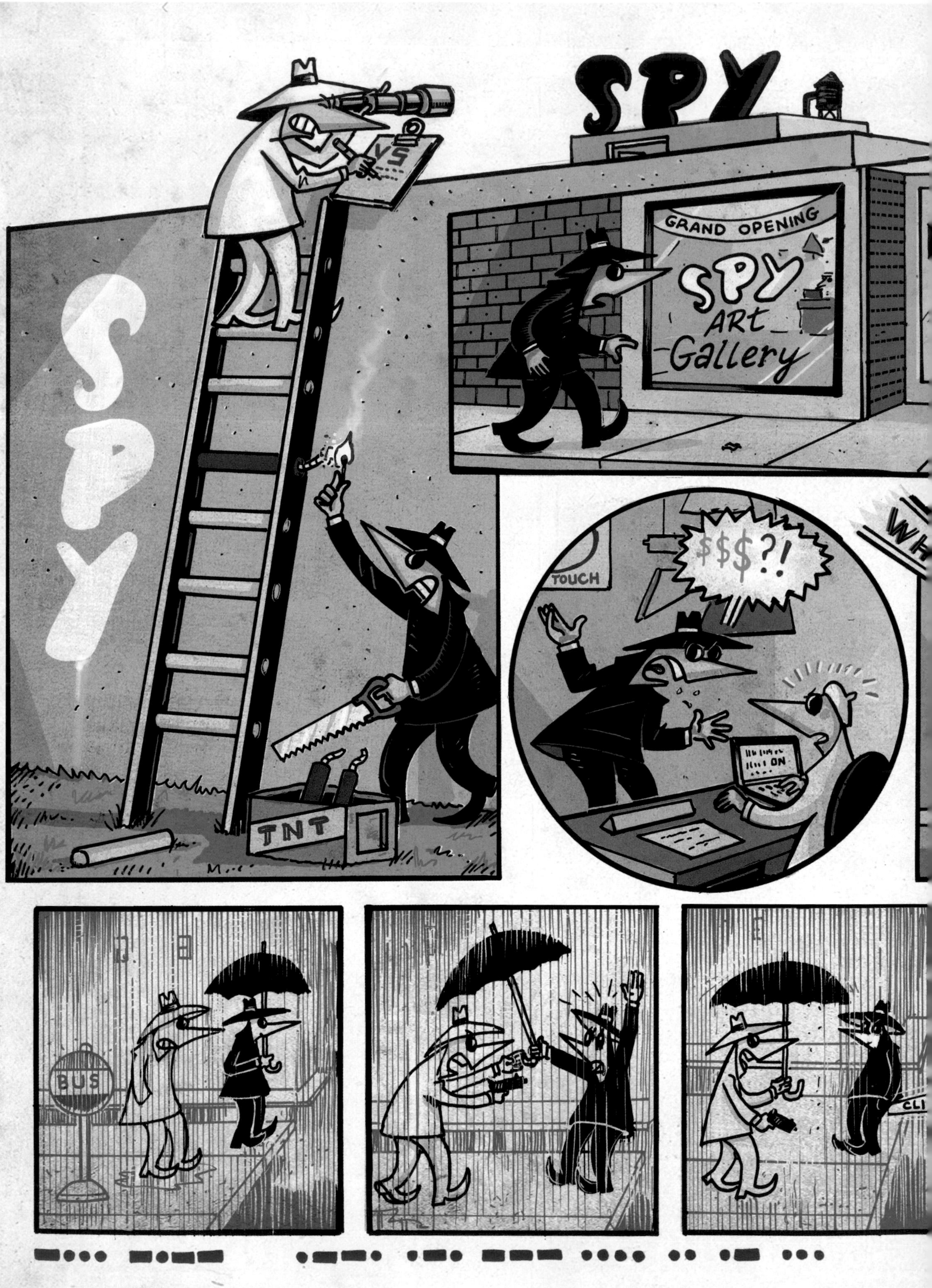
SPY
VS
SPY
GRAND OPENING
SPY Art Gallery
TNT
TOUCH
$$$?!
ON
BUS

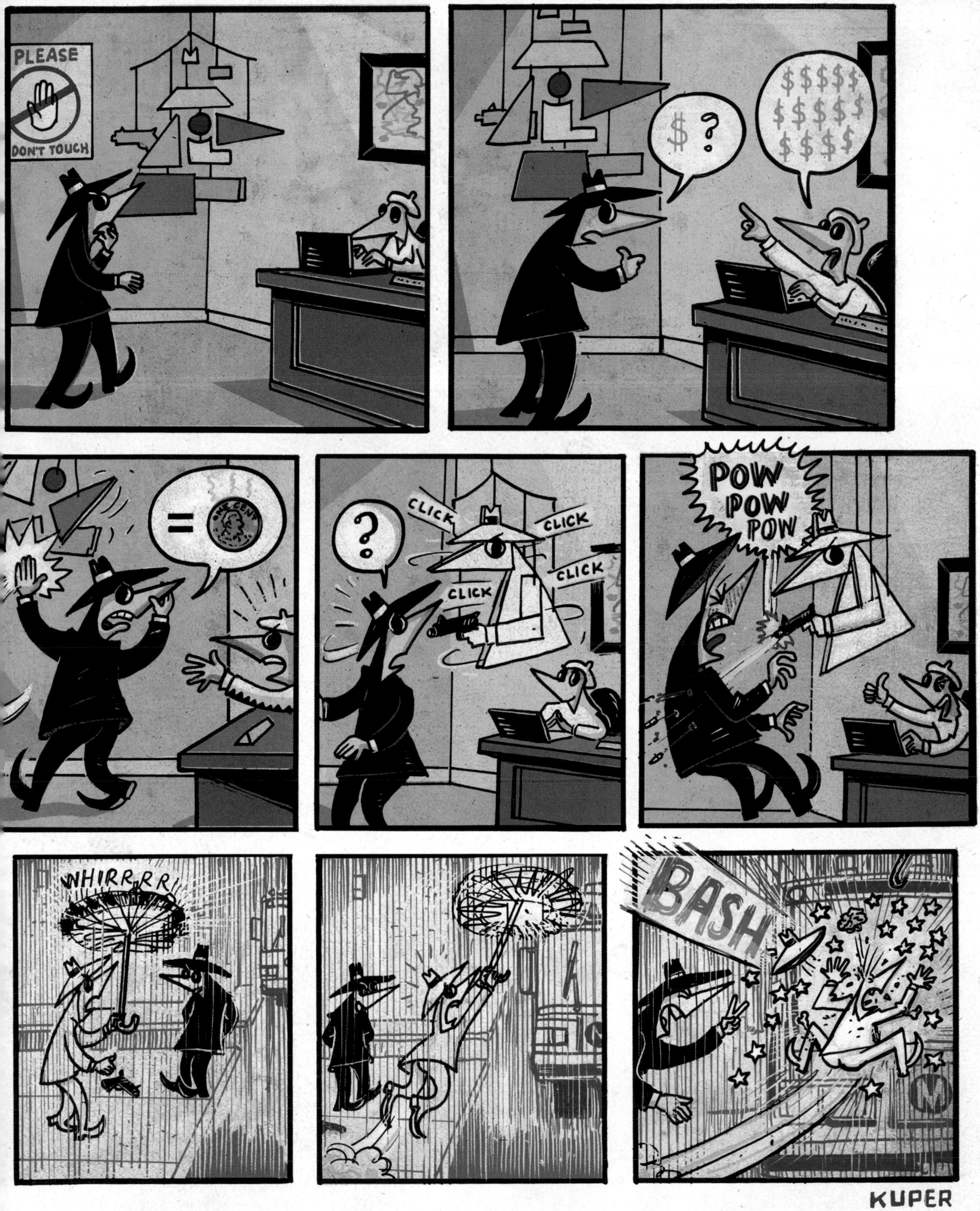
PLEASE
DON'T TOUCH
$?
$$$$$ $$$$$ $$$$
=
ONE CENT
?
CLICK
CLICK
CLICK
CLICK
POW POW POW
WHIRRRR
BASH
KUPER

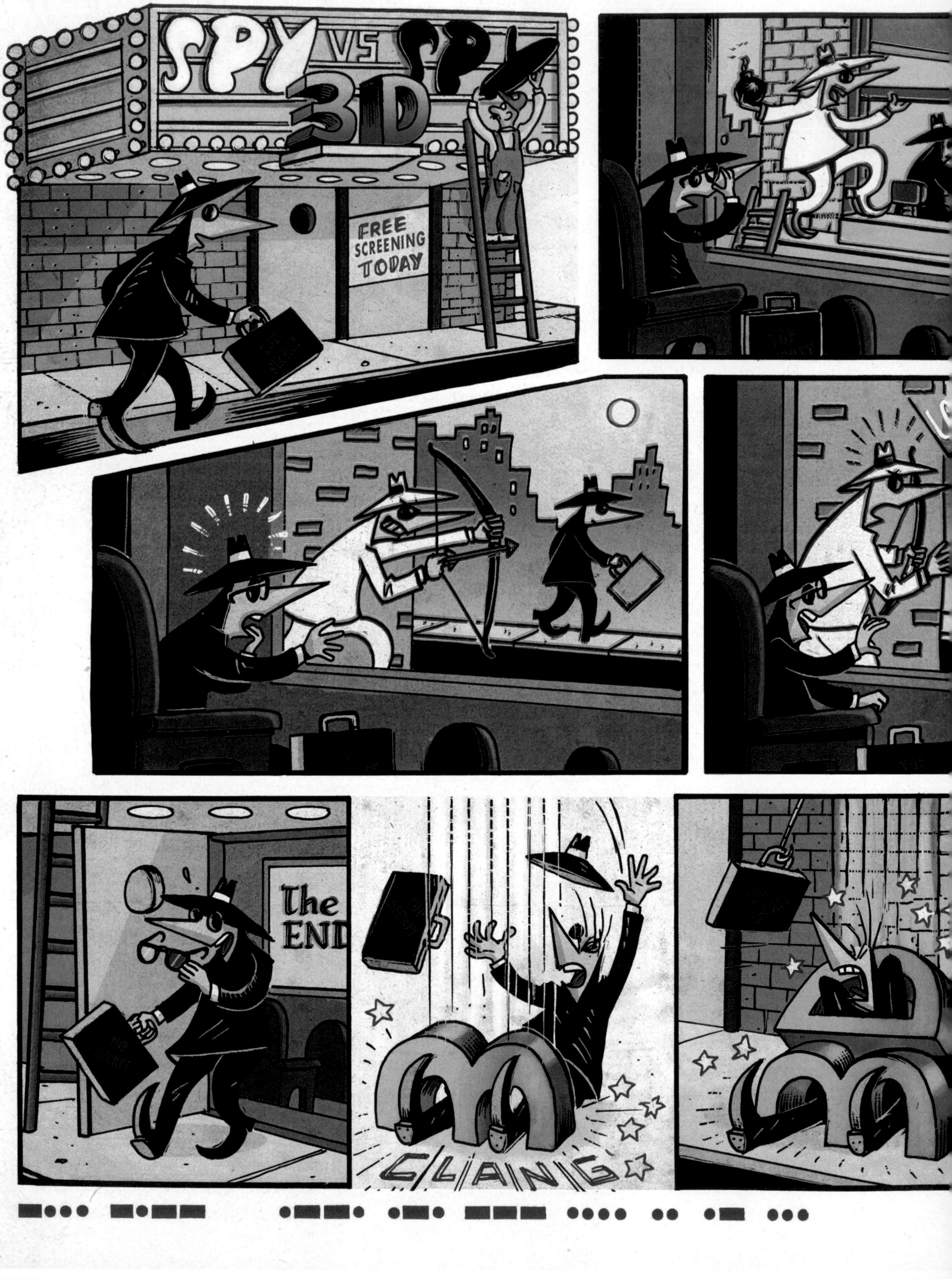
SPY VS SPY
3D
FREE SCREENING TODAY
The END
CLANG

SPY vs SPY

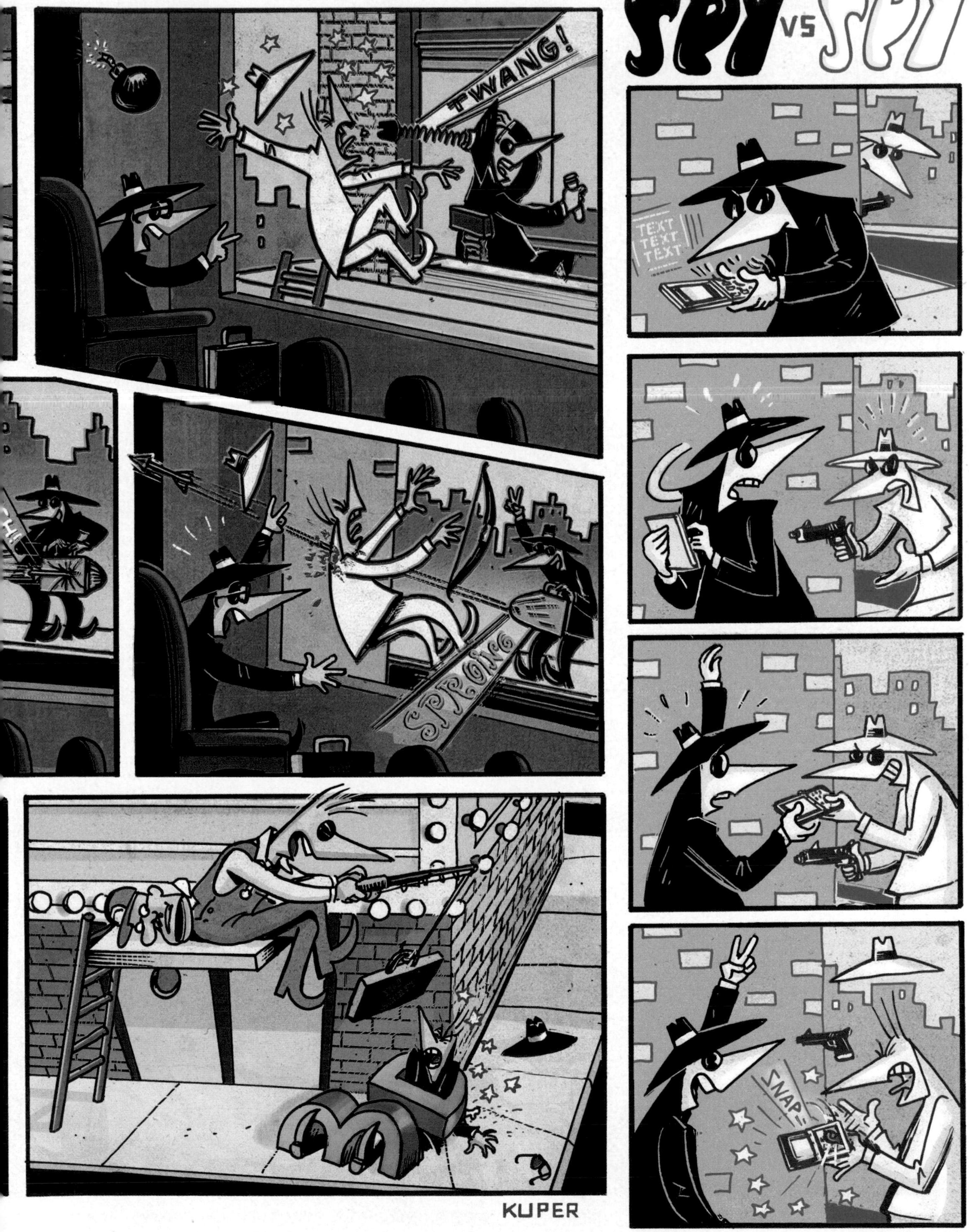
TWANG!
SPROING
TEXT TEXT TEXT
SNAP
KUPER

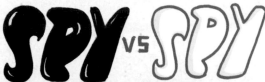

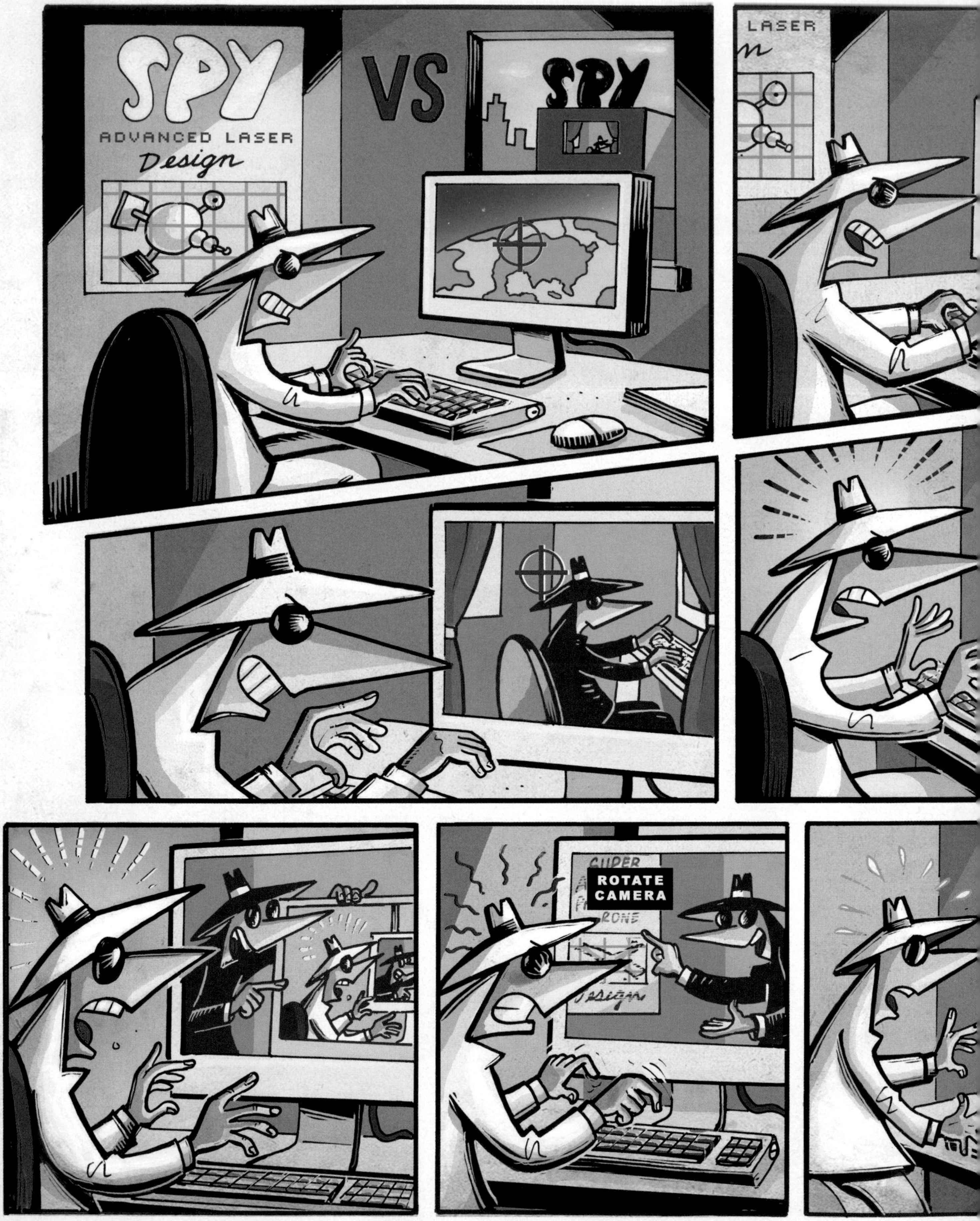
SPY
ADVANCED LASER
Design
VS
SPY
LASER
ROTATE CAMERA

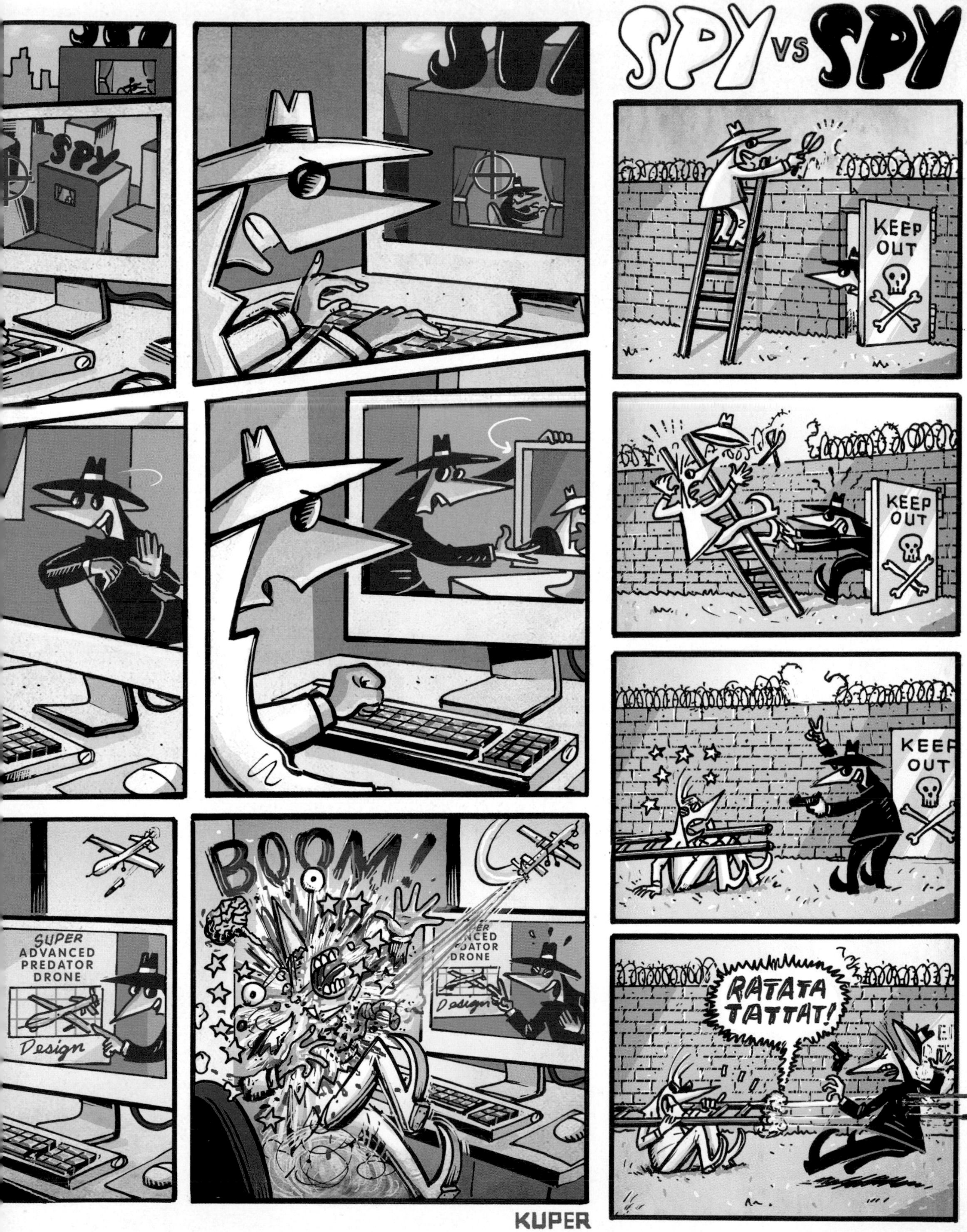
SPY vs SPY
SPY
KEEP OUT
KEEP OUT
KEEP OUT
SUPER ADVANCED PREDATOR DRONE
Design
BOOM!
RATATA TATTAT!
KUPER

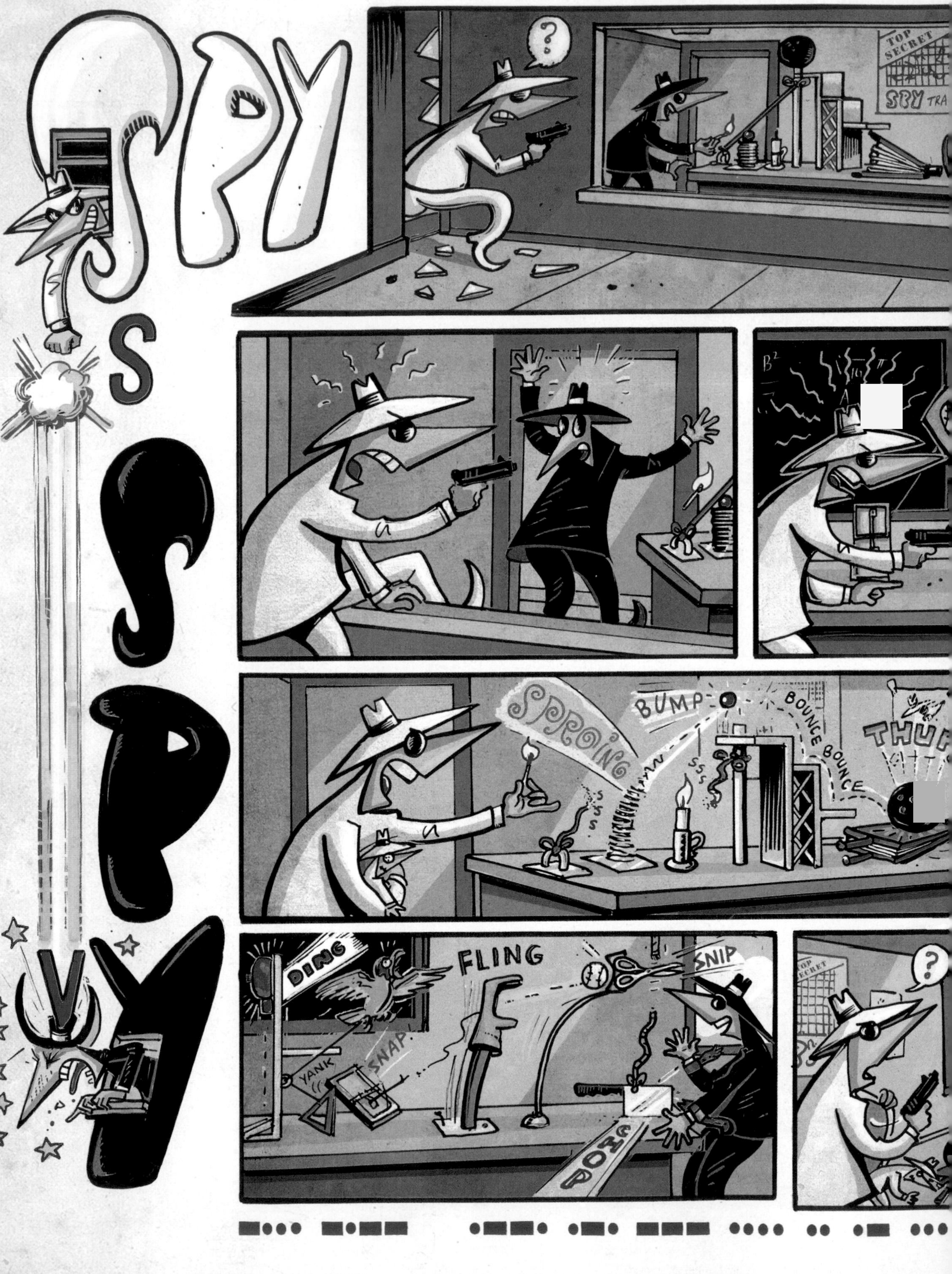

SPY
S
SPY
?
TOP SECRET
SPY TRA
SPROING
BUMP
BOUNCE
BOUNCE
BOUNCE
THU
DING
FLING
SNIP
YANK
SNAP
?

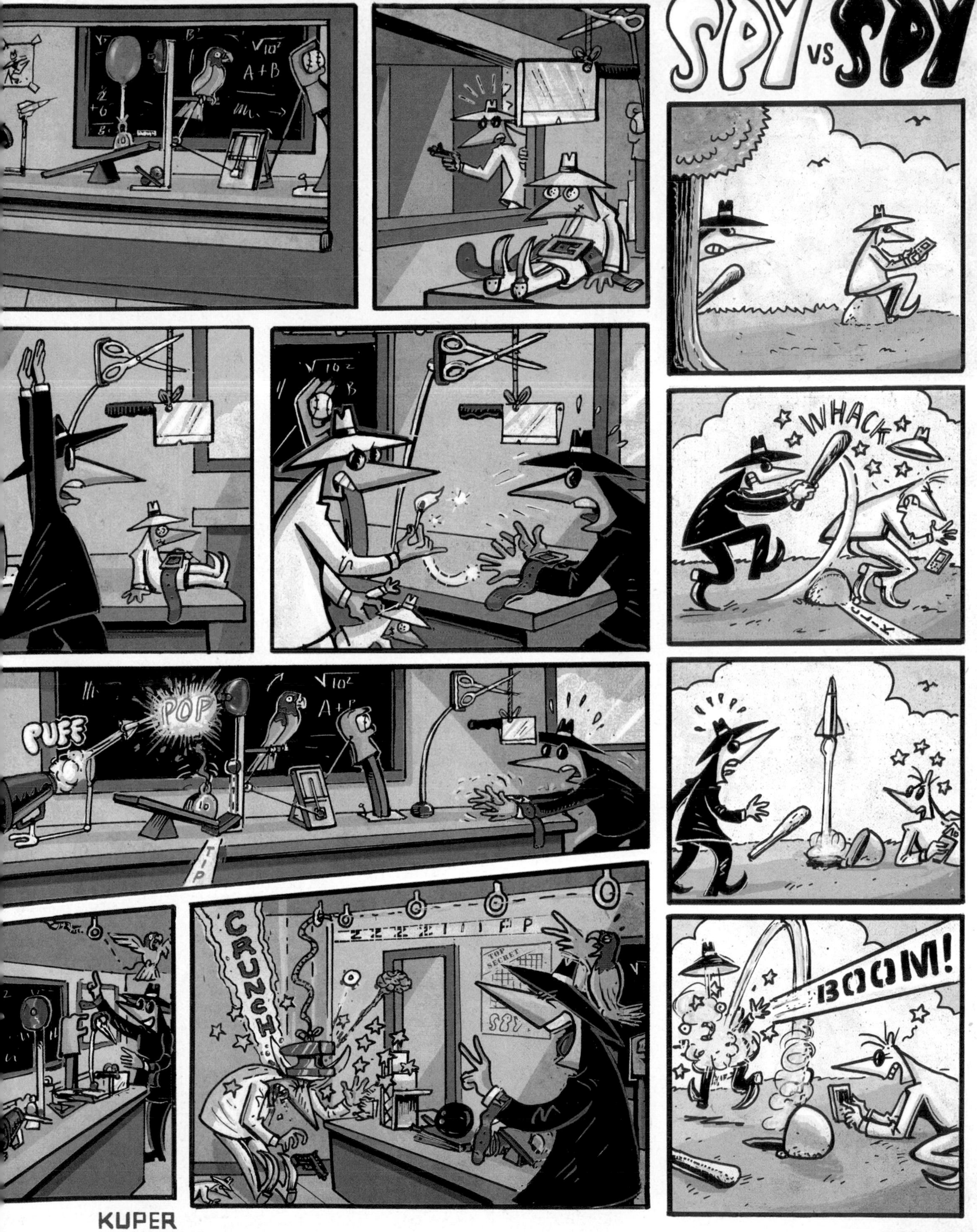
SPY vs SPY
WHACK
BOOM!
PUFF
POP
TIP
CRUNCH
TOP SECRET
SPY

KUPER

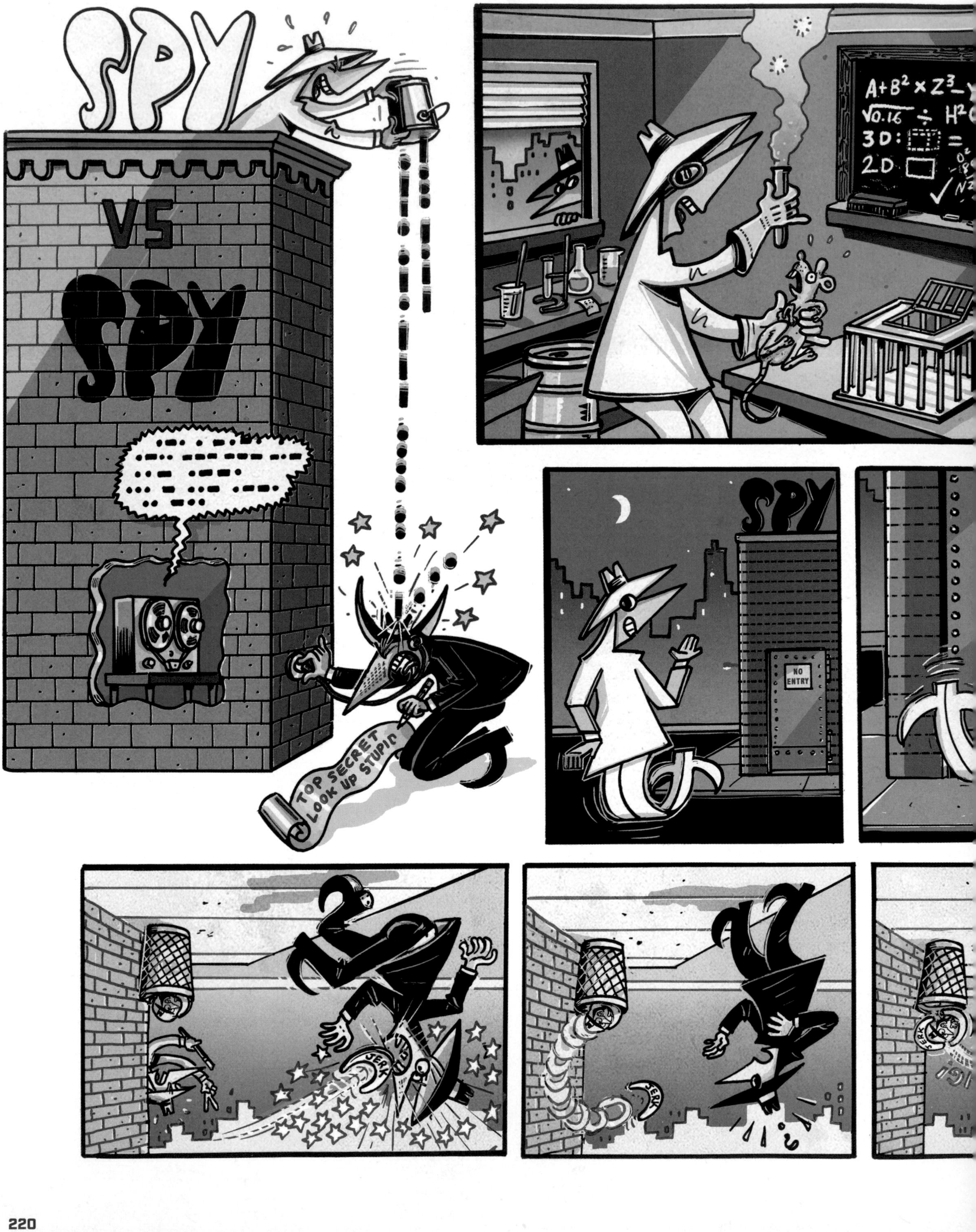
SPY
VS
SPY
TOP SECRET
LOOK UP STUPID
NO ENTRY
JERK
JERK
JERK

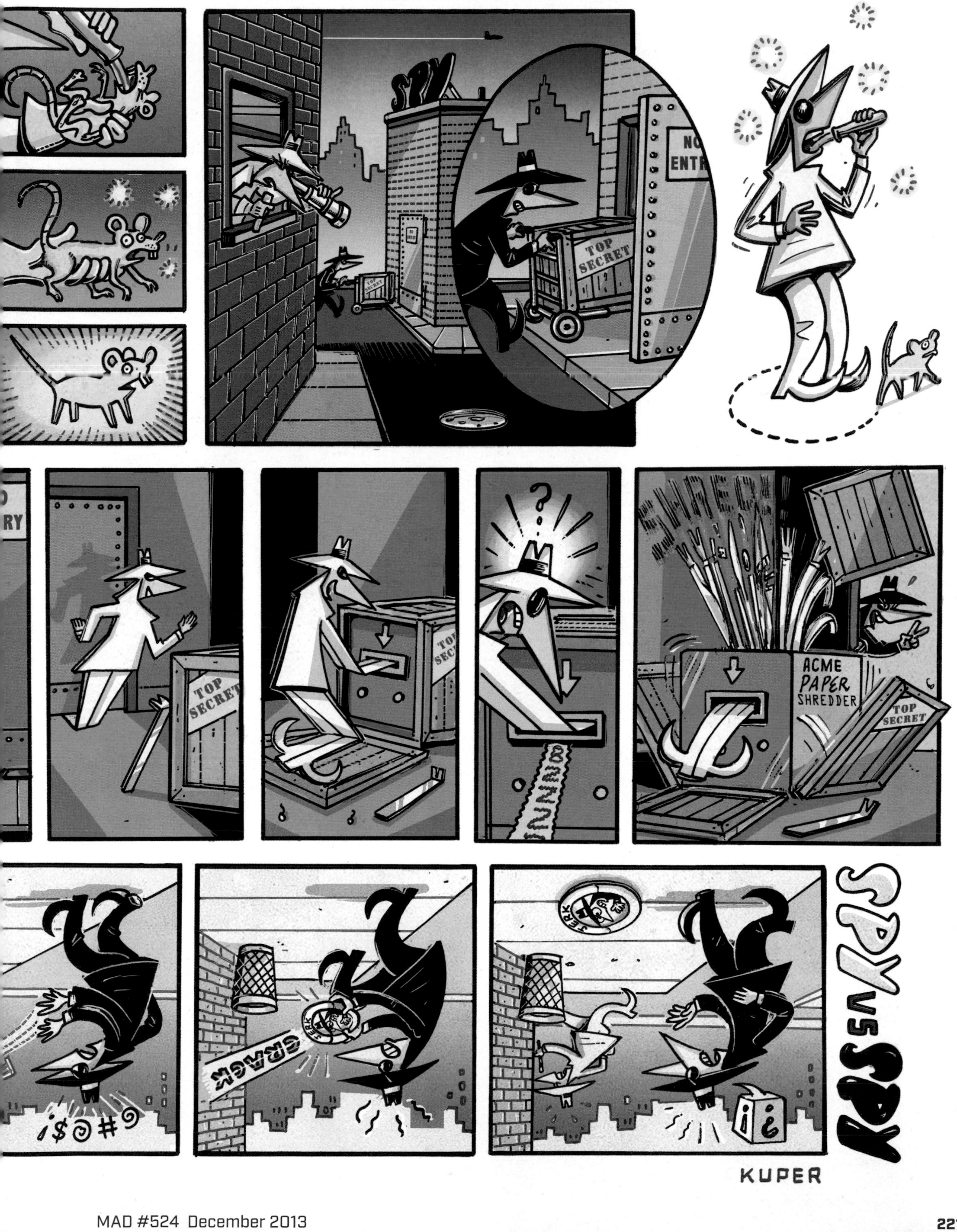
SPY
NO ENTRY
TOP SECRET
TOP SECRET
TOP SECRET
?
ACME PAPER SHREDDER
TOP SECRET
¡$@#@
JERK
SPY vs SPY
KUPER

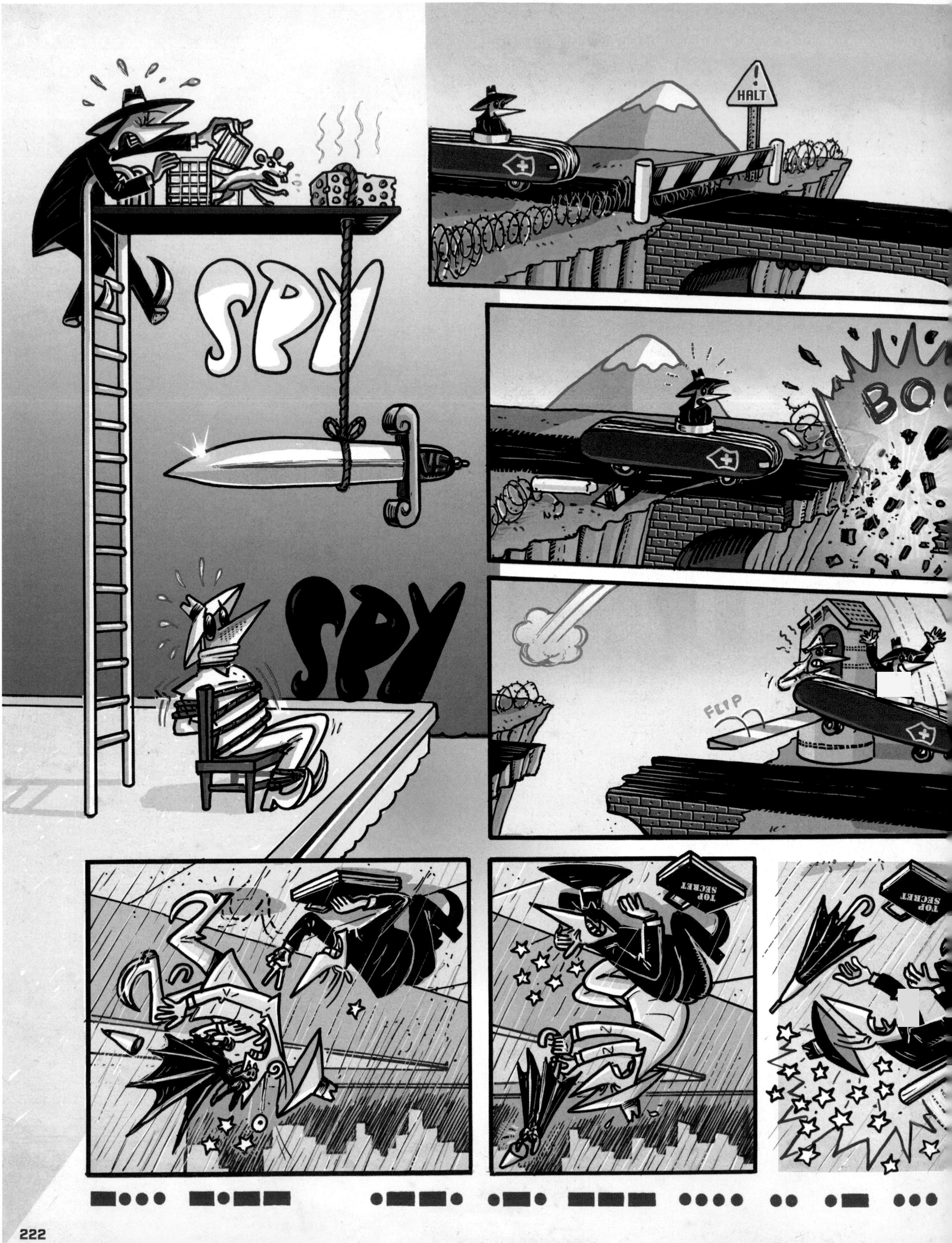
SPY
HALT
SPY
FLIP
TOP SECRET
TOP SECRET
TOP SECRET

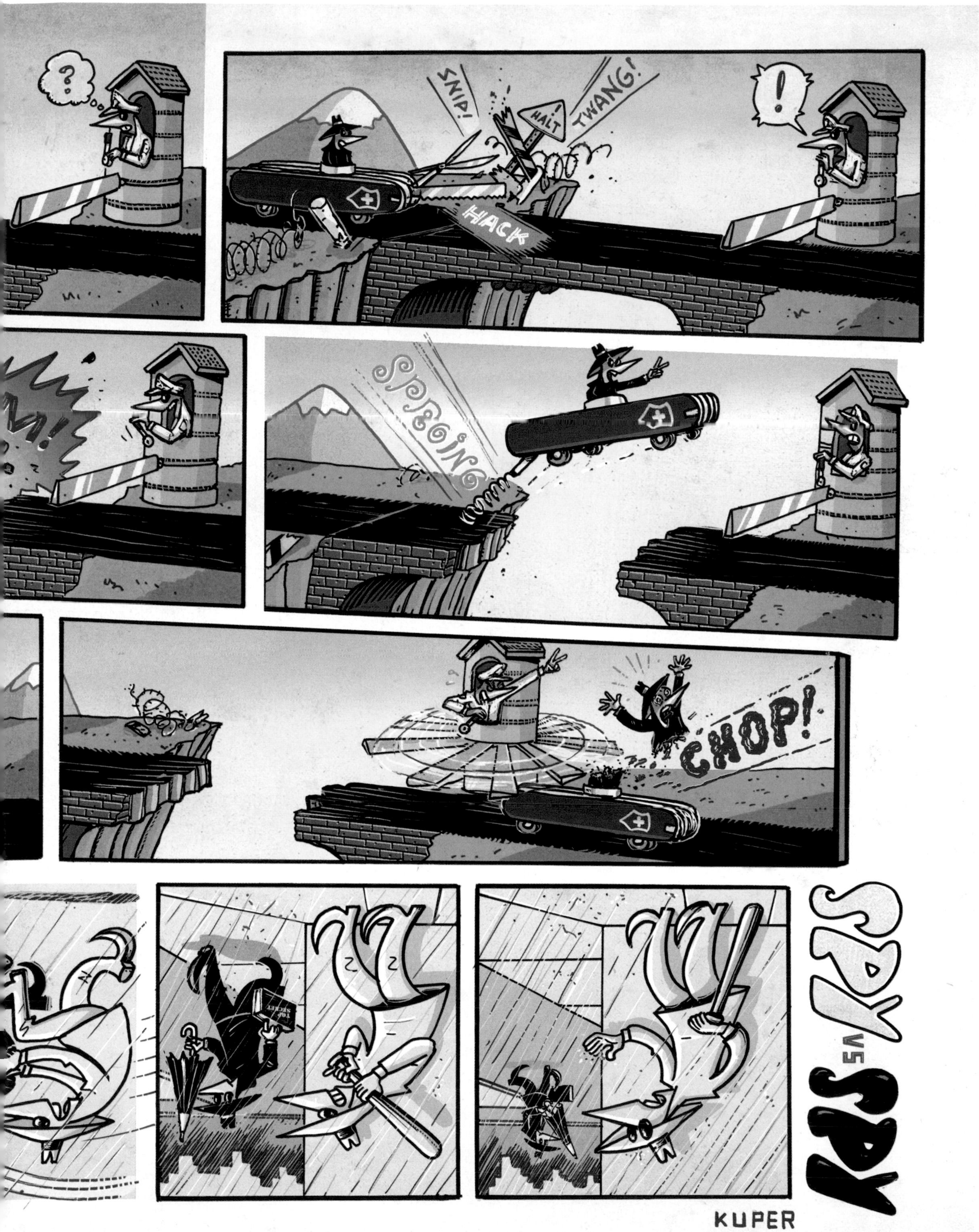
?
SNIP!
TWANG!
HALT
HACK
!
SPROING
CHOP!
TOP SECRET
SPY vs SPY
KUPER

To commemorate the 50th anniversary of *Spy vs. Spy*, MAD commissioned a diverse group of artists to decorate or modify a Spy figurine. Of all the great resulting art, the most touching was from the Prohias family, who transfigured the Spy form into Antonio Prohias himself, working at his drawing board, his ever-present cigarette in hand — a scene they had themselves affectionately witnessed for years.

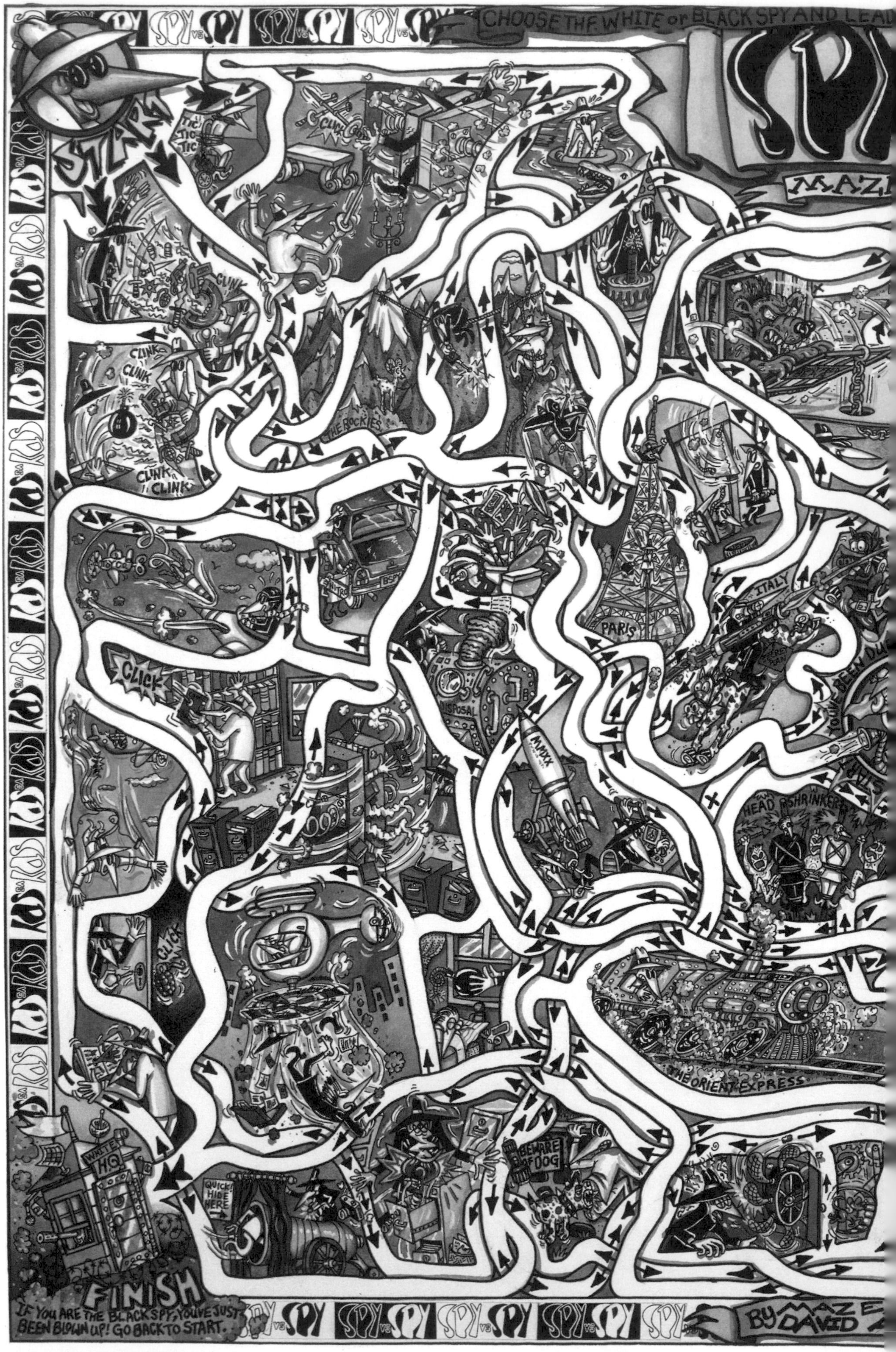
CHOOSE THE WHITE or BLACK SPY AND LEA
START
TIC TIC TIC
CLINK
CLINK CLINK
CLINK CLINK
THE ROCKIES
PARIS
ITALY
CLICK
DISPOSAL
MMXX
HEAD SHRINKER
CLICK
THE ORIENT EXPRESS
WHITE H.Q.
QUICK! HIDE HERE
BEWARE OF DOG
FINISH
IF YOU ARE THE BLACK SPY, YOU'VE JUST BEEN BLOWN UP! GO BACK TO START.
SPY vs SPY
BY MAZE DAVID